AGRIMARKETING TECHNOLOGY

AGRIMARKETING

JASPER S. LEE
Agricultural Educator
Mississippi State, Mississippi

JAMES G. LEISING
Agricultural Educator
University of California–Davis

DAVID E. LAWVER
Agricultural Educator
Texas Tech University

TECHNOLOGY

Selling and Distribution in the Agricultural Industry

AgriScience and Technology Series
Series Editor
Jasper S. Lee, Ph.D.

Interstate Publishers, Inc.
Danville, Illinois

AGRIMARKETING TECHNOLOGY

Cover Photo Credits:

Coffee grading—courtesy Coffee, Sugar, and Cocoa
    Exchange, Inc.

Supermarket shopper—courtesy Illinois Department of
    Agriculture

Florist Shop—courtesy Florists Transworld Delivery
    Association

Trading floor scene at commodity exchange—courtesy
    Chicago Board of Trade

Grain elevator—courtesy Continental Grain Company

Ship being loaded for export from the United
    States—courtesy Continental Grain Company

Order from

Interstate Publishers, Inc.
510 North Vermilion Street
P.O. Box 50
Danville, IL 61834-0050

Phone: (800) 843-4774
FAX: (217) 446-9706

Library of Congress Catalog Card No. 94-77465

ISBN 0-8134-2962-5

1   2   3

4   5   6

7   8   9

Preface

Success or failure in agriculture is largely determined by marketing skills. How well a producer is able to market what has been produced is often the difference between making a profit and losing money. This applies to all sectors of the agricultural industry.

Well prepared people are needed for all levels of work in the marketing process. They need to know the importance of their particular jobs in providing food, fiber, and shelter. In many cases, agrimarketing work does not require a high knowledge of economic theory. It requires people who understand the importance of doing a good job in meeting the needs of consumers.

This book represents a departure from traditional books on agricultural marketing. First, *AgriMarketing Technology* stresses the successful performance of the functions in marketing. The book is based on economic theory, particularly in agricultural marketing in the free enterprise system, but places emphasis on carrying out the marketing functions. The content is organized around what people do in agricultural marketing.

Second, this book departs from traditional agricultural marketing books because it presents marketing in production agriculture as well as the supplies and services and processing areas. All of these areas of marketing are important in assuring a quality supply of food, fiber, and shelter for consumers at the most reasonable cost possible. Agricultural productivity is closely tied to all three areas.

Third, *AgriMarketing Technology* includes information on career success in agrimarketing. Descriptions of career areas and the necessary education and experience are included, as well as how to locate, apply for, and gain employment are included. Further, individuals who choose can use the book to develop entrepreneurship skills and be successful with their own agricultural endeavor.

The overall goal of this book is to introduce agricultural marketing from a broad, agricultural industry perspective. The authors hope that students find this book most useful when studying agricultural marketing. It is their wish that students will be motivated to pursue areas of agricultural marketing for their careers.

Acknowledgements

Many individuals made important contributions in the writing of this book. The authors are most grateful for their assistance. It is impossible to recognize all of them here but several should be recognized for their special efforts.

Two individuals are recognized for their assistance with illustrations. Illustrator Jeanne C. Jones, Senior Research Assistant with the Mississippi Agricultural and Forestry Experiment Station, is acknowledged for her assistance with line art depicting important concepts in graphic forms. Vice President Mary Carter of Interstate Publishers, Inc., is acknowledged for her important assistance with computer-generated graphics.

Professor of Agricultural Economics Warren Couvillion, Mississippi State University and former Louisiana agricultural educator, is acknowledged for his assistance in reviewing the manuscript and providing suggestions on content and sequence.

Special acknowledgement for assistance with figures is given to Davis Lumber and Hardware of Davis, California; Smith & Byars of Starkville, Mississippi; the National FFA Organization, Alexandria, Virginia; and Agri-communication Student Johnny Walker of Texas Tech University.

Appreciation is also expressed to Michelle Newman, Lela Ladner, and Lou Boland of LEE AND ASSOCIATES in Starkville, Mississippi, for their assistance in various ways with the manuscript, library review, and other areas.

Special appreciation is expressed to Interstate Publishers, Inc., for their dedication to agricultural publishing. President Vernie Thomas of Interstate is acknowledged for his enthusiastic support of this book and extra efforts given in its production. Ronnie McDaniel and Dan Pentony, Interstate Vice Presidents, are acknowledged for their important roles in producing and marketing the book.

Many other individuals are acknowledged with the figures and other materials in the book. Without their assistance, the book would not have involved a collaborative effort of agricultural businesses, associations, and agencies.

Contents

PART THREE
Distribution and Selling in Agricultural Industry

Chapter 1

PROVIDING FOOD AND FIBER

The pizza or hamburger you like has a big story to tell! It is the story of marketing—how it gets to you. Not only do you enjoy pizza and hamburger, but they help meet some of your basic needs. All humans need food, clothing, and shelter for survival.

Producing the needed food and fiber has resulted in a marvelous agricultural industry. Providing these in the forms people want is more complicated than many think—it requires much more than good farms. Today, people in the United States want food in convenient, easy-to-use forms. A vast system has developed to handle this demand. This system is

Figure 1–1. Agrimarketing provides an abundance of food for North America. The chef shown here is preparing to serve a large number of people a wide array of food products. (Courtesy, ARA Services, Philadelphia, Pennsylvania)

1

all a part of the agricultural industry, with stress on marketing. It emphasizes getting products to consumers when and where they want them and in the forms they want.

Today, success in agriculture requires considerable understanding of agricultural marketing and many other activities involved in meeting human needs. Further, all of us can be better consumers with some knowledge of agricultural marketing.

TERMS

agribusiness marketing
agricultural industry
agricultural marketing
agricultural revolution
agrimarketing
agrimarketing functions
agrimarketing technology
capital
commercial production
distribution
economy of scale
grading
infrastructure
marketing
non-agricultural marketing
segmentation
self-sufficient
specialization

OBJECTIVES

This chapter provides information about today's food and fiber system. Upon completion, you will be able to:

- Explain three views of marketing
- Describe changes in agriculture that created modern marketing
- Describe the scope of modern agricultural industry
- Explain the functions in marketing agricultural commodities
- Explain agricultural marketing infrastructure
- Identify important marketing concepts for success in the agricultural industry

MARKETING

Marketing is providing the goods and services that people want. But, it is much more complex than such a simple definition. Further, agricultural marketing is different from marketing other products, such as radios and automobiles, because of the nature of agricultural commodities. In agriculture, there are many producers who produce highly perishable commodities.

Marketing is viewed from three perspectives: agricultural marketing, non-agricultural marketing, and agribusiness marketing.

AGRICULTURAL MARKETING

Agricultural marketing is the marketing of food and fiber produced on farms. This includes crops, such as corn, wheat, cotton, and soybeans; livestock, such as sheep, beef cattle, and hogs; livestock products, such as milk and wool; poultry, including eggs; aquacrops, such as fish and water cress; horticultural crops, such as fruit, vegetables, nuts, and ornamental plants; and numerous other crops, including trees and specialty crops. The term, *agrimarketing*, is sometimes substituted for agricultural marketing.

Agrimarketing technology is agricultural marketing that emphasizes the use of technology in the process of marketing food and fiber. Emphasis is on the functions in marketing. Agrimarketing technology does not include emphasis on the economic theory of marketing.

Agrimarketing is a complex process. It begins when the producer (farmer) is deciding what and how much to produce. Farmers should only produce those crops, livestock, and livestock products that consumers will buy. Further, farmers must consider their strengths and weaknesses. They must look at their situations and make the best possible decisions. Factors to consider include climate, available equipment, soil capacity, labor supply, sources of supplies, and how the product will be moved from the farm into the marketing channel. There must be demand for a product at a price level that will cover the costs of production and allow some extra money, known as profit. Unfortunately, some farmers have felt that marketing ended when the ownership of the product changes and the farmer has made a profit.

Today's farmers are involved in *commercial production*. This means that they must produce something that they can sell. If it can't be sold, it shouldn't be grown! In the past, some farmers produced what they liked and ignored marketing. They often lost money and went out of business.

Figure 1–2. Marketing may require considerable technology to get products to the consumer. This shows a fish-haul truck equipped with water tanks and aeration equipment to haul live fish. (Courtesy, James Tidwell, Kentucky State University, Frankfort, Kentucky)

Farm production has many hazards, such as bad weather or insect infestations. All of these production hazards influence the potential to produce food and fiber at a profit even when a good market exists. Decisions about farm production must recognize possible hazards.

More and more, agricultural producers are realizing the importance of marketing. They are approaching production much the same as those in non-agricultural marketing.

NON-AGRICULTURAL MARKETING

Non-agricultural marketing is the activities involved in the flow and production of non-agricultural goods and services (goods that are neither food nor fiber). Product examples include automobiles, televisions, refrigerators, and cosmetics.

Business people consider the total success of a business in terms of marketing. Successful businesses do not view marketing as separate from other functions, such as planning new designs and products. In other words, marketing is a consideration in every decision made by a successful business.

The level of production is often regulated by the manufacturer. Advertising and buyer incentives are often used to increase sales. A good example is automobiles. Manufacturers produce to certain levels. Promotions are used to boost sales. If necessary, the auto assembly plant will be closed for a while or even permanently, when an over supply exists. To some extent, automobile manufacturers try to convince consumers that what they produce is what you need!

AGRIBUSINESS MARKETING

Agribusiness marketing is the marketing of supplies and services to the farm producer. It is a blend of agricultural and non-agricultural marketing. Agribusinesses are typically concerned with providing the supplies and services used by farmers and converting farm products into desired forms for the consumer. Many consider agribusiness marketing similar to non-agricultural marketing. And, since agribusinesses are a part of the agricultural industry, others consider them to be closely related to agrimarketing. Agribusinesses perform many specialized functions in providing the consumer with food and fiber.

Managers of agribusinesses must keep up with what is happening in production agriculture. Changes on the farm impact demand for supplies and services. The quantity of farm supplies sold and profit are shaped by farm trends. Government programs, international markets, droughts or floods, pest invasions, and other factors influence farm yield and profit. Good information is important for success in agribusiness marketing.

CHANGES IN AGRICULTURE

People in the United States enjoy their current standard of living because changes have occurred in how they get food and fiber. A few of the major changes in agriculture in the last 250 years are presented here.

EARLY NORTH AMERICA

When North America was being settled by Europeans, nearly everyone farmed and lived on the land. The first settlers lived by hunting and growing a few crops. Almost everyone is familiar with the teachings of Squanto, a Native American, about the use of fish to fertilize crops.

Inland commerce was slow to develop. Early settlers on the eastern shore gradually moved westward and found fertile soils. Those along streams and rivers produced a few extra crops, such as tobacco and indigo (a plant that produced a blue dye). These were exported to Europe—often in exchange for spices, fancy cloth, and other products.

Early farmers had to save their own seed, provide the fertilizer they used, and try to cope with pests (insects, weeds, and crop diseases) as best they could. Whatever they harvested was theirs to prepare for use, often barely enough for their families.

BEGINNING OF THE AGRICULTURAL REVOLUTION

By 1800, some ways of getting food and fiber had begun to change. However, 90 percent of the people still lived on either small or large farms. These farms were a way of life and often involved considerable manual labor. Farm production was supplemented through hunting and fishing. Many farms were *self-sufficient*, meaning that they produced only for their own needs. Little was available for trade, though some farmers bartered extra crops. (Bartering is exchanging one commodity for another, such as a watermelon for a dozen eggs.)

New inventions resulted in gradual changes in the productivity of farm labor. Workers could get more done using the new equipment. Major impacts were made by Eli Whitney with the invention of the cotton gin in 1793, Cyrus McCormick with the reaper in 1834, and John Deere with the steel moldboard plow in 1837. Draft animals and humans were the major sources of power until steam and internal combustion engines were developed. Farmers were often expected to do some preparation of the produce, such as slaughtering the hogs or separating the seed from the cotton.

AGRICULTURAL REVOLUTION

Beginning in the mid-1800s, numerous industrial developments occurred. Steam engines and railroads had significant impacts on how people lived and the way they made their living. Some historians refer to this time as the "industrial revolution" because factories began to produce steel and other goods. This never could have occurred without increased productivity on the farm and the *agricultural revolution*. The agricultural revolution is all of the changes that occurred in how food and fiber are made available

Figure 1–3. Modern agriculture uses many labor-saving inventions for efficient production, such as this tractor with round hay baler. (Courtesy, KMN Modern Farm Equipment, Inc., West Memphis, Arkansas)

to people. In effect, the industrial and agricultural revolutions occurred simultaneously. Each enhanced the other.

Important new laws were enacted to enhance agriculture. In 1862, the Organic Act established the agency which later became the U.S. Department of Agriculture. That same year, Senator Justin S. Morrill of Vermont authored an important education law which was passed by the U.S. Congress and signed by President Abraham Lincoln. Now known as the Morrill Land-Grant Act, the law set aside blocks of land for states to use in establishing schools to teach agriculture, the mechanical arts, and military science. The first schools were known as A&M colleges. In 1887, the Hatch Act was passed which established a system of agricultural experiment stations in conjunction with the land-grant schools. In 1890, the U.S. Congress passed a second Morrill Act that established A&M schools for black students in 17 states in the southeastern United States. Additional laws that enhanced agricultural education were the Smith-Lever Act of 1914, which created the Cooperative Extension Service, and the Smith-Hughes Act of 1917, which created vocational education in agriculture in the public schools. The agricultural revolution was more a product of increased emphasis on agricultural research and education than anything else.

MODERN U.S. AGRICULTURE

The mid-1900s were great years in the emergence of efficiency on U.S. farms. Gasoline- and diesel-powered tractors and equipment made it possible for farm workers to produce much more. Animal and human power were replaced with mechanical power. Fewer farm workers were needed to produce the essential food and fiber. However, they were needed off the farm to produce the inputs (fertilizer, equipment, etc.) that farmers now wanted and to prepare farm produce for the consumer. The release of the workers from the farms also allowed them to produce luxury items, such as radio and television sets.

The changes that occurred are often referred to as segmentation and specialization. *Segmentation* means that the functions previously carried out on the farms (such as some crude forms of processing) might now be carried out in off-farm agribusinesses. *Specialization* occurred when farms produced only a few products (sometimes only one) for sale to large processors that would convert the products into forms desired by consumers. Most any agricultural commodity can be used to illustrate segmentation and specialization. For example, corn farmers buy seed, fertilizer, equipment, and other inputs from specialized manufacturers, and they may sell their corn to specialized processors who convert it to syrup or corn oil.

New cultivation techniques were developed in the mid-1900s. Hybrid crop varieties increased production. Pesticides allowed for the control of insects, weeds, and crop diseases. Agricultural mechanization allowed one person to care for huge acreages. Irrigation brought new land areas into production. In the late 1900s, biotechnology resulted in more yield and less human effort.

The way of life has changed considerably in the United States. Now fewer than two percent of the people farm; however, many agribusinesses exist. These provide the traditional farm functions, such as producing feed and fertilizer and preparing the products for the consumer. The vastness of agribusiness is often illustrated by comparing employment with that on the farm. In the 1990s, a ratio of 10:1 is the standard. This means that for every worker on a farm there are 10 workers off the farm who provide supplies and services and get the produce to the consumer.

All phases of the agricultural industry involve marketing. Here is an example using corn:

- Fertilizer companies produce the kind of fertilizer farmers use in growing corn (just as the seed companies produce seed and chemical companies produce herbicides and insecticides).

• Farm equipment manufacturers produce the tractors and implements farmers use to prepare the land, plant the seed, control pests, and harvest the crop.

• Farmers produce the kind of corn that can be converted by an agricultural processor into a product that consumers want.

• Processors turn the corn into oil, syrup, starch powder, and other products that consumers will buy.

This is an amazing story with corn. Only a few of the steps and processes have been included. Nearly all other crop and livestock products are similar.

Figure 1–4. Hogs are produced in clean facilities and given nutritionally complete feed to meet consumer demands. (Courtesy, Moorman Feed, Quincy, Illinois)

Farming is a Business

Farming is no longer a way of life; it is a business. The farm owner operates the farm to get a return (money back) on what has been invested.

In doing so, food and fiber are produced for many people off the farm who are involved in non-agricultural and agribusiness work.

The whole notion of farmer has changed. Farmers are agricultural producers; they are in the business of producing food and fiber. They are well educated in the use of the latest technology in producing and marketing their crops, and also in areas of communication. They produce for specific markets, and little for home consumption. And they want to make money! If they don't make money, they will soon quit farming!

AGRICULTURAL INDUSTRY

Agriculture is much more than farming! A vast system has developed to support the needs of humans for food and fiber. This system is often referred to as the *agricultural industry*.

The agricultural industry includes three major areas:

1. Non-farm agribusinesses provide the inputs (supplies, services, and equipment) that agricultural producers need.

2. Farmers and ranchers produce the crops and livestock.

3. Processors and distributors supply the crop and livestock products to the consumer in the desired forms.

Agricultural industry is made up of all the activities that serve to meet the needs of consumers for food and fiber. This includes a vast network of farms, agribusinesses, and agencies.

THE SCOPE OF AGRICULTURAL INDUSTRY

Today's agricultural industry has evolved because of education and research. New technology was developed through research. Education has prepared people to use the new technology. Certainly, the dedication of U.S. citizens to a productive work ethic, the natural benefits of fertile soil and good climate, and a reward-driven economic system helped agricultural industry develop. Employment in the food and fiber industry has undergone huge change!

Farm Trends

The number of farms has been declining steadily for many years. The value of what is produced on the farms has been increasing during this same time. As the number of farms became smaller, the size and productivity of farms increased.

Today, there are 2.1 million farms in the United States. This compares with over 4.1 million farms in 1959 and 2.9 million in 1970. The total value of farm output now exceeds $182.5 billion a year. This can be compared to $55.1 billion in 1970. Another way to look at farm trends is to say that one-third fewer farms than in 1970 produce products valued at over 3.5 times the 1970 value. Much of this increase has been made possible because of the increased development of markets.

Three million people were employed on U.S. farms in 1970. By the 1990s, this number was slightly over two million. The people who work on farms today must be better trained than ever before. Today's worker must know about chemicals, crop varieties, computers, and various areas of marketing. If not, the person will be little more than a farm laborer.

Marketing Trends

Moving farm products to consumers involves activities that add value. Crops, livestock, and livestock products are worth more after they have been made more appealing to the consumer.

Today, 18.6 million people are involved in marketing food and fiber. This reflects a steady increase over the past two decades. Of the people involved in marketing food and fiber, 1.3 million are in food processing; 2.6 million are in manufacturing, such as the garment industry; 6.8 million are in transportation, trade and retailing of food and fiber products; 3.8 million work in eating establishments; and over 4 million are involved in other areas related to marketing. Employment in nearly all marketing categories has been increasing over the last 25 years. The exception is garment manufacturing. A steadily increasing percentage of the work in this industry is occurring overseas. Ratification of the North American Free Trade Agreement (NAFTA) in 1993 was considered a major event in opening new markets in Canada and Mexico for U.S. agricultural commodities.

Marketing adds value to food and fiber. Only a fraction of the retail cost of food and other items goes to the farmer. The majority of the after-marketing value of food and fiber (currently over $750 billion a year) goes to related industries. Another way to look at it is to say that the farm production valued at $182.5 billion brings over $750 billion after marketing. The process of marketing increases the value of farm production over four times!

Supplies and Services Trends

As farmers produce more, there is increased demand for the supplies and services needed to produce. Large employment opportunities exist in those industries that support production agriculture.

Modern farms have large investments in farm tractors and implements. The value of farm machinery now exceeds $182 billion, as compared to 1970 when the value was $34.4 billion. In less than 25 years, the value increased over five times!

Other inputs to farms have also increased. The fertilizer and lime used is valued at over $7 billion a year. Chemicals to control insects, weeds, crop diseases, and other pests are valued at over $4.6 billion a year. Seed, feed, fuel, and other inputs used on farms run into billions of dollars a year.

Figure 1-5. Warehouse filled with bags of feed ingredients waiting for use.
(Courtesy, Moorman Feed, Quincy, Illinois)

Other Areas

Forestry, aquaculture, and related areas account for considerable marketing activity each year.

Forestry involves nearly 500 million acres of land in the United States and is an important source of employment. Over 1.2 million people are involved in producing lumber, paper, and furniture from wood. The products produced are valued at $200 billion a year. This production requires supplies and services for tree farming, but not to the same extent as row crops and livestock.

Aquaculture is the production of aquatic food and other products. Some parts of the United States have had considerable expansion of aquaculture in recent years. Aquacrops require marketing just as agricultural products do. Aquaculture accounts for 18 percent of all fish and seafood consumed in the United States. Aquaculture production is valued at $600 million annually in the United States. Marketing adds a considerable amount to the value, so that aquacrops account for approximately $2.4 billion when consumed.

AGRIMARKETING FUNCTIONS

Agrimarketing consists of various categories, known as *agrimarketing functions*. These are essential in the movement of food and fiber from the farm to the consumer. Ownership of the product may change at several points along the way between the farm and final consumer. Nine major agrimarketing functions are included:

- Planning what to produce
- Assembling the product
- Grading the product
- Transporting the product
- Storing the product
- Processing the product
- Packaging and storing the processed product
- Advertising and promoting consumption
- Selling
- Distributing the processed product

PLANNING WHAT TO PRODUCE

The first function occurs when the farmer is deciding what is to be produced on the farm. A farmer cannot be financially successful unless there is a demand for what is produced. This is not always an easy decision to make. Many factors are involved.

Most farmers begin by assessing the possibilities on their farms. They study the climate, soil capacity, available equipment and labor, government programs and regulations, and available market outlets (places to sell). The final consideration should be personal preferences.

It is important to get information from reliable sources. Other farmers are often good places to begin. Agricultural specialists at universities and private agricultural consultants may be helpful. It is also helpful to check with local buyers (processors, elevators, etc.) of various crops to determine their plans.

In some cases, farmers sign contracts before production is begun. These contracts specify what the local buyer will take, how much will be paid, and the volume to be taken. Contracts can assure a market outlet for what is produced and reduce some marketing risk to the farmer.

The goal is to produce the crop that will result in the greatest returns to the farmer. Returns refers to the amount of money left after all costs of production have been paid.

ASSEMBLING THE PRODUCT

Assembling occurs after harvesting. It involves delivering the produce of farms to a central location to enable other functions in marketing to occur. Several small farms may deliver what has been produced to a location to be combined into a larger quantity. Larger farms may have assembly points where produce is brought from different locations for assembly on the farm. Regardless, assembly involves massing quantities of farm products. Examples include: locations where farmers deliver their produce, such as vegetable packing sheds, grain elevators, and livestock sale barns, and transporters that go from one farm to another, such as bulk milk trucks that pick up raw milk on the farm.

Assembly is important because of the economy associated with larger quantities. This is sometimes referred to as *economy of scale* or economy of size. A processor might offer a better price for a large quantity that makes it profitable to operate a truck to haul the product to the processing plant. Further, processing plants must have adequate supplies of products to make their operations profitable. Several smaller farmers can pool their products into uniform lots of larger quantities. Farmer cooperatives are often formed for this purpose.

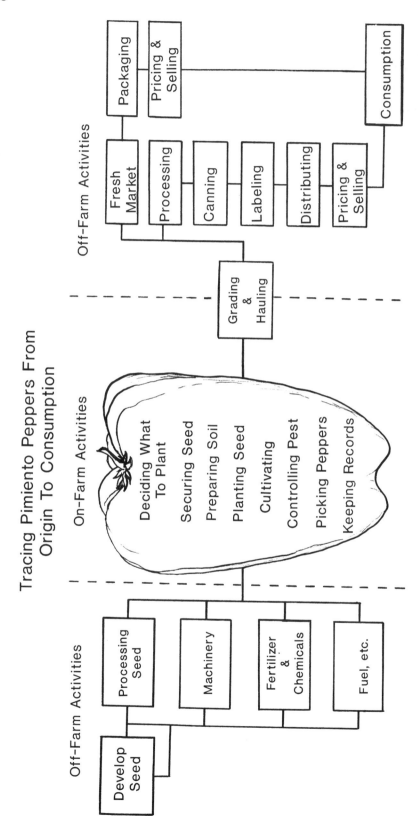

Tracing Pimiento Peppers From Origin To Consumption

Off-Farm Activities

Packaging
Pricing & Selling
Consumption

Fresh Market
Processing
Canning
Labeling
Distributing
Pricing & Selling

Grading & Hauling

On-Farm Activities

Deciding What To Plant
Securing Seed
Preparing Soil
Planting Seed
Cultivating
Controlling Pest
Picking Peppers
Keeping Records

Off-Farm Activities

Processing Seed
Machinery
Fertilizer & Chemicals
Fuel, etc.

Develop Seed

Figure 1-6. Various farm and off-farm activities are used in producing and getting pimiento peppers to the consumer.

GRADING

Grading is an important function that assures uniform quality of agricultural products. This function often occurs at or shortly after assembling. Value is affected by grade and whether or not uniform standards have been used. Most agricultural products have uniform grade standards. A few examples of products with standards include eggs, potatoes, apples, wheat, cotton, livestock, and fruit and vegetables.

Grading assures uniformity. Similar sizes may be grouped together. Damaged products are removed. Products that are beginning to decay are culled. For example, potatoes should be free of decay or damage and uniform in size and variety. White potatoes and red potatoes can't be mixed. Partially rotten potatoes should be removed.

Marketing is enhanced when uniform standards are used. Agricultural products can be sold merely by exchanging information on the standards that are met. Visual inspection may not be needed for the products to be shipped and sold. Of course, all of the people involved must know and follow the appropriate standards.

A good example is cotton. Color of the cotton (how white it is), length of fiber (known as staple), and presence of trash influence the grade. When a sample from a bale is graded by a trained grader, the sale of the cotton is made on the basis of the grader's findings. Visual inspection by the buyer is not needed.

TRANSPORTING

Most agricultural products have to be transported from the farm to places where the next steps involved in preparation for consumption occur. In fact, most products are transported several times in different stages of preparation. For example, green beans may be transported from the farm to a packing shed and from there to a processing plant. After processing, the canned or frozen beans are hauled to a distribution center or warehouse and again to the supermarket or restaurant where they will be bought by the consumer.

Appropriate methods of transportation must be selected to maintain the quality of the product. Freshly picked beans should be kept cool and delivered promptly to the processing plant. Otherwise, the quality will begin to deteriorate. After processing, the beans are transported in a refrigerated truck or trailer if frozen or in a container without refrigeration if canned.

STORING

Agricultural products may be stored on the farm or in central facilities, such as grain elevators, before processing. This is often referred to as raw storage. Storage conditions must protect the product from damage and deterioration. Refrigeration may be needed. Protection from rodents, insects, birds, mildew, and other organisms is needed. Protection from contamination by hazardous chemicals is essential for both human food and livestock feed.

Livestock must often be stored for a few hours at a processing plant. Appropriate feed and water must be provided. Humane treatment of livestock is essential.

After processing, products are stored in several locations. These include large warehouses, distribution centers, and in retail stores. All along the way, quality of the final product must be maintained.

Conditions for storage vary. The qualities of the product being stored must be considered, and storage conditions selected accordingly.

A good example is fish. Harvested fish may be transported to a processing plant where they are "held" (held means the same as stored). While held, the fish are kept alive in vats filled with cool water that has oxygen added to it. After processing, the fish may be stored in refrigerated warehouses if frozen or in the fresh product form. If canned or preserved in other ways, appropriate storage must be selected.

PROCESSING

Processing involves many different activities. It includes all of the changes that occur as the product is prepared for consumption. The nature of the product as well as the demands of consumers influence the extent of processing that occurs. The more that is done to prepare a product for consumption, the greater the value is increased. In general, processing adds considerably to the value of a farm product. A few examples will be briefly discussed.

Beef cattle processing involves slaughtering the animal and preparing it into the desired cuts or food items. In some cases, the carcasses or parts of the carcasses may be made into canned or frozen food products. Hamburger, steak, wieners, and ribs all require different processing procedures.

Potato processing varies widely. Some potatoes are bagged for sale through supermarkets as whole potatoes. Other potatoes undergo considerable processing, such as potato chips and instant mashed potatoes.

Figure 1–7. An automated citrus packing plant packing fresh oranges in boxes for distribution to supermarkets. (Courtesy, USDA)

Cotton processing involves separating the lint (fiber) and seed, weaving the fiber into cloth, and constructing garments or other products from the cloth.

Wheat processing includes milling into flour and baking the desired products. There are many steps along the way to the consumer that ensure a quality, wholesome product.

PACKAGING AND STORING PROCESSED PRODUCTS

Many products are packaged in easy-to-use containers as a near final step in processing. Attractive labeling may be attached to promote consumption by consumers. These products must be carefully stored after processing to protect quality. A few examples are briefly described here.

Cucumbers may be processed in many ways. They may be preserved by pickling, packaged in attractively labeled jars, and stored in protective warehouses until delivery to the supermarket. Some cucumbers are processed into slices or chopped for pickle relish.

Milk must be carefully packaged and stored to maintain its quality. After processing (which includes pasteurizing and homogenizing), the milk is packaged in plastic, paper, or other cartons. These cartons are in con-

Figure 1–8. The display in this dairy case shows many different ways fresh milk can be packaged.

venient sizes for customer use, such as half-pint, pints, quarts, half-gallons, and gallons. Protective packaging also keeps the product fresh. Storage must be in refrigerated areas.

Broilers (young chickens used for frying, roasting, and similar purposes) undergo considerable preparation for the consumer. Processing involves several steps in slaughtering the bird, including removing the feathers and internal organs, preparing the desired cuts, and packaging in a variety of ways for the consumer. Fresh chicken must always be stored under refrigeration or in frozen form.

ADVERTISING AND PROMOTING THE PRODUCT

Advertising and promotion are used to increase the consumption of food and fiber products. Advertising is actually a part of promoting a product. Advertising involves calling attention to a product and encouraging consumers to buy it.

Various approaches are used to promote a product. All consumers are familiar with the grocery ads in the newspaper and the special sales prices that are used to try to lure buyers. Discount coupons, signs, samples of food, and other procedures may be used in product promotion. Large processors or retailers may spend huge sums of money promoting products.

SELLING

Selling is the transaction that takes place between a seller and buyer. A seller is an individual who has something that is of value to others. A buyer is someone who wants what a seller has to offer. An exchange of valuable goods or services for some medium, such as money, is a part of the transaction. Selling occurs several ways in agricultural marketing: supplies and services are sold to the farmer, the farmer sells the produce of the farm, and the processor of food and fiber sells to the consumer or another individual who can reach the consumer, such as a wholesaler.

DISTRIBUTING THE PRODUCT

Once a product has been prepared for the consumer, it must be moved to a location where the consumer will have access to it. This is known as *distribution*. Trucks, railroads, ships, and airplanes are used in distribution. Often these must be specially equipped to ensure a quality product. For example, some products require refrigeration while being transported.

One of the best examples of a popular item that requires considerable

Figure 1–9. Modern refrigerated trucks deliver food directly to supermarkets.

distribution is the hamburger. Bringing together all of the items required in a hamburger requires considerable coordination. Buns, meat, mayonnaise, pickles, onion, and other ingredients originate in many different locations. All of these must arrive at the local fast food hamburger restaurant in good condition so that the consumer can have a delicious, wholesome hamburger. Getting products to the right location in a timely manner is a key to the success of the business producing the product. The best products in the world are of little value unless they can get to the consumer.

AGRICULTURAL MARKETING INFRASTRUCTURE

Infrastructure is the foundation or framework that allows the agricultural industry to function. The network linking the producer with the consumer is built on a huge infrastructure. Infrastructure includes production agriculture as well as the supplies and services needed by producers. It also includes the processing and other steps that occur to convert the produce into the forms desired by consumers. Infrastructure includes the manufacture of farm machinery, chemicals, and other inputs. The various marketing functions exist because of the infrastructure that has developed.

Several parts of the infrastructure that support agricultural marketing are harvesting, transportation, assembly facilities, processing facilities, and capital (finances).

HARVESTING INFRASTRUCTURE

Harvesting is not always an area left to the farmer. Some commodities require expensive, specialized equipment for harvesting. The availability of such equipment to farmers is a part of the infrastructure. For example, many wheat farmers don't own the expensive combines that are needed to harvest wheat. The farmers contract with other farmers to perform the harvesting on a custom basis.

In some cases, processors of agricultural commodities, order buyers, and others involved in marketing processes will provide harvesting assistance. Poultry processing plants may provide specialized equipment and work crews to catch chickens and haul them to the processing plant. Cattle buyers may have a crew of "cowboys and horses" to round up, load, and haul cattle for the rancher. A milk processor may send a truck to collect the milk from farms for delivery to the processing plant.

Farmers couldn't carry on their production without the harvesting infrastructure, particularly with some commodities.

TRANSPORTATION INFRASTRUCTURE

Transportation is an essential function to link the producer with the consumer. In agricultural marketing, roads, railroads, ports that access water transportation, and airports are all important. In addition, appropriate trailers, boxcars, barges, and airplanes must be available. Most agricultural commodities require careful consideration of the unique needs of the products. Some commodities require refrigerated trucks, while others can be shipped on flatbed trailers. Milk can't be hauled in the same truck as wheat!

Agricultural marketing is enhanced when good highways or railroads exist from farm areas to processors and consumers. International marketing depends on river and sea ports accessible by barge and ship. Some high-value items, such as cut flowers, may be transported by air to ensure arrival in good condition.

ASSEMBLY FACILITIES

Assembly facilities include grain elevators, cotton gins and compresses, livestock auction barns, and vegetable packing sheds. These are common assembly facilities that must be in place for farmers to market their commodities. Most farmers can't ship grain and vegetables long distances. They depend on facilities in the local community where they and other farmers can deliver their produce. From here it continues on its way through the marketing channel to reach the consumer.

Assembly facilities also often have specialized grading and packaging equipment. Other than the largest farms, most farmers can't afford such facilities. Their volume of produce is simply not large enough!

Without assembly facilities, many agricultural commodities could not be profitably grown in many areas. For example, if the only grain elevator in a community closes, what will farmers do? There are several options: haul the grain a greater distance to another elevator, build storage facilities on the farm, form a cooperative with other farmers to start another elevator, or switch to another crop. These alternatives are costly and may be impractical for a farmer, particularly if a lot of equipment and other facilities are owned that can only be used with one kind of crop.

PROCESSING FACILITIES

Many agricultural commodities require large, expensive facilities to process the product as it leaves the farm. These facilities are far more than most farmers could afford.

For example, modern cotton gins cost millions of dollars. Some farmers form corporations to construct and operate cotton gins. In addition, specialized work crews must be available to manage and operate the gin. Another example is the vegetable processing plant, which requires a large factory filled with washers, peelers, shellers, retorts, conveyors, boilers, sealers, and other equipment. Again, specialized work crews are needed to operate the plant. Only the largest producers have their own processing plants, such as the Dole Company that produces pineapple in Hawaii.

Processing facilities must be present as an integral link in the marketing of most agricultural commodities. If these are not available, farmers should consider another crop.

Figure 1–10. The water tank at the Dole Company in Hawaii has long been a major symbol of agricultural processing.

CAPITAL

Capital refers to the property that is used in the agricultural marketing infrastructure. Capital can be described as money and what money will provide.

Marketing agricultural commodities requires money to finance the construction of the infrastructure. Harvesting machinery, road construction, building assembly points (such as packing sheds), and processing plants all require considerable capital.

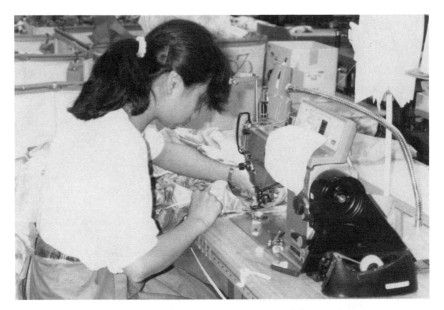

Figure 1–11. Manufacturing clothing requires capital for equipment, raw
material, and labor.

Funding for the infrastructure may come from several sources. Lending agencies, such as banks, may provide loans to finance the establishment and maintenance of the processing plants. In some cases, tax funds are used to build the infrastructure. Examples includes roads, packing sheds, and subsidized packing plants. Sometimes farmers form cooperatives to establish an infrastructure. Foreign investors may provide the needed capital, particularly when the foreign nation can benefit from the investment. Examples of foreign investment range from soybean elevators to forestry port facilities and eel farming packing sheds.

IMPORTANT
MARKETING CONCEPTS

Agricultural marketing involves a number of phenomena, some of which are quite complex. Understanding these fundamentals can help individuals to be more successful in marketing.

Many researchers have studied agricultural marketing. They have attempted to explain the marketing process. One such effort was by The National Council for Agricultural Education, located in Alexandria, Virginia. Four major areas of marketing concepts were identified.

1. *Marketing is an integral function of the food and fiber system.* Understanding the meaning and role of marketing in the agricultural industry is essential. (The focus of this book is on developing an understanding of these functions.)

2. *Consumers demand products that are readily available in the desired form at an acceptable price.* Understanding the concepts of market margin and the process involved in getting products to consumers will support this marketing concept.

3. *Various functions are involved in providing consumer goods.* Under-

Figure 1–12. Consumers can choose from a wide variety of products, such as corn that is frozen in convenient cooking bags, canned, or on the cob.

standing the functions involved in agricultural marketing is essential. Each function provides a valuable service by linking the producer with the consumer.

4. *Vertical integration is an important component in marketing certain agricultural products.* Vertical integration involves control of production and marketing functions to assure a quality product at a competitive price. Vertical integration is very important with certain commodities. Broiler production is a good example. A company may contract with farmers, provide the chicks and feed, process the birds, and deliver the products to supermarkets or restaurants.

SUMMARY

Marketing is the link between producers and consumers. In agricultural marketing, emphasis is on providing consumers with food and fiber when they want them and in the form they want. This requires a huge infrastructure of marketing facilities.

Agricultural marketing is made up of various functions. These begin with the farmer planning what to produce—only those items that can be sold for a profit should be considered. After production, the marketing process includes: assembling, grading, transporting, storing, processing, packaging, advertising and promoting, and distributing.

The marketing functions can be carried out only if a good infrastructure exists. Infrastructure includes the roads, packing sheds, processing plants, capital, and other structures that must exist for marketing to take place.

CHAPTER SELF-CHECK

Match the following terms with the correct definitions:

   a. marketing

   b. capital

   c. specialization

   d. self-sufficient

   e. agrimarketing technology

f. agribusiness marketing

g. agricultural industry

h. infrastructure

i. distribution

j. agrimarketing functions

_____ providing the goods and services that people want

_____ using technology in the process of marketing food

_____ marketing supplies and services to the farm producer

_____ farms that produce only for their needs

_____ when a farm or agribusiness produces only one or a few items

_____ a system of three major areas to meet consumer food and fiber needs

_____ functions in the movement of food and fiber from producer to consumer

_____ moving products so consumers can get them

_____ framework that allows agricultural industry to function

_____ property used in agrimarketing infrastructure

QUESTIONS AND PROBLEMS FOR DISCUSSION

1. What is marketing? Agricultural marketing? Agrimarketing technology? Distinguish between non-agricultural marketing and agricultural marketing.

2. How has agriculture changed in North America? Begin with the 1700s and describe changes through today.

3. Why is farming a business?

4. What are the three major areas of the agricultural industry?

5. How has employment in agriculture changed?

6. The ratio of 10:1 is sometimes used to describe the number of people who work in the agricultural industry. Explain this ratio.

7. Agrimarketing is made up of several functions. List and briefly describe the functions.

8. What is the agrimarketing infrastructure? List and briefly explain several major areas of this infrastructure.

9. How is the agrimarketing infrastructure related to the functions in marketing?

10. Name four agricultural marketing concepts.

ACTIVITIES

1. Select one of your favorite foods and study how it moves through the marketing process to you. Use reference books and other materials to locate the general area where it was grown and the activities involved in preparing it for you. Prepare a written report or poster that describes what you learned.

2. Visit a local farm supplies store or garden center. Note the kinds of products that are available. Read the labels on five products to determine the use of the supply and the precautions to follow in using it. Give an oral report in class on what you observed.

3. Tour a local business involved in agrimarketing. Be sure to make your plans well ahead of time with the manager. Determine the kinds of products that are marketed and the nature of the functions that are carried out. Prepare a short written report on your findings.

Chapter 2

DOING BUSINESS IN FREE ENTERPRISE

Buying your favorite shirt or jeans at the local department store is easy enough. You will probably have a large selection from which to choose. You exchange some money for the items you want and take the clothing with you to wear as you wish. You have a lot of choices about what you can buy. In the United States, there aren't many restrictions on what you (the consumer) can buy and what the store sells.

The choices you and the store have are a part of the way business is done. The store hopes to provide what you want. If you don't find something you like at one store, you can go to another store. You and the store have

Figure 2–1. Ready-made, quality clothing is the result of consumer-oriented agrimarketing that gives people many choices.

29

a lot of choices about styles and types of clothing. These choices are a part of free enterprise and an economic system known as capitalism.

Agrimarketing is a part of the freedom to choose. Success in agrimarketing requires an understanding of the freedoms involved. Of course, there are various regulations and procedures that are in place to assure that the food and fiber system operates smoothly. In a representative government, the people have put the regulations there because they were needed. And agricultural marketers must be able to deal with the regulations!

OBJECTIVES

This chapter provides information about agrimarketing in the United States. Upon completion, you will be able to:

- Describe the economic system in the United States

- Describe the important characteristics of free enterprise

- Describe ways of doing business in the agricultural industry

- Explain how free enterprise is important in agrimarketing

TERMS

capitalism
competition
consumer
cooperatives
corporation
demand
economics
economic system
for-profit business
freedom of choice
free enterprise
marketing cooperative
nonprofit business
partnership
personal property
principle of supply and demand
private ownership
proprietor
purchasing cooperative
real property
sole proprietorship
supply

ECONOMIC SYSTEM

Agricultural industry involves creating and exchanging food, fiber, and related goods and services. Considerable commerce is involved. Commodities are bought and sold in a wide range of situations. Some sort of system must be in place for this to occur. Every nation has a system, but some are more effective than others!

Economics is concerned with the creation of goods and services to satisfy human wants and needs. The focus is on using the most effective means available to produce the goods and services. Various social factors are also involved. Often, people think of economics as focusing on the wise use of resources to produce the greatest possible returns. Economic measures are often stated in terms of money. Typical economic questions in agrimarketing are: How much does it cost? How much will the consumer pay? and How much profit can be made?

The way goods are owned, created, and exchanged forms an *economic system*. The economic systems of all countries are different. Several economic systems have been tried, including communism, socialism, and capitalism. Within each, there are numerous variations. Pure economic systems have given way to mixed systems. Many nations of the world have capitalism in one form or another. The United States uses modified capitalism as its economic system. The modifications are made to assure that the overall good of society is met. In the early 1990s, several communist countries began converting to other systems, particularly forms of capitalism.

A major distinction among economic systems is ownership and control of property. The role of government in establishing regulations on production and ownership is also a part of the economic system. Agrimarketing occurs in all economic systems.

FREE ENTERPRISE

Capitalism, as it has been modified in the United States, is known as free enterprise. It is also referred to as private enterprise. The notion behind free enterprise is that individuals are free to make money. In this usage, "making money" refers to establishing a business to earn a profit, or have money left over after all expenses have been paid. It is felt that if people can invest their time and resources and get back more than they have invested, they will work harder to be more productive. There must be money left over after all expenses have been paid. Profit is a reward for good work! Considerable skill in management and production is often

Figure 2–2. The small fruit stand is one way agricultural products can be marketed in free enterprise.

needed to make a profit. Agrimarketing is an area where in-depth knowledge is essential for a profit.

Free enterprise is the system that allows individuals to organize and conduct business with a minimum of government regulations and to own what they have produced as well as the property used in production.

CHARACTERISTICS OF FREE ENTERPRISE

Free enterprise is based on four important principles: private ownership of property, private ownership of business, freedom of choice, and a minimum of government control.

PRIVATE OWNERSHIP OF PROPERTY

Individuals like to have things (property) that they can call their own, known as *private ownership.* The ability to acquire property is an important feature of free enterprise. The freedom to acquire property is highly motivating.

Property comes in two major forms: real and personal. *Real property* refers to land and the improvements that have been made to it. Real property cannot be easily moved about; it is in a permanently fixed location. *Personal property* refers to the goods that people use in their ordinary life, such as cars, clothing, radios, and household furnishings. These items tend to be easily moved about.

Individuals like to own real and personal property. Ownership means that an individual has legal title to the property. Legal titles are particularly important for real property.

Private ownership in agrimarketing includes the commodities marketed as well as the facilities that are used in the marketing process. Individuals may own farms, elevators, trucks, processing plants, and other components in the food and fiber system. However, some of the infrastructure is not privately owned. Sometimes the government and private individuals may collaborate to establish infrastructure. In the United States and most other countries, the government has provided highways, ports, assembly locations, and other facilities. Agricultural commerce is possible because these have been provided by the government. Further, the facilities serve the overall needs of society. Another way to view the role of government in providing infrastructure is to ask ourselves: "What kinds of roads would we have if the government did not build them?" There probably would be few roads and those available would be in poor condition.

The government may buy huge quantities of some commodities, such as milk and cotton, and ultimately oversee their marketing. This is done in an attempt to keep prices to farmers at levels where some profit can be made and to remove excessive quantities from the market. Though it is sometimes hard for the general public to see the benefits, these measures are modifications of free enterprise that are designed to better serve the needs of consumers and producers. For example, if prices to farmers get too low, many of them would quit farming. Shortages would develop in a few years after the excess had been consumed and no producers were left.

PRIVATE OWNERSHIP OF BUSINESSES

A business is an entity that is engaged in activities to produce goods or services that consumers want. People own businesses. People are free to establish and operate a business with a minimum of government restraint. Businesses can be formed by one person or groups of two or more persons. The owners are free to retain profits (if any). They also risk losing all of the money that they have invested. Businesses can compete with other businesses for raw materials, employees, customers, new products and in many other ways.

In the agricultural industry, farms and agribusinesses are privately owned. Only a few farms in the United States are owned by the government, and these are special situations such as those at schools or prisons. Large acreages of land are owned by the government, such as range land in the western United States. The land is leased to ranchers for grazing. Agrimarketing involves many kinds of businesses, including the farm itself, trucking companies, packing sheds, processing plants, warehouses, advertising agencies, and supermarkets.

Businesses involved in agrimarketing are subject to certain government regulations. These regulations must be followed. Most of the regulations deal with fair practices in employment, taxation, and unfair competition tactics. The roles of managers may be limited in the hiring and firing of employees, particularly in larger agrimarketing businesses.

Figure 2-3. Operating an agrimarketing business requires giving careful attention to records and reports.

FREEDOM OF CHOICE

In free enterprise, individuals are free to choose what they want to produce and to buy and sell at prices they agree upon. This is known as *freedom of choice*. Farmers can try to produce any crop they wish, but this is often not a good approach. They must consider many variables, such as climate, land fertility, availability of equipment and supplies, knowledge of how to produce quality produce, available markets, and labor supply. With freedom of choice, individuals must make careful decisions. The decisions lead to success or failure of a farm or agribusiness.

Freedom of choice also includes the freedom of the seller and buyer to determine a price. Simply, the farmer and buyer can negotiate until they agree on a price. For example, a farmer with a watermelon might want to sell it for $5; the buyer might be willing to pay only $3; but they reach agreement on $4 for the watermelon. The buyer gives the farmer $4 and takes the watermelon. Ownership has changed. The farmer has the money and the buyer has the watermelon.

Due to the high productivity of U.S. agriculture, it is easy for farmers to produce more than can be sold at a profit. This is because the price paid for a commodity goes down as the supply of that commodity increases. In economics, this is often referred to as supply and demand.

Scarce items are usually in greater demand and people are willing to pay more for them. When farms produce an excess of a commodity, the government may establish programs to buy some of the commodities and remove them from the market. This tends to keep prices at a level that is more likely to be profitable to farmers. The government may also enact various programs to establish price levels for farmers to insure that the commodity can be produced profitably. Government policies have often been made to keep prices as low as possible to consumers and as high as possible to producers. Promotional efforts can be made to influence buyers and sellers. Advertising can be used to make consumers aware of products. Special pricing can be used to attract buyers. Attempting to influence people to buy a product is certainly a part of free enterprise.

GOVERNMENT REGULATIONS

Pure free enterprise would involve no government regulations on commerce. Carrying on business with no regulations is often impractical. All people benefit when some sort of order is brought to the marketing process. Standards for products such as eggs and milk protect both the producer and consumer. Regulations on accurately measuring and describing products are essential. Only wholesome products should reach the consumer. No one wants to buy bad food or other inferior products. Many marketing functions are subject to various regulations, though these are kept to a minimum.

Regardless of the regulations, free enterprise allows people to take the

Figure 2-4. Fruit trees are often inspected and certified as disease-free before
they are sold.

initiative to be successful in agrimarketing. They must simply follow the
regulations that are in place. Regulations are established to assure that the
overall needs of society are efficiently and effectively met. For example,
processing plants cannot directly discharge waste water into streams. The
water must be treated so that when it is released the natural water in the
stream will not be changed. Even though a processing plant may have to
spend a lot of money on water treatment, the environment is protected
from pollution by the discharge of its untreated waste water. The costs of
meeting government regulations are passed on to consumers when they
buy a product. Government regulations should be limited to those that
protect public interest and national security.

WAYS OF DOING BUSINESS

In the United States, businesses are established to make a profit for
the owners or as nonprofit businesses that provide services to members or
citizens. Both for-profit and nonprofit businesses are found in agrimarketing.

FOR-PROFIT BUSINESSES

Businesses that are privately owned and intended to make a profit for the owners are known as *for-profit businesses* or profit-making businesses. The free enterprise system allows the establishment of three kinds of for-profit businesses: sole proprietorships, partnerships, and corporations. (The cooperative, a special kind of corporation, is discussed later.)

Sole Proprietorship

The *sole proprietorship* is a business that is owned and managed by one individual. For example, one person can set up a vegetable stand or farm tractor dealership. Some businesses in agrimarketing are relatively small and easily established. Others are large and more difficult for individuals to start.

The *proprietor* (owner) must have the money needed to start the business. This includes the capacity to borrow the money that is needed to begin and operate the business after it has opened. Other duties of the owner include managing the business, buying or renting the land, constructing the improvements (buildings, etc.), hiring employees, buying the raw materials, setting prices, keeping records, submitting government forms and payments, and many other activities associated with the business.

All profits, if any, go to the owner. Likewise, the owner can lose all that has been invested in the business if it fails. Sole proprietorships are a popular form of for-profit business. They tend to be limited by the resources available to the owner. The owner has a lot of flexibility. Decisions can often be made without checking with other people. A sole proprietorship requires considerable personal commitment if it is to be successful.

Partnership

A *partnership* involves two or more people joining together to start a business. The partners are known as co-owners. They are bound by a legal contract. Profit, if any, is divided among the partners but not necessarily equally. The amount of profit to a partner depends on the commitment of each partner. If one partner owns three-fourths of an agribusiness and another one-fourth, the profit would typically be divided proportionate to the extent of ownership. All of the owners assume some risk in the business, including unlimited liability for all the actions of the business. This probably contributes to the low popularity of partnerships in agrimarketing.

Formal legal agreements are needed between the partners. A partnership agreement describes the business and the partners, designates certain practices of the business, such as how the funds will be accounted for, provides for changes in the partnership, and contains the signatures of all partners.

Some variations in partnerships may exist. In general partnerships, all share in the business much like the sole proprietorship. Limited partnerships are sometimes used. In a limited partnership, partners may agree to contribute certain things to the business. This limits the amount of risk that may be involved. For example, in some partnerships one individual will provide the money and the other will assume the duties of operating the business. In this case, the limited partner providing the money risks the amount of money that has been invested and no more.

Partnerships may participate in agrimarketing. Using the earlier sole proprietorship example of a vegetable stand, two or more individuals may go into a partnership to start a stand. Each has a role to fulfill in the success of the stand. A written agreement among all individuals is needed. Good communication and careful attention to planning are essential. All partners in the vegetable stand should understand the roles of the others. Partnerships often get into trouble when individuals don't do what they are supposed to do or when there is a lack of understanding of the roles of the individuals involved.

Corporations

A *corporation* is treated as a legal entity though it is owned by a number of people. Forming a corporation involves establishing a business using a complex process. This includes obtaining a charter from a state government agency, writing bylaws about the corporation, selling stock, establishing a board of directors, electing officers, hiring people to run the business, and complying with other government regulations. A corporation can raise large sums of money by selling stock to invest in costly land, buildings, equipment, and raw materials. The liability of the individuals is no greater than the amount of money they have invested in the stock.

Here is how a corporation works: The stockholders elect a board of directors. The board sets the policies for the business and hires managers to run the business. These managers typically include a president, vice president, secretary, and treasurer. Reports are regularly provided to the board and members on the progress of the corporation. Managers can be replaced if the corporation doesn't do well. Government reports must be completed and submitted. If a profit is produced, stockholders may be paid a certain amount for each share of stock they own. Meetings of stockholders

Figure 2–5. The name of an agrimarketing business often describes the kinds of products it handles as well as the way it is organized to do business. (Courtesy, Office of Agricultural Communications, Mississippi State University)

are held to make decisions about the corporation. Such meetings may be held once a year or more often.

Many agrimarketing functions are carried out by corporations. These are often large businesses, but not always.

Cooperatives

The agricultural industry makes considerable use of farmer cooperatives. *Cooperatives* are associations formed by people to provide a service or meet a need. They are very similar to corporations in the way they are chartered by the government, managed, and operated.

Agricultural industry has two kinds of cooperatives: marketing and purchasing. Both are actually involved in marketing.

A *marketing cooperative* helps farmers market the commodities produced on their farms. Farmers can pool their smaller quantities into larger quantities to attract processors and others interested in large quantities. Dairy farmers often market their milk through a cooperative because a single farmer rarely produces enough milk to justify an expensive bottling plant. When several farms join together, the volume of milk is much larger. Nearly all areas of production agriculture in the United States benefit from cooperatives. Marketing cooperatives fulfill vital roles in linking the producer and consumer. Very few producers could achieve this on their own.

The *purchasing cooperative* is used to help farmers find the most economical sources of supplies and services used on farms to produce crops and livestock. In effect, the purchasing cooperative is an important marketing link between agriculture supply manufacturers and the farmer. Large quantities of farm supplies are usually sold at lower costs than small quantities. By joining together, the volume bought is much larger. Cooperatives also provide supplies and services that other businesses fail to provide.

Here is how a cooperative works: Interested individuals form an association, obtain a charter, elect a board of directors, and hire a manager to run the cooperative. Members each have one vote regardless of the size of their investment. Funds to operate the cooperative are borrowed (often from a government agency) or provided by stockholder members. Stockholders share in the ownership of any property and may receive limited returns if there is a profit. Regular reports are made to the members in meetings, published reports, and by other means. Profits, if any, are divided among the members on the basis of the volume of their purchases or sales if the board of directors declares a dividend. Federal government funding is often available to help start agricultural cooperatives.

Cooperative members usually assume risk equal to the amount they have invested in the establishment of the cooperative. Earnings go to stockholders and patrons. The returns to patrons are sometimes known as patronage dividends. Returns from participation in a cooperative may be low or there may not be any if the cooperative is poorly managed or experiences financial difficulties. The main purpose of a cooperative is to provide services to its members, and usually not to make a profit for its owners.

NONPROFIT BUSINESSES

Nonprofit businesses are often referred to as organization or associations rather than businesses. These businesses do not seek to make a profit themselves but provide services to their members. Credit unions and utility service associations are two examples.

Publicly-owned organizations may be set up to perform services that for-profit businesses don't find feasible. State or federal government agencies establish nonprofit organizations to provide certain goods or services that either aren't being provided or can't be provided by other businesses. Any profits go into the treasury of the government agency forming the organization. Examples include public utility organizations that provide electricity or water. No stock is issued.

Many rural areas of the United States have benefited from water systems. These are typically established in areas where for-profit businesses are reluctant to set up because there isn't much chance of making a profit.

AGRIMARKETING IN FREE ENTERPRISE

U.S. agrimarketing occurs in the free enterprise system. The freedoms and ways of doing business help to form a system that usually functions well. Important individual parts function together smoothly to get food and fiber to the consumer. These operate under certain principles of economics, including supply and demand, competition, and consumer choice.

SUPPLY AND DEMAND

The *principle of supply and demand* is important to producers and consumers. This principle states that price varies with the supply of a product and the demand for it. Individuals involved with agrimarketing need to understand how the principle works. Supply and demand influence the potential for profit.

Supply refers to the quantity or amount of a product that is available for sale in the market. Producers want to be able to sell more as the price goes up. If producers increase the amount available, the price will likely go down. With agricultural commodities, the supply is greatest at harvest season and at harvest the price paid is usually the lowest of the year. Conversely, the price is usually higher just before harvest begins because the supply available is at the lowest point of the year. All of the commodity that was produced last year has been used. Of course, all comparisons must be made with products of similar grade, such as no. 2 yellow corn or choice fed steers.

Demand refers to the quantity of a product that will be bought at a given price at a particular time. As prices go up, demand tends to go down. Fewer people are willing to pay the higher price. They buy other products that can substitute for what they have been buying. For example, as the price of corn goes up, farmers may buy other grains to feed their livestock. The other grains, such as wheat and milo, may not be quite as good as corn, but comparatively they are satisfactory. When the supply of corn increases and the price goes down, farmers may start buying corn again.

Agrimarketing specialists use supply and demand schedules to study the relationships between quantity and demand. These are also known as graphs or curves. The curves show the interaction between supply and demand. The point where the curves cross is where buying and selling will occur. "On-paper" prices can be established using the curves. Further, the quantity that will be bought at a given price can be estimated with curves. Of course, the supply-and-demand curves are graphic depictions and may not actually show what happens in the marketplace.

Market prices are established when the buyer and seller agree on a price. If demand remains constant and supply goes down, the price paid will go up. On the other hand, if the supply of an item goes up and demand remains the same, the price will go down.

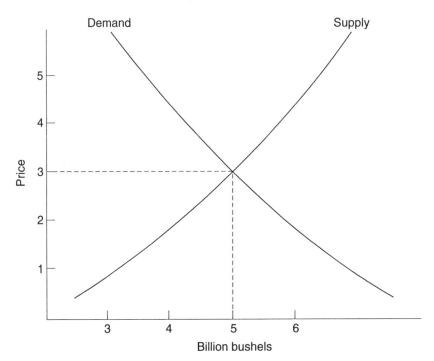

Figure 2-6. A supply and demand curve graphically shows the number of
           bushels of a product that would be sold at a given price. In this
           example, five billion bushels would be sold at a price of
           $3/bushel. The curve also shows that more would be sold at a
           lower price and less at a higher price.

An every-day example: Fresh vegetables tend to be available on a seasonal basis. Prices in supermarkets are lowest when a vegetable is in season. Prices are higher when they aren't in season. Shoppers tend to buy more when the price is lower. Even though available year-round in modern supermarkets, fresh tomatoes are priced higher in the winter than in the summer. This is because the supply available is greater in the summer. Some farmers try to take advantage of the higher winter prices by growing tomatoes in a greenhouse. By using a greenhouse, the farmer is trying to overcome the fact that tomatoes won't grow in cold weather and take advantage of higher prices. (Of course, it is much more costly for the farmer to grow tomatoes in a greenhouse than in an open field!)

COMPETITION

Buyers and sellers often compete with each other. Each wants the best quality product at the lowest price. This creates competition in agrimarketing.

Competition occurs when several producers have identical or similar products and each tries to get people to buy their products. These producers compete with each other for buyers. Competition gives consumers choices. If there are only a few choices, there is little competition and prices tend to be higher.

Consumers have limited money to spend. This applies to individuals buying food and clothing, as well farmers buying seed and fertilizer and processors buying raw products. All want to get as much as they can for their money.

Marketing also involves trying to get consumers to buy products. The functions performed on food and fiber between the farm and consumer reflect efforts to attract buyers. The end result is what the ultimate consumer receives. Eggs are cleaned and graded, placed in protective packages, and labeled to attract consumers. Some foods are prepared into easy-to-cook frozen dinners to attract buyers. Competition results in marketing activities that make a product more appealing to the consumer.

Competition exists in various forms. Pure competition occurs when the number of buyers and sellers is so great that no one individual can materially affect the market price. Imperfect competition occurs when certain buyers or sellers have advantages over the others. They can exert more influence over the price level. Sometimes cutthroat competition arises. This occurs when intense competition results in losses to businesses. Some of the businesses may lose money and have to go out of business. Destructive competition is another form of intense competition. It may lead to prices that are so low that the product can no longer be offered to the public.

Monopolies occur when one individual or company becomes very large and controls the price by limiting the supply that is produced. It is obvious that cutthroat and destructive competition and monopolies are dangerous in the free enterprise system. Electrical power companies that have a monopoly to provide power are regulated by government agencies so that the price is kept reasonable.

Competition occurs among agribusinesses that provide supplies and services to the farm as well as among those who are involved in moving food and fiber to the consumer. The following are a few examples:

- Tractor and implement manufacturers compete for sales of equipment to farmers. Farmers buy from the one that offers the equipment that will do the job at the least cost to the farmer. Other factors may be considered, such as service, personal preferences, and resale value of used equipment.

- Seed, feed, fertilizer, and chemical companies compete for sales of their products to farmers. Farmers will buy from those companies that offer the product at the lowest price. Exceptions may arise when credit practices, delivery, packaging, and other factors are considered. Those who are members of cooperatives will likely buy through the cooperative, but only if this gives the best price.

Competition exists in moving food and fiber from the farm to the consumer. Examples of competition in agrimarketing are:

- Buyers of farm produce who compete with each other to buy the commodities grown on farms. In some cases, farmers may have several possibilities. They sell to the one that offers the best (highest) price.

- Processors of food and fiber compete with each other to get supermarkets to stock what they have produced. In some cases, processors may pay supermarkets for shelf space in the store in order to get their products available to the shopper. A good example is with cucumber pickles. A supermarket may allocate shelf space on the basis of the incentive provided by the processor.

Competition is an important factor in agrimarketing. It must be understood and used to the advantage of society in general. When one or two individuals become too powerful (as in a monopoly), the welfare of society may be ignored.

CONSUMER CHOICES

Consumers are people, farms, agribusinesses, and other entities that use goods and services. Typically, consumers are thought of as the people who buy food and clothing. The food is consumed! But, the word "consumer" has a much larger meaning. It refers to any person or thing that uses goods and services.

In free enterprise, consumers are free to buy as they choose. They can buy from whom they wish at a price they and the seller can agree upon. Those who produce goods and services try to attract consumers. Sellers use incentives to attract buyers. For example, tractor manufacturers may offer discounts to farmers who buy their equipment or supermarkets may advertise food items at lower prices to attract grocery shoppers. Discount coupons may be used to encourage buyers, such as coupon for 50¢ off the price of breakfast cereal.

In agrimarketing, farmers have to cope with buyers who try to buy at the lowest cost. This is a problem, because when crops are ready to harvest, the work must be done! A crop left in the field will deteriorate in quality

Figure 2–7. Consumers can choose from many different food products marketed in a variety of ways. Some of these require considerable preparation, while others can be eaten as they are shown.

if not harvested in a timely manner. Various approaches have been used to alleviate losses: Farmers may contract with a buyer before production is started; farmers may form marketing cooperatives to assist in moving the commodities to the consumer; farmers may establish their own marketing outlets through vertical integration and farmers may use various ways of buying and selling through a complex process of futures and hedging.

SUMMARY

Agrimarketing is carried out under the free enterprise system in the United States. This is an economic system that allows individuals to organize and do business with a minimum of government regulations. Individuals are free to own property privately, choose what they want to produce, and sell the produce as they please. Some government regulations are needed, however, to assure uniformity in the exchange of products and protect the consumer.

In the United States, people structure businesses in three ways: sole proprietorships, partnerships, and corporations. In addition, nonprofit businesses may be established. Producers often set up cooperatives (similar to corporations) to provide services to the members in purchasing and marketing agricultural supplies and products. Any profits from cooperatives are returned to the stockholders and patrons.

Agrimarketing begins when a producer is deciding what is to be produced. Only those items that consumers demand should be considered. Further, only those products that produce a profit for the farmer should be grown. Understanding the role of supply and demand helps the producer make better decisions about what is to be produced. Supply and demand works to establish price. As supply goes up, price goes down because the relative demand for each unit produced is less. As supply goes down, price will go up because there is more demand for each unit. Competition is an important element in marketing because producers compete to sell their products and buyers compete to get what they want.

CHAPTER SELF-CHECK

Match the following terms with the correct definitions:

    a. sole proprietorship

    b. partnership

    c. economic system

    d. free enterprise

    e. consumer

    f. supply

    g. demand

    h. competition

    i. private ownership

    j. freedom choice

_____ a system that allows individuals to operate businesses with a minimum of government regulations

_____ when individuals have things that they call their own

_____ when individuals are free to choose what they want to produce

_____ a business owned by one individual

_____ a business owned by two or more people

_____ the way goods are owned, created, and exchanged

_____ the amount of a product that is available for sale in the market

_____ when several producers have similar products and try to get people to buy their products

_____ people, farms, agribusinesses, and others that use goods and services

_____ the quantity of a product that will be bought at a given price at a particular time

QUESTIONS AND PROBLEMS FOR DISCUSSION

1. What is an economic system? Name three examples of economic systems.

2. What is capitalism? Why is it also known as free enterprise?

3. What are four characteristics of free enterprise? Explain each.

4. What are the ways of doing business for profit in the United States? Describe the advantages and disadvantages of each.

5. What is a cooperative? What kinds are found in agriculture?

6. How does a cooperative benefit a member?

7. What is the principle of supply and demand? How is it related to the price received?

8. What is competition? How is competition a part of agrimarketing?

9. What is the role of consumer choices in agrimarketing?

ACTIVITIES

1. Make a list of the agribusinesses in your town or community by the kind of business they are, for example, sole proprietorship, partnership, and corporation. Include the cooperatives. Use the telephone directory and personal contacts to prepare your list.

2. Interview the manager of an agrimarketing business. Determine the nature of the business and the problems that are present. Write a report on your findings.

3. Prepare a bulletin board or poster that compares and contrasts ways of doing business. Pay particular attention to the agricultural industry.

Chapter 3

SELECTING AND MANAGING AGRIMARKETING TECHNOLOGY

How much are you willing to pay for what you eat and wear? The prices we pay for food, clothing, and other items vary with costs of getting them to us the way we want them. Controlling marketing costs helps keep prices down! Minimizing these costs is also important to the agricultural producer.

Using efficient marketing procedures helps both the consumer and producer. Consumers pay less for what is needed and producers may earn

Figure 3–1. Trading floor activity at a futures market involves the use of hand signs to communicate whether a trader is buying or selling. For example, buyers hold their hands facing inward and sellers hands face outward. (Courtesy, Chicago Board of Trade)

a greater profit from what is sold. How the link between the producer and consumer is established affects profits.

In free enterprise, producers have a number of alternatives in production as well as marketing. Proper organization and performance of the marketing functions is essential to the success of a farm or agribusiness.

OBJECTIVES

This chapter provides information about the selection and management of the marketing process. Upon completion, you will be able to:

- Explain ways agrimarketing occurs in free enterprise
- Describe the role of information in agrimarketing
- Describe how the consumer influences agrimarketing
- Explain the importance of management in agrimarketing
- Describe the role of government in agrimarketing
- Explain how associations are involved in agrimarketing

TERMS

actuating
cash contract
cash marketing
cash price
checkoff
controlling
futures contracts
management
management functions
market information
market intervention
organizing
parity
planning
product uniformity
product wholesomeness
staffing
traders

HOW AGRIMARKETING WORKS

Every agricultural commodity is marketed in ways unique to its culture, characteristics, and consumer demands. The most sophisticated marketing systems are used for milk, cotton, grain, and livestock. Farmers have many choices with some crops and livestock and few choices with others. Farmers also define marketing differently. To some, marketing occurs when a crop is sold by the farmer for the first time. Other farmers become more involved in the marketing process.

Here are three brief examples:

- Cotton farmers have few ways of marketing their crop; however, a fairly complex system involving government and private business exists. After harvesting, the cotton is hauled in trucks and wagons, or as pallets to be ginned. Ginning is the process of separating the seed from the cotton. As harvested, 1,200 pounds of cotton will yield one bale of lint cotton, weighing about 500 pounds, and 700 pounds of seed. The seed is usually sold immediately and often is worth little more than the cost of ginning. In fact, some farmers trade the services of the gin for the seed. The bale of lint may be hauled to a warehouse for additional processing and storage. New ginning techniques are being used that may eliminate the need for the compress. From here, the cotton will eventually be sold to a textile mill and manufactured into cloth. Government programs play a large role in the marketing of cotton.

- Vegetable farmers have a fairly wide range of marketing alternatives. Of course, the kind and quantity of vegetable produced influences the process involved. Cucumbers are considerably different from lima beans, yet both go through similar functions. Vegetable farmers can market in several ways: to processors, to supermarkets, to packing sheds, or through on-farm marketing using roadside stands and pick-your-own approaches. With pick-your-own, customers come to the farm and pick and pay for what they want. A few farmers harvest and haul their vegetables to central farmers' markets where they operate retail stands to sell directly to the public. When farmers market directly to the public, they have added responsibility for managing stands, collecting money, keeping records, and dealing with the public.

- Dairy farmers produce a product that must be carefully handled, stored, and processed for the consumer. There are few marketing alternatives available to the dairy farmer. Milk is typically held in a refrigerated bulk tank on the farm. Large farms may haul the milk to a processing plant, while small and medium-sized farms arrange with a trucker to pick up the milk and haul it to the plant. Many factors are involved in marketing milk, including grade, government price supports, and milk marketing orders. (The latter occurs when the government sets the price for the milk that is marketed in a given geographical area.)

As these examples show, farmers have considerable risk in the production and marketing of agricultural commodities. Once harvested, commodities may be destroyed or damaged, or they may deteriorate in quality during storage. To help minimize some of the risk, various marketing alternatives have been developed.

CASH MARKETING

Cash marketing is the simplest way to sell a crop. The farmer delivers commodities to a buyer and receives payment on the same day. No previous contracts between the farmer and buyer have been signed. The farmer takes what the buyer is willing to pay. In cash marketing, efforts to overcome price changes include on-farm storage and delaying harvesting or selling

Figure 3–2. Hogs being sold at auction are in the cash market. (Courtesy, Marco Nicovich, Mississippi Cooperative Extension Service)

until the price is acceptable. Of course, harvesting can't be delayed too long, or the crop may deteriorate.

An example of a cash market is a livestock auction. Cattle producers bring their cattle and several buyers bid to establish the highest price to be paid. The auction company writes a check to the producer, with commission and other fees deducted from the price received.

Also known as spot price, the *cash price* is the price paid for products that are delivered today. In the above example of the livestock auction, the cash price is what the highest bidder pays for the livestock, often on a per-pound basis.

CASH CONTRACTS

Cash contracts involve the farmer and buyer signing a contract that specifies that a certain quantity of a commodity will be delivered on or by a certain date at a specified price. This form of marketing provides the farmer some protection against a drop in prices. The contract is often signed before the crop is planted; therefore, the farmer knows the price that will be received at the time of harvest.

Contracts are often used by grain elevators and vegetable processors. Not only does the contract protect the farmer, it also assures the elevator or processor of an adequate volume of raw material to operate the facility. Without a contract, the vegetable processor may not have enough vegetables.

A cash contract should be developed by a lawyer and carefully reviewed before it is signed. The contract should contain the following information: names and addresses of buyers and sellers, signatures, dates, price or basis for determining the price, kind of product, quality of the product to be delivered, how the quantity is to be determined, how the payment will be made, and any penalty for default. (Default occurs if the farmer fails to grow the crop as specified in the contract or the buyer fails to buy as agreed upon.)

An example of a cash contract for cucumbers follows. A processor of cucumber pickles may arrange for several farmers in a local community to grow cucumbers. The processor signs individual contracts with each farmer. The farmers know how much they will receive for the cucumbers before they are planted. Likewise, the processor is assured that a sufficient volume of a specified kind of cucumber will be available to operate the pickling plant. (For cucumbers, the processor may furnish the seed for the specific variety to be planted and provide supervision provided throughout the growing cycle to ensure the desired quality of cucumber.)

Figure 3–3. Futures contracts are traded in octagonal areas known as pits.
Traders stand in certain places depending on conditions of the
sale. Hand signals and open competitive outcry (shouting) are
used. The top photograph shows the trading floor during trading
hours. The bottom photograph shows the empty pits at the end
of the trading day. (Courtesy, Chicago Board of Trade)

FUTURES CONTRACTS

Futures contracts are more complex than cash and cash contract marketing. Futures contracts involve using futures markets and are most important for grain and livestock. The contract is an agreement to either make or take delivery of a commodity in the future at a specified price. The futures price is today's price (when the contract is made). No actual exchange of products occurs when the contract is traded and priced. The trading takes place at a futures market, such as the Chicago Board of Trade, Minneapolis Grain Exchange, New York Cotton Exchange, or Kansas City Board of Trade. The contracts for future delivery are known as "futures."

People involved in futures markets are known as *traders*. Traders focus on two areas: speculation and hedging. Speculation involves attempting to anticipate and profit from futures price changes. Speculators typically never own actual products. Some producers feel that speculators are detrimental to farmers, but this is usually not the case. Speculators make good futures marketing possible. Their action provides liquidity in futures marketing. Liquidity refers to the ability to convert assets (owned commodities) into money.

Hedging is taking the opposite of one's position in the cash market.

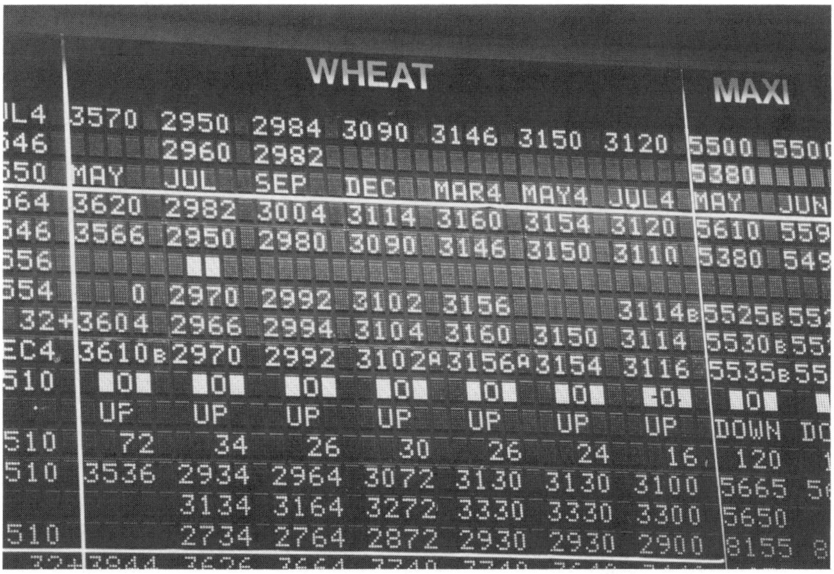

Figure 3–4. Electronic priceboards surround the trading floor at an exchange to keep traders informed on world-wide prices. This photograph shows a wheat priceboard, with futures prices for various months. (Courtesy, Chicago Board of Trade)

A farmer has a crop of wheat that is sold, while a flour mill needs wheat and buys futures. Traders who hedge are more likely to make or take delivery of a product than a speculator is. Hedging is a means of protecting against financial loss if prices decline. Hedging is used to protect against future changes in price.

Successfully using the futures market requires knowledge of the process. The services of individuals who are highly trained in the futures marketing process may be needed. (More details on futures marketing will be presented later in the book in specific chapters on commodities that are hedged.)

INFORMATION IN AGRIMARKETING

Decisions are no better than the information used in making them. A manager must have good information in order to make intelligent agrimarketing decisions.

Market information provides knowledge that may influence marketing decisions. It allows individuals to plan what to produce and when to buy and sell to maximize profit. This applies to supplies and services, farm production, and product processing.

Newspapers, radio, television, newsletters, consultants, and other means

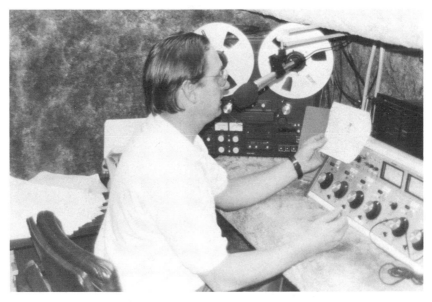

Figure 3–5. Radio is a fast way to get agrimarketing information. This agricultural marketing specialist broadcasts agrimarketing news to a number of stations.

are used to get information. Some of the media have syndicated programs and columns that provide reliable information.

Decision-makers often need and use the following information:

- **Price**—Price refers to the price of the product. Cash and futures prices change daily. Trends can be assessed. Newspapers and marketing newsletters and services are sources.

- **Weather**—Information from other regions of the United States and foreign nations on rain, frost, drought, storms, and floods has an impact on the market. For example, a drought in the wheat producing areas will result in the price of wheat going up.

- **Government policies**—Trade agreements and restrictions on trade impact prices of many agricultural products. If a large amount of a product is imported from another nation, the price will likely decline.

- **Acres planted or head on feed**—The information on acres planted and head on feed provides evidence of the quantity that will be on the market in a few months. U.S. Department of Agriculture reports are regularly issued that indicate the acreage planted and number of head of cattle or hogs on feed.

- **Disease and insect problems**—Sudden disease or insect outbreaks in another region or nation can result in increased prices. Shortages of products may develop. New markets for farmers may arise out of crop failures.

- **New product development**—New products that are appealing to consumers may result in a marked increase in demand. Decision makers need to keep up to date on possible new products.

- **Consumer issues**—Today's consumers are more health conscious. Reports that indicate that certain products may be beneficial or harmful to health may create sudden shifts in the market demand. In some cases, foods may be tainted with residues or other foreign matter which affect demand.

All available information should be used in making decisions. Of course, the information must be accurate and relevant. A good procedure is to determine the reputation of the source of the information. Market information from the U.S. Department of Agriculture is usually accurate and trustworthy. That from commodity associations may be good, depending on the reputation of those involved. Information in magazines and other publications is often based on USDA sources.

Figure 3–6. Newspapers publish reliable commodity market information.

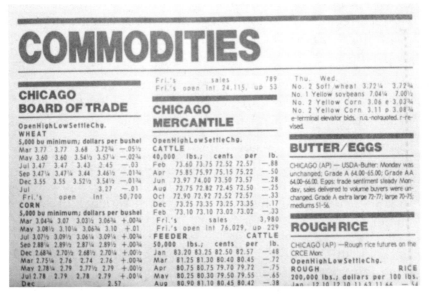

Figure 3–7. Commodity reports in newspapers provide detailed futures
information for the commodities that are traded.

HOW CONSUMERS ARE CHANGING

Consumers change. What they like to buy and use changes. Since consumers don't remain the same, individuals involved in agrimarketing must be aware of how they are changing. The kinds of products produced and the forms in which they are marketed are important agrimarketing considerations. In the United States, consumers are changing in the following ways: the number of older citizens is increasing, there is an increasing disparity of income, there is a larger proportion of ethnic groups, and there is a growing need to cope with technology.

POPULATION CHANGES

Population changes in the United States are a product of two major factors: People are living longer and birth rates have declined.

Overall, the age of citizens is increasing. The average age of people in the United States was a little over 20 years of age in 1960. In the 1990s, it is approaching 30 years of age. With a population exceeding 250 million people, there are still many individuals of all ages. However, a small increase in average age reflects considerable increase in the number of older people.

Older people have different wants and needs. They are more health conscious and want food that is conducive to good health. They will consume fewer items that are damaging to their health, such as tobacco products. Older people are more concerned with comfort and less with the latest style.

Another way to look at increases in the number of older people is to determine their social, economic, cultural, and ethnic backgrounds. Preferences for goods and services and the ability to buy what they want varies with their backgrounds.

INCOME CHANGES

The difference between the incomes of the well-off and impoverished is increasing. Many U.S. citizens live in poverty conditions. One-fourth of the children live in poverty and may lack proper nutrition and clothing. Among the affluent, incomes are continuing to rise. They are able to buy what the want, and have developed appetites for more expensive specialty food and fiber. They are also willing to pay more for services when buying their food, such as the convenience of pre-cooked frozen dinners that can be heated in a microwave oven.

Communities vary in the level of income of the people who live there. Successful marketing of agricultural commodities reflects these social and economic situations. For example, a supermarket located in an area of low income people will stock more lower-priced cuts of beef or pork, while those in higher income areas will stock the more expensive steaks, specialty foods, and fresh vegetables.

ETHNIC GROUPS

The proportion of citizens of identifiable ethnic groups is increasing in the United States. Individuals of similar religious, racial, and cultural origin tend to have particular preferences for food and other agricultural products. Marketing in communities with large proportions of ethnic groups must consider their preferences.

Religious preferences influence choices of foods. In some communities, lamb and mutton may be more popular than pork or beef. In others, specialty vegetables, poultry, and fish may be in more demand. Farmers sometimes produce and market specifically for these groups. This is known as "niche marketing," because the buyers represent an identifiable group.

A good example of producing and marketing to ethnic groups is in aquaculture. Certain species of fish, such as tilapia, may be grown and processed specifically for ethnic groups. Whereas the vast

Figure 3–8. Demand for clothing varies with the population and the preferences of people. (Courtesy, Levi Strauss & Co.)

majority of the U.S. population would want the fish dressed, some niche markets want the fish without any processing—the head and skin are left on and the internal organs are not removed.

TECHNOLOGY

People who are in the mainstream of the U.S. work force must have increased skill in the use of technology. Areas of technology include computers, robots, communication systems, and transportation. Individuals who have skills in these areas will seek goods and services equal to their backgrounds and incomes.

Education is a part of the capacity to use technology. Communities where the citizens use technology will likely have different expectations in terms of agricultural products. Better educated citizens will be more aware of healthy foods and nutrition content and will often choose items that create less danger to the environment.

Technology skills and income level tend to go together. Those with more technological capabilities usually have higher incomes and can afford more expensive food and fiber products.

MANAGEMENT IN AGRIMARKETING

Management is important in all areas of the agricultural industry. *Management* is the use of resources to achieve objectives. The objectives include the process of agrimarketing. When marketing is not included, the farm or agribusiness being managed will likely lose money and go out of business. Efficiency in marketing requires careful attention to the details involved.

Success in agriculture is far more than knowing how to produce crops and livestock. How the products are moved to consumers determines profitability.

Managers have five roles: planning, organizing, staffing, actuating, and controlling. These are known as the five management functions. Good managers are skilled in these areas. Each function depends on the others. All the functions must be performed to meet market demands.

PLANNING

Planning involves deciding on a future course of action. It includes setting goals and objectives and describing ways and means of achieving them. Plans are often written, particularly for large farms and agribusinesses. Small operations may rely on mental plans that aren't written, but it is best to have written plans.

Planning for marketing begins when the manager is deciding what to produce. This is true for agricultural supplies and services, farming, and all aspects of moving farm produce to the consumer. The key decisions focus on producing a product that will return a profit. Plans are often for more than one year.

Planning the marketing of supplies and services involves looking at what farmers will need. Managers study crop and livestock trends, government regulations, international trade, and consumer preferences. There must be a market for the supply or service. Take the example of Anderson Valley, California, where apples were once a major crop. Grapes are now replacing apples. The managers of supplies and services businesses need to consider this and increase emphasis on supplies and services for grape production.

Farm managers begin planning for marketing when they are deciding which crops to grow. Only those crops that can be marketed at profitable prices should be produced. Of course, climate requirements, soil and water availability, tractors and equipment, and personal preferences are also important. Farmers often sign contracts to grow a crop before it is planted. Farmers may change crops and grow other crops if there is the potential for more profit. Take the example of the Mississippi Delta, where cotton has been king. Some farms have switched to aquaculture—water farming. The farmers saw an opportunity to make more profit even though considerable money was needed to construct ponds and other facilities.

Managers of processing plants must have a source of raw product as well as a market. Processing plants are typically located near where the raw product is produced. In some cases, processing is near population centers in large cities. Often, processors find it more profitable to process near farms and ranches, because the raw product doesn't have to be hauled a long distance. A more valuable processed product is then shipped to the population centers. Beef is a good example. Since the 1950s, beef processing has shifted from the large cities to the rural areas where cattle are fed. In addition to the advantage of shipping processed beef over live animals, wastes from processing plants aren't concentrated in the cities.

Without good planning there is little need to go on to the other management functions. Planning must focus on producing products or providing services for which there is a good market.

ORGANIZING

Organizing is the key to putting plans into action. Activities must be identified and sequenced. Some sort of organizational structure may be needed. Organizing larger agricultural units requires more effort. Whether the agribusiness is large or small, organization will help to ensure that the necessary resources are available when they are needed. This is an important step for successful marketing.

Identifying what is needed requires knowledge of the product. Education and experience are essential. In order to grow corn, the farmer must have equipment, seed, herbicides, insecticides, fertilizer, fuel, and labor. Arranging activities in sequence involves doing the steps in the order that is needed to produce a product. Many agricultural products are seasonal and involve a specific process. For example, corn is planted in the spring and harvested in the fall. Supplies and services associated with planting are needed in the spring. Those associated with growing the crop are needed in the summer. Harvesting supplies and services are needed in the fall.

If things get out of sequence, a market may go unfilled or partially filled. Heavy rains in the spring can delay corn planting resulting in fewer acres being planted or reduced yield due to a shorter growing season. This will likely cause market prices to go up. Of course, managers can't do much to regulate the weather. They have to organize around it!

Figure 3–9. Efficient hand grading of carrots requires careful attention in all areas of management. (Courtesy, Citrus & Vegetable Magazine)

STAFFING

Staffing means having workers who can do what needs to be done. In order to meet market requirements, people must produce the desired product. The number of workers depends on the quantity and nature of the product. The workers must also be skilled in performing the work.

Small agricultural units may need few workers. In some cases, the owner is sufficient. Employing more people than needed results in excessive costs which lower or eliminate profits.

Large agricultural units may need many workers with specialized skills. For example, a large sawmill will have a variety of jobs. Workers will perform different activities, depending on their skills and job demands. Some will operate equipment, others will grade lumber, and still others will keep records on the entire process of producing lumber. Of course, one or more individuals must be involved in marketing the lumber!

In some cases, staffing will involve employing people with marketing skills. Large agribusinesses may be organized with a specialized marketing department. Some agribusinesses use the services of public relations and marketing specialists.

ACTUATING

Actuating is getting people to work together toward a common goal. Leadership is an important skill for a manager. A leader should be able to influence people.

Motivating people is a major component of actuating. It involves focusing people's energy so that they want to be productive. It is essential for everyone involved in agrimarketing to work efficiently and enthusiastically.

In recent years, employees have increasingly been involved in making decisions about their work. Emphasis is on producing a quality product. When all else is equal, quality results in more profit in the marketplace. Consumers want the best product they can get for their money.

In order to encourage quality, companies may institute a management approach called "total quality management" (TQM). The workers voluntarily form small groups to discuss problems and develop proposed solutions. Quality begins with the way employees perform their work.

CONTROLLING

Controlling is comparing what was done during the year with the goals that had been set. Though controlling may at first appear to focus on bossing people around, it involves the evaluation of the performance of the farm or agribusiness. Costs and returns are closely studied. Sources of loss and profit are noted.

In agrimarketing, managers compare end-of-year results with plans that were made at the beginning of the year. Profit is always important. Assessing successes and problems helps the manager prepare a better plan for next year. It allows the manager to compare various products, processes, and outcomes.

The cabbage farmer who doubles acreage over the previous year without additional markets may learn the importance of market planning. What do you do with cabbage no one wants?

Controlling provides information needed to revise goals and improve marketing procedures. It may result in changes in what is produced. Controlling helps the producer to see which crops are not making a profit, and which are quite profitable.

GOVERNMENT IN AGRICULTURAL MARKETING

Government assumes a variety of roles in agricultural marketing. The major role should be to enhance the marketing process. Government policies should not stifle marketing in the free enterprise system. Government regulation of product wholesomeness, product uniformity, national security, and infrastructure maintenance are discussed below.

PRODUCT WHOLESOMENESS

Consumers expect to buy products that promote good health. They expect food to be fresh and free of harmful substances. These qualities are known as *product wholesomeness*. Product labels are expected to be accurate and descriptive. Various government agencies are involved in ensuring product wholesomeness.

Federal, state, and local government agencies regularly inspect food processing establishments. The inspections are to ensure that the facilities are clean and that only good products, properly prepared, reach consumers.

Samples of the product are taken and analyzed for any problems. Storage facilities are inspected to determine if perishable items are being stored properly. Foreign substances are not tolerated in foods; however, certain standards allow for a tolerance level. For example, a can of peas may contain a limited number of insects or insect parts. The regulations do not say that absolutely no insects or insect parts are allowed.

Consumers will not tolerate spoiled and unsafe food. The government agencies that oversee food wholesomeness were established to assure quality.

PRODUCT UNIFORMITY

Consumers expect products to be the same each time they buy them. Of course, it is impossible to market an identical product every time, but the product should be uniform. *Product uniformity* describes products that meet certain standards, although they may not be identical.

Products are graded as a part of establishing uniformity. Eggs of similar size and color are packaged together. Potatoes of similar variety and size are bagged together. Beef is graded to assure relative uniformity of the same grade regardless of where it is purchased. In all cases, there is some tolerance for differences.

Weights and measures are expected to be standard. The consumer who buys 5 pounds of potatoes expects to get a full 5-pound weight. Cartons

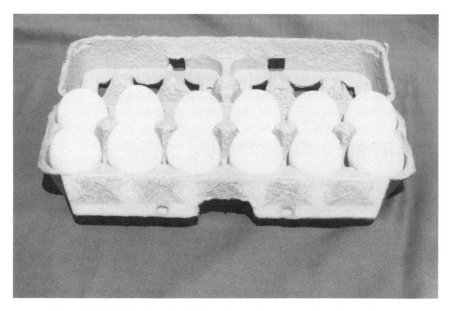

Figure 3–10. Eggs are graded and put in cartons for the consumer.

of milk are expected to be filled to the appropriate level for pints, quarts, half-gallons, and gallons. Cartons of eggs are expected to contain an exact number of eggs. Government agencies inspect scales and other measuring devices for accuracy.

Uniformity enhances the buying and selling of products. Grading allows trading to occur without the buyer actually seeing the product. A good example is cotton. Government classers sample each bale and "class" the sample. Color, presence of trash, and length and strength of staple (fiber) are important factors in classing. Standards have been established for the classes. For example, a sample may be classed as "strict good middling, 1⅛ inch." This means that the cotton is

Figure 3–11. This cotton is being graded according to official cotton standards. (Courtesy, National Cotton Council of America)

white, free of trash with fibers that are 1⅛ inch long. Cotton buyers and sellers world wide can trade cotton that has been accurately classed and know the quality they are getting.

Labels and product information are required on most products. Regulations specify the information to be presented on food labels. Consumers demand nutritional information, product description, and serving instructions.

NATIONAL SECURITY

The security of a nation depends upon citizens having sufficient food and clothing for their needs. Government programs may be initiated to ensure that enough food is available. Sometimes government programs offer subsidies to help regulate production. Payments may be made to farmers or others to encourage them to produce more or less of a certain product. Subsidies are for the overall welfare of society.

International trade is sometimes a matter of national security and human rights. Famines may wipe out food supplies in certain countries. The U.S. government may make food supplies available to the citizens of those countries to prevent starvation.

MARKET INTERVENTION

Market intervention is when the government takes steps to enhance the overall welfare of the nation by regulating certain aspects of marketing. Decisions to intervene must be made carefully to minimize conflict with the notion of free enterprise.

Agricultural leaders have long sought equality of agriculture with other sectors of the economy. This is known as *parity*. The Agricultural Adjustment Act of 1933 established criteria for fair prices.

Over the years, the United States has pursued a cheap food policy. This has involved subsidizing farmers so that the cost of food can be kept low. Regardless, the taxpayers foot the bill for the subsidy. Another related area is the policy of encouraging the maintenance of family farms. Subsidies help farm families earn sufficient money to live. This reduces the movement of rural citizens to problem urban areas.

Several areas of intervention by the government in agrimarketing are:

- **Price and income support programs**—These programs typically provide loans to farmers to store what they have produced. The farmer can later reclaim and sell the product if the price goes up. This gives the farmer an opportunity to have money from the crop at the time of harvest and to realize any price increases that may occur in the months following harvest. The farmer must pay the cost of storage.

- **Purchase and storage programs**—In these programs, the government buys products. When this happens, demand is increased and the prices go up. The government disposes of what is owned in foreign trade, donations to needy families, and in other ways.

- **Direct farm payments**—These programs provide the farmer with cash to make up for low prices. In some cases, various land diversion programs may be used. Farmers are paid for taking land out of production.

- **Marketing orders**—With a few products, particularly milk, regulations are established that set minimum prices buyers of products must pay farmers. The U.S. Secretary of Agriculture issues the orders and prescribes the conditions to be met.

INFRASTRUCTURE MAINTENANCE

Highways, roads, ports, warehouses, and other facilities used in agrimarketing are often established and maintained with government funding. These are know as infrastructure; they facilitate the marketing process.

Programs to build roads for hauling agricultural products have been used in parts of the United States. The notion was that roads were needed to transport farm commodities. Good roads promoted agricultural industry. Supplies and services could get to the farm and products could move from the farm.

Port facilities are often constructed and maintained by the government. These encourage the international marketing of agricultural products. The commerce is said to be good for the nation's economy because money is brought into the United States from other nations. This involves something known as balance of trade. In many years, the United States imports more products than it exports. This creates a negative balance of trade.

Processing plants, warehouses, grading stations, and other facilities may be constructed with government assistance. The assistance may be in the form of grants or loans to individuals or groups. Individuals who operate the facilities may be employed by the government.

ASSOCIATIONS IN AGRIMARKETING

Associations of farmers and other groups may get involved in marketing. In some cases, an association may set standards for a particular product. In many cases, commodity groups promote consumption of a product. Funding of these efforts occurs in several ways: commodity research and promotion programs, dues, and voluntary assessments.

COMMODITY RESEARCH AND PROMOTION PROGRAMS

Commodity research and promotion programs are sometimes known as checkoff programs. Funds are raised by assessing producers fees at the time of sale. For example, a small charge may be made for each head of cattle or hundred weight of milk sold. The checkoff amount is deducted from what the product sells for and is sent to the appropriate agency. The U.S. Congress must approve such programs.

Commodity research and promotion programs have been authorized for beef, dairy products, cotton, eggs, floral products, honey, lamb, pork, potatoes, and a few other commodities.

DUES

Farmers, agribusinesses, and others may form associations to serve useful roles in marketing commodities. The associations may also conduct educational programs on the latest production practices. Some associations have lobbyists to help assure favorable legislation for their members. Association members are typically assessed dues on the basis of the size of their farms or businesses—the larger the volume of commerce, the more the dues.

Agribusinesses may band together to help solve common problems and promote their products. For example, grain elevators in the United States may join the National Grain and Feed Association. The association conducts research and development activities and develops product promotion campaigns.

Farm producers may form associations for particular commodities. For example, the American Tilapia Association is an organization of individuals interested in the production of tilapia—a hardy warm-water fish. Educational programs and product promotional campaigns are developed with the dues of the members.

A few associations represent the general interests of agriculture. These associations do not focus on a particular commodity. An example is the Farm Bureau. Local and state Farm Bureau associations are affiliated with the American Farm Bureau Federation.

VOLUNTARY ASSESSMENTS

Farmer associations may voluntarily assess themselves fees to promote markets that are beneficial, sometimes known as *checkoff,* because the costs are assessed when a commodity is sold or a supply is bought. The amount of fee is typically based on the size of the farm or volume of product produced.

In some cases, supplies going to the farm have an added charge. A good example is the aquaculture industry of the Mississippi River Delta. A small amount is added to each ton of fish feed sold. This money is sent to an independent agency that promotes the consumption of the fish products through advertisements, recipe development, cooking contests, and other means.

Checkoff for rice, soybeans, livestock, and other commodities involves deducting a small charge from the sale of the product. The money from the checkoff supports research on the commodity as well as marketing efforts.

SUMMARY

Agrimarketing begins when a producer is deciding what to produce. Only those items that consumers demand should be considered. Further, only those products that produce a profit for the farmer should be grown. Agrimarketing typically occurs in several ways: cash, cash contracts, and futures. The cash market is the easiest to understand—the producer delivers a product and gets paid for it. With cash contracts, the producer and the buyer sign a contract specifying the amount of a product to be delivered later at a specified price. Futures contracts involve buying and selling in the cash and futures markets. This is a complex marketing method.

The agrimarketing manager must be capable in five roles: planning, organizing, staffing, actuating, and controlling. These are critical to the success of all agrimarketing enterprises. These must also be carried out so that government regulations are followed. The benefits provided by commodity associations should also be explored in managing the agrimarketing process.

CHAPTER SELF-CHECK

Match the following terms with the correct definitions:

    a. cash marketing

    b. cash price

    c. cash contract

    d. futures contract

    e. management

f. parity

g. market intervention

h. product uniformity

i. checkoff

j. product wholesomeness

_____   when the government regulates marketing for the
           overall welfare of the nation

_____   voluntary assessment made when products are sold

_____   equality of agriculture with other sectors of the
           economy

_____   delivering and receiving payment for products on
           the same day

_____   agreement between seller and buyer specifying that
           a certain quantity of a commodity will be
           delivered on a certain day at a specified price

_____   agreement to make or take delivery of a commodity
           in the future at a specified price

_____   using resources to achieve objectives

_____   qualities of food and other products that are fresh
           and free of harmful substances

_____   products that meet certain standards but aren't
           identical

_____   price paid for products the day they are delivered

QUESTIONS AND PROBLEMS FOR DISCUSSION

1. Name and distinguish between the three ways of marketing products.

2. Why is information important in marketing? What kind of information do decision makers often need?

3. What media provide market information?

4. How are consumers changing? Why are these changes important in agrimarketing?

5. What are the roles of managers in agrimarketing? Explain each.

6. What is planning for marketing?

7. How is organizing important in marketing?

8. What are staffing and actuating? How are they related?

9. What is controlling? Why is it important?

10. Why does the government get involved in agrimarketing? What major areas are included?

11. Why is product wholesomeness important to consumers?

12. What is meant by "cheap food policy?"

13. How is government involved in infrastructure?

14. How are associations a part of agrimarketing?

ACTIVITIES

1. Locate the market report in a daily newspaper. Identify the cash and futures prices of selected commodities such as corn, soybeans, beef, and wheat. Describe your observations in a paragraph. Keep a record of prices for two weeks. Note how the prices varied.

2. Investigate the agrimarketing associations that are found in your area. Interview farmers, agribusiness managers, and others to identify the associations.

Chapter 4

FINDING A CAREER IN AGRIMARKETING

Your favorite foods are possible because of the people who work in agrimarketing. Take the taco you buy for a few cents at the local fast food eatery. Many people have worked at various levels to make it possible!

Exciting and rewarding careers are a part of getting your taco just the way you want it—meat, lettuce, tomato, onion, taco shell, and spicy sauce. Tracing the ingredients back to the farm and to the supplies and services needed to produce them reveals a complex process. Following the ingredients from the point of production through all of the marketing functions is amazing!

Figure 4–1. Designing packages used in agrimarketing requires specific skills in communication and graphics. This person is preparing a new layout for feed bags.

All people in the food and fiber system have a role in marketing. Providing for the needs and wants of consumers requires a quality product at the right time and place at an affordable price. Some jobs require people with specific marketing skills. These individuals need to perform their jobs well. If not, agrimarketing loses efficiency and effectiveness. The result may be lower quality products at higher prices.

The focus of this chapter is on careers in agrimarketing. Some of these are full-time marketing positions. Others incorporate marketing along with a number of other responsibilities. There is probably one that is just right for you!

TERMS

apprenticeship
career
career advancement
career ladder
job
level of education
level of work
managerial occupation
occupation
professional occupation
semi-skilled occupation
skilled occupation
unskilled occupation
work ethic

OBJECTIVES

To help understand the careers in agrimarketing, several important objectives are covered in this chapter. Upon completion, you will be able to:

- Describe the process of choosing a career in agrimarketing
- Explain major career areas in agrimarketing
- Describe the nature of the work in agrimarketing careers
- Describe career ladders in agrimarketing

CHOOSING A CAREER IN AGRIMARKETING

Choosing the direction for your life is important. One of the most important life decisions is about work—the career you pursue. The choice is important because it determines what you spend your time doing and the level at which you live.

If an individual works 40 years in his or her career, many hours are spent at work. At 40 hours per week and 52 weeks a year, there are 2,080 work hours in a year. In 40 years an individual works 83,200 hours. Because this is a huge amount of time, people need to feel good about their careers. Further, their earnings are related to the nature of their work. And earnings dictate the standard of living you have!

AGRIMARKETING CAREERS AND OCCUPATIONS

A *career* is the general course of your life's work. Since people begin at one level and advance to another, we often hear about career patterns or ladders. Career ladder refers to the sequence of preparation and occupations an individual follows in a career. (More information on career ladders is presented later in the chapter.) For an individual in agrimarketing, we could say that they followed an agrimarketing career. Many times marketing is one part of a career. For example, the farmer performs many roles in addition to marketing.

Careers may be composed of a number of different occupations. Careers encompass broad areas. An *occupation* is specific work that can be given a title, such as grain inspector or seed salesperson. Further, occupations have certain duties (often known as competencies) that people must have to perform the occupation. On the other hand, a *job* implies specific work, such as inspecting grain or selling seed. Further, jobs often involve specific sites and employers. An individual can change employers and keep the same occupation and career. Occupations often include a number of different jobs.

People may change occupations and sometimes change careers. Changing occupations is easier than changing careers. People make changes because of new opportunities and the desire to experience new things. Changes may be needed to gain career advancements.

The following example will help explain careers, occupations, and jobs. Assume Cybil McRae enters an agrimarketing career at a vegetable receiving station. The occupational title is assistant receiving clerk. The job is with XYZ Veggies, Inc. It involves greeting farmers who are delivering vegetables, weighing trucks, recording weights, using a computer to enter information, and related duties. Cybil works hard and performs well. After a few months there is a job opening for a receiving clerk. Cybil applies for and gets it. Cybil now has an assistant receiving clerk who helps her. Cybil's job and occupation have changed but the career is still in agrimarketing. Cybil continues to perform well. In a couple of years, Farm Fresh Fruits, Inc., located a few miles away has an opening for a receiving clerk. Since Farm Fresh is a larger company, the position is an advancement and pays better even though it is the same occupation. Cybil applies and gets this job. She has a new job but continues the same occupation and career.

Figure 4–2. Marketing forestry products involves many occupations at a sawmill.

WORK ETHIC

Views of work vary. Our *work ethic* is how we view work. In the United States, work has been viewed as a natural and integral part of life. People are expected to be productive and make contributions to society. They are expected to earn the money to buy what they need. Of course, exceptions are made for the young and elderly and those who are unable to work because of a handicap.

Careers in agrimarketing allow individuals to make useful contributions to society. The work helps provide for the basic human needs of food, clothing, and shelter.

Success is often viewed in terms of the work ethic. Individuals who work hard, do a good job, and live a good life will be rewarded. Of course, there is more to career success than just hard work, but it is certainly important.

THE PROCESS

Choosing an agrimarketing occupation and career is a process. Individuals go through a process similar to setting goals. It typically involves a series of decisions. People assess their likes and dislikes. They learn the nature of the work involved through education and experience. They eliminate certain careers and include others. Plans may change as new opportunities become available and people get more information. It is always okay to change plans, but it is important to think for yourself.

The process must include an understanding of what is involved in the

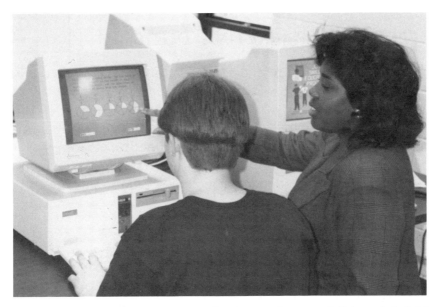

Figure 4–3. Computer programs and assistance from specialists are helpful in making career decisions.

occupation. Here are seven questions to answer that will help you understand an occupation better:

1. How much education is required?
2. Am I willing to get the needed education?
3. What kind of experience is needed?
4. What is the nature of the work?
5. What are the opportunities for advancement?
6. Will I like doing the work?
7. Am I committed to being a responsible, productive worker?

After studying information about careers and occupations that may interest you, answer the above questions. If the answers appear to meet with your expectations, an agrimarketing career may be for you!

OCCUPATIONS AND CAREERS

Occupations and careers in agrimarketing can be classified in several ways. Four classifications are presented here: time spent in agrimarketing, areas of the marketing activities, amount of education required, and level of responsibility.

TIME SPENT ON MARKETING DUTIES

Some occupations require the use of agrimarketing skills all of the time and others make use of these skills only part of the time. Those that require marketing skills part of the time are usually full-time occupations but the remaining time is spent performing other duties. Many farm-based agricultural occupations require being involved with marketing part of the time. In addition to occupations that require marketing skills, many occupations support marketing functions but don't require any specific skills in marketing.

Occupations Where All of the Work Time Is Spent on Agrimarketing

Full-time agrimarketing occupations require people to use all of their work time on marketing. These occupations are often found in businesses that provide supplies and services to farms and in companies that move farm products to consumers. People in these fields deal with agricultural commodities. Individuals who work for marketing companies that don't need marketing skills aren't included in this category.

Occupations Where Part of the Work Time Is Spent on Agrimarketing

People who spend part of their work time using agrimarketing skills are usually employed full time but are involved in marketing only a part of that time. These workers perform a variety of duties, only some of which involve agrimarketing. The amount of time spent on marketing varies considerably. Performing all of the work well is important to overall success. The ability to market competently is no less important, even though these individuals have other duties.

AREAS OF MARKETING

In this book, agrimarketing is divided into three areas: marketing

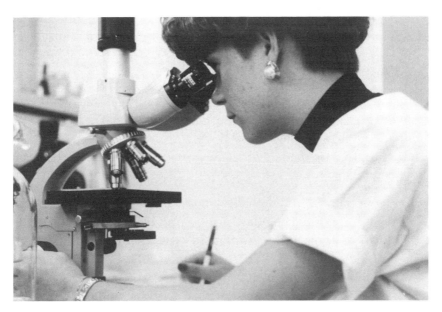

Figure 4-4. People who test food products for spoilage must have appropriate education and be willing to work in laboratories. This person is using a microscope to study the microorganisms that cause kiwi fruit to spoil. (Courtesy, National FFA Center)

supplies and services to agricultural producers, marketing the products of farms and ranches, and marketing after the product has left the farm or ranch. Each of these areas is important in providing food and fiber. Each supports the other. The areas may overlap. Certainly, each must understand the needs and directions of the other. The major emphasis is on effectively producing what consumers want.

EDUCATION

Education prepares people to work in various levels of agrimarketing. Both the level achieved and the areas studied are important.

Level

Level of education refers to the number of years and degrees of formal education completed by an individual. Some occupations require individuals with college degrees, while others have no specific level of education requirements. The typical levels of education are:

- **Less than high school**—This includes those individuals who attended high school, but dropped out before completing diploma requirements. These individuals are typically limited to low levels of occupations; however, their work is essential in the marketing of food and fiber.

- **High school**—This level is made up of individuals who have completed high school, but do not have additional education. The occupations available for these people are typically at the lower levels. Individuals can get some advancement by proving themselves as good workers.

- **Postsecondary**—This typically involves two years of education beyond high school. The education is provided at community colleges, technical schools, and similar institutions. The training may be specialized so that individuals are able to fill occupations that involve considerable responsibility.

- **Baccalaureate**—This level typically requires completing four years of college and earning a baccalaureate degree. Colleges and universities offer a number of programs that can provide important education for success in agrimarketing. These occupations are often at the technical level and above, including sales, product development, and management.

- **Graduate degree**—Occupations at this level require education beyond the baccalaureate degree. They often involve high levels of responsibility in planning marketing strategies, product development, and other areas.

Areas of Preparation

Agricultural marketing occupations include a wide range of duties. Individuals with preparation in a number of areas are needed. Many occupations require education in agriculture, specifically agrimarketing. In some cases, individuals with training in general areas of marketing are

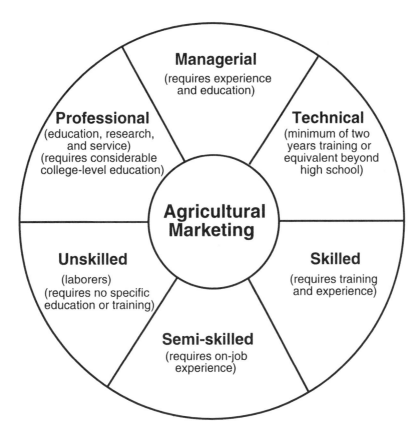

General Clusters of Agricultural Marketing Careers

Figure 4–5. Clusters of agrimarketing occupations by level of responsibility are shown here.

needed. However, a background in agriculture is considered important. Understanding how food and fiber are produced helps individuals relate better to those in the agricultural industry.

In addition to formal education, specialized on-the-job training is often needed. Workshops, seminars, and other means of providing training are used. New employees are often trained to do their jobs. Experienced workers need training in order to keep up to date. Workers who don't stay current often lose their ability to be productive.

LEVEL OF RESPONSIBILITY

Agrimarketing occupations are often classified by the amount of responsibility involved. The duties can be referred to as the *level of work*. The level is based on the amount of skill required, extent to which decisions are made, and other aspects of responsibility. Occupations are often clustered into five levels of responsibility. Sometimes an occupation will appear in more than one level. The difference is based on the amount of responsibility. For example, farmers with very large operations might be in the first level, while those with smaller farms would be in the second level.

Professional and Managerial

This level includes the top managerial and professional agrimarketing occupations. People in these occupations are often the policy makers and top decision makers. Those in managerial occupations are responsible for top-level management activities in large agrimarketing firms. A high level of education is often required. The professional occupations, such as food scientist and agrimarketing researcher, usually require education beyond the baccalaureate degree level. Extensive experience is usually needed. People often advance to the managerial level after considerable time working at lower levels. Except for certain professional occupations that require high levels of education, the occupations in this level are entered only after considerable experience. Individuals in the occupations in this level receive the highest earnings for their work. Agrimarketing researchers, managers of large agrimarketing firms, and similar occupations are included in this level.

Semi-professional and Small Business

These occupations typically have a low degree of responsibility except in the case of small business managers. Education requirements may be at the baccalaureate degree level. Many individuals are entrepreneurs operating smaller agrimarketing firms, such as grain elevators and cattle buying services. Some farmers and ranchers are in this level. The amount of income can be quite good depending on the size of the business or extent of responsibility.

Skilled

Skilled occupations in agrimarketing require specialized training or experience. Entry-level education may be at the postsecondary level or the high school level with vocational training and some experience. People who sample grain, class cotton, and perform related functions are at the skilled level. Individuals often enter at a lower level and advance to the skilled level. In some cases, an apprenticeship is required. An *apprenticeship* is a period of training under the direction of a highly skilled worker. Some schools have established school-to-work transition programs which are similar to apprenticeships. The rate of pay can be good but is usually below the semi-professional and small business level.

Semi-skilled

Semi-skilled occupations in agrimarketing require some skill and job training but less than those at the skilled level. A high school education that includes vocational education is often needed. Experience can make up for a lack of education. Individuals who operate equipment, make deliveries, write job orders, and perform related duties in agrimarketing are at the semi-skilled level. The rate of pay is below the skilled level.

Unskilled

Unskilled occupations in agrimarketing do not require specific education or experience. They usually involve performing simple activities under close supervision. The education requirements are usually the ability to read, write, and do simple mathematics. Sometimes vocational training or on-the-job training may be provided. These individuals are usually paid the lowest of any level. The work they do is important and definitely contributes to the marketing of agricultural products. Typical occupations involve cleaning facilities and equipment, moving supplies and products, and loading and unloading rail cars and trailers.

NATURE OF WORK
IN AGRIMARKETING

Work duties in agrimarketing vary considerably among the occupations. Some occupations require a great deal of interaction with people. Most involve considerable awareness of marketing information. Abilities in analyzing information and making decisions are essential in many of the occupations.

OCCUPATIONS THAT INVOLVE AGRIMARKETING ALL OF THE TIME

Several occupations in which agrimarketing is the primary area of duty are included here.

Traders

These people work in commodity exchanges selling corn, coffee, sugar, cocoa, wheat, cotton, and other commodities on the exchange. Considerable knowledge of trends and events that impact marketing is needed. Since there are only a few exchanges, the number of opportunities in this field is limited. Most traders have baccalaureate degrees and considerable experience in marketing. Some agricultural background is beneficial. The work is usually in large cities where the exchanges are located. Communication with buyers and sellers is most important. Traders are expected to keep up to date on trends that effect the market and follow the rules of trading, including dressing appropriately. (Some exchanges require traders to wear coats of certain colors and other identification.)

Sales Representatives

These people may sell supplies to farms and ranches or sell the produce of farms and ranches. Sales representatives need to know a lot about what they are selling and be aware of the needs of those they are selling to. A good knowledge of agriculture is needed, especially of the crops or livestock

Figure 4–6. Traders must know the rules of trading and stay up to date on commodity prices. This shows traders on the trading floor of a commodity exchange. (Courtesy, Chicago Board of Trade)

Figure 4–7. Sales representatives often call on farmers and others in the agricultural industry. This shows an agripharmaceutical sales rep calling on a sheep farmer. (Courtesy, Merck & Co., Inc.)

they are selling. If their work involves selling to farmers, they need to understand farming and the nature of the farm work. It is essential to be able to relate to people, particularly the clients. Individuals in sales must be self-starters. They must be highly motivated. Salespersons must often work without direct supervision. A baccalaureate degree is often required. Experience and on-the-job training are essential for success. The work is typically in locations near farms and ranches. Some of the work may be in large cities where the headquarters of large companies are located.

Figure 4–8. Agrimarket news reporters receive information from many sources. They must have an excellent knowledge of marketing processes. (Courtesy, Progressive Farmer Radio Network)

Market News Reporters

The work involves gathering information and preparing newspaper and magazine articles or radio and television stories about agrimarketing. Market news reporters must often travel to agricultural meetings. They must be able to interview experts and prepare the interviews into written articles or broadcast stories. Deadlines often require reporters to work under pressure to prepare stories. Education usually includes a baccalaureate degree in agricultural communication or a related area. Reporters must be good in written and spoken communication. A background in agriculture is beneficial and often required for employment. Some market news reporters own their businesses, while others are employed by larger firms.

Government Marketing Specialists

This work includes a wide range of duties, such as collecting market information, preparing reports, or developing new markets. These specialists typically work with the federal and state governments. They are responsible for collecting information on the acres planted and harvested, how the products are marketed, amount received for the products, and trends in the population. The reports they prepare must be accurate. In many cases, deadlines for issuing reports must be met. Some marketing specialists work to develop new markets and products. A baccalaureate degree is usually needed; masters and doctoral degrees may be required. The work is performed in large cities, small towns, and rural areas. Most opportunities are in areas where agricultural products are produced and marketed.

Procurement and Purchasing Agents

These people buy raw products for feed manufacturing mills, food processors, dairy plants, and other areas of agricultural industry. Procurement and purchasing agents are responsible for following all policies of the agency or company in making purchases. They often spend a lot of money, and their decisions are important in determining how profitable a company will be. A baccalaureate degree is usually required. Experience related to procurement and purchasing is needed. The work is typically found in areas where agricultural supplies and services are manufactured or farm commodities are processed.

Buyers

Buyers typically purchase farm products for processors. In some cases, they buy for other farmers or for supplies and services businesses. These individuals may specialize in one area, such as buying cattle at auctions, buying vegetables at packing sheds, or buying flowers at wholesale terminals. Buyers must know quality products. They must be able to appraise a shipment and quickly decide if the quality meets the needs of the client or employer. Buyers typically work in areas where crops and livestock are produced. They need a good background in the commodities they are buying. A baccalaureate degree is often required. The education is usually related to what they buy. For example, cattle buyers are generally required to have a college degree in animal science, or flower buyers in horticulture or floriculture. Experience in work related to buying is often essential.

Inspectors and Graders

Inspectors and graders examine products to determine their quality. They compare products with the standards that have been set. They must know the standards well. These individuals perform valuable services in marketing and often specialize in one product, such as cotton (often known as classers), hogs, corn, poultry, and aquacrops (fish and other crops grown in water). Work is found where agricultural products are produced and sold. A baccalaureate degree is sometimes required. Extensive on-the-job training and experience may be needed. Inspectors and graders are often found at grain elevators, packing sheds, processing plants, and similar places where agricultural products are sold or processed. Inspectors and graders often work for federal or state government agencies. In some cases, they work for associations or for food manufacturers.

Figure 4–9. Eggs are here being inspected and graded before being placed in a hatchery facility.

Dealer Trainers

These individuals train local dealers how to merchandise and sell supplies, services, and products. For example, a farm machinery manufacturer may provide training for the salespeople in the local dealerships. The work often involves travel to places where dealers are located. Trainers must be able to relate to the situations of dealers. They need some understanding of the nature of agriculture and the kinds of problems faced in growing food and fiber. Dealer trainers are typically required to have a baccalaureate degree. Considerable experience is needed, often working as a dealer or in a dealership.

Agrimarket Researchers

These individuals collect information about trends in consumption, production, and other areas. They provide reports that are used in planning production and product development. Agrimarket researchers are responsible for providing information that is very important in agrimarketing. Accuracy is essential. Inaccurate reports can result in poor decisions that cause farms and agribusinesses to lose money. Agrimarket researchers typically have graduate degrees at the masters or doctoral level. Their studies are highly specialized in agricultural economics, marketing, or general economics. A background in production agriculture is beneficial. The work is located at research facilities, typically found at universities, research centers, or government agencies. Larger agribusinesses employ agrimarket researchers, and some work independently.

OCCUPATIONS WHICH INVOLVE AGRIMARKETING SOME OF THE TIME

Many agricultural occupations require skills in marketing as well as skills in many other areas. A few examples of occupations are presented here.

Farmers and Ranchers

Farming and ranching is a business. Farmers and ranchers must perform many duties associated with economic success of the business. Marketing duties are extremely important to financial success. All farmers and ranchers must deal with marketing to some extent. As a manager, the farmer and rancher has many decisions to make. In all decisions, marketing plays an important role. The farmer or rancher who only knows about the cultural requirements of crops or livestock will likely produce quality products but will not have given consideration to marketing. Marketing is where income to the farm is generated. The level of income is related to the farmer's

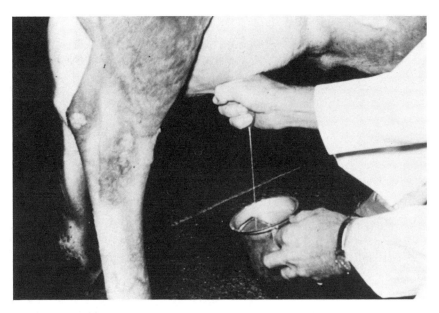

Figure 4–10. A milk sample is being collected by the dairy producer to assure
that the milk meets marketing standards.

marketing skill. Education and experience levels of farmers vary considerably.
Those who operate successful farms and ranches use both education and
experience to guide them.

Field Service Representatives

Individuals in these occupations work for agribusinesses that process
farm products. They work with farmers and ranchers to ensure that the
products are up to the standard needed. The work of field service representatives varies considerably, depending on the commodity being produced.
The work typically focuses on helping farmers and ranchers produce a
product that is in demand. For example, vegetable processors may have
field service personnel who advise farmers on how to grow their crops, or
broiler processors may have specialists who oversee the growing of chickens.
Field service representatives must have considerable experience in their
particular fields. They are typically required to have a baccalaureate degree
in an area closely related to their work. Using the above example, vegetable
processors would hire field service personnel who have studied horticulture
or a closely related subject. The work is located in farming and ranching
areas. Some travel may be required. The ability to relate to farmers and
ranchers is essential.

Figure 4–11. A field representative for animal medicines calls on a
veterinarian in his office. (Courtesy, Merck & Co., Inc.)

Elevator and Warehouse Operators

These individuals are in charge of facilities where grain, cotton, and
other products are stored. They oversee a wide range of duties related to
receiving, storing, and shipping products. Some of their duties involve
marketing skills, such as planning when and what to buy and sell. They
often deal with farmers and processors of raw products. Good human
relations skills are needed. The ability to perform overall management
functions is essential. Preparing accurate written and telecommunication
records is important. Education is often at the baccalaureate degree level
though individuals with high school and postsecondary education may
operate elevators and warehouses. Experience is essential, especially for
those with lower levels of education. The work is performed near marketing
centers for agricultural products.

Farm Cooperative Managers

A cooperative generally employs someone to operate the business. Most
managers perform a wide range of duties, but part of their time focuses
on marketing. The exact nature of their work depends on the purpose of
the cooperative—marketing or purchasing. Regardless, they often oversee

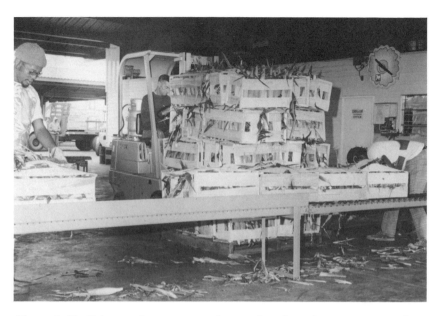

Figure 4–12. Using equipment to receive produce is an important part of
operating a packing shed. This sweet corn is being placed in
crates for shipment. (Courtesy, *Citrus & Vegetable* Magazine)

the work of those specifically involved in marketing. The occupations are
located in areas where farmers and ranchers have formed cooperatives. They
are typically in small towns and rural areas, though not always. Most farm
cooperative managers are expected to have a baccalaureate degree. Their
degrees are typically in some area of agricultural management. Farm cooperative managers often begin in lower-level jobs and advance to be
managers. Human relations skills are essential. Farm cooperative managers
should be good organizers. They must be able to relate to farmers and
ranchers as well as other clients of the cooperative.

Food Scientists

These individuals develop new products or new ways of presenting
products. Their work assures a quality food product at a reasonable cost.
They work in laboratories or with the public testing proposed new products.
Food scientists usually must have baccalaureate and graduate degrees in
areas related to food science. They must be skilled in using laboratory
analytical equipment and processes, accurately recording information, and
designing development processes. Chemistry and other areas of science are
important.

OCCUPATIONS THAT SUPPORT AGRICULTURAL MARKETING

Agrimarketing is supported by many occupations which require simple marketing skills. These are important occupations because they facilitate the marketing functions. Individuals in agrimarketing depend on those in supportive occupations to do their jobs well so that quality products reach the consumer. A few examples are given here.

Truck Drivers

These individuals operate trucks that transport agricultural supplies, products, and manufactured goods. The do not apply many marketing skills. However, it is helpful for them to understand the nature of what they are transporting. For example, under-

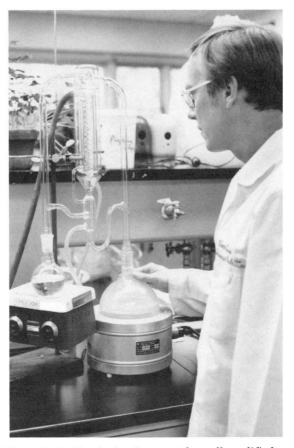

Figure 4–13. Food scientists must be well qualified to use laboratory equipment. This shows a distillation extraction unit being used in food analysis. (Courtesy, American Association of Cereal Chemists)

standing how to maintain the quality of fresh oranges can help ensure the delivery of top quality oranges. Truck drivers must usually complete specialized training in truck operation and have the appropriate commercial vehicle operator's license.

Line Workers in Processing Plants

These individuals work in food and fiber processing plants. They perform a variety of important duties that assure a quality product for the consumer.

Figure 4–14. Food processing plant workers have important roles in assuring
that a quality product reaches the consumer. This processing
line is preparing whole catfish for freezing. (Courtesy, Delta
Pride Catfish, Inc.)

In many cases, little training is needed. What is needed can often be given
in a few minutes by a supervisor.

Clerical Workers

These individuals operate the offices that support the marketing functions. They operate computers, prepare letters and orders, handle communications, keep records, and perform many other essential duties. Clerical
workers must be skilled in their work but they don't need to have many
skills in agrimarketing.

Farm Employees

Farm employees perform a variety of duties in the production of food
and fiber. They contribute to the quality of a product so that it will meet
consumer demands. They work hard in production but do not get heavily
involved in marketing.

Figure 4–15. People in retail markets perform a variety of work activities, such as this person who is preparing a display of fish in a supermarket.

Loan Officers

These individuals work for banks and other lending agencies. They are not specifically involved in agrimarketing; however, a knowledge of the process can help them relate to farmers, ranchers, and others involved in the marketing process.

CAREERS LADDERS IN AGRICULTURAL MARKETING

Career ladder is the term applied to the upward advancement of people in agrimarketing careers. They start at a lower level and move upward. Of course, advancement is not automatic. It comes about when people prove themselves in the job they are in. Advancement is closely linked to the goals that individuals set for themselves.

Career advancement is moving to higher levels of work. This often brings more responsibility and better pay and benefits. The personal demands also may be greater.

Individuals normally begin low on the ladder and move upward. As they move upward, the amount of responsibility and rate of pay increase.

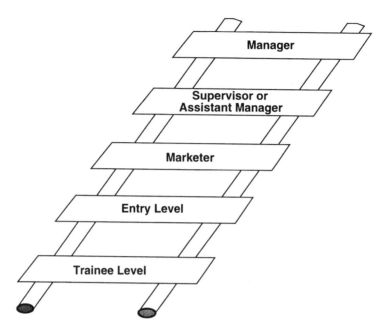

Career Ladder in Agricultural Marketing

Figure 4–16.   Illustration of a career ladder in agrimarketing.

The usefulness of the occupation may not change a great deal. It is definitely appropriate for individuals to have career ladder advancement goals!

Some employers and occupations don't offer much opportunity for advancement. In this case, individuals must change their employers or seek new occupations. Individuals who own small agrimarketing businesses advance by expanding the size of their businesses or by finding ways to make the businesses more profitable. Large farms may offer opportunities for advancement. Medium and small farms require expansion in size in order for advancement to occur.

HOW INDIVIDUALS MOVE ON THE CAREER LADDER

As previously mentioned, several factors influence movement on the career ladder. These include experience and productivity as an employee, additional education, expansion in the agrimarketing area, and changing jobs, occupations, or careers.

Experience and Productivity

Large agrimarketing firms can provide advancement for individuals who demonstrate productivity. The worker must show that he or she can perform at a higher level. Experience is a valuable teacher, and definitely a part of advancement. Doing a good job with the duties assigned is essential for advancement.

Additional Education and Training

Career advancement is more likely to come to individuals who get additional education and training. The better prepared a worker is, the more productive he or she should be!

Market Growth

Expansion in an area of agrimarketing can provide career ladder opportunities. Agricultural production tends to go through cycles of high and low opportunity and profit. These affect career ladders in agrimarketing. Government policies, international trade, crop failures, and other events have influence on the growth or decline of agrimarketing.

Individuals who keep well informed of developments that influence the market can take advantage of changes. They study information, look for trends, and make judgments based on what they observe.

Changing Jobs and Occupations

Sometimes people advance on the career ladder by changing to another employer. This offers opportunity for some individuals to advance who could not do so otherwise. Of course, there are many uncertainties in changing employers. Individuals often lose some benefits. They must carefully study the situation before making a change.

An important principle: Never quit a job until you have another! If you quit a job, you may have difficulty getting a new job. Just think what would happen when you stop getting paid!

Changing jobs involves a number of activities. A job must be open and you must apply for it. The employer will usually hire the best person available to fill the position. This means that you must compete with the other job applicants. Your ability to be a productive worker must be demonstrated better than the other applicants. Decisions about changing jobs are not easy to make.

SUMMARY

Career opportunities in agrimarketing are found throughout the agricultural industry. Individuals need to consider the relationship of careers, occupations, and jobs. Finding and advancing in an appropriate career will involve setting goals, assessing personal interests, determining living preferences, and getting the needed education and experience.

Many individuals enjoy highly successful careers in agrimarketing. Success begins with being prepared educationally. Advancement is based on the ability to work with people, dedication to the work, and enthusiasm for what you do.

Agricultural marketing occupations are found in many places. The supplies and services sector employs individuals who market to farmers, ranchers, and home owners. Farmers and ranchers market the crop and livestock products to consumers, processing plants, jobbers, and others who move the products toward consumers. Food and fiber product manufacturers market their products to consumers through a variety of means.

CHAPTER SELF-CHECK

Match the following terms with the correct definitions:

a. career

b. occupation

c. job

d. work ethic

e. managerial occupation

f. professional occupation

g. skilled occupation

h. career ladder

i. career advancement

j. apprenticeship

_____ moving to higher levels of work with more responsibility

_____ graphic way of showing upward advancement of people in agrimarketing careers

_____ general course of a person's work life

_____ specific work by site and employer

_____ how we view work

_____ require high levels of education and involve advanced work

_____ involve top-level management activities in agrimarketing

_____ require specialized training or experience

_____ specific work that can be given a title

_____ a type of on-the-job training under the direction of a skilled worker

QUESTIONS AND PROBLEMS FOR DISCUSSION

1. Distinguish between career, occupation, and job.

2. What is work ethic? Briefly describe the work ethic found in the United States.

3. What are the ways of classifying agrimarketing careers?

4. How are occupations classified according to proportion of duties in marketing?

5. What levels of education are related to entering careers in agrimarketing?

6. How are agrimarketing occupations classified according to level. Briefly explain each level.

7. List three occupations in agrimarketing. Briefly describe the nature of the work. (If time permits, interview people in the local community who are in these occupa-

tions. Write two or three paragraphs that report the findings of your interviews.)

8. What are the sources of information about job openings in agrimarketing?

9. What is a career ladder? How do individuals move up the career ladder?

10. Seven questions were listed in the chapter as being important in making a decision about entering a career in agrimarketing. Which of the questions is most important? Why?

ACTIVITIES

1. Interview a personnel officer in a firm involved in agrimarketing. Determine the jobs that are present, trends in openings and qualifications, rate of pay and other benefits, nature of the work, and how to go about applying for a job. Further, write a letter of application and prepare a sample personal data sheet for critique by the personnel officer.

2. Review the section of a newspaper where job openings are listed. Prepare a list of those that involve agrimarketing some of the time, all of the time, or support agrimarketing work. Classify them by educational and experience requirements.

3. Develop a list of schools, colleges, and universities in your area that provide education to prepare people for work in agrimarketing. With the help of your teacher or school counselor, write or visit one of the schools to get information on the agrimarketing education program. Share what you learn with other members of the class.

4. Make a poster showing a career ladder in agrimarketing. Use career information materials, interview people who work in agrimarketing, and find other sources of information.

Chapter 5

BEING SUCCESSFUL IN
AN AGRIMARKETING CAREER

People can succeed or fail in their work. Most people want to be successful. How they go about their work has a lot to do with success in agrimarketing.

Success is achieving worthy goals. Setting agrimarketing career goals requires careful thought and good information. Once goals are established, ways and means of reaching them must be stated. Dates for certain activities need to be specified. Assessment should be made along the way to determine progress and areas where additional planning is needed. The important thing to remember is that you can be successful!

Figure 5–1. A successful agrimarketing career may begin with showing a beef animal in high school agricultural education class.

The focus of this chapter is on things you can do to be successful in an agrimarketing career.

OBJECTIVES

To help understand the careers in agrimarketing, several important objectives are covered in this chapter. Upon completion, you will:

- Identify qualities of individuals who are successful in agrimarketing careers

- Explain educational requirements for entering and advancing in agrimarketing careers

- Explain how to find an entry-level job in agrimarketing

TERMS

agricultural education
agrimarketing career
baccalaureate degree
continuing education
employment application
  form
goal
goal setting
interest inventories
job interview
letter of application
personal data sheet
placement service
postsecondary education
success
task orientation

MAKING AGRIMARKETING CAREER CHOICES

Choosing an *agrimarketing career* is an important decision. Individuals need to give careful consideration to a number of factors. Gathering information will require some effort. Comparing your goals with what you learn from the information is an important first step. Several areas to consider are discussed here.

An agrimarketing career is a progression of jobs in agricultural marketing that leads to your personal success as well as success in agrimarketing. The first step is to begin setting goals.

GOAL SETTING

A *goal* is a level of accomplishment you want to achieve. Setting goals requires careful thought. We must feel comfortable with our goals and the direction they take us in life.

Individuals often set three kinds of goals (based on the length of time required to reach them)—short-term, intermediate-term, and long-term goals. Short-term goals are often for one year or less. Intermediate goals are for more than one year but usually no more than 4 or 5 years. Long-term goals are for more than 4 or 5 years. Short-term goals contribute to intermediate- and long-term goals.

Goal setting is describing what we want to accomplish in life. Individuals must look inward at the values they have for their lives. Sometimes people set goals that aren't realistic for them. As time passes, goals often need to be revised. New situations and opportunities result in a need to change goals.

As goals are being developed, ways and means of achieving them must also be identified. A goal is of little good if we don't have a strategy (ways and means) to go about achieving it. Ways and means often include gaining practical work experience, getting specific education, and making progress one step at a time. Further, goals need to have dates by which you want to accomplish them. Target dates can be revised as situations change, just as goals and ways and means are revised.

Begin setting goals by writing down what you want to accomplish. Beside each goal, write the ways and means you will use to achieve the goal as well as the date you want to reach the goal. Decide if the goals are realistic for you. Revise them if you need to. Share your goals with people

Guide for Goal Setting

Instructions: Write your goals below. Follow each goal with a list of the steps to accomplish it and the ways and means for accomplishing each step. Indicate a deadline date by which the ways and means are to be completed. Regularly evaluate how well you are doing in achieving your goals. Revise goals, steps, and ways and means as necessary.

Name _____ Date _____

Goal Number One: _____
_____

Steps to Achieve Goal	Ways and Means for Steps	Date
1. _____	a. _____	_____
	b. _____	_____
2. _____	a. _____	_____
	b. _____	_____
3. _____	a. _____	_____
	b. _____	_____

Goal Number Two: _____
_____

Steps to Achieve Goal	Ways and Means for Steps	Date
1. _____	a. _____	_____
	b. _____	_____
2. _____	a. _____	_____
	b. _____	_____
3. _____	a. _____	_____
	b. _____	_____

Figure 5–2. A handy form for writing goals and ways and means of achieving them.

who are in positions to help you. Talk with parents, your agriculture teacher, and other individuals who have insight into your potential.

PERSONAL INTERESTS

People are happier with their careers if they are in an area that is interesting to them. Unhappy people are not productive workers and will have difficulty being successful.

Assess your interests. Determine if your interests are in line with what is required in agrimarketing. Observe people working in agrimarketing and compare what you see with your interests. Part-time work in agrimarketing can be most beneficial. Many schools have programs that assist students in gaining part-time jobs.

Due to the wide range of careers involving agrimarketing, opportunities exist for people with many different interests. People who enjoy working outside can find opportunities in agrimarketing. So can those who want to travel, work with people, use equipment, operate laboratories, or organize materials. People with a wide variety of interests can find opportunities in agrimarketing.

Sometimes people take special tests that help assess interests. These tests are actually *interest inventories* that help people understand themselves better. Specific occupational inventories are also available. Vocational teachers and counselors often have access to reliable information to help students assess their interests.

LIVING PREFERENCES

Where people live and the way they live are often associated with their careers. Those who want to live in or near large cities can choose from agrimarketing occupations found there. Those who want to live in rural areas will have other choices. Sometimes people limit themselves by an unwillingness to move. Career advancement often requires moving.

Living preferences are related to the amount of income from work. Some agrimarketing occupations offer higher salaries than others. This is not to say that one job is more useful to society than another but that levels of responsibility are rewarded differently. Of course, people must remember that they enter a career at one level and can advance to higher levels of responsibility. Advancement is based on performance. Productive, responsible people are given opportunities to move up.

EDUCATION

Occupations in agrimarketing often require specific education. Individuals who aren't willing to gain the necessary education will not be considered. If they do get a job, they may have difficulty being successful because they don't have the needed job skills. (Another section of this chapter treats education in more detail.)

Figure 5–3. The stair stringer is sometimes used to show the progression in goal setting and success.

EXPERIENCE

A background in agriculture and related areas is often needed to be successful in agrimarketing. Part-time jobs in the summer and after school hours can help provide entry-level experience. Advancement will be based on experience in lower-level work. Individuals may work for many years before promotion to higher levels.

Individuals who start their own agrimarketing businesses can benefit from experience working for another person. On-the-job experience is valuable education.

ACHIEVING AGRIMARKETING CAREER GOALS

Success involves achieving worthy goals. It begins with goal setting, as discussed earlier in the chapter. Of course, your values are an important part of goal setting and assessing success.

People want to be successful. No one wants to fail. By observing a few general guidelines, you can be successful. Regardless of how involved you are in agrimarketing, the areas presented here will be useful in your career success.

BE PREPARED

Knowing what to do and how to do it is important for success in any job. Education and experience are both particularly important. Once you have a career goal, involve yourself in education programs to develop needed skills.

On-the-job experience teaches a lot about agrimarketing. Experience can be obtained on a part-time basis after school hours, on weekends, and during the summer. Young people who are just out of school often begin in lower-level, learner-type positions. Their employers invest time and resources in preparing them for the full responsibilities of their jobs.

Once into a career, people must keep up with new developments. In agrimarketing this requires daily study of new developments and trends. Awareness of market trends involves regularly reading market reports, attending educational events, and using other types of communication systems to keep informed.

LEARN TO WORK WITH PEOPLE

Good relationships with other people are essential for success in most jobs. Understanding ourselves helps us relate better to other people. More people lose their jobs because they do not get along with people than for any other reason.

Here are a few tips. Be interested in people. Be cheerful and demonstrate a positive attitude. Show people you are interested in them. Find things to like in other people. Be understanding and helpful. Be a team player.

Common everyday courtesies can be useful. The following are four examples of simple things you can do.

Figure 5-4. Most occupations involve working with people. This marketing representative is helping a feeder pig producer. (Courtesy, Moorman Feed, Quincy, Illinois)

- Ask people their opinions on matters related to their work.
- Compliment people on the work that they do.
- Use the word "please" frequently when seeking help.
- Use the words "thank you" frequently when others help you.

BE DEDICATED

Dedication to your work means productivity for the employer or for you as the owner of your own business. It is also known as *task orientation*, which includes being at work on time, using your time to perform your job duties, working a full day, and staying with a job until it is done in a quality manner.

People who do the best they can with their work are more likely to be successful. They are the first to be considered for promotions and increases in pay.

Some people view dedication as an expression of respect for the employer. Others view dedication as a demonstration of how you feel about yourself. Loyalty to the employer is definitely needed. Honesty in all work matters is essential.

The resources provided by an employer should be used in a productive manner. Wasting materials, time, or other resources reflects a lack of dedication to your work.

SHOW ENTHUSIASM

Being excited about what you do is important. You will be more productive and get more enjoyment out of what you do. Enthusiasm often "rubs off" on other people.

Enthusiasm is showing positive energy for what you are doing. It involves making positive comments to others rather than complaining about your work. It represents you and your employer well. Develop more enthusiasm for work by concentrating on what you like the best. Of course, all jobs have some aspects that are less desirable than others, but do not dwell on them.

Enthusiasm involves being willing to try new things. Don't be afraid to learn new ways of doing your work. Have a positive attitude about new things that come along.

EDUCATION REQUIREMENTS

Education provides much of the preparation people need to work in agrimarketing careers. Different careers require different levels and areas of education. Individuals interested in working in agrimarketing careers need to pursue the education that is needed.

Education determines the level at which an individual enters a career. The education required for job entry may not be sufficient for advancement. Individuals must view education as a life-long process. Seminars, workshops, adult education classes, and other means must be used to keep up to date. Success often depends on learning new skills and adapting to new technology.

The classification of occupations in agrimarketing by level of education was discussed in Chapter 4. The focus here is on specific areas of study and educational needs.

ENTRY LEVEL EDUCATION

Entry level education prepares an individual for initial employment in agrimarketing. Additional education is needed for advancement and to keep up to date. Several areas of education are presented here.

High School

In addition to preparing for entry into lower-level jobs, high school education also prepares individuals for postsecondary and college study.

Individuals interested in agriculture should take *agricultural education* courses in high school regardless of their education plans beyond high school. Nearly 8,000 high schools in the United States offer agricultural education, with 750,000 students enrolled in the classes. In many cases, these classes have instruction in agrimarketing. Regardless, the classes teach many of the background skills needed in agrimarketing. Increasingly, the emphasis is on agriscience—the combination of science and agriculture instruction. The instruction helps students understand the broad nature of the agricultural industry. High school agriculture programs often have student organizations where individuals can develop personal skills as well as enhance their agricultural skills. A central part of many programs is supervised practice, which is also known as supervised agricultural experience. Students develop practical skills participating in programs in agricultural businesses or on farms. Their experiences are closely related to their life goals and the instruction they receive at school.

Figure 5–5. These students are presenting a marketing plan as a part of their high school agricultural education class. (Courtesy, National FFA Organization)

Some high schools have adopted areas of agrimarketing education as a part of their curriculum. Three areas increasingly receiving attention are agricultural selling, marketing planning, and commodity marketing. These three areas have competitive activities for teams of students to demonstrate their mastery of various agrimarketing skills. The National FFA Organization of Alexandria, Virginia, sponsors these competitions.

Students should select classes which help develop the needed skills. English and communication are important. Mathematics and science classes develop important basic skills. Students interested in agrimarketing should take classes in economics and government. These courses provide an understanding of business in a capitalistic system. Other useful classes include bookkeeping (accounting) and computer applications. High school students who are planning to go to college should be sure to meet the admissions requirements of the college they plan to attend.

A few high schools are starting technical preparation programs. These are sometimes referred to as tech-prep. Certain eleventh and twelfth grade classes are carefully sequenced with the curriculum in agriculture at a nearby community college or other postsecondary institution. Students are able to move from high school to the community college in an efficient manner. They have the preparation needed to enter and be successful at the community college.

Postsecondary

Community colleges and postsecondary institutes typically offer two years of education beyond high school. This education is often referred to as *postsecondary education* or junior college education.

Nearly 500 postsecondary schools in the United States offer education related to agrimarketing. The instruction typically is designed to help students make a smooth transition from high school and on to successful employment. Further, the curriculum is often planned so that students who wish to do so can transfer credits to four-year colleges or universities.

Postsecondary schools offer general education courses as well as specialized technical education. All agrimarketing occupations require some ability to read, write, and perform mathematics. Students should take a mix of general and technical courses. Also, students should complete the degree that is offered, often the Associate of Arts Degree.

Many postsecondary schools offer agriculture courses in various areas of production, horticulture, and agribusiness. Students who know they will transfer to a four-year college or university should take courses in the postsecondary schools that will be accepted by the college or university and applied toward a degree. It is a good idea to complete as many of the general education courses as possible at a postsecondary school.

For the first two years of college, postsecondary schools often offer superior educational opportunities. Classes are typically smaller than those at universities. The classes are taught by faculty who are dedicated to teaching and not by graduate assistants or researchers. Postsecondary schools offer students the opportunity to develop good study habits and settle into academic success. Students who complete postsecondary education can enter a wide range of careers in agrimarketing. The occupations they begin with are often at the lower level but advancement is possible with hard work and dedication.

College and University

Education at a college or university provides the four-year *baccalaureate degree*. Sometimes more than four years is required. Some colleges and universities offer masters and doctoral degrees.

Every state has at least one public college or university with a baccalaureate program in agriculture. Some have specialized programs in agrimarketing. Colleges that offer agricultural degrees usually offer courses in agrimarketing. Students can major in different areas of agriculture, such as animal science, agronomy, agricultural education, and horticulture. In each of these majors, they can usually take courses in agrimarketing. Education in agriculture is essential in many agrimarketing careers.

Individuals with baccalaureate degrees enter more responsible jobs than those with less education. However, they often begin as assistants or in trainee positions. They advance when they have completed the entry-level work and have proven that they can be productive.

Individuals with masters or doctoral degrees enter at higher levels of responsibility. Of course, many agrimarketing occupations don't require this level of education. Those with masters and doctoral degrees often work in research, development, and related areas for large agribusinesses or government agencies. Even with higher levels of education, experience is very important to success.

EDUCATION FOR ADVANCEMENT

Advancement occurs when people have proven that they can perform in advanced positions. *Continuing education* is the education that an individual gets throughout a career. It is essential to remain up to date. Individuals have a responsibility to stay current. Agrimarketing firms must keep their employees up to date or the firms ability to compete will decline. Many firms provide incentives for their employees to participate in educational activities.

Various approaches are used for continuing education. Individuals can attend seminars, workshops, field days, and other programs. For example, the National Agricultural Marketing Association (NAMA) has educational programs to keep its members informed on new developments. NAMA sponsors national meetings as well as local and regional meetings. The association also works with student groups in colleges and high schools to promote agrimarketing education.

Individuals have a personal responsibility to keep themselves up to date. Reading journals, reports, and other materials about agrimarketing is helpful. Reviewing the market reports published each day in newspapers or broadcast on radio or television is important. Special newsletters also can be helpful.

Career success comes to those who keep up to date. Being enthusiastic about new developments and trying new things is definitely beneficial. Innovators are the first people to adopt new technology. They do so before most other people but only after careful consideration of how the new technology will affect their abilities in agrimarketing.

FINDING A JOB
IN AGRIMARKETING

Young people have to start their careers some place. They must often go through a search process. Landing the first job isn't always easy. Even with good preparation, opportunities in agrimarketing may not be available just as you would like.

Finding a job includes locating opportunities, making an application, going for an interview, and responding to a job offer, if any.

Agrimarketing jobs can be located in several ways. How you approach the search depends on your situation. If you are just finishing school, one strategy might be used. If you are already employed, another strategy might be the best. Several sources of information about job opportunities in agrimarketing are discussed here.

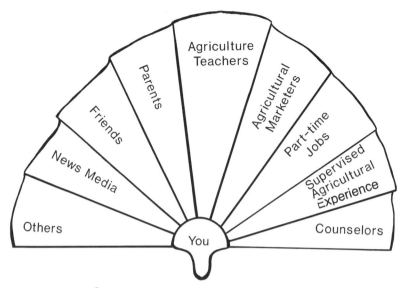

Sources of Career Information

Figure 5-6. Information about agrimarketing careers can be obtained from a number of sources.

PLACEMENT OFFICES

Placement services help people find jobs and are typically associated with high schools, postsecondary schools, and colleges and universities. The services generally are offered at no charge to students completing a program of study. A few private placement services are available. They usually charge a fee.

Many schools offer career placement services. Career interest assessment may be made. Counseling may be offered. Instruction is often provided in how to apply for a job. Students learn how to fill out job application forms, develop personal data sheets, and go for interviews. The schools may schedule interview days with potential employers. In some cases, schools maintain files of materials that can be used in locating prospective jobs. Agriculture and agrimarketing teachers often have good contacts with employers. In some cases, employers will call teachers when they need to fill a position. Share your plans with your agriculture teachers and ask for their help.

EMPLOYMENT AGENCIES

There are two kinds of employment agencies: public and private. Public employment offices are operated by agencies of local and state government.

Private agencies are operated by people who want to make a profit helping others find jobs.

At public agencies, individuals go to the office, discuss their wishes with a counselor, fill out application forms, and wait for referrals to prospective employers. These offices may maintain lists of job openings. Public employment offices do not usually charge fees for their services. Refer to the local telephone directory for the location of the nearest public employment agency or ask a counselor for information.

Private employment agencies usually charge fees for their services. They provide many of the same services as public employment offices. Some job seekers feel that private employment agencies are more diligent in helping people locate suitable employment because they are paid on the basis of placements. In some cases, employers pay fees to find employees. Individuals using the services of private agencies should determine the charges for the services first thing. Do not wait until after you get a job to ask about costs.

MEDIA

Newspapers, magazines, radio, television, and other media may be used to help locate jobs in agrimarketing. Many newspapers have want ads that advertise job openings. Some ads are placed by employers. Others are placed by agencies that charge fees for filling a position. Magazines also may have advertisements which announce job vacancies.

Local radio and television stations, including cable networks in towns and cities, may offer information about employment opportunities.

Carefully assess any advertisement before responding. Ads that fail to give sufficient information may be misleading. Those that glamorize a job without giving duties and needed qualifications should be viewed as suspicious. Respond only to ads that appear honest and for positions that match your interests.

FRIENDS AND FAMILY

Personal associates may know about job openings. Your friends and family members are good sources of information.

Not only can family and friends help with information about openings, but they can describe the work environment and qualifications needed to get a job. These individuals can also tell you how to apply for a job. They often know where the employment office is located and who to see for an application. Of course, some employers have regulations that limit the employment of relatives.

Another point to consider is whether to inform the employer of your source of information. If you feel that your source of information is viewed positively by the employer, mention the name of the friend who told you about the job. Your work qualities will be associated with those of your friend. If your friend is a good employee, you will be thought of as having associates who know how to be productive workers.

DIRECT CALLING

Job seekers can contact employers to ask if agrimarketing job openings exist. The contacts can be by telephone or in person. Larger businesses have personnel offices. In smaller operations, make contact with the manager. Some firms will only discuss possible job openings at certain times. Individuals should abide by these regulations. (After all, if you don't follow this regulation, what would you do if you were employed there?)

APPLYING FOR A JOB

After an opening has been located, you must then apply for it. Application procedures vary. Some employers require that a job application form be filled out. Other employers ask for letters of application. In some cases, an oral inquiry may be sufficient.

When applying for a job, do what you are told to do. Many employers have *employment application forms*. The completed forms provide information about education, experience, and goals. Read the instructions on application forms or job announcements. Determine the deadline for sending an application. Be sure yours arrives on time.

Carefully prepare the application. Make it neat. Spell correctly. Provide the information requested. In most cases, an application should be filled out in ink or with a typewriter.

A *letter of application* is a business letter that indicates that you are applying for a job. If one is requested, write a one-page letter that represents you well in the screening process. The letter should indicate the job you are applying for, summarize your qualifications, and state a willingness to come for an interview. The letter should be factual; do not over-sell yourself. Letters of application should be typewritten.

A *Personal data sheet* (or résumé) is a written summary of your education,

P. O. Box 393
Raymond, MS 39154
February 15, 1995

Mr. James W. Smith
Personnel Manager
Carson-Scott Packing Company
15 Windham Road
Columbus, MS 39701

Dear Mr. Smith:

Please accept this as a letter of application for the position of assistant cattle buyer with Carson-Scott Packing Company. Ms. Pamela Jenkins, agrimarketing instructor at Hinds Community College, indicated that your company would be filling the position later this spring. I feel that I have the education and experience for the position.

In May of this year, I will complete the Agrimarketing Technology Program at Hinds Community College. I have considerable emphasis in livestock marketing and management. As you may know, my college has a beef cattle performance testing program for producers in the area. Students gain practical experience in their classes by using the facilities for teaching. My grade point average is currently 3.4 out of a possible 4.0.

In addition to my education, I have worked part-time for a local cattle company after school hours and during the summer while in college and high school. More information about my qualifications is presented on the enclosed personal data sheet.

My education, experience, and sincere interest in working as an assistant cattle buyer are reasons I believe I have the necessary qualifications for the position at Carson-Scott Packing Company.

I would be pleased to meet with you at your convenience to discuss my qualifications in more detail. I can be reached at 601-323-6103 during the evening hours.

Sincerely,

Susan Ann Sloan

Figure 5–7. Sample letter of application.

experience, and goals. It is often submitted with a letter or provided later upon request by the employer. Follow good procedures in preparing your personal data sheet. Be sure it is accurate and represents you well. All words should be spelled correctly. Personal data sheets should be typewritten. Computer word processing systems can be used to create individualized personal data sheets that will interest employers.

GOING FOR AN INTERVIEW

An interview is a normal part of getting a job in agrimarketing. *Job interviews* are personal conferences that allow the employer to assess the job applicant and the applicant to assess the prospective employer. Being asked to come for an interview is a positive sign. Your credentials have been reviewed and appear to match what the employer wants.

A job seeker needs to make a good impression during the interview. The following tips will help you make a good impression.

- **Study the employer before you go.** Learn about the business so that you can show genuine interest in its welfare. Think about answers to possible questions, such as: Why did you apply for this job? What are your qualifications for the job? What are your goals for the future? If selected, when can you begin work?

- **Dress appropriately.** The clothes you wear and your grooming should be appropriate for the nature of the job you are seeking. If it's work in a warehouse, wear the clothing that you think the employer would want you to wear to work if you get the job. Clothing should be clean, in good repair, without words or pictures, and of good quality.

- **Take a pen, note pad, personal data sheet, and your Social Security Number to the interview.** Do not bring your friends or relatives unless specifically asked to do so by the employer.

- **Arrive on time or a few minutes early for the interview.** Never be late, as this might be seen as a sign of how you would report for work if you get the job.

- **Be personable.** Show good manners. Introduce yourself to people you don't know. Speak clearly and confidently. Use good grammar and show enthusiasm for the work. Be sure to look into the eyes of the employer. Sit and stand with good posture—do not slump in the chair or lean against a wall when standing. Do not use tobacco products or chew gum during the interview.

Wholesome food is important for human growth and development.

Homes are furnished with many products that involve agrimarketing technology.

Attractive clothing is important in our lives. (Courtesy, Smith & Byars)

2 FOR $2 SPECIAL
2 SAUG EGG BIS
2 DBL CHEESEBURG

Homes are built of quality forestry products.

Convenient fast-food products are important in our lives. This sign uses color, shape, and lettering to uniformly advertise a food product.

Meeting the Needs of Producers

Quality seed are carefully produced and packaged for distribution to growers of grain crops. (Courtesy, DEKALB Plant Genetics, Dekalb, Illinois)

Poultry producers depend on hatcheries to produce quality chicks that will grow-off fast. This photo shows newly-hatched chicks being carefully de-beaked (removal of tip of beak to prevent pecking each other). (Courtesy, Michael Stevens, McCarty Farms)

Fruit and nursery growers use carefully produced improved trees in landscapes and orchards.

Tractors and implements are used on most farms. This dealer has a display of several different models.

Various chemicals are used to control weeds and other pests.

Animal producers may use commercially-manufactured feed. (Courtesy, Kent Feeds, Inc., Muscatine, Iowa)

Establishing a poultry farm with houses, feed systems, and other equipment must be based on the ability to market poultry at a profit for a number of years.

Tree farmers must consider the long-term market situation.

Beef cattle production may involve producing calves for the feeder market. Most cows produce only one calf a year. Brood stock are selected on the basis of the kind of beef that is in highest demand.

Grain sorghum can be produced in one growing season and should be grown only if a market is available.

As a fruit crop, several years are required for fig trees to grow large enough to bare figs.

Harvesting Is Important in Marketing

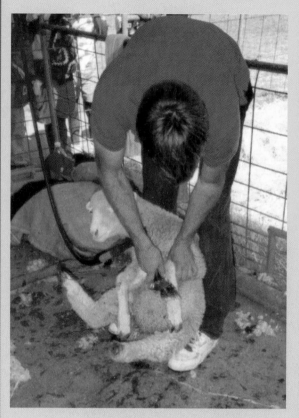

Turf may be harvested in long strips which are rolled and placed on pallets for marketing.

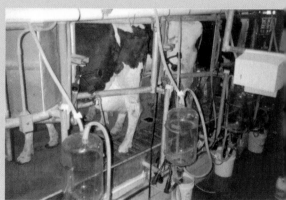

Wool is removed from sheep by shearing.

Cows are milked in clean dairy barns to assure a wholesome food product.

Cotton is harvested with mechanical pickers.

Trees are cut and the logs collected for sawing into lumber.

Marketing Channels

Produce may be sold to the consumer through a retail stand.

Fruit and vegetables may be marketed through a central farmers market where a number of different growers are at one location.

Some producers operate retail markets on their farms.

Producers may store grain crops on the farm until a more favorable market situation develops.

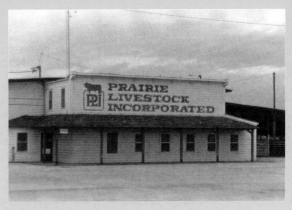

Cattle producers often market through centrally located livestock buyers and auctions.

Many commodities are marketed through processing facilities that convert the raw materials into oil, meal, and other products. (Courtesy, Lauhoff Grain Co.)

Processing Converts Raw Products

Poultry is processed in clean facilities that use automated processing lines. (Courtesy, McCarty Farms)

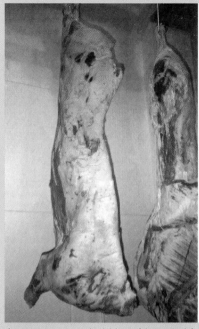

Beef carcasses are held in refrigerated facilities until made into the appropriate cuts.

Wheat is milled into flour and other products. Wheat is here being examined after the first break in the milling stage. (Courtesy, Cargill, Minneapolis)

Processing involves packing products in convenient containers, such as milk in plastic jugs.

Cotton is first processed by ginning and baling. (Ginning involves separating the lint from the seed.) Bales weigh 500 pounds.

Food products are produced with careful attention to quality. (Courtesy, Cargill, Minneapolis)

Specially equipped trucks and trailers are used to haul cattle.

Barges may transport grain. (Courtesy, Cargill, Minneapolis)

Rail cars provide economical transportation of many commodities. (Courtesy, Cargill, Minneapolis)

Oils and other products may be transported in tank cars. (Courtesy, Cargill, Minneapolis)

Large containers may be used in shipping agricultural products. This container is being lifted on to a trailer for delivery of the produce. The container will be returned and placed on a ship to get another load.

Specially-designed crates filled with chickens are being lifted from a truck at a processing plant. (Courtesy, Michael Stevens, McCarty Farms)

Many Opportunities in AgriMarketing

Individuals with many different skills are needed in agrimarketing, such as this pasta machine operator. (Courtesy, ARA Services, Philadelphia, Pennsylvania)

Agrimarketing information is broadcast by radio to producers and others. (Courtesy, Bob Wade, Progressive Farmer Network)

Attractive containers promote the consumption of products.

Television is used to provide agrimarketing information.

Market information can be received by facsimile machine and other means.

Labels give important information about products.

SUSAN ANN SLOAN
P. O. Box 393
Raymond, MS 39154
601-323-6103

CAREER OBJECTIVE: To obtain a position in livestock buying with opportunities for increased responsibility and advancement based on ability and performance.

EDUCATION:

1993–1995   Hinds Community College, Raymond, Mississippi
Associate of Science Degree in Agrimarketing Technology. Expected date of graduation is May 1995. 3.4 grade point average (out of possible 4.0)

1989–1993   Clinton High School, Clinton, Mississippi
Graduated with Honors. Class rank was 12 out of 491.

EXPERIENCE:

1992–present   Bovina Cattle Company, Clinton, Mississippi
Part-time work included all areas of managing and marketing cattle.

1991   Frank's Meat Market, Clinton, Mississippi
Part-time work bagging meat products for customers, cleaning, and stocking.

COLLEGE ACTIVITIES:

1994–1995   President, AgriTech Club
Member, Phi Theta Kappa (scholastic honorary)
Member, Agriculture Marketing Plan Team
Member, Agriculture Ambassadors

1993–1994   Member, AgriTech Club
Editor, AgriTech Club Newsletter
Recipient, Academic Award from AgriTech Club

HIGH SCHOOL ACTIVITIES:

President, Clinton FFA Chapter, 1992–1993
Vice President, Beta Club, 1992–1993
Member, Debate Team, 1991–1993
Staff Member, school newspaper, 1992–1993
Delegate, State FFA Convention, 1992
Member, FFA Marketing Plan Project Team, 1991–1993
Winner, State FFA Public Speaking Contest, 1993

REFERENCES: Available upon request.

Figure 5–8. Sample personal data sheet.

- **Conclude the interview on schedule.** Notice cues from the interviewer about ending the interview. Express thanks for the interview. Determine when a decision will be made on the job offer.

- **After some interviews it is appropriate to follow up with a letter thanking the interviewer for the interview.** This is also a good opportunity to further sell yourself to the potential employer.

RESPONDING TO
A JOB OFFER

If you are lucky enough to have a job offer, you will want to handle it properly. Here are a few suggestions:

- Thank the person who contacts you for their trust in you.

- If not included in the offer, ask when the work would begin (date and time), where you would go to report to work, what you need to bring with you for the work, and the rate of pay.

- Determine when the employer wants an answer from you about accepting or rejecting the job offer.

- If you are employed elsewhere, be professional about resigning. Follow the policies on resignations. These usually require two to four weeks or more notice.

- You may want to talk to others before making a decision. Parents, teachers, friends, and other trusted associates can often be helpful.

SUMMARY

Career opportunities in agrimarketing are found throughout all of agricultural industry. Finding and advancing in an appropriate career involves setting goals, assessing personal interests, determining living preferences, and getting education and experience.

Many individuals enjoy highly successful careers in agrimarketing. Success begins with the proper education. Advancement is based on the ability to work with people, dedication to the work, and enthusiasm.

Getting a job requires following certain steps in locating, applying, and interviewing for a position, and responding appropriately to an offer.

Productivity and work ethic are driving forces in moving up the agrimarketing career ladder.

CHAPTER SELF-CHECK

Match the following terms with the correct definitions:

 a. baccalaureate degree

 b. goal

 c. interest inventory

 d. task orientation

 e. goal setting

 f. agricultural education

 g. continuing education

 h. letter of application

 i. personal data sheet

 j. job interview

_____ level of accomplishment you want to achieve

_____ education throughout a career that keeps a person up to date

_____ personal conference with a prospective employer

_____ degree received from a college or university after the equivalent of four years of study

_____ written summaries of an individual's education, experience, and goals

_____ describing what we want to accomplish in life

_____ qualities of an individual that show dedication to work

_____ education in agriculture offered in high schools

_____ tests that help people understand themselves

_____ business letter that indicates that you are applying for a job

QUESTIONS AND PROBLEMS FOR DISCUSSION

1. What are the major areas to consider in choosing a career in agrimarketing? Briefly describe each.

2. What is success?

3. What are four important factors in an individual's career success? Briefly describe each.

4. Describe sources of education in agrimarketing.

5. Explain the role of continuing education in advancement in agrimarketing careers.

6. What are the sources of information about job openings in agrimarketing?

7. What are the ways of applying for a job?

8. What important things should be observed when going for a job interview?

9. What should be considered in responding to a job offer?

10. What are the major parts of a personal data sheet?

ACTIVITIES

1. Prepare a personal data sheet for yourself. Ask your teacher or school counselor to provide suggestions on how it can be improved. Neatly type the personal data sheet and use it when you apply for a job or go for an interview. File it on computer diskette so that you can easily revise it and print additional copies.

2. Write a sample letter of application for an agrimarketing job. Use one of the following sample job openings: assistant grain sampler, sales trainee for fertilizer, or cattle buyer.

Chapter 6

SELECTING
A MARKETING APPROACH

In the business of agriculture, decisions are made every day. Farmers must decide what to plant, when to plant, when to irrigate, when to apply chemicals, when to fertilize, and when to harvest. Ranchers must decide what breeds of animals to raise, when to breed, when to wean, and when to vaccinate. People who operate agribusinesses make decisions as well. They must decide which products to sell, how to advertise, how to display the products, and how many people to employ. These decisions only represent a small number of the day to day decisions that a farmer, rancher, or agribusiness person must make. The challenge in making these decisions

Figure 6–1. The decision to raise Christmas trees should be the result of a clear understanding of all aspects of this agricultural enterprise.

is that most of the time the profitability of the farming or agribusiness enterprise is at stake. For example, when the producer chooses a particular crop to raise, a major consideration is whether there will be a market for that product. Producers must be good managers and they must have a very clear understanding concerning all aspects of the farming enterprise.

Good decisions are important when running any business. Producers of agricultural products cannot expect to be successful if poor decisions are made. One area of decision making that often is overlooked or not given the attention it deserves is marketing. Marketing activities must be incorporated into every phase of agriculture. Everyone involved in the business of producing, transporting, processing, or selling food and fiber should be fully aware of the importance of agrimarketing.

TERMS

commodities
comparative advantage
current market values
forward contracting
market niche
market places
marketing approach
marketing objectives
method of delivery
method of exchange
opportunity cost
price maker
price taker
product form
risk
value-added
volume of production

An agribusiness person must choose a marketing approach that will maximize the profitability of the business, whether that business is a farm, ranch, or store. Intelligent marketing approaches require, perhaps even demand, some basic information. This information will aid the agribusiness person in making choices to effectively select a marketing approach which is right for the business.

OBJECTIVES

There are many decisions that must be made when selecting a marketing approach for an agribusiness. Upon completion of this chapter, you will be able to:

- Explain common approaches in agrimarketing
- Describe how government programs influence agrimarketing
- Explain comparative advantage
- Describe how value is added in agrimarketing
- Explain factors in selecting marketing alternatives

Figure 6–2. Through processing, grapes are marketed as juice products.

MARKETING APPROACH

Marketing was defined in an earlier chapter as providing goods and services people want. Therefore, *marketing approach* may be defined as the result of all marketing decisions. A marketing approach can be very complex. It may include where and how agricultural products or *commodities* are sold, the timing of sales, the setting of prices, volume (how much is produced or manufactured), product form, method of delivery, and method of exchange.

WHERE COMMODITIES ARE SOLD

The traditional place of sale for agricultural commodities includes auctions, forward contracting on futures markets, and direct private treaty sales. The problem with these traditional *market places* lies in the fact that the producer is more a *price taker* than a *price maker*. In other words, the producer is providing a product without being able to negotiate for a better price. The producer's only decision at this point is whether to accept the offered price or to take the product home. The typical producer does not have the option of not selling at the offered price. This producer ends up accepting what is offered whether it is profitable or not.

More and more producers of agricultural commodities are using innovative ways of selling their products. These innovators are identifying specialty markets that allow them to better control the price they take. These markets are usually much smaller, but the price usually more than makes up for what is lost in volume. These specialty markets include on-the-farm restaurants where the producer may serve catfish just a few yards from were the fish were grown. Pick-your-own fruit and vegetables are popular in some areas. There are numerous places across the country where consumers can go out into producers' fields or orchards and pick anything from peas, beans, and strawberries to peaches, apples, and pecans. Some producers market specialty products such as hormone-free beef and organic fruits and vegetables. These fit the lifestyles of a growing segment of the population that selects and consumes food that is perceived to be more healthful.

TIMING OF SALES

Most agricultural commodities are seasonal in nature. The commodity becomes available when harvest is occurring. Many commodities, particularly those grown for human consumption, are perishable and must be delivered in a timely manner so that freshness is maintained. Unfortunately, harvest time is not always the most profitable time to sell. During harvest, oftentimes the market becomes flooded and prices of a particular commodity fall dramatically. Some commodities experience more price volatility than others at harvest time. Vegetable prices seem to be particularly prone to this problem.

Agricultural producers must seek ways to shift the timing of sales in order to maximize profit. *Forward contracting* is one way of shifting the timing of the sale. With forward contracting, the producer and a buyer enter into an agreement well before the actual harvest date. Typically, the producer agrees to supply a set amount of a certain commodity on a certain day. The buyer agrees to pay a set price provided the commodity is delivered in the proper amount. These contracts often specify not only the price and quantity but also the quality of the commodity. The advantage to this approach is that the producer can "lock in" a price that will guarantee a profit. On the other hand, the producer takes a chance of "locking in" a price that is below what the product would bring on the open market. However, most of the time the producer is wise to lock in a reasonable profit rather than speculate that the price may be better later. At harvest time, if the open market prices are exceeding the forward contracted prices the producer may think it was a bad decision. In the short run, this may be true. However, over the long run, producers who forward contract should experience better performance in the market place.

Another way of shifting the timing of the sale is to store the commodity until a more profitable price occurs. The commodity can be stored on the farm or in a commercial storage facility such as a grain elevator. Storing crops for better prices can be risky. The producer must recognize that the cost of storing the commodity may exceed the additional revenue earned. Before producers decide to store a commodity, they must consider at least two factors. The first is how well the commodity stores. Obviously, fruits and vegetables for human consumption have a limited storage life. On the other hand, traditional agricultural commodities, such as corn or wheat, can be kept for longer periods without damaging the quality of the product. The second factor is the cost of storage. Even on-farm storage can be expensive. Many times

Figure 6–3. Baby pigs can be forward contracted to lock in favorable market prices early in the production cycle. (Courtesy of the Dept. of Agricultural Education and Communications, Texas Tech University)

the producer must use electrical energy to run fans and drying equipment to control the moisture content of the crop. Also the producer must control pests which may damage the crop. Rodents and insects can greatly diminish the value of the commodity if they are not dealt with in a proper manner.

Additionally, when producers store crops, they are not earning interest on the money they would have received if the crop was sold. However, interest payments on any outstanding loans the producer has must be paid. If the crop were sold at harvest the producer could have invested the revenue in interest-bearing accounts or paid off loans. This represents the *opportunity cost* of not selling the crop at harvest.

Figure 6–4. While crops can be stored for later sales, cattle must be marketed when they reach market weight. (Courtesy of the Dept. of Agricultural Education and Communications, Texas Tech University)

SETTING OF PRICES

Farmers and ranchers traditionally have had very little to say about the value of their crops and livestock. Historically, prices for agricultural commodities have been determined by *current market values*. In earlier times, ranchers would drive cattle hundreds of miles to market. These cattle drives would take weeks or even months. The ranchers started the drive anticipating that it would be financially rewarding. However, there were no guarantees. The buyer was often times in a position to take advantage of the ranchers who had just arrived after a long cattle drive. The buyers knew that the rancher must sell the cattle. The rancher could try to negotiate a fair price, but the buyer knew that the rancher was not about to take the cattle back home. Farmers and ranchers were, and still are, at the mercy of the traditional market. They are often price takers instead of being price makers.

Agricultural producers who find other ways of marketing their commodities are more likely to become price makers. The key to becoming a price maker is to find a *market niche*. Producers with a unique market niche are better able to set their own prices. A catfish producer who operates a catch-your-own business is able to set a price because some people like to fish. These people are willing to pay more for the product because they get to experience catching the fish. Other consumers are willing to catch their own fish because the idea of eating freshly caught fish is appealing. The catfish producer also has the option of operating a restaurant which serves fish produced on the farm. Again, this is appealing to many people because of the freshness of the product. A catfish producer who operates a catch-your-own business or an on-site restaurant has more power to set the price than the catfish producer who sells to a packer.

Figure 6–5. Ostrich production is an example of a unique agricultural enterprise that is gaining popularity in parts of the United States. (Courtesy of the Dept. of Agricultural Education and Communications, Texas Tech University)

VOLUME

The *volume of production* for the typical agriculture producer is usually determined by the availability of resources. These resources include capital, equipment, land, and time. In most cases, the producer must seek financing in the form of loans. The ability of the producer to borrow money for production is often the limiting factor in determining the volume of production. Equipment can also be a limiting factor. With row crop production, the farmer must be able to cover the number of acres necessary to produce the crop. Agricultural equipment is expensive, and the producer may not be able to invest in more equipment. Land is one of the most expensive resources. Obviously, the farmer or rancher cannot produce more than what the available land will support.

PRODUCT FORM

Product form at the time of marketing plays a large role in the profitability of agricultural enterprises. Agricultural products can be sold in many forms. However, in traditional marketing approaches, agricultural commodities are sold at the site of production in unprocessed, natural conditions. In other words, the producer sells the commodity in a bulk form that needs processing. Some commodities are well suited to on-site processing by the producer. Producers who change the form of their commodity in some way have more options in marketing. Pecan producers have been very successful in changing the form of their commodity. Many pecan producers have on-farm stores where they sell not only pecans in the shell but also cracked pecans, pecan halves, pecan pieces, and products which have been made with the pecans such as candies and cakes. Each time the form of the commodity changes, the value of the commodity increases. The higher value translates into increased profitability for the producer. It may be difficult for all but the very largest producers of some commodities to take advantage of this concept. Even though wheat is highly processed before it is ready for human consumption, it would be impractical for individual producers to own and operate flour mills and bakeries.

Figure 6–6. Most cotton producers market their crop in an
unprocessed, natural condition.

METHOD OF DELIVERY

Method of delivery refers to the transportation of agricultural commodities. Raw agricultural products are transported using include trucks, trains, barges, and ships. For bulk, raw agricultural products, such as grains and livestock, it typically is more cost effective to move massive volumes of product. Producers should figure out the per unit cost when considering alternative means of transportation. That is, the producer should compare the different available methods of transportation according to the cost of transporting each unit (bushel, hundredweight, etc.). As commodities become more and more processed, transportation methods may change. Certain perishables are shipped by air, but others can be transported by freight companies. Producers must keep in mind that transportation is a significant cost in the marketing of their products.

Producers who limit transportation costs are likely to increase the profitability of their enterprises. One way to limit transportation costs is to market the commodity in such a way that the consumer comes to the site of production. The producer who markets vegetables with pick-your-own operations not only limits harvesting costs but will have no delivery expenses.

METHOD OF EXCHANGE

Method of exchange refers to the way the seller is paid. In earlier days, it was not uncommon for producers of agricultural products to barter (trade). Barter is a form of exchange which is rare today. Sometimes the seller will finance the sale of the commodity and accept payment at some later date. Of course, the buyer and seller must develop a contract which specifies payment schedule and interest rates. Most often, however, the seller demands to be paid at the time of delivery.

COMMON APPROACHES TO AGRIMARKETING

A key to selecting a marketing approach is to know your *marketing objectives*. These objectives guide the agricultural producer in marketing. Producers who formulate, record, and review their marketing objectives are more likely to market successfully.

SELLING AT THE HIGHEST PRICE OF THE YEAR

This can be a rather unrealistic goal. Even the most sophisticated forecasting techniques cannot predict commodity prices with 100 percent accuracy. Sometimes market analysts will predict that prices will go higher, when in fact the highest price of the year has already occurred. Foreign production, weather patterns, the economy, production estimates, plus other factors make identifying the highest price of the year very difficult. Trying to sell at the highest price of the year often leads to failure in the achievement of objectives.

SELLING ABOVE THE AVERAGE PRICE

This is a realistic objective for most producers. The producer who watches the market can become quite good at determining the average price of the year. However, producers must realize that selling above the average price does not necessarily guarantee a profit. Conditions can be such that prices never reach the levels necessary to cover the cost of production.

NET SELLING ABOVE THE AVERAGE PRICE

This objective accounts for additional costs that occur when a crop is stored beyond harvest. Producers will often choose to store a crop beyond harvest to try to get a better price. Storage cost and interest cost on the money invested in the commodity represent additional costs of production. The producer's objective is to sell the commodity at a market price high enough to cover storage and interest costs. Again, producers must recognize that the average price is not necessarily a profitable price.

MAKING A PROFIT

Profit is one of the primary objectives of an agribusiness manager. One way that agribusiness managers seek to meet this objective is to compute potential profits at various prices. Producers who use partial budgeting are able to project profits and losses. By doing this, they are able to discover the price needed to cover their costs plus meet a profit objective. If managers do not determine the price needed before selling, they may sell at what appears to be a profitable price that is in fact below the break-even price. When producers sell below the break-even price, they experience a loss.

SELLING TO MEET CASH FLOW NEEDS

Producers often sell their commodities at whatever the prevailing price is in order to meet current cash needs. Producers have needs for cash at all times of the year even though a particular commodity may be harvested and ready for sale at only one time during the year. Unfortunately, this is the time when prices are not likely to be at the most profitable levels. A wise agribusiness manager always maintains a cash flow statement to anticipate demands on cash. Using a cash flow statement, the producer can time heavy demands on cash so that there is cash available. Also, the producer can work with an agricultural lender to arrange for credit to meet cash demands.

MINIMIZING RISK

Producers with a high debt load are especially concerned about minimizing risk. Producers who buy land and equipment for production have invested large

Figure 6-7. Agricultural producers should determine their marketing objectives before production of a commodity.

amounts of capital, many times incurring very large debt loads. Those who are able to manage the risk of agricultural production usually are the most successful. Some producers minimize price risk by forward contracting or hedging on the commodity market. The manager who takes advantage of forward contracting or hedging may not be able to take advantage of the very highest commodity prices but is guaranteed a fair price for the commodity. This removes most of the price risk associated with marketing.

COMPARATIVE ADVANTAGE

Just as individuals have different talents which allow them to excel at certain skills, farmers and ranchers have particular expertise at raising certain commodities. In fact, this phenomenon is true for entire regions,

Figure 6–8. Some regions of states and countries are well
suited to cotton production. These regions have
a comparative advantage.

states, and countries. Many things contribute to the ability to be successful
with certain commodities. On an individual basis, it may be a keen interest
in a particular crop. On a regional, state, or international basis, many more
contributing factors must be considered. Variables such as climate, soils,
available labor, and government subsidies may give an advantage to one
region, state, or nation in the production of certain commodities. This is
called *comparative advantage*. The total agricultural output can be increased
when each individual, region, state, or nation specializes in producing that
commodity for which it has the greatest advantage or the least disadvantage.

If the theory of comparative advantage is reality, then trade must occur.
Trade occurs because governments, businesses, farmers, and consumers realize benefits from trade. Trade allows access to items that would otherwise
be too expensive or maybe not even available. With comparative advantage,

everyone has the benefit of doing what they do best, plus trade occurs which provides products that are needed.

VALUE-ADDED

To understand the term *value-added*, consider the following question. How is the value of a loaf of bread determined? If you were to add the value of the products needed to produce a loaf of bread, you would see that the total of all the values of the individual components would be less than the value of the bread in the supermarket. Why is this? Between the time the wheat leaves the field and when the bread reaches the consumer's table, many steps occur. At each step, value has been added to the commodity. At each step the value increases more than the additional input. For example, when wheat is milled into flour, the value of the flour is more than the value of the wheat plus the cost of turning the wheat to flour. Furthermore, when the flour is made into bread, the value of the loaf of bread is more than the flour and other ingredients that go into the bread. By the time the bread reaches the consumer, the wheat has been transported, milled, baked, packaged, marketed, displayed, and sold. Each of these processes adds value to the commodity.

Traditionally, adding value to agricultural products was done after the commodity had left the site of production. Farmers and ranchers were, and often times still are, so intent on the production of the commodity that they failed to see the advantage of adding value to their product. Producers who are able to discover a way to add value experience success. Producers who fail to be innovative in marketing sometimes go out of business.

Value-adding can occur at any point during marketing. Value is added if the product is transported to a better marketplace. Likewise, value is added when marketing is timed to coincide with particular events. For the producer, however, most value is added when the product form is changed. In other words, if the producer can complete part of the processing before selling the commodity, value is added.

The earlier example of the pecan producer is a good illustration of various stages of value-adding. The typical pecan producer with an on-site store sells pecans in a number of ways. The most obvious product form is the whole uncracked pecans. These can be purchased for less per pound than pecans that have been further processed. By simply putting the whole uncracked pecans through a cracking machine, the producer can add value. Cracked pecans sell for more than uncracked pecans and the cost to the producer for cracking the pecans is very slight. In most cases, the cracking

Figure 6–9. Ginning adds value to cotton.

operation will add more value to the crop than it costs to crack them. The pecan producer can further add value by having the pecan nut meats separated from the shells. This is typically done by hand. However, pecan nut meats, particularly pecan halves, are a relatively valuable product. The value of the pecans is increased enough to compensate the producer for hiring the labor to separate the pecan nut meats. The pecan producer can further add value by manufacturing prepared food products with the pecans. A popular pecan candy product is pecan pralines. Pralines are relatively simple to make. They contain a small amount of pecans, and the other ingredients are relatively inexpensive. By making pralines, a producer can increase the value of the pecans by tenfold.

A particularly important value-adding consideration in today's market-place is packaging. Packaging formerly served a very practical function—containing and transporting. Today, because many consumer buying decisions are made at the point of sale (instore), packaging in eye-catching, appealing ways is very important. In other words, packaging can help in the advertising part of marketing. Some of the functions that packaging can perform in adding value to an agricultural product are:

- **Providing name brand identification**—Easily recognized logos and graphics provide name brand identification. This is important in the promotion of particular products. Brands which deliver quality products dependably over time build images that consumers rely on for future purchases.

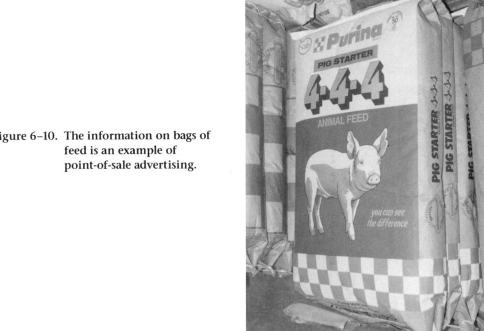

Figure 6–10. The information on bags of
feed is an example of
point-of-sale advertising.

- **Advertising at the point of sale**—The package is the best and maybe only source of information about a product at the point of sale. The package should provide the information that consumers use to decide which product to purchase.

- **Transporting the product with the least damage**—Consumers expect to receive undamaged products. Packaging should be designed to limit damage as much a possible. Packaging which protects the quality of fresh fruits and prevents the breakage of fragile items should enhance the desirability of certain products.

- **Increasing home shelf life**—Consumers appreciate products that remain fresh and usable for long periods of time. Recent developments include vacuum packaging for fresh meats, aseptic packaging for juices (drink boxes), and individualized serving size products such as fruit cups. All of these innovations in packaging increase the usable shelf life of products and add value.

- **Convenience**—The TV dinner was probably the most innovative packaging concept that has ever been developed. The TV dinner is becoming more and more sophisticated. Today's version can be either microwaved or prepared in a conventional oven.

GOVERNMENT PROGRAMS

The United States government, through the United States Department of Agriculture (USDA), exerts tremendous influence on agrimarketing. Government programs such as price supports, subsidies, acreage allotments, and loans are sometimes foremost in the mind of the producer as he/she makes production decisions. Many producers believe that the USDA should exist to help only the producer. However, the government's role in agrimarketing is broad. Government programs serve to make the market more stable and help to insure an adequate and safe food and fiber supply for the American consumer. Because of government programs, the typical American family spends only twelve percent of its income for food. The various services provided by the USDA are discussed below.

AGRICULTURAL MARKETING SERVICE (AMS)

The Agricultural Marketing Service (AMS) of the USDA provides marketing programs, marketing services, and regulatory functions for U.S. agriculture. The AMS aids the movement of food and fiber from the producer to the consumer. There can be many stages between the time that the food and fiber leaves the farm and the time the consumer selects the product at the supermarket or department store. The AMS assists in the complex process of moving food and fiber products from producer to consumer. Its programs and services promote an efficient, effective, and equitable agrimarketing system.

AMS Marketing Programs

The U.S. government purchases vast amounts of food through the AMS Food Purchasing program. This food is distributed to schools, institutions, and other eligible recipients by the USDA's Food and Nutrition Service. This food includes products that are perishable and in temporary surplus and foods that are purchased specifically to help schools meet nutritional requirements. Meat and meat products, poultry and poultry products, egg products, fish, and processed and fresh fruits and vegetables are among the foods that are purchased. The AMS increases demand on the open marketplace by reducing the available supply while also providing badly needed nutrition to those who might not otherwise have access to adequate food. Because of this and other USDA programs, schools are able to provide free and reduced cost breakfasts and lunches to students.

Government Food Quality Assurance Program (GFQAP). Because the AMS is responsible for the purchase of food for consumption by military installations, Veteran's Administration hospitals, schools, correctional institutions, and other agencies the Government Food Quality Assurance Program (GFQAP) was started. The GFQAP, within the AMS, has developed uniform and simplified specifications to insure the quality of food which federal agencies purchase. These specifications insure the quality of food that is purchased for use by these agencies.

Grade Standards Program. The quality of agricultural commodities is a very important consideration in marketing. When a producer markets superior products, better prices are justified. When a producer markets inferior products, the producer can expect to receive lower than market price. There must be a way to determine and describe the quality of a commodity. The Grade Standards program of the AMS helps to insure that purchasers of agricultural commodities receive the quality they want and pay for. The AMS maintains grade standards for cotton, dairy products, fruits, beef, veal, calf, lamb, pork, mohair, poultry, rabbits, shell eggs, tobacco, vegetables, and wool. These standards describe the entire range of quality for each product and are the basis for quality grades. From the producer's viewpoint, premiums are received when the quality of their commodity is exceptional. Likewise, if their commodity is of a lower quality, they will be penalized at the marketplace in terms of lower prices or perhaps even rejection of the commodity. The quality of grain, for example, is at its peak when the crop matures in the field. As the crop is harvested, transported, and sold it tends to experience a loss in quality. It is difficult to maintain the quality of grain. Declines in grain quality can be due to a number of factors: (1) drying and storage practices; (2) mechanical damage due to harvest and storage equipment; (3) micro-organism and insect damage; and (4) contamination with foreign materials. The grade standards developed by the AMS address these factors when grades are assigned to crops.

AMS Marketing Services

Upon request, the AMS will provide grading services. The Grading and

Acceptance Services assesses a fee to the requester of the service. Grading provides buyers and sellers with an impartial appraisal of the quality of the commodities being sold, and assists producers in receiving fair prices for their products.

Market News Service reporters gather data by visits to trading points and by telephone. The report on qualities and quantities of products sold, prices paid, demand, movement, and trends. The AMS uses satellite communication, earth stations, and microcomputers to send out 700 to 900 market news messages and reports daily. These are made available to the agricultural industry as well as the print and electronic news media. Automatic telephone recordings also are employed to provide current market information. Market news services are operated cooperatively with state departments of agriculture.

Agricultural Marketing Service researchers with the Market Research and Development Service explore new techniques and methods for improving marketing, including handling, processing, packaging, storage, and distribution of agricultural products. Local governments and food industry groups cooperate with researchers to identify existing problems, to design improved facilities, and to assist in the development of modern, efficient wholesale food distribution centers and farmers' markets. Studies are also conducted at the state level through a matching funds grant program.

AMS Regulatory Functions

Commodity Research and Promotion Programs enable producers to solve production and marketing problems; finance their own coordinated programs of research; create producer and consumer education; and develop promotional programs to improve, maintain, and develop markets for their commodities. The U.S. Congress has authorized research and promotion programs for beef, cotton, dairy products, eggs, floral products, honey, lamb, mohair, pork, potatoes, watermelon, and wool.

Dependable sources of supplies, reasonable prices, and protection against unfair business practices are important to producers, marketers, and consumers alike. The AMS administers regulatory laws through the Fair Trade Practices program. The laws which are administered are the Perishable Commodities Act, the Federal Seed Act, the Plant Variety Protection Act, and the Agricultural Fair Practices Act.

To help stabilize markets, Marketing Agreements and Orders programs are administered by the AMS. These programs are initiated by farmers. The farm commodities affected are chiefly milk, fruits, vegetables, and certain specialty crops like nuts, raisin, and dates.

Egg Products Inspection and Shell Egg Surveillance conducts mandatory, continuous inspection in all plants processing liquid, frozen, and dried egg products. They ensure that products reaching the consumer are wholesome and pure. Also, the disposal of certain types of shell eggs which do not meet grading standards is controlled.

NATIONAL AGRICULTURAL STATISTICS SERVICE (NASS)

Some producers feel that government crop and livestock reports depress market prices and that they would be better off without them. However, the National Agricultural Statistics Service (NASS) provides a needed and valuable service to U.S. agriculture. The crop estimates provided by the NASS are used by farm organizations to plan programs. Legislators use estimates to justify legislative action. Advance indication of supply helps to prevent severe price adjustments that might otherwise occur at harvest-time. Without the advance notice, uncertainty would cause food marketers and suppliers to increase their costs and producers would receive lower prices.

SELECTING MARKETING ALTERNATIVES

Agricultural producers use a variety of approaches to select marketing alternatives. These can vary from highly complex, computer-aided marketing plans to simple logic. Selecting a successful marketing alternative requires a combination of business skills, planning, analysis, and action.

Before agricultural producers can successfully select marketing alternatives, they must examine factors that affect that decision. It is important that these factors be examined in a structured way. Because marketing plays such a vital role in the production and distribution of agricultural commodities, it is imperative for the producer to plan before taking action. This decision-making process can be structured by determining (1) the current situation, (2) the goals or objectives of the enterprise, and (3) how to achieve or reach the goals or objectives.

Determining the current situation can be a difficult, time consuming task. However, it is the foundation for all decisions and must be done.

Figure 6–11. Marketing alternatives for this field of grain sorghum must be considered early, even before the production cycle begins.

Assessment involves examining the market, your own financial situation, and available alternatives.

Market assessment is more than just forecasting prices. To do a market assessment the agricultural producer must have a basic understanding of how supply and demand affect the pricing of various commodities. Also, the producer must be aware of the current market situation. What is the current price trend for the particular commodity? Is there a shortage or an oversupply of the commodity? What are the consumer biases for the commodity? What are the current crop projections? Additionally, one should consider local competition.

In addition to analyzing the market situation, producers must assess their financial situations. Current debt load, cash flow requirements, plus the profitability of the commodity being considered should impact the assessment of the financial situation. One key to controlling the financial situation is the use of a good record keeping system. Good records can help to determine the profitability of producing a commodity. Good records can also be useful when approaching an agricultural lender for production capital. Banks and lending agencies are in a better position to provide assistance if they can see that good records are being kept.

The available marketing alternatives should be considered. The traditional alternatives may or may not satisfy the needs of the individual producer. Regardless, the producer should at least consider some of the

Figure 6–12. Some agricultural enterprises are riskier than others. In semi-arid regions, irrigation may be needed before planting so that the seeds will germinate. (Courtesy of the Dept. of Agricultural Education and Communications, Texas Tech University)

more nontraditional alternatives that are available. These alternatives will vary in their flexibility, riskiness, simplicity, and efficiency. As a result, the final selection should be based upon the market assessment and the financial situation of the producer.

By determining the goals or objectives for the marketing alternative, the producer is able to provide guidance to the selection process. The development of desired and realistic marketing alternative objectives enhances the process. Without clear, realistic objectives, the producer can drift aimlessly through marketing alternatives. By developing objectives, the producer is able to examine each alternative in light of the goals or objectives.

By determining how to reach the objectives the producer is putting the marketing alternative into action. To take action the producer must (1) use the assessment results to analyze market outlook and price-determining factors, (2) evaluate the ability of various marketing alternatives to deal with market conditions and the outlook, (3) examine the financial status and requirements of the farm business, and (4) establish market or price objectives.

SUMMARY

As you can see, people in the business of producing food and fiber have a need for the intelligent selection of a marketing approach. Businesses at all levels, from the individual farmer or rancher to large corporations, have a need for marketing strategies to complement the strategies for production and financing. Of course, the large corporation can devote more resources to developing marketing alternatives than the individual producer. Producers need to have a clear understanding of governmental programs that affect their operations. Governmental programs can enhance the chances of a successful agricultural enterprise. Whether the farming or ranching operation is large or small, proper planning is very important. The agricultural producer has many decisions to make throughout the production cycle. Many of those decisions should be made before production ever starts.

CHAPTER SELF-CHECK

Match the following terms with the correct definitions:

a. market niche

b. comparative advantage

c. price maker

d. forward contracting

e. marketing approach

f. commodities

g. value-added

h. method of delivery

i. method of exchange

j. price taker

_____ the result of all marketing decisions concerning how goods and services are provided to customers

_____ products of agricultural production

_____ agricultural producers who must accept the price offered for their agricultural products

_____ people who set prices for agricultural products

_____ shifting the timing of sales of agricultural products

_____ unique market places

_____ ways of transporting agricultural products

_____ compensation received by the seller of a commodity

_____ the progression of agricultural commodities through the marketing system. At each step the worth of agricultural commodities is more than the additional input.

_____ particular expertise in raising certain commodities

QUESTIONS AND PROBLEMS FOR DISCUSSION

1. What decisions are made in determining a marketing approach?

2. When are agricultural producers price takers? Price makers?

3. What typically happens to prices for agricultural commodities at harvest time? Why?

4. What can agricultural producers do to shift the timing of sales of agricultural commodities?

5. How are current market prices for agricultural commodities determined?

6. Describe how a unique market niche can be beneficial to the profitability of an agricultural enterprise?

7. How do agricultural producers determine how much of an agricultural commodity they can produce?

8. How does transportation add to the value of agricultural commodities?

9. How does an agricultural producer's marketing objective affect the way a commodity is marketed?

10. What are some marketing approaches that help the agricultural producer to minimize risk?

11. What is the role of the United State Department of Agriculture in agricultural marketing?

12. Describe how value is added to agricultural commodities as they progress through the marketing system?

13. Name five ways that packaging adds value to agricultural products.

14. What are the three steps to selecting a marketing alternative?

15. What are four things an agricultural producer must do to put an agrimarketing alternative into action?

ACTIVITIES

1. Visit a local agricultural producer and determine the agricultural products which are produced and marketed. Interview the producer to determine what approach is being used. Prepare a written report on what you learned.

2. Choose a common agricultural commodity that is grown locally. Study that commodity to determine what kinds of products, including by-products, are made from that commodity. Prepare a flow chart which shows how your commodity moves through the marketing system from the time it is harvested until it reaches the final consumer.

3. Choose two agricultural commodities, one that is grown locally and another that is grow in another state or region. Find out why one commodity is grown locally and why the other is not. Also, find out why the commodity that is grown elsewhere is produced. Prepare an oral report to be given to the class on what you found out.

Chapter 7

MARKETING AGRICULTURAL SUPPLIES AND SERVICES

Agricultural supplies and services are those inputs that are consumed in the process of agricultural production. Agricultural production requires many different supplies and services. In earlier times, farmers were basically self sufficient and required few supplies and services from off the farm. For example, farmers usually purchased very little seed because they saved some of the previous year's crop to plant for the next year's production. Also, little to no fertilizer was purchased. If fertilizer was used, it was usually manure from animals raised on the farm. Today, fertilizer purchases represent a major production cost. With technological advances, farmers have become more productive and fewer people work in agricultural production. However, more people (about 20 percent) are involved in other

Figure 7–1. Modern farm equipment is essential to production agriculture in the United States.

agricultural occupations. A large portion of today's U.S. population is involved in occupations unrelated to agriculture and agricultural production.

OBJECTIVES

In today's modern agriculture very few supplies and services have their origin on the farm on which they will be used. Even grain for livestock feeds may be purchased from a feed company or other producers who specialize in grain production. Consequently, there is a need for the marketing of agricultural supplies and services (inputs) used to raise livestock and grow crops. This chapter contains information about the marketing of agricultural supplies and services.

TERMS

agricultural chemicals
agricultural input industries
agricultural pharmaceuticals
bank financing
company financing
competition
custom farming
dealer financing
debt structure
financial backing
inputs
leasing
market area
market share
sales potential
trade leakage

- Define agricultural supplies and services

- Describe the role of agricultural supplies and services in the agricultural industry

- Explain sales potential

- Explain market share

- Explain competition

- Describe agricultural equipment marketing

- Describe seed, feed, and fertilizer marketing

- Describe agricultural chemical marketing

- Describe agricultural pharmaceutical marketing

AGRICULTURAL SUPPLIES AND SERVICES

Agricultural supplies and services represent everything the farmer or rancher uses to produce food and fiber. Economists refer to these supplies and services as *inputs. Agricultural input industries* include those businesses that manufacture, process, and/or supply feeds and feed additives, seed, tractors, tillage equipment, planters, harvesting equipment, fertilizer, insurance, insecticides, herbicides, lubricants, fuels, veterinary supplies and services, consulting services, custom operations, financing, and a host of other inputs. Roughly 75 percent of the total inputs used by agricultural producers are provided by these businesses. The other 25 percent include items such as hay, livestock, and grains that are produced and used on the farm or ranch.

Figure 7–2. Seed wheat is an example of an agricultural supply.

Examples of Agricultural Supplies and Services

Seed	Chemicals	Fertilizer
Fuel	Tractors	Planters
Tillage equipment	Sprayers	Land
Seed treatments	Labor	Combines
Custom operations	Trucks	Aerial applicators
Accountants	Mechanics	Feed
Veterinarians	Lubricants	Equipment parts
Insect scouts	Veterinary supplies	

The agricultural supply and service industry extends far beyond those directly associated with the production of food and fiber. Lawn care services are an important part of this industry, particularly in urban and suburban areas. Lawn care services perform many functions in addition to simply mowing the grass. Many of these business also remove thatch; prune trees and shrubs; apply fertilizers and pesticides; plant trees, shrubs and seasonal bedding plants; and apply water. Another example of agricultural supply and service industries that are not directly involved in the production of food and fiber are those associated with the recreation business. Increased interest in outdoor sports such as golf has opened opportunities for industries specializing in the building, operation, and maintenance of golf courses. Golf course employees perform such duties as establishing and maintaining turf; applying herbicides, fungicides, insecticides, and fertilizers; land leveling; and irrigation. Many municipalities with parks, sports complexes, and other public outdoor areas have entire divisions of employees who are responsible for establishing and maintaining them.

ROLE OF AGRICULTURAL SUPPLIES AND SERVICES

Advances in technology have had great impact on agriculture as an industry. Included in this are all the industries that supply inputs for production agriculture. The latest technologies have resulted in highly

Figure 7–3. Agricultural supplies contribute to the efficient production of agricultural commodities.

productive, cost-reducing inputs for the efficient production of agricultural commodities. Agribusiness firms exist for the exclusive purpose of supplying inputs (supplies and/or services) for agricultural production. Farmers and ranchers are able to buy, rather than make or raise, more and more of the many supplies and services necessary for agricultural production. With the shift in the source for agricultural supplies and services, there has been unprecedented gains in agricultural productivity. Each producer is able to increase volume because of greater capacity and greater yields.

The total level of inputs used in agricultural production has changed very little since the end of World War II. However, there has been a shift in the mixture of inputs used. Chemicals and machinery have replaced a large portion of the labor that once was commonplace in agricultural production. It is not uncommon for one or two people to operate a farm or ranch that once would have required labor from several people. Farmers are now able to produce more output for less cost with less labor. Farmers once produced enough food and fiber to feed and clothe their families. The average U.S. farmer now produces enough food and fiber to feed and clothe 125 people.

SALES POTENTIAL

One of the outcomes of fewer people being involved in the actual business of agricultural production is that more of the population is available to provide other services. Some of the population which is released from production agriculture may decide to enter businesses that specialize in the sale of agricultural supplies and services. These businesses must carefully examine the *sales potential*, or the predicted sales volume, of their product before entering business. Obviously, entering or starting a business that specializes in a product with little sales potential is foolish. Predicting the volume of sales is much more complex than it appears on the surface. However, the difficulty of predicting sales potential does not lessen the need to attempt this task. Certain failure awaits those who fail to recognize that there is no sales potential for the product they wish to market.

The first step in determining sales potential is to estimate the total current sales in the *market area* for the supply or service being considered. Defining the market area represents a major problem in determining sales potential. There are many factors to consider in determining market area. Location of major cities must be considered. Oftentimes, major cities have many businesses already providing the supply or service being considered. If the major city is close to your market area, you can expect some *trade*

Figure 7–4. Agricultural services are available in small rural
communities across the United States.

leakage as people travel to the city to take advantage of the things that
cities have to offer. Also to be considered is the mobility of consumers.
There seem to be regional differences in the willingness of consumers to
travel to purchase supplies and services. It is entirely possible that some
from within your market area will leave to purchase supplies and services,
while others from outside your market area will come to you, particularly
if you develop a reputation for exceptional products, customer service, and
prices. This willingness of the consumer to travel greater distances for
higher quality products, or some other aspect which is unique, figures
greatly into the determination of market area.

Once the market area is determined, you can begin the task of estimating
total sales potential. By visiting businesses that currently provide the agricultural supply and/or service you are thinking of marketing, you can begin
to develop an understanding of the sales volume that is available in a
particular market area. Things like number of employees, inventory, merchandise condition, and cleanliness of the business, offer clues to the sales
volume of each business. Of course these indicators are only clues. You
must be careful not to be misled because of misinterpretation of some of
the above characteristics.

Also important to the task of sales potential determination is a description of the population in the market area. Information such as per
capita income and age distribution are available from census data. This
information is used to develop a profile of the consumers in the market

area which aids in the prediction of sales. Also, since agricultural supplies and services are the items to be marketed, it is of utmost importance to know production information from the area. Things like number of acres of each crop grown, livestock numbers, and amounts of commodities sold will be invaluable in determining total sales potential.

MARKET SHARE

If it is determined that the total sales potential is favorable, the next step is to determine the share of the market that is available for the new business. In most cases, new businesses, unless they are marketing a never-before-marketed supply or service, must capture a share of the market from existing businesses. This means that the new business may have to compete with businesses that have been in existence for years. Capturing a *market share*, or a portion of business, from established businesses can be one of the most difficult and formidable aspects of starting a new business. Usually, a new business will have to provide supplies and services in such a way that it is to the consumer's advantage to do business with them. This is where the new business often determines its success or failure.

Location is vital to the business' ability to capture a share of the current market. Ease of access, location of competitors, direction of growth of the city, and direction of growth of the market should be considered. It is nearly essential for a business to be centrally located to the market targeted for capture. It is also advantageous for the business to be easily accessible. Businesses which are difficult to find very seldom succeed. Generally speaking, your business should be more centrally located and more easily accessible than the competition's business.

It is important to estimate the time it will take for the business to reach its sales potential. Existing businesses that change owners or management usually experience very little down time in terms of sales potential. New businesses, however, are at a disadvantage and can expect to take longer to reach this potential. This time period is vital to the health of the new business. This is why new businesses have grand openings and sell certain products at greatly reduced prices. With the expense of starting a new business, it is important that the business reach its potential sales as quickly as possible. The success of a new business is highly dependent upon the business' ability to meet financial obligations such as payroll, payment to suppliers, financing, and advertising. If potential sales are not reached quickly enough, the business may fail early.

COMPETITION

Businesses in the agricultural supply and/or service industry must be fully aware of the *competition* or businesses that offer the same or similar products. Unless you are offering a new supply or service, the success of your business is dependent on your ability to capture a portion of the market from competitors. If competitors are strong and well established, capturing a market share can be particularly challenging. Competition may be measured in a number of ways, but questions to be answered should include: (1) How many competing businesses are there and what size and type are they? (2) How much equity do owners have in their businesses? (3) What is the financial strength and backing of each? (4) What level of managerial skill does each appear to have?

NUMBER, SIZE, AND TYPE OF COMPETING BUSINESSES

The number, size, and type of competing businesses is very important to consider when analyzing the competition. The number of competitors has an obvious impact on competition. There is a limited amount of sales potential. The greater the number of competitors, the more fragmented the market becomes. This leaves less sales potential for each business. The goal

Figure 7–5. Businesses that sell agricultural supplies must stock a wide variety of products.

that each competitor should have is to capture more than their share of the business.

Size is important because generally, larger businesses have lower per unit costs. Larger businesses receive volume discounts and have the opportunity to utilize specialized equipment that smaller competitors may not be able to afford. This may allow larger businesses to market supplies or services at greatly reduced prices. Many family owned local businesses have failed because large company-owned discount businesses have moved into a community. These businesses can be a sizable challenge to small independent businesses.

Type of business refers to the structure of the competitor. Is the competitor a single, independently owned business or is it part of a large chain of businesses? Typically, businesses that are part of a chain have advantages related to volume purchasing power. However, franchising costs are sometimes prohibitive.

COMPETITORS DEBT STRUCTURE

Determining the *debt structure* of a competitor may be relatively easy or it may be impossible. It is important to know the debt structure of a competitor because it can offer some clues to how strong the competitor is. A competitor with debt-free, modern, well-designed facilities can be tough competition for a new business. On the other hand, businesses with highly leveraged facilities may have trouble selling enough to pay expenses, mortgages, and salaries.

Information about the debt structure of competitors may be common knowledge or it may be a closely guarded secret. Sometimes bank loan officers may supply some clues as long as the information does not infringe upon the relationship of the competitor with the bank. Credit bureau newsletters can sometimes carry lists of real estate transfers with information about the size of loans and to whom the loan was made. The county clerk or county recorder generally has information about real estate and non-real estate debts. However, the amount of information one can obtain varies from state to state.

FINANCIAL BACKING

It is sometimes helpful to know something about the *financial backing* of the competitor. Sometimes competing businesses have the backing of funds external to the business, such as other sources of family income. Or perhaps the business is located on unusually valuable property which may be considered good collateral for loans. Businesses with substantial financial backing other than the usual bank loans are typically more resistant to times of tough competition and may be able to survive longer than new businesses that do not have as much backing.

MANAGERIAL ABILITY

The ability of competing managers and their staffs to manage a business is perhaps one of the most important indicators of how strong competition will be. The skill and ingenuity of competing businesses may be the most important factor. Good management can offset higher operating costs and disadvantages in finances.

Figure 7–6. Well-managed agribusinesses are organized.

Well-managed businesses have a decided edge in competing for sales. Managerial skills are not always apparent, but the general condition of the business may give some clues. How well the manager demonstrates the ability to apply recognized good practices generally tells something of his or her ability to compete. Customer loyalty may be an indicator of managerial skill.

AGRICULTURAL EQUIPMENT MARKETING

The agricultural equipment industry has undergone many changes throughout history. However, most of these changes have occurred recently. Until 1850, agriculture changed very little from generation to generation. Most of the jobs that were done on the farm or ranch were very labor intensive. Planting, tilling, and harvesting all were done by hand. When you consider that up to 90 percent of all people in the United States were engaged in agricultural production, it is evident that more people were necessary just to feed the farm family, let alone have extra for sale or export. In modern agriculture, production per person is up dramatically. This is primarily due to the increased mechanization of agriculture. Today, less than two percent of the population in the United States is engaged in agricultural production. Yet this two percent is able to produce enough food and fiber to feed and clothe their families, with enough left over to supply the rest of the United States and export to the world's markets.

The marketing of agricultural equipment is very competitive because of the small number of potential purchasers. In response to this competitiveness, agricultural equipment dealers provide many services in addition to selling equipment. These services provide a competitive edge for the agricultural equipment dealer. Of course, many of these services provide additional income for the equipment dealer. In times of poor production

Figure 7–7. Modern agricultural producers require the use of a wide variety of specialized agricultural equipment.

or poor prices, the equipment dealer may rely entirely on these services for income.

Generally speaking, farmers who require agricultural equipment obtain it in one of two ways. The traditional way is to take ownership. In other words, the farmer purchases the equipment. Taking ownership of agricultural equipment represents a very significant portion of farmers' capital expenses. Consequently, one of the services equipment dealers provide is helping the buyer obtain financing. Financing can be arranged from one or more of three different sources. *Dealer financing*—the equipment dealer lends the money to the buyer and is the owner of the note—is sometimes available from well-established businesses with ample financial backing. More common are either *bank financing* or *company financing*. For bank financing the dealer often helps the buyer complete all the paper work and actually submits the loan request to the bank. Company financing is available from larger equipment manufacturers. Again, the dealer helps the buyer to complete and submit the necessary paper work. Of course buyers can choose to obtain financing on their own. The dealer simply helps obtain financing as a customer service and, unless the dealer finances the purchase, realizes no income from this service.

Leasing agricultural equipment has become an attractive alternative to ownership. When leasing, the farmer has the use of the equipment without ownership. Leasing agreements vary from state to state and with the type of equipment being leased. Usually, the lease agreement is based upon hours of use, days/weeks/months of use, acres worked, or units harvested. On a tractor, the hour meter on the control panel provides a true indicator of use. For other machinery, such as tillage equipment, other measures must be used. Typically, such equipment is leased by the day, week, month, or year. Some equipment, such as a hay baler, has a counter which keeps track of the number of bales made. Consequently, the lease agreement for a hay baler may be based on this count.

With typical lease agreements, the lessee (farmer) is responsible for everyday servicing and damage due to excessive use or mistreatment. The lessor repairs normal wear and tear. Leases are particularly advantageous for farmers who are just starting and for farmers who have debt loads that prohibit further borrowing. Additionally, leases can be used under abnormal conditions such as when untimely extreme rainfall delays planting or harvesting. Under these circumstances the farmer may need to plant or harvest during a compressed time period. The lease option allows the farmer to complete these operations by putting more equipment in the field. Leasing also provides a farmer with the opportunity to conduct an extended "test-drive" to help decide whether to purchase a particular piece of machinery or not.

Businesses that market agricultural equipment generally sell replacement parts. Therefore, equipment dealers must maintain a substantial inventory of replacement parts for all the equipment they sell. Inventory maintenance is an important factor due to the expense of keeping parts in stock. Timeliness is of utmost importance when providing parts for farmers. During busy times of the cropping season, even a few lost hours due to breakdown can reduce a farmer's profit. Equipment dealers who develop a reputation for quickly providing hard-to-get replacement parts have an advantage toward capturing a share of the market.

Another service that equipment dealers provide is mechanical repairs. Most equipment dealers have shops where anything from simple preventative maintenance to major overhauls can be performed. Simple preventative maintenance includes oil changes and tune-ups. However, most farmers perform these jobs themselves. Major overhauls, on the other hand, are often left to the mechanics in the equipment dealer's shop to perform. Due to the expense of owning agricultural equipment, farmers may have their equipment overhauled rather than replaced. Timely service is important due to the seasonality of agricultural production. Skilled, efficient mechanics are valuable assets to the equipment dealer. Repair shops that are known to have quick turnaround for repairs are sought by agricultural producers. Efficient service enhances a dealer's ability to market equipment.

Figure 7–8. Agricultural equipment dealers provide new equipment and repair services.

Some manufacturers provide services that help dealers to market equipment. A combine manufacturer in Independence, Missouri, provides a unique service to farmers who purchase its combines. Every combine sold is assigned to one of the employees at the plant where the combine was made. This employee contacts the owner of the combine just after the farmer accepts delivery, forming a direct link between the manufacturer and the farmer. This employee helps the customer resolve any problems that may occur and answers questions about service and maintenance of the machine. The manufacturer benefits because the employees are motivated to build quality machines and problems with the machines are corrected earlier. The farmer benefits because the manufacturer is concerned about customer service. The dealer benefits because the manufacturer backs up the product.

Another service provided by a manufacturer is making parts available for custom harvesters as they follow the wheat harvest. Custom harvesters begin harvesting wheat in June in Texas. As the grain ripens they follow the wheat harvest north into Minnesota, North Dakota, Montana, and perhaps even into Canada. Custom harvesters travel great distances from the dealers where they purchased their combines. To overcome this problem, the manufacturer sends truckloads of replacement parts to follow the harvest. As combines break down and replacement parts or warranty repair work is needed, the mobile parts inventory is usually only a few miles away. This is a much appreciated service because custom harvesters are trying to harvest as many acres of wheat as their machines and crews can handle. The mobile replacement parts service reduces the downtime that the custom harvester might otherwise experience.

An important service related to the agricultural equipment industry is that provided by custom farmers. The previous discussion referred to the specialized service performed by the custom harvester—harvesting grain crops. *Custom farming*, however, is much more general in nature. Custom farmers perform any number of the jobs necessary for the production of food and fiber. They till, plant, cultivate, spray, and harvest crops. Custom farmers that provide a wide range of services are more likely to cover a limited territory. Specialized custom farmers, like custom harvesters, tend to be more mobile and will travel many miles following agricultural jobs.

Farmers use custom farming services for a number of reasons. In the case of custom harvesting, several factors justify the use of custom farming. Combines are very expensive to purchase, service, and maintain. New modern combines sell for more than $100,000. Many farmers, especially wheat farmers, would find it difficult to purchase these machines. Using custom harvesting, farmers get their wheat harvested without the burden of owning expensive combines. Another factor that makes combines expensive to own is the fact that they are very specialized in the operation they perform. They are used only a few weeks out of every year. The rest of the year, they may sit idle in a machinery shed. Also, timeliness plays a role in the decision to use custom farmers to harvest the crop. Most custom harvest crews provide more than one combine. Some provide six or more. By providing multiple combines, the harvest is performed more quickly, lessening the chance that the crop might be lost due to some disaster such as hail, excessive rainfall, or even fire.

Other custom farming services are provided for many of the same reasons that custom harvesting is so popular. Custom operators often can perform services quickly and at a reasonable cost. This allows the farmer to concentrate on other aspects of the farming enterprise.

Figure 7–9. Some farmers rely on the custom application of fertilizer to avoid the cost of owning highly specialized equipment.

A farmer may not have a large enough operation to justify owning a particular piece of agricultural equipment. This farmer may use the equipment on neighboring farms in exchange for a fee. Then, due to increased volume, the producer can justify the expense of owning the equipment. A common example of this sort of situation is the farmer who needs to harvest hay. A farmer may have need for a sizable amount of hay for farm use. However, the cost of equipment needed to harvest the hay may be prohibitive. If this farmer can arrange to mow, condition, rake, and bale hay for neighboring farmers, perhaps the increased volume in bales of hay harvested will help the farmer justify owning the equipment.

The rates that custom farmers are paid for their services vary according to the service. For instance, custom wheat harvesters are paid by the bushel harvested. A custom farmer who provides tillage operations might be paid by the acre and the custom farmer who harvests hay will likely be paid by the bale or ton. At any rate, custom farming provides a way for a farmer to experience the benefit of the service without the cost of ownership. Moreover, the operation may be completed in a more timely manner. The custom farmer, on the other hand, owns the equipment. Because of the volume of work performed, the custom farmer is able to lower the per unit cost of ownership. Therefore, the custom farmer can justify owning agricultural equipment that otherwise might be much too expensive.

SEED, FEED, AND
FERTILIZER MARKETING

At the beginning of the twentieth century, farm families produced a variety of livestock and crops and were nearly self sufficient. Grains, fruits, and vegetables were raised for food to feed the farm family and for the production of livestock. Horses and mules ate the feed and provided power to pull and operate machinery to grow crops. Animal manure was used for fertilizer. Pesticides were not used at all. Farm children provided the unpaid supplemental labor that was needed to run the farm. Nearly all the food and most of the clothing needed by the farm family was produced on the farm.

When farms were operated as described above, corn yields were 25 percent or less of what they are today. Early farmers had fewer acres in production when compared to modern counterparts. Crop and livestock diseases, insects, and other pests were very difficult for the earlier farmer to overcome. Together with open-field-pollinated seeds, it is easy to see why more farmers were necessary to meet the demands of consumers of agricultural products.

In the 1930s hybrid seeds were first developed and made available. This was a major breakthrough for agriculture. Vast improvements were made by carefully breeding for desirable crop traits such as yield and disease resistance through controlled pollination. Hybrid seed resulted in plants that nearly doubled corn yields with a minimal increase in costs. This advancement resulted in the formation of businesses that specialize in the production of hybrid seeds. New hybrid seed must be produced each year. In the past, farmers used a portion of the current crop as seed for the next year, but a crop raised from hybrid seed is not suitable for seed. Farmers no longer devoted a portion of their acreage to the production of the next year's seed which increased the total production of grain available for marketing. This increased the gross income on the farm. Farmers became less dependent on their own ability to provide the inputs necessary for agricultural production and began to rely on outside sources.

Advances are still being made in the development of new and better seed for all agricultural crops. Agricultural experiment stations and private seed companies, using the latest biological technology, are continuously making improvements in crop varieties. Seed companies also are improving varieties. Efforts are currently being made to develop seeds that are resistant to new diseases, pesticide resistant insects, and other undesirable conditions. The Plant Stress Laboratory at Texas Tech University is developing varieties of crops that are more resistant to drought, insects, diseases, and other conditions that stress plants to the point of being unproductive.

The marketing of seeds is carried out in many ways. Many agricultural supply stores sell seeds. Seed companies market seeds through agricultural supply stores and farmers who sell seed as a supplement to their farming enterprises. Demonstration plots are commonly used to show the advantage

Figure 7–10. Research provides new, more efficient ways of producing crops.

of particular varieties. Seed companies establish test plots and host field days to show why their varieties should be used.

The improvements in livestock feeds have been less dramatic than those made in other areas of agriculture. Probably the most important advancements are in feed additives. Additives are used to supply vitamins, minerals, and medications. The use of additives enhances feed efficiency and the rate of gain so that returns from livestock production will be maximized. Farmers and ranchers strive to raise animals that reach market size in as little time as possible. Medications in feed are important because they aid in keeping livestock healthy. Healthy livestock are more likely to gain at an acceptable rate. However, medicated feed must be carefully regulated to insure that proper withdrawal periods are used. Animals that have been fed medicated feed should not be marketed or slaughtered until the withdrawal period has expired. All animal medication should be labeled with withdrawal periods to insure that contaminated meats and livestock products do not reach the consumer.

Figure 7–11. Feeds are available for nearly every species of livestock and poultry imaginable.

Feeds are marketed much the same as seed. Agricultural supply stores and grain elevators sell feed. Other stores sell feed exclusively. Some farmers have distributorships for certain feeds. Demonstrations are used in the marketing of feed and feed additives just as they are used in the marketing of seed. Feeding demonstrations often include several pens of livestock which are fed rations with varying amounts of grain, minerals, vitamins, medicines, and other additives. The results are then published and used to justify to the farmer or rancher the use of certain feeds and additives.

The wartime economy of the 1940s brought about a tremendous demand for nitrogen, which was used for the manufacturing of explosives. After World War II, nitrogen plants built to satisfy the wartime need were idle. These plants were sold to private firms that converted them to the production of nitrogen for fertilizer. This provided farmers and ranchers with access to low-cost chemical nitrogen. This chemical fertilizer replaced the natural, organic fertilizer (animal manure) that had been used up to that point in time. Here again, farmers replaced an input that had its origin on the farm with an input that was purchased from off the farm.

The major components of fertilizer—nitrogen (N), phosphorus (P), and potassium (K)—are produced in separate operations. Most nitrogen for fertilizer is a form of ammonia and is produced from natural gas. That is why the price of nitrogen is so closely tied to the price of natural gas and energy prices in general. Both phosphorus and potassium are naturally occurring minerals. There are major deposits of phosphorus in Florida, North Carolina, South Carolina, Africa, and Chile. Phosphorus is mined and then processed for agricultural use. Potassium is found naturally in Canada. At one time potassium was produced by collecting the ashes from burning wood in iron pots. This ash was called potash, hence the common name used to refer to potassium today.

The effects on productivity from increased fertilization are well documented. Fertilizer has helped to boost crop yields. Abundant supplies of fertilizer have kept prices relatively low and made it profitable for farmers to use large amounts. Suppliers have met farmers' needs for plant nutrients by providing fertilizer at the time, in the place, in the form, and in a way that made possession easy and convenient. In short, they did a good job of marketing their products.

Figure 7–12. Farmers should be responsible in the use of fertilizers and chemicals.

Marketers of agricultural fertilizers must be aware of the effect that over application of chemicals has on the environment. Runoff from over-fertilized agricultural lands seriously damages the ecosystem. An example of this problem can be seen in the Chesapeake Bay. When too much nitrogen enters the bay, an overabundance of algae is formed. This algae consumes too much oxygen from the water. Entire species of fish are disappearing from waterways partially because of agricultural runoff. People who sell *agricultural chemicals* should make sure that the farmers who purchase the fertilizers are aware of the problem and they should try to educate farmers as to how to lessen the problem.

AGRICULTURAL CHEMICAL MARKETING

The addition of chemical pest and weed control has been one of the most important and dramatic introductions to the agricultural input industry. With the introduction of DDT and 2,4-D farmers had the means to control the insects and weeds that affected the ability of the farmer to be profitable.

Unfortunately, too little was known about the side effects of these two chemicals. It has since been determined that DDT and 2,4-D were too hazardous to the environment. The good news is that environmental concerns are now of utmost importance as each new chemical becomes available for entry into the market. Chemicals now undergo extensive testing to see that the environmental effects are minimal.

Agricultural chemicals are marketed in much the same way as seed, feed, and fertilizers. Demonstration plots where the producer can actually observe the effectiveness of the chemicals are impressive ways to document the control of insects and weeds. However, chemical dealers must abide by governmental regulations as they sell and/or apply chemicals. Some chemicals are restricted in their use. This means that only certain trained individuals are allowed to purchase and/or apply these chemicals. Agricultural chemical dealers should inform purchasers of the proper use for chemicals and offer advice about application methods.

Agricultural chemicals are often marketed by custom applicators who sell and also apply the chemicals. These chemicals can be applied from spray trucks and tractors or they can be applied from airplanes and heli-copters. Many custom applicators offer their services as insect scouts to inspect crops periodically for outbreaks of detrimental insects. When these insects are found in populations large enough to inflict damage and affect the profitability of the crop, these consultants recommend application of an insecticide to control the insect. Custom pesticide applicators who use airplanes have the advantage of being able to cover many acres in a short period of time. This is important because large outbreaks of insects can cause irreversible damage in a short time.

AGRICULTURAL PHARMACEUTICAL MARKETING

The health of livestock is very important to everyone. Farmers know that healthy livestock are profitable livestock. Consumers want healthy livestock that provide high quality and safe food products. The general population wants healthy livestock that is treated as humanely as possible.

Animal health is enhanced by the use of *agricultural pharmaceuticals*. Agricultural pharmaceuticals are medicines and other substances that are used to control parasites, prevent diseases, and treat sick animals. This in turn allows the livestock to be grown as efficiently as possible. Some of the parasites that affect animals are lice, ticks, worms, and grubs. There are many treatments specific to particular species of livestock that control a particular parasite. Some diseases can be prevented in livestock through vaccination programs. They include black leg, brucellosis, and tuberculosis

Figure 7–13. Products are available that enhance the health of animals. Healthy animals are more productive than unhealthy animals.

in cattle; and cholera, brucellosis, erysipelas, and pseudorabies in swine. One way to prevent these diseases is with an immunization program. Animals are immunized to prevent them from contracting the disease. Diseases in animals are treated primarily with injectable antibiotics, although a preventative program with medicated feed is used by many farmers and ranchers.

The marketing of agricultural pharmaceuticals is done primarily through farm supply stores. Some agricultural pharmaceuticals are available by prescription only and must be dispensed by a veterinarian. Labels should be consulted to determine correct doses, withdrawal periods, and injection sites. Marketers of these drugs must be aware of this information and be able to advise the purchaser as to the correct dosages.

SUMMARY

The agricultural supplies and services industries have developed significantly since the end of World War II. These industries exist because the inputs they sell are less expensive and more productive than those produced on the farm. The development of these industries has permitted farmers to concentrate on production. Input firms are a major force in agribusiness. Agricultural input industries have made a major investment of time and money in the development of highly technical and sophisticated inputs. They have a great interest in the efficient and effective marketing of their products, in order to insure the continued health and profitability of the food and fiber system.

CHAPTER SELF-CHECK

Match the following terms with the correct definitions:

    a. market area

    b. trade leakage

    c. bank financing

    d. agricultural input industries

    e. sales potential

    f. custom farming

g. inputs

h. leasing

i. debt structure

j. market share

_____ everything farmers and ranchers use to produce food and fiber

_____ businesses which manufacture, process, and/or supply feeds and feed additives, seed, tractors, tillage equipment, planters, harvesting equipment, fertilizer, insurance, insecticides, herbicides, lubricants, fuels, veterinarian supplies and services, consulting services, custom operations, and financing

_____ predicted volume of sales

_____ geographic description of the range of customers

_____ sales lost to other market areas

_____ portion of sales potential available for an agricultural business

_____ the financial condition of a business or individual including outstanding loans

_____ loans from banks

_____ using agricultural equipment without ownership

_____ performing farming operations for hire

QUESTIONS AND PROBLEMS FOR DISCUSSION

1. What roles do agricultural supplies and services play in the production of food and fiber?

2. What are some examples of agricultural input industries?

3. Why is it important to determine the sales potential of an agricultural supply or service before entering business?

4. What are three factors that should be considered when determining a market area?

5. What factors may make capturing a market share difficult for new businesses?

6. What four questions should be answered when analyzing the competition?

7. Describe the services a farm equipment dealership might provide in addition to selling farm equipment.

8. Distinguish the differences between custom farming and farming for yourself.

9. How might feed, seed, or chemical companies use demonstrations to help market their products?

10. What roles do agricultural pharmaceuticals play in production agriculture?

ACTIVITIES

1. Select an agricultural supply or service that you would be interested in selling or performing. Determine the sales potential, market share, and competition for that supply or service. Prepare a written report on what you learned.

2. Visit a local agricultural equipment dealer. Determine the types of equipment that are sold. Determine the services the dealer provides in addition to selling. Prepare a poster illustrating what you learned.

3. Collect labels from feed, chemicals, fertilizers, and pharmaceuticals. Determine restrictions on use, labeled uses, withdrawal periods, and emergency procedures. Prepare an oral report to be given to your class.

Chapter 8

MARKETING FARM AND RANCH COMMODITIES

Farmers and ranchers are not always in a position to set the price that they will receive for their commodities. Instead, farmers and ranchers are accustomed to accepting the price that buyers of their products will pay. Farmers and ranchers have historically been "price takers" rather than "price makers" and thus have been at the mercy of current market prices. Unfortunately, current market prices do not guarantee that the production of livestock or a particular crop will be profitable. Farmers and ranchers can do little to control the profitability of their agricultural enterprises unless

Figure 8–1. Cattle feeders must make correct marketing decisions to increase the profitability of their operations. (Courtesy of the Dept. of Agricultural Education and Communications, Texas Tech University)

173

they approach marketing as a vital component of producing agricultural commodities.

In modern agriculture, marketing is at least as important as the actual production of the commodities. Correct marketing decisions can mean the difference between success and failure of the agricultural enterprise. Therefore, at least as much time and effort should be spent on marketing animals and crops as is spent on their production. Marketing is a management component of the agricultural enterprise. The time and effort expended on marketing is a different sort of work than the farmer or rancher is accustomed to. Production usually implies physical labor whereas marketing, for the most part, involves dealing with people.

TERMS

cash market
cost-price squeeze
farm/ranch problem
food and fiber marketing
    sector
free-rider
hedging
industry fragmentation
pricing efficiency
private treaty
producer sector
production control
production flexibility

OBJECTIVES

This chapter contains information which can be used in the marketing of farm and ranch commodities.

- Explain the importance of marketing to financial success in farming and ranching
- Distinguish selling and marketing
- Describe markets available for farm and ranch commodities
- Identify strategies to increase revenues in marketing
- Identify marketing alternatives
- Describe the role of financial position and risk taking
- Explain how to select the best marketing alternative

THE IMPORTANCE OF MARKETING TO FINANCIAL SUCCESS IN FARMING AND RANCHING

Financial success in farming and ranching is directly related to the producer's management ability. The farmer or rancher must be able to (1) manage the crop or livestock program, (2) make decisions about machinery and equipment, (3) manage agricultural structures, (4) supervise the labor supply, (5) manage financial matters and taxes, and (6) perform general administrative duties.

All of these abilities have a direct impact on financial success. The skills that successful producers need to market their commodities are often overlooked. Unfortunately, marketing is usually an afterthought for producers. Generally speaking, the earlier in the production cycle that producers consider marketing problems, the more profitable their agricultural enterprises will be.

American farmers and ranchers are better producers of agricultural commodities than producers anywhere else in the world. Barring unforeseen problems—such as not enough rain, too much rain, outbreaks of detrimental insects, or other natural disasters—the American farmer/rancher can expect yields that are unparalleled by anyone. The *farm/ranch problem*, generally speaking, is not one of low production. The farm/ranch problem is associated with unstable and relatively low farm/ranch prices and incomes. Some of the factors that contribute to this problem are:

- Lack of production control

- Lack of production flexibility

- Industry fragmentation

- The free-rider problem

- The cost-price squeeze

- Superior bargaining power of buyers of agricultural commodities

- Market pricing efficiency

- Separation between the production sector and the food marketing sector

Figure 8–2. Agricultural producers in the United States are very
skilled at producing high-yielding, high-quality crops.

LACK OF PRODUCTION CONTROL

Farmers and ranchers are not able to exercise *production control* to the same degree as nonfarm firms. Agricultural commodities come from many independent units (farms or ranches). Even if the farmer or rancher is very skilled at growing food and fiber commodities, production is largely dependent on weather and biology. The producer may wish to change output by adjusting the number of acres planted or the number of livestock bred, but weather, disease, and other uncontrollable factors affect yields per acre and the productivity of animals. Producers' attempts to adjust production are really just best-guess estimates of what the yields will be if all goes as planned. Farmers and ranchers simply cannot quickly shut off or turn on agricultural production. This means that, in the short run, buyers, processors, and consumers of agricultural commodities must adjust to supplies of agricultural commodities because farmers cannot adjust to the buyers, processors, and consumers. Farmers and ranchers could expect more control over the profitability of their enterprises if they could exercise more control over production.

LACK OF PRODUCTION FLEXIBILITY

It takes long periods of time to change the production of certain

Figure 8–3. Pecan production requires a long-term commitment. It took several years for these trees to yield profitable crops.

agricultural commodities. Fruit groves are planted years in advance of their coming into production. Orange and grapefruit trees in the lower Rio Grande Valley region of Texas were badly damaged and even destroyed by an unusually harsh winter freeze in the winter of 1989. That region of the state experienced a nearly complete loss of citrus production for two to three years. It was the winter of 1993 before new trees were mature enough to bear fruit at marketable levels.

The lack of *production flexibility* is particularly troublesome. The market situation may change during the period between deciding to grow or raise a particular commodity and being able to put it on the market. The expansion of milk production is a slow process. Unless lactating dairy cows are available from another source, the gestation period for a dairy cow is nine months. This means that after the decision is made to expand production, several months will pass before the dairy farmer can actually start marketing more milk. Even decreasing production of milk is slow and difficult. Once the investment is made in buildings, equipment, and the herd, changes are very difficult and expensive to make.

Historically, swine production has been one of the easiest agricultural enterprises for adjustment of production. Modern, high-tech swine production can involve facility investments that make even swine production particularly inflexible. Modern farrowing facilities are not well suited for anything but farrowing. Pig nurseries and feeding floors are not particularly flexible in their use. This means that unless they are used for swine production, they are likely to be idle. Even though these facilities may be idle, fixed costs such as depreciation, interest, repairs, taxes, and insurance continue. Swine producers who have made large investments in modern swine production facilities are not likely to be willing or able to adjust production.

The inability to adjust quickly to changing conditions creates a high-risk element in agriculture. The market for which a long-term production plan is made may change by the time the product is finally available. Changes in consumer tastes may find large amounts of agricultural resources being devoted to the production of something that is no longer greatly desired. High prices resulting from shortages of production may reduce the consumer market for that product when it finally arrives at the marketplace.

INDUSTRY FRAGMENTATION

Because farms and ranches are mostly independent businesses, production agriculture in the United States is subject to *industry fragmentation*. Farmers and ranchers face difficulty in improving their prices through independent or group activities. Even though attempts at collective bargaining have been made, for the most part farmers and ranchers are price-takers. They cannot individually influence the price of their products in traditional marketing settings. In order to raise prices through the control of *supply* or advertising programs, farmers and ranchers must act as a group. The large number of farmers and their differing economic circumstances frequently frustrate attempts to organize and act jointly.

Farmers and ranchers who specialize in raising commodities that are not commonly grown throughout the country are in a better position to organize and act as a group. For example, farmers who raise catfish in the Mississippi Delta established processing and marketing facilities specifically devoted to catfish. This smaller group of producers who raise a regionally unique product were able to reduce the fragmentation that is so prevalent in other segments of the agricultural industry.

THE FREE-RIDER PROBLEM

When farmers and ranchers attempt to organize in order to influence farm prices, the *free-rider* problem usually surfaces. Free-riders receive the benefit of an action without sacrifice for the overall welfare of the group. When benefits associated with organized effort go to everyone regardless of their participation in the group, free-riders are bound to surface. For instance, farmers may try to raise their prices through voluntary supply-control programs, advertising efforts, or bargaining associations. The results would benefit all farmers whether they have contributed to the program or not. Because of this, it is sometimes difficult to achieve the group participation necessary for success.

Many free-rider conflicts exist in agriculture when what is best for a single farmer may differ from the best interests of farmers as a group. For example, if prices and profits for a commodity are high because of voluntary production constraints, individual farmers will have an incentive to expand output. A few can do this without consequence. However, if all producers attempt to expand to take advantage of favorable prices, current market prices will fall due to excess supply. Because current market prices have fallen, profits will fall also, jeopardizing the ability of individual farmers and ranchers to stay in business.

THE COST-PRICE SQUEEZE

The competitive nature of agriculture tends to keep farm prices close to the costs of production. This is called the *cost-price squeeze*. Falling farm prices would not be so critical if they were accompanied by falling input costs. Increased dependence of farmers on off-farm-produced supplies leaves the farmer little leeway for adjusting to falling farm prices. This is com-

Figure 8–4. Costs of agricultural production remain relatively stable while prices received can fluctuate.

pounded by the tendency of production costs to rise as commodity prices improve.

Rising commodity prices attract farmers to more profitable enterprises which, in turn, places more *demand* on the inputs necessary to produce. Because more producers are raising a particular commodity, they tend to bid up the costs of production. This was particularly evident in the early 1980s when farmers experienced unprecedented profits. As more and more farmers sought to expand their enterprises, the demand for agricultural land skyrocketed. Along with the demand for land came greatly inflated land prices. Simultaneously, interest rates were very high. Even though prices for agricultural commodities were particularly good, increased land prices and interest rates raised the cost of production to a point where profits were negligible. When the prices for agricultural products fell sharply later in the 1980s, farmers were left owing too much money for land that was not priced on its ability to produce. Unfortunately, many producers were forced out of business by bankruptcy and foreclosures.

SUPERIOR BARGAINING POWER OF AGRICULTURAL COMMODITIES BUYERS

The superior bargaining power of agricultural commodities buyers is seen by many as a serious farm problem. Food marketing firms are usually

Figure 8–5. Through membership in a cooperative, farmers are able to take advantage of marketing cottonseed oil. This cottonseed oil is processed by a cotton cooperative.

larger and normally have better market information than the farmers from whom they buy. Understandably, firms that buy agricultural commodities are in business to make money. One of the ways they can maximize profits is to purchase agricultural commodities for as low a price as possible. U.S. agricultural producers are so good at producing that invariably there is an abundance of agricultural commodities. Because supplies are usually good, prices tend to be lower. Unless large groups of individual producers organize to participate in collective bargaining, the buyers of agricultural commodities have the edge in marketing. In addition, through contracts and other arrangements, food marketing firms are thought to gain some control over farm decisions and farm markets.

FOOD MARKET PRICING EFFICIENCY

In the past, farmers did not need to be concerned with food marketing because competitive conditions assured all farmers a fair, or at least equal, price. When competitive conditions exist there is usually a large degree of *pricing efficiency*. Pricing efficiency occurs when every producer can expect nearly the same price for commodities of the same quality. A producer of number one hogs is paid for number one hogs and a producer of number three hogs is paid for number three hogs. However, in today's direct negotiation and contractual arrangements, there is no longer any assurance of a high level of pricing efficiency in food markets. As a result, farmers must be more skilled in marketing decisions. This means that all farmers who market agricultural products should strive to negotiate and enter contractual agreements. Farmers who do not get involved with direct marketing to food and fiber firms receive the current market price. Typically, the current market price will be below prices which are negotiated directly.

SEPARATION BETWEEN THE PRODUCER SECTOR AND THE FOOD AND FIBER MARKETING SECTOR

Agricultural producers should be aware of the separation between the *producer sector* (farmers and ranchers) and the *food and fiber marketing sector* (firms involved with marketing food & fiber). Farmers have a commodity production orientation, whereas food and fiber marketing firms stress a merchandise orientation. Farmers are interested in producing and marketing raw commodities rather than products which are ready for consumption. That is, farmers like to produce vast quantities of their commodities. Even farmers who produce commodities that require little processing to be consumer ready, like vegetables, are most interested in providing the product in bulk to food marketers. It may be impractical for farmers to participate in many food and fiber marketing activities; however, some cooperatives make it possible for individual farmers to participate in value-adding opportunities. For example, members of the Plains Cotton Cooperative Association in western Texas benefit from an agreement with Levi Strauss.

There are many factors that contribute to unstable and relatively low market prices and incomes. Some of the more traditional marketing activities, like selling at current market prices at harvest, are not the most profitable. However, when producers go beyond traditional marketing activities, there are many extremely profitable alternatives.

Figure 8–6. These cotton modules are waiting to be ginned. These farmers marketed their crop by selling at current market prices. (Courtesy of the Dept. of Agricultural Education and Communications, Texas Tech University)

SELLING VERSUS MARKETING

Traditionally, agricultural producers have taken commodities not used on the farm to town and sold them for whatever a local buyer would pay for them. Sometimes, when the offered price was less than what the farmer wanted for the product, the farmer could try to bargain for a higher price. The buyer was usually in a position to buy any amount of that particular commodity at the posted price. There was usually little incentive for the buyer to offer more than the posted price. The farmer could take the crops or livestock back to the farm if the offered price was not acceptable. Given that some of the commodities may have been perishable or that storage facilities were not available or that there may have been a need for cash to meet financial obligations, the farmer usually settled for the offered price.

The previous scenario describes a farmer selling rather than marketing a commodity. When an individual farmer was operating on a small scale and the amount of excess commodities was also small, the difference between selling and marketing didn't matter much. The farmer may not have been very happy with the outcome but would always be back next year to repeat the same sequence of events.

Most modern farmers cannot afford to dispose of their commodities by simply accepting current prices at harvest. Modern producers have larger farms and specialize in the production of only a limited number of commodities. The quantity of commodity produced and sold is large. A small price difference per bushel or pound can have a large impact on the profitability of the farm enterprise. The modern farmer is also at a disadvantage because of the degree of specialization that is common today. Some farmers produce only one marketable crop that is harvested only one time per year. This can create cash-flow problems that only the best managers can overcome. Management skills are of utmost importance to modern agricultural producers.

Too often, when the crop is harvested or is ready for market, the farmer hauls it to the local market and takes whatever price is offered. Sometimes the price is good and the farmer does well. Other times the supply of the particular commodity is great and demand is small. This results in low market prices. By relying on current market prices, the farmer is selling the crop rather than marketing it. In competitive markets the farmer has little to no control over the price because there is no way to bargain for a better price. One farmer cannot change the price. On the other hand competitive markets, because they are based on supply and demand, can be very efficient in controlling the total volume of production for specific commodities. Since most of the agricultural marketing system in the United States is based on a competitive market, it is in the best interests of producers to look for ways to improve the prices they receive for their commodities.

Many farmers are now marketing rather than selling. Successful farmer/marketers of agricultural commodities begin the process of marketing long before the crop is planted or the livestock is bred. Many decisions must be made before production begins. These decisions include:

1. What to produce and how to prepare it for sale. For example, certain varieties of crops or species of livestock are in more demand than others. Additionally, some harvesting, hauling, and storing practices may have a serious effect on crop quality. Farmers who contract with companies to raise popcorn must be careful during harvest not to damage the kernels because popcorn will not pop if the seed coat is damaged.

Figure 8–7. This grower decided to produce grapes only after
determining that there was a viable market.

2. When and where to buy or sell. For each agricultural commodity there is a traditional time of the year when prices are high or low. With some commodities it is possible to adjust production and storage practices to take advantage of the high prices. Sometimes the producer can discover alternative buyers for the commodity. Perhaps high-quality grain sorghum would be worth more if sold directly to poultry producers for feed than if the crop were sold to the elevator.

3. How much of the marketing job should be done by the farmer, either as an individual or as a member of a group? Hauling may either be hired or provided by the farmer. Similarly, someone may be hired to do the selling and other marketing, or the farmer could choose to perform these chores. In the case of some specialty crops, the farmer may own the entire marketing system. This is the case for a catfish producer who owns and operates a restaurant where the fish appear fresh daily on the menu.

4. What can be done to expand markets? Many advertising strategies and other techniques for enticing consumers may be applied. A knowledge of human nature and what influences people can help to determine which alternatives might be most effective. For example, with today's concern for safe food, perhaps offering low-fat, low-cholesterol, hormone-free beef would be successful.

5. What marketing arrangements are desirable? Farmers are offered many different methods of selling their products. Some proposals guarantee returns in exchange for permitting the marketing firm to make certain operating decisions on the farm. Many contractual possibilities exist. Farmers need to know how to appraise different opportunities to make sure that they choose an alternative which is right for their particular situation.

6. How can changes necessary to correct undesirable practices be secured? New laws are often proposed as a means of improving the marketing machinery's operation. Sometimes government intervention may be desirable; other times there are better means of accomplishing objectives. Decisions in this area often have far-reaching implications.

MARKETS AVAILABLE FOR FARM AND RANCH COMMODITIES

There are two basic categories of markets that are available for farm and ranch commodities. These categories are based upon how ready the product is for final consumption by the consumer when it leaves the farm or ranch. The two categories are (1) traditional marketing of raw agricultural commodities and (2) nontraditional marketing of agricultural commodities in various stages of consumer readiness.

TRADITIONAL MARKETING OF
RAW AGRICULTURAL COMMODITIES

Traditional marketing includes several markets ranging from local elevators to the futures market. The key distinguishing factor that makes these markets traditional is that the product is in the same raw form when it changes ownership as it was when it left the farm or ranch. The product may be trucked immediately from the field to the new owner at harvest or it may be stored for a time. In some cases the commodity may be delivered to buyers some distance away from the production site. In these markets, all stages of processing the agricultural commodity occur while the commodity is owned by someone other than the producer.

Figure 8–8. This module of cotton is ready to be ginned. After ginning, the cotton is sold and becomes the property of someone else. The producer was able to add value to the crop before transferring ownership.

A classic example of this type of market is the local grain elevator. Most of a grain elevator's buying is done at the time of harvest. In many cases the grain is trucked directly from the field to the elevator. Unless other arrangements have been made (such as *forward contracting*), the grain is sold to the elevator at the current market price.

Grain producers can sometimes improve their profitability by storing crops for a time. Two types of storage are normally available: (1) on farm and (2) off farm. With on-farm storage, the producer owns the storage facilities, while with off-farm storage, the storage facilities usually are located at the elevator where the grain eventually will be sold. Regardless of where the grain is stored, there are costs associated with storage. These costs include (1) utilities, (2) rent, (3) opportunity costs, and (4) grain treatments. When storing grain for future sale, the grain producer is gambling that in the future the market prices of the grain will rise sufficiently to cover the costs associated with storage and provide more profit. Particularly with off-farm storage, the costs often exceed any increased revenue realized by waiting to sell.

A traditional market for livestock is the local livestock auction. Producers transport animals to the auction. After arriving at the auction, the livestock are bid upon by buyers. The producer can usually predict, within a range of prices, what the livestock will be sold for. However, there is no guarantee that the animals will sell within that range. At auction sales, the producer becomes a seller and not a marketer.

Other methods exist for selling grain and livestock. For example, some livestock feeders may buy grain by *private treaty*, a market agreement arrived at by a buyer and seller in private negotiations, directly from the grain producer. A beef feedlot may purchase feeder cattle by private treaty.

Livestock can be marketed at various stages in the animals' growth and development. For example, in swine production the animals can be marketed as feeder pigs when they are 40–60 pounds, as finished hogs at 220–240

Figure 8–9. Private treaty is a common way to market breeding
   animals.

pounds, or as breeding stock. An important consideration when deciding at what point to market swine is whether the increased costs associated with keeping the swine longer will pay off in terms of increased revenue. Another consideration when deciding to market finished hogs is that there is little flexibility. When finished hogs reach market weight, they must be sold to maximize returns on the investment.

Forward contracting of agricultural commodities can prove to be a valuable marketing tool. Forward contracting is any technique that permits the buyer or seller to fix the price of a commodity prior to the actual physical exchange. The advantage to the producer lies in the fact that once prices reach a target level that has been predetermined, the producer can "lock in" that price, thus guaranteeing a profit. Conversely, the buyer can also agree to a price in advance. The disadvantage of forward contracting for both the buyer and seller is that they must forgo advantageous prices later on. Buyers who agree to forward contracting of agricultural commodities include elevators, feed lots, mills, and packing plants.

NONTRADITIONAL MARKETING OF AGRICULTURAL COMMODITIES IN VARIOUS STAGES OF CONSUMER READINESS

When considering nontraditional marketing of agriculture commodities, it is important to make the distinction between commodities which are suitable for human consumption and those which are not. Many grain crops are not suitable for human consumption without processing, which is probably beyond the ability of ordinary agricultural producers. For instance, corn, one of the major cash crops grown throughout the Midwest, is not the same type of corn that you find in the grocery store. Field corn is grown primarily as animal feed. Sweet corn, which is grown for human consumption, has a higher sugar content and is more palatable than field corn. Field corn is processed to manufacture corn sweeteners and cornstarch products. However, this processing is beyond what the average agricultural producer can expect to do independently. Other common crops that are not fit for human consumption unless highly processed are grain sorghum, soybeans, oats, and wheat.

Agricultural commodities that are well suited to nontraditional marketing include almost all fruits and vegetables, most meats, dairy products, and poultry. The characteristic that makes these commodities more suitable for nontraditional marketing is the ease with which they can be made ready for human consumption. The goal is to add value to the commodity while expending minimal costs to make the product consumer ready.

Perhaps the simplest value-adding, nontraditional marketing approach is the pick-your-own operation. The concept is simple. The producer grows a typical garden crop on a large scale, then allows customers to pick their own. Examples of fruit and vegetables that can be found at pick-your-own operations include strawberries, raspberries, peas, green beans, sweet corn, tomatoes, pecans, apples, peaches, plus just about any other fruit or vegetable.

Pick-your-own operations appeal to people for a variety of reasons. People like to eat food that is as fresh as possible. There is no question as to freshness when you get to pick the food yourself. Also, some view picking or gathering their food as a wholesome family activity. In other words, there is a certain amount of entertainment value that is achieved through pick-your-own activities. Others like to preserve fresh fruits and vegetables for consumption later on in the year. Although people who preserve foods are unlikely to experience a great deal of financial savings, they may prefer to eat foods that they have canned or frozen.

A variation of the pick-your-own concept is fish farms that allow anglers to fish for a fee. Catfish and rainbow trout are typical species of fish that are available this way. Some fish farm operations charge a fee to fish plus a per pound fee for any fish caught. Others simply charge a per pound fee. Some per pound fees include cleaning the fish while other operations charge an additional fee if you want the fish cleaned. Customers patronize fish farms for a number of reason. Some people are willing to pay to catch fish because of the entertainment value. Children, in particular, enjoy catching fish. Others like to purchase fish this way because they enjoy the taste of freshly caught and prepared fish. They perceive fish marketed this way as superior to fish found in supermarkets or in fish markets.

Roadside fruit and vegetable stands have long been a way of marketing fruits and vegetables that are a surplus to those who have grown them. Some producers grow fruits and vegetables for the express purpose of selling them in roadside stands. Some producers purchase fruits and vegetables from others to market in addition to the produce that was grown on their farms. Some roadside stands have become major businesses. Some you-pick operations have roadside stands for those customers who do not care to pick their own. Consumers like to purchase food from roadside stands because of the perceived freshness and wholesomeness of the fruit and vegetables. Some customers are actually willing to pay more for produce

Figure 8–10. Roadside stands are popular places to purchase fresh
fruits and vegetables.

at these businesses because of the quality. Roadside stands are seasonal
businesses in most parts of the country, unless they purchase produce from
other sources that have access to produce grown in parts of the world with
longer or different growing seasons.

Farmer's markets can be found in many parts of the country. At farmer's
markets, several producers of agricultural commodities (especially fruits
and vegetables) will transport their produce to a central location. Each
producer sets up a sales area. The advantage of farmer's markets to producers
is that the marketing channel is shortened to include only the producer
and the consumer. The advantage to the consumer is that they can go to
one central location to purchase most, if not all, of the fresh produce they
need. As with pick-your-own operations and roadside stands, the produce
at farmer's markets should be fresher than that which could be purchased
at the supermarket.

Pick-your-own operations, roadside stands, and farmer's markets have
certain disadvantages for producers. It is much more time consuming to
market vegetables through these means. It must be remembered that time
has value and the value of time depends upon alternative uses for that
time. The farmer may have 1,000 acres of cotton that needs attention at
the same time the roadside stand or farmer's market needs attending. The
time would be better spent tending to the cotton crop in this case.

Another approach to marketing agricultural products is to satisfy consumer wants with specialty products. An example of this is the producer

Figure 8–11. Farmer's markets provide an outlet for the sale of fresh
fruits and vegetables.

who raises fruits and vegetables without the use of chemicals. Fruits and
vegetables which are grown without chemical fertilizers, herbicides, or
insecticides are referred to as "organically grown." There is a growing
segment of the U.S. population that is interested in eating only foods that
have been grown without the aid of chemicals. These people feel that food
grown organically is more healthy and wholesome than food that is grown
with chemicals. This type of specially grown food could be marketed in
any number of ways. You-pick operations, roadside stand, and farmer's
markets could serve as outlets for these products. Supermarkets will often
display organically grown fruits and vegetables.

Another specialty item which is meant to satisfy the wants and desires
of the health conscious consumer is beef that is grown without the use of
growth stimulants and other medications. This type of beef is referred to
as "hormone free" beef. Some consumers are willing to pay a premium
for food products that are perceived to be healthier for their families. Much
concern has been raised about the use of hormones to stimulate growth
in beef animals. Some producers of "hormone-free" beef have established
a market by selling beef directly from the farm.

There is also a market for beef that is low in fat and cholesterol. Some
breeds of beef animals have a tendency to produce meat that is naturally
lower in fat and cholesterol. Beef producers have capitalized on this trait
by using these breed exclusively and by using these breeds in cross breeding

programs. Like hormone-free beef, this beef is most often sold directly from producer to consumer.

Another strategy for shortening the separation between producer and consumer is that of the catfish producer who markets fish through an on-farm restaurant. The producer of the catfish has the advantage of removing several layers of "middle men." By doing this, the producer has the advantage of marketing a value-added product. Patrons of the restaurant enjoy dining on fresh fish that has never been frozen.

Wineries represent another type of value-added marketing strategy. Many, if not most, wineries have their own vineyards for growing wine grapes. Some wineries also purchase grapes on contract from other producers. Wineries convert a relatively low-value crop into a high-value beverage. Some wineries also bottle nonalcoholic juices to satisfy customers who do not consume alcohol.

Figure 8–12. Some wineries contract with local growers to purchase grapes.

STRATEGIES TO INCREASE REVENUES IN MARKETING

If farmers and ranchers are to become successful marketers of their agricultural products, there are some key strategies which should be followed.

Farmers and ranchers should carefully examine the market area to determine what agricultural products are needed. Farmers need to be well attuned to current events and trends to identify market niches which they could fill. Ranchers that supply hormone-free beef and low fat/cholesterol beef meet a consumer demand for healthier foods just as those who grow organically grown produce have done. These products typically can be sold for more than the conventionally grown products.

Farmers and ranchers should purchase agricultural supplies and services (inputs) as inexpensively as possible. The cost of production should be lowered so that profits can be maximized. If possible, agricultural producers should purchase inputs in amounts that allow quantity discounts. This may mean purchasing supplies in cooperation with other producers. Producers should take care to not purchase more inputs than necessary. Carrying large inventories of supplies over from one season to the next is usually not a good idea.

Farmers and ranchers should strive to shorten the marketing channels between producer and consumer. By shortening the marketing channel, producers can realize additional revenue that would otherwise go to middlemen. Producers can assume middlemen roles by getting involved in such functions as storage, transportation, financing, and processing.

Farmers and ranchers should time the sales of commodities to receive the best prices. This can be done by forward contracts or by storing harvested

Figure 8–13. Through cooperatives, producers can receive some of the benefits of processing their crops. This cotton has been ginned and baled and is now ready for shipment to a textile mill.

grain crops for later sales. At harvest time, the market becomes flooded with the particular commodity that is being harvested. As the market becomes flooded, prices normally fall. Usually, the farmer can sell at higher prices as the supply of the commodity lessens throughout the market year. Prices may rise continuously until just before the new crop hits the market in the following year.

Farmers and ranchers should market agricultural products where they are most needed. Businesses that need agricultural products are willing to pay the best prices. By doing some research, farmers and ranchers can find outlets for their commodities that will increase revenues. Typically, grain terminals and processing plants offer more for commodities than local elevators. One should use caution, however, to insure that any increase in revenue more than compensates for the additional transportation costs associated with delivering commodities to more lucrative markets.

In short, farmers and ranchers can become marketers rather than sellers if they strive to minimize production costs and maximize the prices they receive. By identifying products that are in demand for their market areas, by paying as little as possible for inputs, by shortening the marketing channels, by timing sales to best prices, and by delivering commodities where they are in the greatest demand, farmers and ranchers can usually increase revenues.

MARKETING ALTERNATIVES

Several alternatives for marketing nontraditional agricultural products were discussed earlier in this chapter. This section will specifically cover marketing alternatives for traditional grain and oilseed crops. Following is a discussion of marketing alternatives which are available to grain and oil seed producers.

Farmers can always sell commodities in the *cash market* at the time of harvest. With this option, the commodity usually is taken directly from the field to the local elevator. Sometimes this is very time consuming. Invariably, other producers utilize the same market alternative which means that there could be a lengthy wait at the elevator just to unload a commodity. The price received is the price that is posted at the elevator. This price will typically fall as the harvest progresses.

Selling in the cash market at harvest time offers some advantages to the farmer. For one, the farmer does not have to own expensive storage facilities and drying equipment. Another advantage is that the farmer will receive payment for the crop much sooner than if some of the other marketing alternatives were used. However, the lowest price of the year for any given commodity normally occurs during harvest time.

A farmer may decide to store at harvest and sell later in the year. On-farm storage of grain has become a very popular marketing alternative. Encouraged by government programs, there is now more on-farm storage of grains than off-farm storage. The storage of grains at harvest allows the farmer to sell commodities at times of the year when the best prices are realized. Harvest time prices are usually the lowest prices of the year. As the harvest time surplus of grain is used up in the commercial grain markets, price tend to rise.

Storage of grain does have disadvantages. Increased prices may not be enough to offset the increased production cost associated with storage. Even storing grain on-farm incurs costs. These costs include electricity to operate drying and aerating equipment, fumigants to protect the quality of the grain, dockage for grain that looses quality while stored, not to mention the opportunity costs associated with financial resources that could be otherwise invested.

Farmers can and often do elect to sell grain before it is harvested. This is called cash forward contracting. Some farmers actually sell the grain before it is even planted. All that is necessary to cash forward contract is to find a buyer who is willing to commit to purchasing a set quantity of grain at a given price. The price agreed to normally is the price at the time the contract is made.

Producers who cash forward contract know exactly what price they will receive for their crops upon delivery to the buyer. The disadvantage is that if the prevailing market prices rise after the contract is signed, the farmer is not in a position to take advantage. However, the farmer is also protected should the prevailing price fall after the contract is signed.

Cash forward contracts specify the quantity of grain that is to be delivered. Should yields be reduced by some unforeseen circumstance, the farmer is still obligated to deliver the contracted amount. This could mean that the farmer must purchase grain from someone else just to fill the contract.

Another form of forward contracting is called *hedging*. Hedging involves the use of the futures market in order to lock in a price. Much like cash forward contracting, when the farmer sees an acceptable selling price on the futures market, he acts to lock in that price. To lock in the price, the farmer sells futures contracts at the acceptable price on a certain quantity of grain. At harvest time, the farmer sells harvested grain on the cash market at the current cash market price. Immediately, the farmer lifts the hedge by buying back the futures contract he previously sold. Any profits or losses in the futures market are offset by the difference between the cash selling price and the locked in price. In other words, when hedging, the producer takes equal but opposite positions on the futures and cash markets in order to guarantee an acceptable price.

Grain farmers have the option of processing their grain before it leaves the farm. By marketing grain as livestock feed the farmer can add value to it. Instead of selling the grain to someone else, the grain is transferred from the crop enterprise to the livestock enterprise. The value of the transfer is the current market price.

Marketing grain as livestock feed adds value to the grain. The farmer takes a relatively low-value agricultural commodity (grain) and converts into a relatively high value commodity (livestock). This is a particularly attractive option when grain prices are unusually low. However, there is a danger. If livestock prices, which might be quite favorable when the decision is made to market grain in this manner, have fallen to unprofitable levels when it is time to sell. Some farmers will hedge in combination with this marketing alternative to protect livestock prices as well.

Another marketing alternative available to grain farmers is to sell to the government. Through the government's farm program, loans are available to protect the farmer from erratic markets that can affect price and farm income. To participate in this program, the farmer places grain in approved storage and receives a loan at the current loan rate per bushel. The grain serves as collateral for the loan. The farmer can then use this money to pay off debts, as operating capital, or for just about any other purpose. When the market price exceeds the loan price, the farmer takes the grain out of storage. The farmer then pays back the loan plus storage costs. Any excess money is pocketed by the farmer as profit. If the market price never exceeds the loan price, the farmer has the option of allowing the government to take ownership of the grain. Since the loan is a nonrecourse loan, the government will not seek repayment. The government, in effect, has purchased the grain at the loan rate. Grain and other agricultural commodities that the government owns due to the farm programs are kept in reserve. They are also distributed to agencies through various government programs designed to feed needy people.

The marketing alternatives discussed all have the same effect. That is, they all serve as ways that grain producers can turn agricultural products into cash. Individual producers will find that some of these alternatives work for them and that others do not. Regardless, agricultural producers should have a marketing plan in mind before production starts.

THE ROLE OF FINANCIAL POSITION AND RISK TAKING

Farmers and ranchers are risk takers by nature. Agricultural producers gamble that the weather conditions are going to be favorable for growing a crop or that the market will be favorable. Farmers and ranchers who are well established and not heavily in debt are in a better position to assume additional risks. Producers with good financial circumstances may choose a more risky marketing alternative. They are able to do this because the assets they own serve as protection against making wrong decisions. Conversely, poorly established or heavily leveraged producers cannot afford to take the same risks as the debt-free producer. Should the poorly established, debt-ridden producer make risky marketing decision that prove to be wrong, they do not have the assets to protect them. Consequently, it is very important for producers to carefully analyze their financial positions and willingness or ability to accept risk when considering marketing alternatives. Producers may choose to utilize a mixture of marketing alternatives. By mixing and choosing, a producer can tailor a marketing plan that meets individual needs.

Figure 8–14. Using irrigation, producers can remove some of the risk that is present for those who must rely on the weather to provide adequate moisture.

SELECTING THE BEST MARKETING ALTERNATIVE

There is no one best marketing alternative that fits every individual producer and situation. Selecting an acceptable marketing alternative is dependent upon various factors. Producers should keep in mind that just because a marketing program works for a neighboring producer there is no guarantee that the same program will work for them. Individuals have different financial situations or requirements. They also have different levels of acceptable risk. Some marketing alternatives may not be viable just because the producer does not handle risk well. It is important to choose a marketing alternative that the individual can live with. In any case, decisions concerning marketing alternatives should be considered long before harvest.

SUMMARY

Producers of agricultural products have many things to consider in marketing. The key concept is that producers should strive to become marketers rather than sellers. Producers who are marketers are proactive in their approach to converting agricultural products into cash. They understand that when marketing channels between the producer and the consumer are shortened that more profits can be realized by the producer. When producers can find ways to make their product more valuable through transportation, storage, or processing, more revenue is available for profit. Successful marketers of agricultural products plan well in advance of harvest.

CHAPTER SELF-CHECK

Match the following terms with the correct definition.

    a. hedging

    b. cost-price squeeze

    c. food and fiber marketing sector

    d. private treaty

   e. forward contracting

   f. cash market

   g. free-rider

   h. producer sector

   i. supply

   j. farm/ranch problem

_____ farmers and ranchers

_____ providing benefits to all farmers regardless of
             whether they participate in programs

_____ availability of agricultural commodities

_____ when falling farm prices are not accompanied by
             falling input costs

_____ firms which advertise, process, package, and mer-
             chandise agricultural commodities

_____ using the futures market to lock in a price

_____ low farm and ranch commodity prices and income

_____ purchase of commodities directly from the producer
             through negotiation

_____ fixing the price of a commodity prior to the actual
             physical exchange

_____ selling a commodity for current market prices

QUESTIONS AND PROBLEMS FOR DISCUSSION

1. Why is marketing important to financial success in farm-
    ing and ranching?

2. What is the distinction between selling and marketing?

3. What are the factors which contribute to the farm/ranch problem?

4. How does industry fragmentation affect agrimarketing?

5. Explain the cost-price squeeze, the free-rider problem, and production flexibility.

6. What affect does the separation between the producer sector and the food and fiber marketing sector have on agricultural prices?

7. Under what conditions would a farmer store a crop?

8. What are the advantages of selling commodities in the cash market at harvest? What are the disadvantages?

9. What is cash forward contracting?

10. What affect does marketing grain as livestock feed on your own farm have?

ACTIVITIES

1. Visit a successful local farmer or rancher. Determine marketing strategies which are used on that farm or ranch. Prepare an oral report to be given to the class which details strategies.

2. Select an agricultural commodity. Visit local elevators, stockyards, or other marketing outlets to determine marketing alternatives that are available for your commodity. Prepare a written report.

3. Select an agricultural commodity. Using daily market and futures reports, graph the daily prices for your commodity for one month. Prepare a poster which shows the trends for your commodity.

Chapter 9

MARKETING HORTICULTURAL CROPS AND SERVICES

Horticultural crops and services are a major industry. Horticulture is a very broad area of agriculture which includes the growing of fruits, nuts, and vegetables; production of ornamental shrubs and plants, lawn and landscape care; golf course management; landscaping; interior plant services; flower production; and more. With the exception of the marketing of fruits, nuts, and vegetables, the marketing of horticultural crops and services is somewhat different than the marketing of farm and ranch commodities.

Figure 9–1. Methods of marketing horticultural crops and services include sidewalk fruit and vegetable displays. Shown here is a sidewalk display of fruit and Christmas trees outside of a small store in France. (Courtesy, Stephen Lee, Emory University)

This chapter contains information about the marketing of horticultural crops and services.

OBJECTIVES

To help understand marketing of horticultural crops and services, several objectives are covered in this chapter. Upon completion you will be able to:

- Explain the nature of horticultural crops and services
- Describe how markets are identified and developed
- Identify strategies to increase revenues in marketing
- Identify marketing alternatives for horticultural crops
- Describe the role of financial position and risk taking
- Explain how to select the best marketing alternative

TERMS

acclimatization
balled and burlapped
bare root
bedding plants
commercial greenhouse
commodity commissions
container grown
direct marketing
farmers' market
landscape contractor
landscape design
mail order
pick-your-own
retail nursery
roadside markets
terminal markets
wholesale marketing
wholesale nursery

THE NATURE OF HORTICULTURAL CROPS AND SERVICES

Horticultural crops and services are very diverse. Horticultural crops and services are part of businesses that provide landscaping; businesses that produce horticultural plants; businesses that design floral arrangements and interior landscape; and businesses that produce fruit, nuts, and vegetables.

LANDSCAPE DESIGN, CONSTRUCTION, AND MAINTENANCE

People like to have pleasing surroundings. They like to take trips to the country to see grass, trees, and shrubs as they occur in nature. People also like to have pleasing surroundings at home, at work, and at places for recreation. An entire industry exists that seeks to address this desire to be surrounded by an environment that appears to be natural.

Landscape Design

Landscape design helps people to create a union between nature and their built environment. Landscapes should to be pleasing to look at (aesthetic) and functional. The designing process combines aesthetics and functionality. Although landscape design seeks to compliment nature, it is important that the landscape designer considers people and their enjoyment of the environment. Landscape designers cannot disregard the needs and desires of people.

Landscape designers market their landscaping ideas in several ways. The most common method is with drawings. Many designers are now using computer technology to further enhance their ability to communicate with the client. There are many computer aided design (CAD) programs that are intended for the purpose of landscape design. These are particularly important to the designer because they make it easy to adapt designs if changes are required.

Landscape Construction

Once a client has approved a design, construction of the landscape

Figure 9–2. Landscape designs are not complete until high-quality
plants are installed.

design can begin. A *landscape contractor* is often hired to complete the
landscape. The contractor does not necessarily have to be affiliated with
the designer but many times they work very closely together. The first
concern the landscape contractor has is to select the highest quality plants
available. Landscape contractors understand that the ability of their businesses to market services in the future is dependent upon the quality of
the plant material they install.

Landscape Maintenance

Many homeowners choose to maintain their landscape themselves. However, there are many opportunities for people to be involved with the
business of maintaining landscapes. Homeowners and businesses may hire
landscape maintenance businesses. Landscape maintenance can be as simple
as mowing a lawn or as complete as watering, fertilizing, pruning, and
applying chemicals. Some landscape maintenance businesses are very specialized. There are some that only apply fertilizers and pesticides. Other
businesses are very general in nature. These businesses offer a full line of
services. Some provide planning, installation, and maintenance services.

Golf courses and parks are prime examples of areas that require intensive
landscape maintenance. With the rising popularity of golf, many new
courses are being built, and established courses are experiencing unprece-

dented pressure from the increased number of rounds being played. Golf course managers typically hire many people to perform different maintenance jobs on the plant materials associated with golf courses. Some of the jobs that must be performed include mowing, fertilizing, watering, planting, pruning, and applying pesticides.

HORTICULTURAL PLANT PRODUCTION

This is a broad area of horticulture. *Commercial greenhouses* are primary producers of horticultural plants. Commercial greenhouses produce plants in an artificially controlled environment. Some commercial greenhouses produce plants exclusively for wholesale, while others market their plants to retail customers. Some greenhouses rely very heavily on producing seasonal plants such as poinsettias grown for the Christmas season and Easter lilies. Many commercial greenhouses produce *bedding plants* throughout the late winter and spring seasons. Bedding plants are seedlings that will be transplanted into flower and vegetable gardens. These bedding plants include vegetables such as tomatoes, peppers, cabbage, onions, and flowers such as petunias, impatiens, geraniums, and pansies. Other greenhouses specialize in producing cut flowers to be used by florists for bouquets and in flower arrangements. Cut flowers are also available to private individuals through some outlets. Cut flowers include gladiolas, cannas, and ginger. Still other greenhouses specialize in the production of house plants. House

Figure 9–3. Landscape maintenance requires the use of specialized equipment. This shows a display of mowers, tillers, and choppers which make landscape maintenance easier.

plants are very popular because they enhance the interior environments of homes and businesses. Favorable growing conditions allow greenhouses to produce bedding plants, cut flowers, and house plants quickly. Faster production in the greenhouse business leads to marketing efficiency.

FLORAL DESIGN AND INTERIOR LANDSCAPE DEVELOPMENT

This segment of the horticultural industry provides plant materials to beautify interior spaces. Cut flowers, dried flowers, silk flowers, and foliages are used for floral design. Cut flower arrangements, dried flower arrangements, corsages, boutonnieres, and holiday arrangements are the primary products of floral design. Floral designers understand design principles, color harmony, material selection, and floral construction techniques. They also know how to increase the keeping quality of their products.

Interior landscape design involves working primarily with living plants. Interior landscapes can be as simple as house plants or as complex as atriums for large hotels. People who work with interior landscapes must

Figure 9-4. Cut flowers are an important segment of the floral design industry. Cut flowers can be sold individually, as shown, or they can be used in floral arrangements.

Figure 9-5. Hotels, shopping malls, convention centers, and other public areas make extensive use of interior landscaping. This hotel atrium is an elaborate example of interior landscaping.

know what types of plants grow well under certain conditions and how to combine them effectively. Other aspects of interior landscape design include watering and fertilizing interior plants and pricing of interior landscape services.

FRUIT, NUT, AND VEGETABLE PRODUCTION

This is the part of the horticulture industry that produces food for human use. Fruit, nut, and vegetable production can be on a small a scale (a patio tomato plant) or a large a scale (commercial growers who produce hundreds of acres of a particular crop). Some growers, such as the citrus growers in the Lower Rio Grande River Valley in Texas, specialize in one or two crops. Other growers produce a variety of crops. Almonds grown in California represent a very important segment of the nut production industry. In tropical climates, coffee and pineapples are very important commodities.

IDENTIFYING AND DEVELOPING MARKETS

Progressive horticultural producers constantly look for ways to increase the profitability of their operations. Identifying and developing new markets is one way they can increase profitability. Sometimes a *commodity commission* will participate in this. Commodity commissions are organizations formed by producers and others for promotion and research dealing with a particular commodity.

Commodity commissions conduct market research, advertise, develop new products, evaluate consumer preferences, develop foreign markets, and perform other activities to promote product sales. Boards of directors usually serve as administrators for commodity commissions. Typically, boards of directors are composed of growers, processors, handlers, and other business men and women who are involved with commodities at the various stages in the marketing process. The commodity commission regulates product quality and monitors firms that are doing business with the commission. Funding for commodity commissions comes from industry-wide excise taxes on the commodity as it moves through commercial marketing channels. Most of the revenue is used for advertising and promotional activities. Commodity commissions identify and develop markets by using a four step process.

STEP ONE — ANALYZING THE MARKET SITUATION

To analyze the *market situation* there must be an understanding of changing consumer lifestyles, tastes, and preferences. Market situation refers to purchasing tendencies of the consumer. Each population group eats different foods at different places, and each buys somewhat differently. Young and higher income households tend to eat out more often. They also differ from older and lower income people in their food selection habits. Households with growing children tend to purchase more dairy products. Elderly households tend to purchase more fruits and vegetables. Certain segments of consumers are more likely to purchase flowers or house plants. It is important to know and understand these and other consumer characteristics as you go about identifying a segment of the consumer population to target with your marketing program.

STEP TWO — FORMULATING A MARKET STRATEGY

After analyzing the market situation, one can formulate a market strategy for a specific commodity, product, or market. A market strategy is based on systematic, coordinated decision making. Sometimes growers of a specific commodity organize to advertise through a commodity promotion program. This is called *generic promotion* or generic advertising. Generic promotion is targeted toward a specific commodity without regard to brand names. An example of this is the generic promotion used by the Florida Citrus Commission. Their strategy was to try to increase the consumption of orange juice at meals other than breakfast. You may remember the slogan—"It isn't just for breakfast anymore." After the product was promoted, brand-name companies began their own advertising.

STEP THREE — DEVELOPING SPECIFIC ACTION PLANS

Action plans include the advertising and promotion that are targeted to specific audiences. Children, teenagers, and working women are examples of specific audiences. Another term for action plan is advertising campaign. Before an advertising campaign is used nationwide, it is often pretested on a small scale to evaluate its effectiveness.

Specific action plans also can be used to create a pre-consumer demand for a commodity. The Potato Board is an example of a commodity commission that tries to develop new uses for its commodity. Potatoes are used as a food binding agent in pasta, as an emulsifier in salad dressings, and as a nutritional supplement in processed foods. Potatoes are also used to stop ice crystal development in ice cream.

Sometimes specific action plans target international markets. A prime example is the action plan developed by Blue Diamond Growers of California. Blue Diamond Growers is a cooperative of growers who specialize in producing almonds. Blue Diamond was able to successfully market almonds to Japan. Japan is now second to Germany as the world's biggest importer of California almonds. Almonds are now California's number one food export. This is a very important part of California's economy because in many years California produces up to 40 percent of the world's supply of almonds.

STEP FOUR — EVALUATING PROGRAM PERFORMANCE

To evaluate performance, firms and commodity commissions conduct surveys to determine the effectiveness of marketing programs. Another indicator of marketing program performance is demand for the particular horticultural product. However, it is often difficult to determine if demand increased because of the program or for some other reason. Industries monitor the impact of media, coupon promotions, merchandising, and public relations to gain more understanding as to why demand increases.

STRATEGIES TO INCREASE REVENUES IN MARKETING

The key to increased revenues in horticultural production is to base production decisions upon the existing market. Producers must have a clear understanding of the horticultural industry and of what the customer wants and is willing to purchase. A producer of horticultural crops, whether ornamental or for food, must consider several factors.

CONSIDER ALTERNATIVES

Producers should look for alternatives in their production programs. They must consider other enterprises that will help maximize profits. Typical alternatives include (1) getting out of horticultural production; (2) changing management techniques, labor relations, or marketing alternatives; (3) considering new crops or commodities; or (4) adding value to existing crops or commodities.

GOVERNMENT PROGRAMS AND POLICIES

Growers should keep up with current programs and policies. They should also work to develop the ability to anticipate changes in programs and policies. Subsidies, price supports, health and environmental regulations, tariffs, quotas, and trade barriers influence the production and profitability of various crops. For example, a trade agreement for Washington apples was agreed to with a foreign trade partner. This helped to enhance profitability for Washington apple growers.

CONSUMER TRENDS

Growers must be aware of consumer needs, wants, and trends. Since horticultural enterprises are market oriented, it makes sense that producers be attuned to the consumer. Growers of horticultural products should be aware of how the consumer has changed in recent years. For example, today's consumer is much more aware of food quality and nutrition than in times past. Additionally, the growing number of single-parent and dual-income households has placed more emphasis on convenience foods.

MARKET PROMOTION

It is in the best interest of grower groups to promote their products. This can be done through programs to increase consumer awareness and demand for their crops. Programs aimed at market promotion can start as grass roots efforts by commodity groups. Cooperatives sometimes get involved in market promotion. These efforts should be aimed at informing the consumers about how the particular product can enhance their lives. The Florida Citrus Growers is an example of an effort to promote Florida citrus products.

COST REDUCTION

Everyone involved in agricultural production should look for ways to reduce production and marketing costs. Reducing costs is vitally important to the success of any agricultural enterprise. Production, marketing efficiency, and cost reduction should be coordinated to make the product more competitive in the marketplace. Producers can reduce costs by purchasing supplies in quantities to take advantage of price breaks, combining opera-

Figure 9-6. One revenue increasing strategy is market promotion.
Packaging provides an opportunity for site-of-sale
promotion. Shown here are macadamia nuts in the
shell, shelled, and packaged.

tions to make production more efficient, employing labor saving devices, and joining cooperatives to reduce the cost of ownership of specialized equipment.

QUALITY CONSIDERATIONS

Current grading standards in the United States provide producers the opportunity to receive the best price for the best product. In other words, producing high-quality products creates a price advantage for the producer. Consumers are willing to pay more for products that receive high grades because of the assurance that the product will be of the best quality. However, producers and commodity groups must be aware that grades and standards in the United States may not reflect foreign tastes, cultures, and needs. This must be considered when establishing foreign markets for U.S. products.

TOXIC CHEMICALS

The use of chemicals has been one of the major contributors to the success of agriculture in the United States. Chemicals aid the producer in growing large quantities of high-quality foodstuffs. However, many con-

Figure 9–7. High quality means premium prices. Produce that is of high quality and attractively displayed will yield the best price.

sumers are now concerned about the use and abuse of chemicals. Although much of the concern is unfounded, a scare over a single chemical can ruin profits for producers for several years. The announcement about Alar found on apples almost ruined the apple industry in the Northwest and California. Even growers who did not use Alar had difficulty selling their apples. Some producers may want to capitalize on the consumer's desire to obtain organically-grown and chemical-free foods. Organic, chemical-free foods often sell for higher prices in the marketplace.

INFORMATION ACCESS

There are several ways that producers can reduce risk. Some of the ways deal specifically with how the crop is marketed. Producers can use the futures and options market to reduce risk. Forward contracting, long term contracts, and other arrangements can also help to reduce risk. Reliable sources of information are important to the producer's ability to use these methods of risk reduction. New data bases, information bases, and university and private research facilities have been developed to improve production efficiency and marketing strategies. These will aid producers in forecasting prices and production based on current situations, trends, and economic and political factors.

MARKETING ALTERNATIVES
FOR HORTICULTURAL CROPS

DIRECT MARKETING ALTERNATIVES
FOR FRESH FRUITS AND VEGETABLES

In *direct marketing* (also known as retail marketing) of fresh fruits and vegetables, the produce is transferred directly from the producer to the final consumer. Producers who direct market are usually operating on a smaller scale than those who market indirectly.

Pick-your-own Operations

One of the more popular marketing alternatives for fresh fruits and vegetables is the *pick-your-own* business. With pick-your-own marketing customers are expected to harvest the produce they want to purchase. This is a popular alternative for those who enjoy getting outside to pick fresh fruits and vegetables. Because food safety and quality are a large issue today, people like the opportunity to see where their food is coming from. There are some advantages from the producer's point of view as well.

One of the advantages for the producer is that harvest costs are eliminated. For some produce, harvest costs are a major cost of production. When customers pick their own fruit and/or vegetables, they effectively assume the harvest cost. Customers are willing to assume this cost because they perceive benefits from picking their own fresh fruits and vegetables.

The cost of transporting the crop to market is another production cost which is eliminated in the pick-your-own operation. Again, customers assume the transportation costs when they transport the crop from field to home.

There are usually other costs associated with selling produce. These costs may be in the form of commissions or advertising. With the pick-your-own operation, the cost of selling is represented by the need to have some sort of field manager. The field manager should be available to offer harvesting instructions to the customer. The field manager is also responsible for collecting payment for the harvested produce. Another selling cost associated with the pick-your-own operation is advertising. Advertising is particularly important when establishing a new business. Advertising is one way that new operators inform the public of the opportunity to purchase. As word of mouth spreads and the business become established, less advertising may be needed. However, advertising can also serve the function of informing the public that a particular crop is in season and ready to harvest.

With the pick-your-own operation, agricultural producers are inviting the public onto their property. Unfortunately, the chance for an accident to occur makes this type of operation risky. Producers need to be adequately covered by insurance. They also must make sure that any potential hazards are removed or minimized. The producer is also liable for any damage to the property or crop.

The producer must make market investments to effectively operate a pick-your-own enterprise. The producer will need to provide containers for the customers to use. The use of uniform containers expedites charging customers for the produce picked. Also the customer knows exactly how much their produce will cost as they are picking. The producer will also need to provide parking and location signs.

In order to minimize waste and maximize profits the producer needs to accurately predict the amount of produce to grow. For someone just starting a pick-your-own operation, this can be a very difficult task. Ideally, the producer should grow enough to satisfy demand without having waste. It may help to visit existing operations to determine demand. Also, the Cooperative Extension Service or other governmental agencies might have some guidelines to follow.

The price received at pick-your-own operations may be lower than received through other marketing channels. However, the producer must remember that harvesting and transportation costs have been assumed by the customer. This means that the producer may still realize more profit even though prices may be lower. Also, some customers are willing to pay nearly as much at pick-your-own operations because they have the opportunity to get the freshest produce possible. Before setting the price at pick-your-own operations, it is suggested that producers visit supermarkets, roadside markets, and farmer's markets to find out what the going price is for particular crops. Producers may see the need to adjust the price of crops as the harvest season progresses.

If a producer has done a good job of raising the crop, the quality of the crop should exceed the quality available elsewhere. The producer needs to have an effective irrigation, fertilization, and disease and pest control program in order to raise the highest quality produce. At pick-your-own operations, the customer tends to pick only the best and leave the rest in the field. If quality is suspect, this means the producer can experience loss by virtue of the produce being left. One way to control the amount of crop left in the field is to only open small sections of the field to the customer at a time. The field manager should continually check the open parts of the field to assess the progress of the harvest. Only when the crop is sufficiently harvested to satisfy the producer should the customer be allowed to enter other parts of the field. This removes the customer's temptation to pick only the easiest to reach or the best produce. The field manager should instruct the customers to "clean-pick" the produce as much as possible.

It is in the best interest of the producer to raise the highest quality possible. Some of today's customers are only interested in produce that has been raised without the addition of chemicals. Producers may want to consider raising the crop using organic farming methods. If produce has been raised organically, it may be an effective marketing strategy to publicize that fact. Depending on the characteristics of the customer base, organic produce may be priced higher. If chemicals are used it is very important to follow the application instructions. Chemicals should be used only on the crops for which they are labeled. Also, chemicals have specified withdrawal periods. This means that a minimum amount of time must pass before the produce is to be used for human consumption. If a chemical is used, **READ, UNDERSTAND, AND OBEY THE LABEL!**

It is difficult to achieve a balance between the number of customers and the amount needed. Uncontrollable factors during growing may affect the maturity of the crop. Also, unfavorable weather such as rain when the crop is ready to harvest could be devastating. To minimize these risks, it may be wise to schedule planting or to choose varieties so that the maturity of the crop can be staggered. This way, not all of the crop will be ready for harvest at once. This also allows the producer to open only small portions of the field to customers at a time.

Roadside Markets

Roadside markets are another popular way to sell fruits, nuts, and vegetables. This method of marketing can be very effective. Although most people purchase fruits and vegetables at supermarkets, roadside markets usually develop very loyal customers. These customers feel that they receive a superior product at a better price.

Harvesting costs for roadside markets are the usual costs which are expected with most other marketing strategies. The producer must harvest the crop to provide it for the roadside market. Hand harvesting is required for some crops. This may mean that the producer has to hire people to

Figure 9–8. Direct marketing of horticultural produce should mean
increased revenue for the producer and fresher fruits
and vegetables for the consumer.

help. Other crops may be mechanically harvested. The producer must either
own the harvesting equipment or hire a custom harvester. Either way there
is a cost associated with harvesting. This cost is hopefully passed on to
the customer.

Roadside markets are typically located at or near the point of production. This means that transportation costs may be low. The crop is transported only a short distance from field to market. Not only does the
producer realize a cost savings but the quality of the produce is protected.
Much of the product deterioration occurs during transportation. The quality
of the produce is enhanced when the crop is not transported as far.

A check-out attendant is required at roadside markets. This represents
a selling cost. The check-out attendant is responsible for displaying the
produce in an attractive way. Much of the business roadside markets do is
with people who just happen to pass by. Consequently, it is important for
roadside markets to be located on well-traveled roads and highways. Advertising in the form of newspaper ads and signs can be effective. These also
represent a selling cost to the roadside market.

Liability is of great concern for roadside markets. Accidents involving
automobiles and pedestrians are a real possibility. Producers should carry
sufficient liability insurance. The best way for producers to protect themselves is to try to eliminate the potential for accidents. Locating the market
well off the road with adequate parking is one way to do this. Also, the

producer should locate the market so that people can leave and enter safely. Place entrances and exits so that automobiles do not have to leave and enter traffic at blind spots. In other words, do not locate entrances and exits just beyond curves or crests in the road. Producers also must prevent accidents in the roadside market proper. Producers must carefully analyze the arrangement and construction of the roadside market to eliminate potential hazards.

Market investments for roadside markets can be very small or quite extensive. Some roadside markets are as simple as the tailgate of a pick-up truck. Others are permanent buildings. The volume of business expected has a great impact on the investment in structures. If only one or two short season crops are to be marketed, a simple stand may be in order. If several crops are expected to be marketed for longer periods of time, more elaborate structures may be indicated. Other marketing investments include containers for the produce and possibly parking areas.

Roadside markets are only successful if they entice customers to stop. One consideration in attracting customers is the volume of produce. There has to be enough produce displayed to provide customers with a selection. If only a small amount of produce is visible customers may fail to stop. Another concern related to volume is the variety of produce available. If there are several crops displayed, customers are more likely to stop.

The producer sets the price for produce at roadside stands and must be aware of prices at other markets. In other words, the producer must be aware of demand and competition. Prices at supermarkets, other roadside markets, and farmer's markets must be studied in order to determine fair market value. Generally speaking, roadside market prices should be some-what less than supermarket prices. Although the producer is incurring harvest costs, the transportation cost is small. The producer can afford to pass some of this savings on to the customer.

The customer expects to receive only the highest quality fruits and vegetables when shopping at roadside markets. Because the market is close to the fields, the produce should be very fresh. Also, as discussed earlier, produce will probably not be damaged during transportation. Should there be variations in the quality of available produce, the producer can opt to classify the produce into grades. If this option is taken, the producer can then sell at more than one grade.

Roadside markets provide a unique opportunity to market more than just produce. Many roadside markets sell other items to supplement income. Things like arts and crafts, and food items made from the produce being sold complement the produce.

Farmers' Markets

A third direct marketing alternative for fresh fruits and vegetables is *farmers' markets*. These markets are popular in cities and towns that have strong rural agricultural roots. Many times the city or town will supply space for the farmers' market. In other cities or towns, the Cooperative Extension Service has assisted in arranging for farmers' market space. The farmers' market allows producers in the area to bring their produce to a central point. Producers who want to use the farmers' market can set up booths to sell their produce.

Just like roadside markets, the usual costs of harvest are incurred by those who market with farmers' markets. Some crops need to be harvested by hand while others are best harvested mechanically. Either way, harvesting costs are part of the cost of marketing.

Transportation costs for producers who decide to use farmers' markets depend upon the distance from the point of production to the farmers' market. However, distances traveled to farmers' markets are usually relatively short. There is usually a farmers' market within the county in which the produce was grown.

At farmers' markets someone must be available to assist the customer with their purchases. The check-out person is responsible for calculating the cost of purchases, attractively displaying the produce, and answering any questions about the produce being sold. The check-out attendant should

Figure 9–9. Farmers' markets provide an excellent source of high-quality, fresh produce. This producer has several varieties of tomatoes, peppers, garlic, and gourds for sale.

be able to answer questions about where the produce was grown, when it was picked, and whether or not the product was grown organically.

Grower liability is somewhat less at farmers' markets. The owner of the market, the local government or an individual, becomes the responsible party. For this reason, the owner of the market usually expects the participating producers to follow certain rules and regulations. Common sense dictates that the producers use good judgment in eliminating hazards.

Participants in farmers' markets usually rent or lease booth space. This represents part of the selling cost. This cost is usually very minimal. Other costs include containers for the produce.

Volume produced and marketed through farmers' markets should be dictated by the distance the produce must be transported and the cost of space in the farmers' market. In any case, the producer will want to have enough produce to warrant the time spent selling the produce, the distance traveled to get the produce to market, and the cost of the space. Producers should determine a break-even point to insure that these requirements are met. Otherwise, the costs associated with marketing the produce may exceed returns.

Producers who use farmers' markets are free to set their own prices. However, there may be others at the farmers' market selling the same produce. This competition will also determine price. Of course, producers also need to be aware of current supermarket, roadside market, and pick-your-own prices. Supply and demand play a large role in determining the price of produce sold through farmer's markets.

Quality of the produce offered for sale is important. Producers must strive to have the highest quality produce available in the market. Competition at the farmers' market will determine how well produce sells. Obviously, the higher quality produce will receive the most competitive prices. Lesser quality produce must be discounted.

Some customers at farmers' markets want to buy larger quantities of produce for canning or freezing. Bushels of produce are just as likely to sell as individual fruits and vegetables. To promote bulk purchases, many producers offer quantity pricing. A bushel of tomatoes will be sold for less per pound than the single pound rate.

WHOLESALE MARKETING ALTERNATIVES FOR FRESH FRUITS AND VEGETABLES

In *wholesale marketing*, fruits and vegetables go from producer to some other business or businesses before finally reaching the consumer. These businesses provide a marketing outlet. Value is added to the produce with each successive progression through the marketing system. Value is added by changing the form of the produce in some manner such as transporting, assembling, processing, etc.

Terminal Markets

Terminal markets offer the advantage of assembling large quantities of produce in one location. The terminal market provides the equivalent of "one-stop shopping" for people who buy large quantities of produce.

Harvesting costs for producers who use terminal markets are similar to costs associated with other marketing alternatives. However, harvesting costs vary greatly depending on the particular fruit or vegetable. Some produce requires the use of labor-intensive methods such as harvesting by hand. Hand harvesting means that there will be significant labor costs. On the other hand, machine harvesting usually requires specialized equipment, which is often expensive to own.

Transportation cost is largely determined by the physical distance from the site of production to the terminal market. Terminal markets can be great distances from the site of production. This means that hauling can represent a significant cost of production. Hauling can be accomplished by hiring custom truckers or with producer-owned trucks. The advantage to hiring the hauling done is that the producer does not have the expense of owning the truck. However, producers who own trucks can sometimes be more timely in delivering produce to market because trucks are available at all times. They can also supplement income by providing custom trucking for other producers.

At terminal markets, the producer becomes a price taker rather than a price maker. Buyers at a terminal market can usually purchase all of the particular crop they need at the going market price. This means that the producer is under significant pressure to deliver the crop when prices are favorable. Vegetable growers are much more susceptible to market fluctuations than are fruit growers. Vegetable growers sometimes have no choice but to let an entire crop waste in the field if the market price will not cover the cost of harvesting and transporting the crop.

Large volumes are required to market produce through terminal markets. The entire terminal market is based upon economies of scale. In other words, the terminal market system can operate more efficiently when large quantities move through the system. Terminal markets purchase large quantities and they sell large quantities.

Transportation is the main investment in terminal marketing. The producer must arrange for transportation of the produce to market. Either the producer owns trucks or hires the hauling done. Specialized containers are needed for some produce. For instance large wood crates are used when oranges are picked to transfer the fruit to the trucks for hauling. These containers are owned by the producer.

Buyers in the terminal markets set the quality standards they expect. U.S. grade standards exist for most fruits and vegetables. The terminal market can use the grade standard to insure that only produce that meets or exceeds a certain grade will be purchased. This also aids producers, as they can expect to get the best price for produce that meets the higher grade standards. On the other hand, produce can be rejected if it does not meet standards.

Cooperatives/Private Packers

If an individual producer does not have the volume to take advantage of terminal markets, that producer has the option of participating in a cooperative or selling to a private packer. Cooperatives offer the advantages of having a standardized product, assembling large enough quantities for terminal markets, providing valuable market information, making supplies and equipment available at lower prices due to wholesale purchasing, and pooled advertisement and promotion.

Some cooperatives make harvesting equipment available to their members. This has the effect of spreading the cost of ownership of specialized equipment over several producers. However, during particularly busy times of the year, it may be difficult to gain access to the equipment during peak harvest times. The producer must risk being able to harvest at the most advantageous time.

Some cooperatives also provide transportation. Again, the effect of spreading the cost of ownership of trucks over several producers represents a sizable savings. Similarly, with cooperatively owned trucks, the risk exists that the equipment may not be available in the timeliest manner. Particularly with fruits and vegetables, this could be a problem. Fruits and vegetables are perishable commodities that need to be transported carefully and on time in order to preserve quality.

As with terminal markets, cooperatives must insist on delivery of produce which meets buyers standards or U.S. grading standards. Buyers are more likely to return for future purchases when they are satisfied with the quality of previous purchases. Consequently, cooperatives should offer

Figure 9–10. Supermarkets and grocery stores sell large quantities of fresh produce. Many supermarkets and grocery stores buy their supplies of fresh produce directly from cooperatives and packers.

lower prices for lower quality produce and perhaps even reject produce that does not meet standards. Because cooperatives are member owned, they should help members to grow the best produce possible. Educational efforts are offered by some cooperatives to help members to meet grading standards.

Direct Selling

Another wholesale marketing alternative which may be available to some producers is selling directly to grocers or restaurants. The grower, through private treaty, peddles produce directly to businesses that represent the final step in the marketing process. Growers who take advantage of this opportunity are bypassing steps in the marketing chain, thereby reducing cost to the grocer or restaurant and increasing revenue to the grower. Ideally, both seller and buyer benefit from such agreements. The grocer or restaurant receives the freshest, highest quality produce while the producer receives a premium price for providing it.

Harvest costs for this marketing alternative differ very little from other marketing alternatives. However, because the objective is to provide high-quality fruits and vegetables, the grower may have an incentive to take extra care in harvesting the produce. This may result in higher harvesting cost.

Transportation costs for marketing directly to grocers and restaurants depends on the distance traveled. Also, as with harvesting, the objective is to provide unusually high quality. Consequently, extra care may be necessary in transportation. Higher transportation costs may result.

The obvious goal of selling directly to grocers or restaurants is higher prices. The price is arrived at through negotiations with the buyer. The producer in a favorable position may be able to set the price without negotiation. However, the producer must have alternative outlets for produce should the potential buyer decide to try to find the produce for less. Of course, high quality is mandatory. Produce which ends up in the produce section of the supermarket must have a pleasing appearance or customers will not purchase it. Similarly, successful restaurants are interested in only the most eye-appealing foods. A restaurant that does not serve attractive foods is in danger of failing.

Volume of production for direct selling to grocers and restaurants is determined by the number of outlets and the size of those outlets. The producer needs to do some work in advance of the harvest. This work should be aimed at estimating the quantity to produce based upon the number and size of supermarkets and restaurants.

The investment for this marketing alternative is similar to most of the other alternatives. The producer must invest in specialized containers to transport and market the produce. Also, most deliveries are made by the producer. This means that producers must own their own means of transportation. Trucks for transporting produce can be a sizable investment.

In direct selling to grocers and restaurants, the grower can expect to develop a long-term outlet assuming a high quality product is consistently delivered. One drawback is the difficulty in entering this market. A lot of hard work on the part of the producer is required to enter this market and to develop customers that will be a consistent outlet for the grower's produce.

Wholesaler/Broker

Another market alternative is the wholesaler/broker. The wholesale/broker acts as a middleman between the grower and the buyer. Chain store buyers, restaurants, hotels, institutions, and exporters want and need a constant supply of produce. Wholesalers and brokers are able to provide this service.

Harvesting costs for this marketing alternative are typical. Whether

Figure 9–11. Packers handle large amounts of produce. This shows the
grading and boxing of oranges. (Courtesy, Florida
Department of Citrus)

the producer harvests by hand or machine, harvesting is a cost of production. The producer either incurs a labor cost for hand harvesting or a machinery cost of mechanical harvesting. The producer has the option of owning the equipment for harvesting or hiring a custom harvester.

Transportation costs vary from time to time. In some instances, the producer is responsible for delivering the produce to an agreed upon location. At other times, the wholesaler/broker arranges for the produce to be picked-up at the site of production. In general, the producers hope to receive higher prices when they are responsible for delivery to offset transportation costs. When the produce is picked-up at the site of production, lower prices may be received.

Wholesalers and brokers usually operate at large enough volumes that they can set the prices they are willing to pay. Consequently, when marketing to wholesalers and brokers, the producer is a price taker. However, the convenience offered by this means of marketing often offsets the disadvantage of being a price taker. Also, the producers are free to sell their produce by other marketing alternatives. If the price offered by a wholesaler or broker is not adequate, producers can look elsewhere for favorable prices.

Brokers and wholesalers are typically interested in large volume transactions. Consequently, brokers and wholesalers are usually interested in only truckloads or train car loads of produce. This means that producers who wish to market to wholesaler/brokers must operate on a rather large scale.

The market investment associated with marketing to wholesaler/brokers is usually minimal. The grower will need specialized containers in which to transport produce. Specialized containers aid in the safe transportation of fruit and vegetables through the marketing system.

Produce marketed through wholesalers and brokers must meet U.S. grading standards. In this marketing alternative, grading standards aid in the handling of the produce. Produce of the same grade can be handled in bulk. Because of bulk handling, the efficiency of the system is enhanced.

Brokers do not take title of the produce. They simply act as agents between buyers and sellers. Brokers provide their services for a fee. Wholesalers, on the other hand, purchase the produce from the grower and take legal title to the produce. With either the wholesaler or the broker, there is the ability to sell produce quickly at good prices. Wholesaler/brokers have many contacts which enable them to market massive quantities of produce. Producers who choose to market produce this way need to develop long-term relationships with wholesalers/brokers.

DIRECT MARKETING ALTERNATIVES FOR NURSERY PLANTS

Retail Nurseries

The most common direct marketing alternative for nursery plants is the *retail nursery*. Retail nurseries sell directly to the end user of the plant.

Figure 9–12. Garden centers are often found in combination with retail nurseries. This garden center has a small retail nursery where customers can select plants for home landscapes.

One popular type of retail nursery is the garden center. They maintain an inventory of plants that is acquired in a variety of ways. Some retail nurseries expend much energy in production. These nurseries grow much, if not all, of the plants that they market. Others purchase much of the plant material they market from wholesale nurseries.

Retail nurseries must have employees that are very skilled at working with customers. Customers of retail nurseries need answers to questions concerning growth habits, care, planting, and pruning of plants. This means that employees must be knowledgeable about the plants they work with.

Advertising is very important to the retail nursery. Local newspapers, word of mouth, radio, or television may provide effective promotion. Retail nurseries also practice a kind of passive advertisement. The appearance of the business as customers pass by can be an effective means of advertisement. It is important that retail nursery managers keep the exterior of the business looking like a nursery. It is equally important that the retail nursery look organized and efficient. The business should take care to display a variety of available plants.

Mail Order

Another alternative for the retail nursery is to operate a *mail order* business. With mail order businesses, customers purchase plants, seeds, and other supplies through the mail or with telephone orders. Many mail order businesses accept fax orders as well. Mail order nurseries usually operate on a very large scale. In fact, they often participate in wholesaling as well. Mail order nurseries must advertise effectively. This usually is accomplished by publishing a catalog. The catalog should be full color to take advantage of the beauty of the plants offered. Since plants and the accompanying soil may be carriers for disease and insects, federal and state regulations control the movement of plant materials. Mail order nurseries should be well aware of the regulations and follow them rigorously.

INDIRECT MARKETING ALTERNATIVES FOR NURSERY PLANTS

Wholesale Nurseries

A *wholesale nursery* markets plants to individuals and businesses that sell the plants to the final owner. Wholesale nurseries perform eight activities in marketing nursery plants. Those eight activities are discussed below.

Production Planning. The nursery manager must decide if potential customers are large retailers like chain stores or landscape designers, family owned businesses, or a combination. The manager must determine if customers will be interested in only a few varieties, small plants, large plants, or unique varieties. The manager must be conscious of buyer preference trends. Computerized records of the plants purchased by specific customers help to pinpoint trends. Finally, the nursery manager needs to be aware of which plants seem to be particularly profitable for the business.

Advertising. Established nurseries that have a reputation for consistently high-quality plants at good prices do not have to advertise as much as new businesses. Since wholesale nurseries sell to a distinct population, word-of--mouth reputation goes a long way in promotion. Also it is easier to target promotions to customers that purchase in wholesale quantities than it is to target promotion to the general public.

Selling. Nursery stock is sold a number of ways. Sales at the wholesale nursery may be made on-site, by telephone, or through mail-order sales. Larger nurseries may have district or area sales forces or field representatives who travel to make direct contact with customers. Wholesale nurseries may use brokers and title wholesalers. Brokers provide a link in the marketing system that moves the plant material from producers to retailing customers. Brokers do not take title to the plants. Title wholesalers produce a limited number of their own plants and supplement their inventory with purchases from other producers. Wholesale nurseries may also use plant locators that simply locate potential buyers or producers of specific plants.

Inventory Control. Nurseries must have a detailed inventory that describes the types, sizes, and quantities of the plants in stock. In addition to tracking what is in stock, inventory control also shows existing sales trends and aids planning for future demands for plants.

Pricing. Unlike production agriculture, nurseries can establish the prices for plant material they offer for sale. Determination of this price is very important. Three factors should be considered when pricing plants: (1) exact production costs plus a reasonable profit, (2) inventories held by competitors, and (3) demand for specific types of plants.

Grading. Grading provides the means by which plant materials can be

Figure 9–13. Nursery stock can be sold as bare root, balled and burlapped, or container grown. These balled and burlapped trees have a protective plastic wrap to prevent excessive escape of moisture.

sorted into uniform groups of plants. Nurseries can choose to participate in the voluntary plant standards as published by the American Association of Nurserymen. Grading also refers to the marketed form of the plants. Plants can be marketed *bare root, balled and burlapped,* or *container grown.*

Bare root plants are marketed without soil around the roots. Balled and burlapped trees and shrubs are grown in the field. The roots are carefully dug as to not distrub them. Burlap is used to keep the root ball intact. When trees are grown in containers, they are referred to as container grown.

Labeling. Each plant or bundle of plants must be properly labeled. Labeling helps to ensure that plants are correctly identified by specie and variety. Labels usually list both the common and scientific names of the plant. Labels can also include the grade of the plant.

Packing and Shipping. Lightweight bare root plants can easily be shipped long distances. Balled and burlapped and container plants are not as easy to ship. They are usually shipped in trucks carrying only nursery plant materials. At any rate, all nursery stock must be carefully packed and shipped to insure the viability of the plant. When shipping, all federal and state regulations that apply to the shipping of plant materials and soil must be observed.

FLOWER MARKETING

Horticultural growers who produce cut flowers or foliage and flowering plants usually sell their plant materials directly to retailers or to wholesale distributors. Wholesale distributors then sell directly to retailers. Therefore, customers of commercial cut flower or commercial house plant growers are either retailers, such as garden centers and florists, or wholesale distributors.

Cut Flowers

Examples of plants grown for cut flower production include carnations, chrysanthemums, roses, snapdragons, tulips, and orchids. Although these plant materials may be of high quality when they leave the commercial grower, they have the potential of declining in quality if proper precautions are not taken. Cut flowers have a relatively short life once they have been cut from the plant. Special storage techniques are used to slow down respiration so that the useful life of the flower is prolonged. Some cut flowers, such as tulips, may be held in storage for as long as 50 days. Others, such as roses, have a maximum storage life of approximately 15 days.

Shipping is also of major concern when marketing cut flowers. Most cut flowers are shipped from growers to wholesale distributors by truck. Wholesale distributors then ship the flowers in refrigerated trucks on to retailers and florists. Refrigerated trucks keep the flowers cool during hot weather and protect them from freezing during cold weather. Special vapor-proof, reinforced cardboard boxes are used to protect the flowers.

Foliage and Flowering Plants

Plants grown for their foliage include scheffleras, palms, corn plants, ficuses, pothos, rubber plants, philodendrons, and peace lilies. African violets, azaleas, begnoias, Easter lilies, geraniums, gloxinias, hydrangeas, and poinsettias are common flowering plants. As with cut flowers, it is important to protect the quality of these house plants as they move through the

Figure 9–14. Retail flower shops design and sell bouquets to the public.

marketing process. A period of *acclimatization* is necessary as these plants complete the production schedule in the greenhouse. Acclimatization is the climatic adaptation of a plant to its new environment. This is done slowly to reduce the shock that plants experience when they are moved from the greenhouse to homes, offices, and other places.

For shipping, foliage and flowering plants must have proper moisture, temperature, humidity, and shipping materials. Generally, house plants should be watered two days before shipping. They should not be watered again until arrival at the final destination. Temperature should be maintained at less than 75°F but at least 50°F. Humidity should be maintained at 80–90 percent during shipping. Most foliage and flowering plants are shipped in boxes or sleeves. These packaging materials protect plants from damage during handling and shipping.

THE ROLE OF FINANCIAL POSITION AND RISK TAKING

Just as farmers and ranchers are risk takers, so are producers of horticultural products and people who provide horticultural services. Horticultural producers gamble that weather conditions are going to be favorable for growing fruits, vegetable, or plants and that the market will be favorable when the crop is ready for harvest. Providers of horticultural services also gamble that the economic climate will be such that their business will be a success.

Horticulturists who are well established and not heavily in debt are in a better position to assume additional risks. Producers and service providers with stable financial circumstances may choose a riskier marketing alternative. They are better able to do this because the assets they own serve as protection against making wrong decisions. Conversely, poorly established or heavily leverage producers and service providers cannot afford to take the same risks. Should poorly established, in-debt producers make risky marketing decision that prove to be wrong, they do not have assets as protection.

It is very important for producers to carefully analyze their financial positions and willingness or ability to accept risk when considering marketing alternatives. Producers may also choose to use a mixture of marketing alternatives. By mixing and choosing, producers can tailor marketing plans to meet individual needs.

SELECTING THE BEST MARKETING ALTERNATIVE

There is no one best marketing alternative that fits every situation. Selecting an acceptable marketing alternative is an individual decision that is dependent upon various factors. (1) Producers must realize that we are living in a changing world. As the world changes, producers must be willing and able to adapt to a changing market. This means that a producer may need to select a completely new marketing alternative. (2) Growers of horticultural crops and providers of horticultural services must decide upon a mixture of marketing strategies that will make their business as profitable as possible. (3) People who grow horticultural crops and provide horticultural services must understand what buyers want. Careful study of the marketplace is necessary in order to produce and supply crops and services that are in demand. It may require the development of new or better products. (4) People in the horticultural crop and service industry must strive to deliver quality products. The marketing of quality products will help to insure business with repeat customers and will enable the development of other markets. (5) When selecting marketing alternatives, attention should be paid toward the promotion of goods and services. Promotion plays an important role in marketing horticultural goods and services.

Producers should keep in mind that just because a marketing program works for a neighboring producer that there is no guarantee that the same program will work for them. Individuals have different financial situations or requirements. They also have different levels of acceptable risk. Some marketing alternatives may not be viable just because the producer does not handle risk well. It is important to choose a marketing alternative that suits individual needs, desires, and objectives. In any case, the point is that decisions concerning marketing alternatives should be considered long before harvest.

SUMMARY

Horticultural crops and services make up a very broad agricultural industry. Fruit and vegetable production, nursery production, floriculture, and landscaping are all examples of components that make up the horticulture industry. Everybody, in one or more ways, is a consumer of horticultural crops and services .

New markets for the horticulture industry can be identified and developed by adopting a model that is used by commodity commissions. This model consists of (1) analyzing the market situation, (2) formulating a marketing strategy, (3) developing specific action plans, and (4) evaluating program results.

A clear understanding of the horticultural industry and an understanding of what the customer wants and is willing to purchase will aid the producer in adopting strategies that will help to make the business profitable.

Marketing alternatives for horticultural crops are many. Basically, they can be placed in two different categories. The first is direct marketing, which includes alternatives where the final consumer is the purchaser of the commodity. The second category is indirect marketing. In this category, the commodity is marketed to various stages of the marketing chain where the commodity, in one way or another, has value added to it's worth.

The financial position and the ability of the horticultural producer or service provider play a major role in selecting the best marketing alternative. The best alternative for one producer is not necessarily the best alternative for another. Individual likes and dislikes, debt-structure, and other factors will greatly impact the selection process.

CHAPTER SELF-CHECK

Match the following terms with the correct definitions:

a. commodity commissions

b. wholesale marketing

c. retail nursery

d. commercial greenhouse

e. direct marketing

f. mail order

g. farmers' markets

h. terminal market

i. pick-your-own

j. roadside markets

_____ a type of horticultural business that sells directly to the end users of plants

_____ performs activities that promote agricultural products

_____ a form of direct marketing in which consumers do the harvesting

_____ marketing through the mail

_____ marketing from the producer to the consumer

_____ a type of direct marketing of fruits and vegetables where the market site is provided by the producer of the crops

_____ a type of direct marketing of fruits and vegetables where the market site is provided by a city, town, agency, or an individual

_____ marketing fruits and vegetables to other businesses before they reach the final consumer

_____ a type of horticultural business that specializes in the production of horticultural plants

_____ involves assembling large quantities of produce in one location

QUESTIONS AND PROBLEMS FOR DISCUSSION

1. What are some examples of crops, businesses, and services that are included in the horticultural industry?

2. What is the purpose of a landscape design?

3. Give some examples of businesses that are part of the horticultural plant production industry?

4. How do commodity commissions identify and develop potential markets for horticultural produce and products?

5. List and describe five strategies that can be used to increase revenues in horticultural production.

6. What are some ways that fresh fruits and vegetables can be marketed directly from the producer to the consumer? Give advantages and disadvantages for each.

7. Differentiate between retail and wholesale marketing of fresh fruits and vegetables.

8. What advantages do cooperatives offer in the wholesale marketing of fresh fruits and vegetables?

9. Describe the eight activities that wholesale nurseries perform in the marketing of nursery plants.

10. How does risk impact the decisions that horticultural producers make?

ACTIVITIES

1. Divide the class into groups. Pick a commodity such as apples or onions and set up a marketing strategy to sell the product. Plan an advertisement for the school newspaper, draw posters, and prepare informational bulletins. Do a marketing survey to see which group was most successful in advertising and promoting their product.

2. Go on a field trip to various producers of horticultural crops. Ask the growers about their marketing strategies. Write a short paper reporting what you learned.

3. Visit a nursery. Interview the manager to find out how production planning, advertising, selling, inventory control, pricing, grading, labeling, and packing and shipping is accomplished at that nursery. Prepare and give an oral report to your class on what you learned.

Chapter 10

MARKETING
AQUACULTURE PRODUCTS

Do you have a favorite fish? Is it one you catch or do you buy it in a supermarket or restaurant? If you enjoy seafood, you are much like many Americans. Of course, nearly all of us have our favorites, such as shrimp, oysters, or a particular fish. Some of us like water plants such as water chestnuts or water cress. Others prefer the unique products of fish, such as caviar (fish eggs) or surimi (artificial crab and lobster made from processed fish).

Americans consume a wide range of food, fiber, and related products.

Figure 10–1. Following proper harvest procedures is an important first step in marketing aquacrops. This shows seined catfish being lifted to a haul truck. Note that scales above the basket weigh the fish. (Courtesy, Delta Pride Catfish, Inc.)

Some of these products are produced on land; others are grown in water. Demand for products grown in water is increasing faster than what nature can supply from rivers and oceans. Prices have risen as a result of reduced supply greater demand. Today, farmers culture fish and related products and find it to be a profitable area of farming!

Marketing is as important to the producer of plants and animals grown in water as it is to producers of crops grown on the land. Since "water farming" is relatively new in the United States, marketing "water crops" is often a greater challenge. Water farmers often must be more creative in marketing and they face additional risk.

The focus of this chapter is to introduce the marketing of aquaculture products.

OBJECTIVES

This chapter includes several important objectives related to marketing aquaculture products. Upon completion of the chapter, you will be able to:

- Describe the scope of aquaculture
- Explain the ways aquaculture products are marketed
- Explain factors to consider in selecting a market
- Explain product forms in aquaculture
- Describe the role of consumer preferences in aquaculture
- Identify the roles of producers in product quality
- Describe the role of promotion in marketing

TERMS

aquacrop
aquacrop label
aquacrop processing
aquaculture
aquaculture niche market
aquatic
bait and tackle stores
baitfish
brackish water
custom order aquaculture
    marketing
fee lakes
freshwater
hydroponics
live hauler
off flavor
ornamental aquacrop
preparation
preservation
product form
recreational aquaculture
    marketing
saltwater
seafood
terrestrial
uniform species
water structure

AQUACULTURE

Aquaculture, much like other kinds of farming and ranching, is the culture of plants and animals. However, there is an important distinction: Aquaculture focuses on *aquatic* crops. These are the plants and animals that normally grow in water. Water is their environment. Aquatic plants and animals usually die rather quickly when removed from their water environment.

Most farmers and ranchers produce *terrestrial* plants and animals. These normally grow on land and need water for their survival. Terrestrial plants and animals also require certain nutrients for survival and growth. Farmers and ranchers who are successful with terrestrial crops and livestock find aquaculture quite different. The major reason for the difference is that the environment for aquatic plants and animals is water. Careful management of the water environment is needed for the aquatic crops to survive.

Wild crops captured from rivers, lakes, and oceans have long been a source of human food. In recent years, these natural stocks have been depleted. More were harvested than nature could replenish. As this occurred, consumer demand was greater than the supply available. Prices increased. Creative farmers looked for ways to increase their farm incomes and started aquaculture enterprises. Aquafarmers often began on a small scale and increased the scope of their enterprises as they learned techniques of production and developed markets.

Figure 10–2. Harvested fish ready for the next step in marketing.
(Courtesy, MFC Services)

Seafood is the term applied to a wide range of aquatic animals used for human food. It usually refers to wild fish, shell fish, and other species that are harvested from oceans. In some cases, cultured aquacrops are considered a part of the seafood category. People in aquaculture usually prefer that cultured crops be treated separately from wild seafood.

Figure 10–3. Value-added products result when aquacrops undergo additional steps to prepare them for the consumer. These fillets were seasoned and made ready for cooking during processing. (Courtesy, Delta Pride Catfish, Inc.)

KIND OF WATER

Aquatic species are suited to three different water environments: saltwater, brackish water, and freshwater. The types of water used for aquaculture are divided based on salt content.

Saltwater has a high salt content and is often found in oceans, seas, and large lakes. Saltwater species include oysters, shrimp, and salmon. Over 60 percent of the shrimp consumed in the United States are imported because very little shrimp farming is practiced. Some wild shrimp harvested from oceans, bays, and gulfs are used in the United States, but the amount is declining. Oyster culture is increasing in some areas of the United States where proper water conditions exist. A good example is in Washington, where some bays have ideal oyster conditions.

Brackish water is found where freshwater meets saltwater, such as where rivers flow into oceans. Brackish water is a mixture of freshwater and saltwater. Species grown in saltwater are often found in brackish areas.

Freshwater has little or no salt. It is found in most streams and small lakes. Freshwater is also obtained from wells drilled into the earth, runoff from rain or snow, and discharge from manufacturing plants. U.S. aquaculture relies heavily on water pumped from beneath the surface of the earth. Catfish, trout, and crawfish are the major freshwater species cultured in the United States. In recent years, farmers have developed interest in other species, such as tilapia, striped bass, and sturgeon.

WATER STRUCTURES

Various structures are used to grow aquacrops. A *water structure* is the kind of water facility that is used. Aquacrops may be grown in tanks, ponds, or other structures.

Tanks are used on a limited basis to grow aquacrops. Most tanks are of metal, concrete, or fiberglass. They are typically 3–6 feet deep and may be round or rectangular. Small round tanks of 4–8 feet in diameter are often used in laboratories and research facilities. Larger round tanks that are 20 or more feet across are used on farms. Rectangular tanks may be 4 feet wide and 10–20 feet long. Water in tanks requires careful attention so that good quality is maintained. Various ways of circulating, filtering, and adding oxygen to the water are used. An aquarium for ornamental fish is an example of a small tank.

Ponds are earthen structures varying in size from less than an acre to 20 or more acres. Many commercial farmers use ponds. The fish are stocked at rather high densities. Careful attention to feeding, water management, and other factors is required. Ponds must have smooth bottoms and be free of obstacles so that the fish can be harvested by seining. (Seining involves pulling a long net-type screen across a pond so that all of the fish are isolated in a small area of the water.)

Other systems of production include raceways, which involve flowing water. Some raceways are rather large earthen structures; others are small tank-type systems.

Some farmers use pens and cages in ponds, streams, or other water structures. Cages restrict the fish so they cannot swim away and escape harvest. Salmon is one of the few species cultured to any extent in cages.

WATER TEMPERATURE

Aquatic species require varied water temperature. Some thrive in warm water and will die in cold or cool water. Most aquacrops are grown in water ranging from 50° to 90°F. Of course, warm water species may not survive in water below 60°F, and cool and coldwater species may die in water above 70°F. The predominant species grown in the United States, catfish and crawfish, prefer warm water. Trout and salmon prefer cool or cold water.

HYDROPONICS

Hydroponics is growing terrestrial plants with their roots in water solutions. It is not the same as aquaculture. In some cases, hydroponic plants (an example is lettuce) are grown on the surface of the water while aquaculture crops are grown in the same water. Sometimes growers try to establish a water balance so that the hydroponic crops derive nutrients made available by the aquacrop in the water. Balancing hydroponics and aquaculture in a long-term system has been tried many times but has had only limited success.

IMPORTANCE OF AQUACULTURE

Since 1970, aquaculture has been the fastest growing area of agriculture in the United States. During some years production increased by 20 percent or more. Most of the increase involved catfish, crawfish, and salmon. Strong interest is developing in other species—tilapia, striped bass, oysters, and prawns. Trout have been grown for several decades at a fairly steady level of production.

Aquaculture has been practiced in other countries much longer than in the United States. For example, China has been growing fish and other aquacrops for thousands of years. Many of the species consumed in the United States are imported. Shrimp farming is well established in China and some South American countries. Frogs, salmon, and several other species are being produced in various countries. Many of these are imported to the United States.

Catfish, crawfish, salmon, and trout account for 90 percent of the aquaculture in the United States. Catfish make up the largest part of the industry. Nearly 500 million pounds of catfish are grown annually, primarily in the southern states. These catfish are valued on the farm at nearly $400 million. Ninety million pounds of crawfish valued at $55 million are grown each year. A little over ninety million pounds of salmon are cultured, with a value of $40 million. Nearly 70 million pounds of trout are produced each year. Trout often sell for more per pound than catfish, crawfish and salmon. U.S. value of cultured trout is about $81 million annually.

Baitfish and ornamental fish are also popular. Though not consumed as human food, *baitfish* are used by sport fishers to catch other fish and aquatic animals. Minnows and goldfish are the major baitfish. Many species of ornamental fish are found in the United States. Local pet stores usually have a wide range of ornamentals, including plants and non-fish aquatic animals, such as snails. Hobbyists spend millions each year on ornamentals and the equipment needed to keep them, such as aquaria and filters. Aquaculture accounts for nearly $900 million of production each year in the United States. By the time the products are marketed, the value has increased considerably. Opportunities exist for people who specialize in aquaculture marketing. Individuals who aquafarm need to understand their markets and often require help to develop them.

Figure 10–4. Cultured pearls are the most valuable aquacrop. This shows a novelty retail pearl business where the consumer buys an oyster and removes the pearl. Every customer is guaranteed a pearl!

WAYS AQUACROPS
ARE MARKETED

An *aquacrop* is an aquatic plant or animal that is farmed. Every producer needs to locate a market before the crop is produced. Establishing the facilities to grow aquacrops requires a considerable investment of money. Such investments shouldn't be made if a market for aquacrops doesn't exist.

Aquafarmers are sometimes able to develop small local markets. In some cases, aquafarmers may use *aquaculture niche markets* that are located many miles away. A niche market is a fairly small, specialized market for certain aquaculture products. For example, aquacrops are sometimes grown for marketing to ethnic groups in large cities, such as Chinese Americans in New York City. These individuals desire certain kinds of products that make up niche markets.

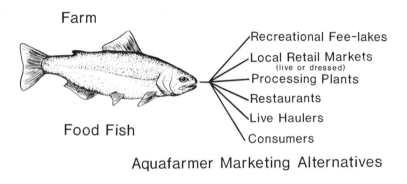

Figure 10–5. Aquafarmers have a number of marketing channels for
fish crops.

Large aquafarms need marketing channels that can handle large volumes of produce. Farmers need to be sure these are available before establishing farms with large capacities. It is as simple as this: What will a farmer do with thousands of pounds of costly fish if there is no market?

The general marketing channels for aquacrops are roadside and retail markets; local restaurants; custom orders; processing plants; live haulers; recreational facilities; hobby stores; laboratories and educational consumers; and bait and tackle stores.

ROADSIDE MARKETS

Roadside markets are on-farm stores that sell directly from the farm to the consumer. These are sometimes known as fish stands or outlets. Roadside markets are typically located on major roads or highways so the public can conveniently get to them. Success depends on advertising to the public and developing a good reputation. Consumers must always get quality products and the facilities must be clean. Most roadside outlets market fairly small volumes of aquacrops compared to that which can go through a processing plant.

At roadside markets aquacrops may be sold without any preparation just as they are harvested. They may also be available as partially processed, fully processed, or, in some cases, cooked and ready-to-eat products. The farmer who is considering opening a roadside store must carefully consider the situation. Sufficient customers must be available to make the store profitable. Aquacrops must be continually available so that the store always has something to sell. In most cases, roadside outlets only sell what is grown on the farm. A part of the crop must be regularly harvested. A few farmers open roadside markets only during certain times or seasons of the year when they have aquacrops available.

Roadside marketing adds an additional responsibility for the farmer.

Figure 10–6. An on-farm retail market and restaurant for shrimp and prawns is popular on the Island of Oahu in Hawaii. The growing ponds are located behind the restaurant. Note the picnic tables on the right where customers can eat.

He or she must operate a retail store in addition to the farm. A store facility must be constructed and properly equipped. Employees must be hired to run the store or the owner must do it. Government permits must be obtained and reports sent to agencies.

RETAIL MARKETS

Retail markets are small stores that specialize in selling a wide range of seafood and aquacrops to the consuming public. These stores are not on the farms where aquacrops are produced. They are usually in shopping centers, located along major streets and in ethnic neighborhoods. In some cases, they may be located in areas of a city near the port area where commercial fishers come in with their boats.

The retail markets may be operated by individuals not involved in aquafarming who buy the products from farmers, suppliers, and wild fish harvesters. The local fish market is most likely a good example. Of course, species other than fish may be sold, including shrimp, crabs, oysters, and crawfish.

Fish markets may offer many species from a wide range of sources. Both cultured and wild fish may be stocked in the store. These are often wholesome products. In some cases, the market owner may buy fish from sources of unknown quality. If poor quality products reach consumers, they are not likely to be repeat customers.

Fish markets may have products available in a variety of forms. Some carry live fish; others carry products that vary in the extent of processing. Live fish require proper tanks and water management. Fresh dressed products require refrigeration. Frozen products require freezers that will maintain the product at the right temperature. Electrical service must be dependable. Electric power failures could result in the loss of products.

A few markets cook products for the customer. For example, crawfish are often kept alive until they are boiled to order. These markets have the necessary cooking equipment. In addition, the people who work in the store know how to season and cook the product.

Some supermarkets have elaborate fish markets. They are usually separate from the meat market which sells beef, pork, lamb, and chicken. The products sold in supermarkets may have come from many sources and been shipped long distances by fish wholesalers. A reputable supermarket usually offers good-quality aquacrops and seafood. They often have well-trained buyers and employees.

RESTAURANTS

Some aquafarmers sell their products directly to local restaurants. Other farmers sell to processors or haulers who deliver to the restaurants. In a few cases, farmers use overnight transportation to ship products to specialized restaurants that are willing to pay a higher price for a very fresh product.

Restaurants located near aquafarms may specialize in a certain product. The restaurant may buy directly from a farmer who assures them of a uniform product on a year-round basis. The product may be processed on the farm or at the restaurant. Many restaurants prefer to get ready-to-cook products that are in exact size portions. They want cuts of fish that are of uniform weights and shapes. Ethnic restaurants may want unprocessed fish.

Figure 10–7. A restaurant that specializes in aquacrop food.

Restaurants often obtain fish and other seafood from local distributors. The distributors get them from processing plants. Chain and franchise seafood restaurants often purchase their fish and seafood this way.

The type of restaurant may influence the way aquacrops are marketed. More expensive, "white table cloth" restaurants may pay premium prices for certain products. They also set high standards for processors and producers.

CUSTOM ORDERS

Custom order aquaculture marketing involves farmers (or on-farm fish stores) taking orders from customers for certain products. The customer knows ahead of time the quantity of fish or other product that they will need on a certain date. If an individual plans to serve fish to a large group, an order for the product may be placed several weeks ahead of time. For example, if a civic club plans to hold a fish fry, they likely will order their fish at the time plans are made for the event. This assures them of the product they want when they want it.

In this approach to marketing, the farmer may be required to prepare the product for cooking. This means that processing facilities must be available. Some farmers prefer not to take custom orders because of the required investment in equipment and the labor needs to prepare the product.

PROCESSING PLANTS

Marketing aquacrops through processing plants is popular. More product is marketed this way than any other. Farmers that produce large volumes of aquacrops like this approach because they can sell their crops quickly. Of course, producers must schedule the harvesting and hauling of their aquacrops with available plants. Large processing plants can handle several tons of fish a day.

Processing plants take products as they are harvested on the farm and prepare them for selling to wholesalers, supermarkets, restaurants, and directly to consumers. Some U.S. processors may operate refrigerated trucks that deliver fresh products from coast to coast. Others may export products to various nations around the globe.

The nature of processing varies. With some species of fish, the heads, internal organs, and skin or scales are removed. The product is then cut into sizes and shapes desired by the consumer. In some cases, seasoning (salt and spices) and breading (flour or meal coating) may be added to make the product tastier and easier to cook. Processing also includes packaging, labeling, and refrigerating or freezing the prepared product.

Processing plants are typically highly automated. Machinery has been developed that will handle large volumes of fish or other product with a minimum of labor. However, even with automation, considerable hand labor is often involved.

Farmers who intend to produce aquacrops for processing must work out the details ahead of time. Written contracts are often signed between producers and processors. The contract may specify the species, size, quantity, price, and anticipated date the product will be ready for processing. Processors often deal with a number of farmers. In some cases, these farmers supply all the product the processing plants want. The processor may not need the products from another farm. The smart farmer will make arrangements with a processing plant before beginning production. For new enterprises, marketing arrangements need to be made before the production facilities are constructed.

Processing plants want good-quality products of uniform size. Most processors require aquacrops to be delivered live. Proper hauling procedures must be followed to keep products alive and free of injury. Dead fish and those with sores or injuries are rejected by processors. Most processors want fish of the same size, as this makes processing more efficient. Farmers need to grow their crops accordingly.

LIVE HAULERS

Live haulers buy live fish from farmers and haul them to another location to be sold. The live fish are sold to fish markets, recreational lakes, farmers, and other outlets. The volume of fish marketed in this manner is small compared to the amount sent to processing plants. However, there are excellent opportunities for a few producers who establish good reputations with live haulers.

A live hauler typically uses a truck with a large tank. The tank is specially equipped to circulate and aerate the water. Oxygen cylinders may be located on the tank to assure that the fish have sufficient oxygen to keep them alive and in good health.

RECREATIONAL FACILITIES

Recreational aquaculture marketing is using ponds or other places where people pay a fee to catch fish. It substitutes for sport fishing in streams, lakes, and oceans for wild fish. Such businesses are frequently known as fee lakes, pay lakes, or fish-out ponds. Fishers often like *fee lakes* because they are more likely to have a good catch. These facilities require considerably more fish than can be grown in them. Operators of recreational facilities usually buy fish from fish farmers or live haulers and stock them in the ponds. Some aquafarmers do well supplying recreational fish. Far fewer fish are used for recreation than are processed.

Figure 10–8. Sign promoting a recreational aquaculture business.

Farmers may operate fee lakes on farms where food fish are grown. Typically, sport fishing is not allowed in food fish ponds. Fish can be injured and diseases transmitted by sport fishing.

Fee lakes must be conveniently located in areas where people take a considerable interest in sport fishing. Advertising is necessary to inform the public of the facility and good roads make it easier for them to get to the business. Ponds must be easy to walk around and kept free of weeds. The grounds need to the mowed regularly and kept clean of debris such as bottles and cans. The water in the facility must be relatively clear and free of harmful substances. Sport fishers usually want to be able to take their catch home for cooking and eating! Some fee lake operators also offer fish cleaning services so that the customers don't have to go home and dress their catch.

Charges for fishing are typically based on a flat rate for admission and a rate per pound of fish caught. Additional charges are made for dressing the fish. Some fee lakes also sell fishing supplies, snack foods, beverages, and other items.

Operating a fee lake is confining. Someone must be on duty at all times when it is open to collect fees and assist the public. Good relations with the public are essential for repeat business. In some cases, operators provide advice on how to catch fish, what equipment to use, and the best bait. Fee lakes must acquire the necessary permits and required reports must be completed.

Figure 10-9. Customers line the bank of a popular fee lake. (Courtesy, James Tidwell, Kentucky State University)

HOBBY AND PET STORES

This area of aquaculture focuses on the marketing of ornamental aquacrops such as fish and related animals, aquatic plants, and equipment. Common ornamental aquacrops include all of the pet and hobby types, such as goldfish, tetras, barbs, guppies, and more exotic species. Ornamental fish production is often highly specialized and the crops are produced intensively in fairly small operations. Farmers may sell directly to retail stores or to distributors who move the aquacrops to retailers.

Hobby stores may be located in shopping centers or as departments in large stores. In addition to aquatic pets and supplies, stores may handle other pets, including dogs, cats, snakes, and hamsters.

Opportunities for hobby and pet aquaculture are found all over the United States. In many cases, the best opportunity is operating a local pet store rather than actually producing the aquacrops.

LABORATORIES AND EDUCATIONAL MARKETS

Some aquafarmers produce aquacrops for laboratory, educational, and nonfood use. Laboratory aquacrops are used for research and teaching purposes. The opportunities are fairly narrow and often involve marketing through biological supply houses or other specialized marketing arrangements. Species include fish, oysters for pearls, alligators for hides, and frogs for laboratory use.

Some species of fish grow rapidly. This makes them extremely suitable for laboratory use. A good example is the Japanese medaka. This is a small fish that reproduces profusely and grows rapidly. It is often used in instructional and research settings.

The aquacrops produced by these operations typically are not used for human food. However, species used in laboratories must be of good quality—free of disease and injury.

A producer interested in producing specialty aquacrops should arrange a market or develop one locally on a small scale before beginning production. Production of species for these markets is definitely a specialized situation.

BAIT AND TACKLE STORES

Bait and tackle stores (sometimes known as bait shops) are often located near recreational and commercial fishing areas. They provide the supplies and equipment sport or commercial fishers need. They are often fairly small stores that sell many items in addition to those needed by fishers. In some cases, bait is handled by convenience stores that sell many other products.

Opportunities in this area of aquaculture are limited to producers of species appropriate for use as bait. Bait refers to fish and other species that are used by sport and commercial fishers to catch other fish. Minnows, crawfish, and shrimp are some of the species that are used as bait. Some farmers specialize in producing these species.

Bait and tackle stores must have a good source of bait. The stores must be equipped to keep the bait alive. This often requires tanks with aerated water. Fishers want healthy, active minnows that will attract game fish. A farmer may deliver bait directly to a bait store or to a live hauler, who serves as a distributor.

SELECTING A MARKET

Some aquacrops are marketed in various ways, such as fish for food or for recreational facilities. The aquafarmer must select the market and produce the crop accordingly. In some cases, only a few markets are available.

Selecting a market involves the following considerations: convenience and location; price and profit; volume that can be accommodated; nature of the product; and personal preferences, including integrity and investment.

CONVENIENCE AND LOCATION

Aquafarmers need to market their products easily and economically. Hauling crops long distances requires equipment, fuel, and labor. Long distance hauling can also result in damage to or loss of the product. Hauling is expensive. Most farmers prefer markets that are close by unless the price paid more than covers the cost of hauling.

Processed products are more likely to be hauled long distances. It is more economical to haul frozen fish fillets than live fish. The value of the product is much greater. Most processing plants are near farms where aquacrops are grown.

PRICE AND PROFIT

Farmers want to make the most profit possible from their aquacrops. They choose the marketing alternative that will provide the most returns on their investment and hard work. Higher prices in distant markets may be more profitable, but the cost of transportation must be considered. Aquafarmers with niche markets can often afford to transport their products longer distances because the higher prices more than pay the cost of hauling.

Producers of large volumes of aquacrops typically want to move them into market channels that are near their farms. Processors want to be close to the supply of aquacrop. They can pay more if the product arrives in good condition and is of uniform quality.

VOLUME

Sometimes a farmer produces more of an aquacrop than one market channel can accommodate. If this happens, other marketing alternatives must be investigated. Some fish farmers began small. They operated on-farm retail stores. As they increased the size of their farms, new market channels were needed. Often they sold to processors or to live haulers who would take the crop to another location.

Processors want to have a sufficient amount produced in the local area to justify the cost of the plant. A large processing plant is very expensive to build. The plant should be of adequate capacity to handle the crop but not larger than needed. In some places, aquafarmers have formed cooperatives or partnerships to build processing plants where none were available. This helped aquafarming to develop in the communities served.

NATURE OF THE PRODUCT

Some aquacrops are more profitable than others. Species of fish that demand a premium price in a niche market are sent through that marketing channel. Lower value aquacrops that are produced in large quantities generally go to processors.

Non-food aquacrops may have highly specialized markets. Oysters may be grown for pearls. Spirulina, a species of freshwater algae, may be grown as a food source for baby aquatic animals, such as fish or shrimp, as well as for additives to human food and animal feed.

Nearly all aquacrops will readily spoil if not properly handled in marketing. There are a few exceptions, but fish crops won't keep long if improperly handled. This means that the appropriate facilities must be available to handle the product through the marketing channel.

REPUTATION AND PERSONAL PREFERENCES

Personal factors are often involved in marketing aquacrops. All people involved must have good reputations. They must be honest and fair in their business dealings. Buyers who shortchange farmers develop reputations for dishonesty. Aquafarmers soon learn to use those who are honest.

Some aquafarmers like to produce products for specific marketing channels. A few like the personal contact of operating an on-farm store. Others like dealing with customers at a fee lake.

Regardless, the success of an aquafarm as a business depends on profit. Personal preferences can sometimes result in less than the most profit. In fact, preferences in producing products that consumers don't want can result in the loss of money and bankruptcy.

PRODUCT FORMS

Product form refers to the way a consumer wants to buy a food aquacrop. In most cases, it refers to the changes made as it is processed and how the product is preserved. Some aquacrops are not changed at all; others require extensive processing to get them into forms that consumers want. It is essential to supply products in the forms desired by consumers. If not, consumers won't buy them and the aquafarmer won't have a market for the crop.

Aquacrops are supplied in several ways: live; chilled, but unprocessed; and processed in various ways.

LIVE PRODUCTS

Some food aquaculture species are marketed to the consumer live. These are known as live products. Many people have seen live lobster in a tank in a restaurant or seafood shop. The customer selects the desired lobster from the tank and it is prepared by the chef or market sales clerk. The lobsters are kept alive until preparation. This assures a tasty product for the consumer. Crawfish, crabs, and a few others are also kept alive until ready for cooking.

In addition, some fish stores sell live fish. Customers may buy the fish and take it home for dressing. Others have the store dress the fish and get it ready for cooking. This assures a fresh product for the customer.

The marketing facility must properly handle aquacrops. They must be kept healthy and free of disease. The water must be clean and properly aerated or the aquacrop may die. Tanks or vats with aeration equipment and a supply of quality water are needed.

NO PREPARATION

Though not kept alive, some species undergo no processing. The head, skin, or scales and internal organs are left in place. Fish may be harvested and chilled for shipping to the customer. Chilling quickly kills some species of fish, particularly tilapia. The cold temperature prevents spoilage.

Preparation for cooking is done by the consumer or the chef in the restaurant. In some cases, only the internal organs and skin or scales are removed. With trout, the head and eyes are often left in place. Their presence serves to identify the product. Without the head and eyes, a dishonest person could substitute another species of fish for a more valuable trout.

Oysters, shrimp, and crawfish are additional species that may have no or very little preparation before reaching the consumer. "Oysters on the half shell" (raw) are a treat to some people. These are fresh oysters whose shells are opened (known as shucking) just prior to eating. The oysters aren't cooked when served in this manner. For shrimp and crawfish, the shells, heads and other parts may be removed or left on. The amount of processing depends on how the consumer will prepare it.

Regardless of the amount of preparation, a product must reach the consumer in a wholesome form. Refrigeration or other methods of preservation must be used to prevent spoilage.

PROCESSED

Processing varies by species and product being prepared for consumers. Aquacrop processing is all of the steps taken to get products into forms that consumers want as well as preserving, packaging, and labeling. Wholesome products must reach the consumer!

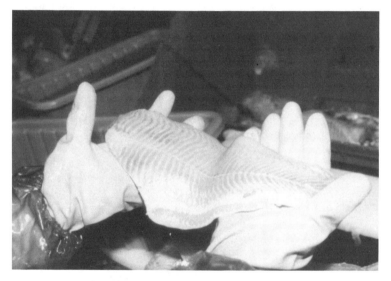

Figure 10–10. This boneless fish fillet has undergone considerable preparation and demands a premium price. The quality of the product is outstanding. (Courtesy, Delta Pride Catfish, Inc.)

Preparation

Preparation refers to the changes that are made in the aquacrop to meet consumer preferences. Most consumers want products that are convenient and easy to prepare. They do not want to spend a lot of time getting ready to cook. Restaurants also want products in uniform portions that are ready for cooking or, in some cases, pre-cooked products that only require heating.

Figure 10–11. Automated equipment is used in processing cultured fish.

For fish, processing typically involves removing the head, skin or scales, and internal organs. Fins may also be removed. Since loss occurs during processing, the value of the remaining product increases considerably.

Most fish dress at about 60 percent of harvested weight. This means that 40 percent of the weight of the fish is lost as head, internal organs, etc. A fish weighing 2 pounds (32 ounces) when harvested would yield a little less than 20 ounces of processed fish. If the fish is processed further, such as into boneless cuts, additional weight is lost. The more weight lost (fish parts discarded) the higher the value of the remaining product. Operators of processing plants want to keep the loss as low as possible. Of course, fish by-products are used in fish meal and other products which provide some value to the processing plant.

There are several forms of fish preparation.

Drawn Form. This form involves little preparation. The fish is left whole with only the internal organs removed. In some cases, the skin or scales may be removed.

Dressed Form. This form goes a couple of steps beyond drawn. The internal organs, head, scales or skin, and some or all of the fins are removed. This is a popular form.

Cut Forms. Several cuts are typically made, depending on the species and

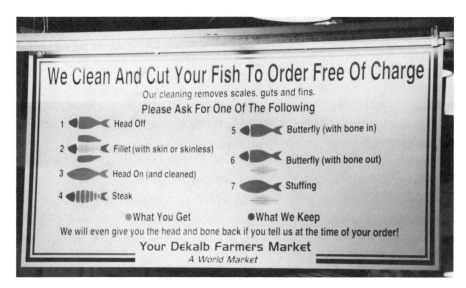

Figure 10–12. Forms of fish preparation for customers at the Dekalb Farmers Market in Georgia. (Live fish are held in tanks. Customers select the individual fish they want and request cleaning and cutting by number.)

size of the fish and the preferences of the customer. The steak cut involves cutting across a dressed fish. The steak contains a cross-section of bones and flesh. The fillet cut involves cutting parallel with the backbone to produce a portion that has no bones. Fillets may be further cut into strips, nuggets, and other forms.

Preservation

Preservation is how the product is kept wholesome until it reaches the consumer. Without preservation, most processed aquacrops will spoil in a short time. Preservation methods are used to prevent the growth of bacteria and other microscopic organisms. If these grow, the product may cause food poisoning.

Several methods of preservation are typically used.

Refrigeration. Refrigeration involves keeping fresh products at low, but above freezing, temperatures. Low temperatures prevent the growth of organisms that cause spoilage. Fish products should be refrigerated at temperatures below 40°F. Once processed, the product should be immediately chilled and kept under refrigeration until time for cooking. Refrigeration can be used to preserve fish products for a few days, with a week often the maximum time. Species that are refrigerated include catfish, trout, striped bass, tilapia and shrimp.

Freezing. Freezing involves storing products at temperatures well below 32°F and often below 0°F. Products should be quickly frozen after processing and not allowed to thaw until the time of preparation. Frozen products can be stored for several weeks—even months—with little product deterioration. Products may be frozen in individual, portion-size pieces or as solid blocks in containers. A number of species are frozen, including trout, catfish, and tilapia.

Canning. Some fish products are preserved by canning. This involves placing the product in cans or jars and heating to kill any spoilage organisms which may be present. The can or jar is tightly sealed so that air and organisms can't enter to spoil the food. Canned products can be stored for months and sometimes years without loss of quality. Salmon and sardines are frequently canned, as are other cultured and wild species.

Other Methods. Some aquaculture products are dried, smoked, salted, pickled, or preserved in other ways. The method selected must result in a product that is wholesome for human consumption.

Packaging

Packaging involves placing fish products in appropriate containers for delivery to consumers. Obviously, products that have been canned are in jars or cans. Frozen and refrigerated products may be in plastic or paper containers.

Containers should be made of durable materials that protect the product. Plastic keeps moisture in the product and prevents outside moisture from entering. Most packages are biodegradable, meaning that they decompose rapidly after use when placed in a landfill. Some papers and plastics can be recycled.

Containers should be of an appropriate size for the consumer. Restaurants may buy large boxes of product, while a two-member family would likely buy a package with only a couple of portions. (A portion is the amount served one individual at a meal.) Packaging serves to provide consumers with the quantity they want. Most processors use sizes that meet the demands of their customers.

Labeling

An *aquacrop label* is the written description on a package that identifies the product. All aquacrop products should be appropriately labeled.

Labels usually include the name of the species of the product or species used in making the product as well as weight, nutritional information, and name and address of the processor. Bar codes and/or written prices may be on a label. In addition, labels often have a date stamped on them. For fresh products, this is the date by which it should be used. For canned products, it is the date the product was processed. In some cases, instructions on preparation of the product are on the label. U.S. Government agencies specify the minimum information to be presented on a label.

CONSUMER PREFERENCES

Meeting consumer demands is essential. Success in marketing aquacrops depends on knowing what the consumer will buy. If the consumer won't buy it, don't grow it!

Consumer preferences change over a period of time. It is important to remain aware of these changes. Several important areas related to consumer preferences for aquaculture products are health concerns, socioeconomic levels, product species, and product preparation.

HEALTH CONCERNS

U.S. citizens are increasingly concerned about eating foods that contribute to good health. Most fish and seafoods are known as beneficial to good health. Some people avoid red meat and meat with a lot of fat. In addition, cultured aquacrops are produced in water that is as free of pollutants as possible. This gives crops grown in well water and other water of known origin an advantage over wild fish and seafood caught in oceans and rivers.

Educating people on how to prepare foods for good health promotes fish and seafood consumption. Preparation instructions on labels often focus on broiling, roasting, and boiling rather than frying in an oil that might be high in cholesterol. Aquaculture associations, universities, and others are searching for improved ways of preparing aquaculture foods.

SOCIOECONOMIC LEVELS

The term socioeconomic refers to the income or financial resources and social orientation of people. Those with higher incomes generally buy more expensive products and eat at more expensive restaurants. Individuals with lower incomes buy inexpensive species of fish and seafood.

Studying a community or neighborhood will provide useful information in determining what to produce. People with lower incomes will buy products that have had less preparation, including fish that are live or whole. Some species are in greater demand than others and sell at higher prices. These should be placed in stores and restaurants where people with higher incomes shop.

Another area often associated with socioeconomic level is ethnicity. Some people have grown up eating certain kinds of products, and they continue to do so as adults. Regional differences exist in the United States. For example, people in the South eat little trout and more catfish and crawfish. Those in the North eat more trout and salmon. Of course, those near fish producing areas or along coastal areas where commercial fishing is practiced eat more of the species grown and caught locally than of other species.

Ethnic groups may be found in large numbers in some cities. These groups often have specific preferences for food. The astute aquaculture marketer will note these preferences and provide products accordingly.

SPECIES

Many people prefer certain species of fish or seafood. It is a part of regional and ethnic differences. Some individuals feel certain species have too many bones. Other people like bony fish. People who live near rivers, lakes, and oceans are more likely to eat what is native in those waters. Aquafarms are frequently started because of a shortage of a species in the local area. The farm produces the species to compensate for an inadequate amount of wild product. Successful marketers carefully study the species preferences of their potential customers.

PREPARATION

Consumers want aquaculture products prepared in certain ways. People who eat catfish often want fillets that contain no bones and are easy to cook. Those who eat trout want whole fish with all the trademarks of being

Figure 10–13. Popular combination restaurant and retail store on the
Maui Island of Hawaii.

a trout (head with eyes left on the fish). In addition to associating a species with certain preparation, ease and convenience of use are important.

People in the work force don't have a lot of time to spend preparing fish. They want to get products they can cook in a few minutes with a minimum of effort. They do not want to have to dress a fish and cut it into portions. They often want the portions seasoned and breaded for cooking. Popular new seasonings, such as lemon pepper and Cajun, are increasing the consumption of certain fish.

PRODUCT QUALITY
BEGINS WITH THE PRODUCER

The quality of the product that reaches the consumer can be no better than the quality of the product on the aquafarm. Many things can happen between the farm and consumer to lower quality. These can influence demand in both the short and long runs. A consumer who buys a product that doesn't taste right or makes them sick will buy other products for awhile. All individuals involved in production and marketing must be conscious of quality.

Practices that assure quality are stocking uniform species, following approved cultural practices, carefully harvesting the crop, checking crops and products for off-flavor, and hauling live and processed products properly.

UNIFORM SPECIES

Consumers want to be assured that they get the product they buy. One who buys trout wants to get trout! *Uniform species* means that all fish in a tank, pond, or other water facility are of the same species. It further means that all of the processed fish in a box or other container are of the same species. Farmers who produce seed stock need to make every effort to avoid mixing species. Aquafarmers should likewise avoid mixing species in food fish facilities. Mixed species often have to be sorted at the time of harvesting and processing. Closely related to species uniformity is size uniformity. Processors and consumers alike prefer uniform size.

CULTURAL PRACTICES

Aquacrops respond to cultural practices just as other crops. Aquafarmers should use those practices that produce quality products. The water should be of appropriate quality. Proper feed should be provided. Diseases should be controlled. Injuries to fish and other species should be minimized.

Aquacrops that aren't fed properly won't grow well. They will develop slowly and may not be of good quality. For example, researchers have found that crawfish that aren't fed properly will have "hollow tails." This means that the shell may be empty or only partially filled with the most desirable part of the crawfish.

HARVESTING PRACTICES

A quality product can be damaged in harvesting. Seines, lifting bags, haul tanks, unloading chutes and other equipment can damage fish. Skin can be punctured creating a wound. Fins, backbones and other parts can be broken or crushed. These injuries result in fish that are unacceptable to the consumer. The farmer or processor will have to cull fish injured in harvesting.

In large ponds, several hours may be required for harvesting. Oxygen levels may get low in the water and the fish might die. Dead fish must be culled upon arrival at the processing plant.

OFF FLAVOR

Some aquacrops and processed products can develop an undesirable flavor. *Off flavor* is when the product doesn't taste the way it should. Products with off flavor should not be marketed.

For some fish, checking for off flavor is a standard procedure at the time of harvest. This involves taking a sample of fish before harvesting and cooking it to determine if it has the right flavor. Upon arrival at the processing plant, this process is often repeated. A person trained in product tasting does the testing. Off flavor products can damage demand for a long time if they reach the consumer. The exact cause of off flavor is unknown. Producers should adjust management practices to eliminate off flavor.

Processed products can develop off flavor, particularly if not stored properly. Packages that aren't tightly sealed can allow the product to be exposed to undesirable substances. Products that are stored too long may lose their flavor although they aren't spoiled. Of course, spoiled products will likely have an undesirable flavor.

Figure 10–14. A specially-trained tester is smelling and tasting a sample of fish for flavor. (Courtesy, Delta Pride Catfish, Inc.)

HAULING

Aquacrops are hauled before and after processing. Before processing, rough handling can damage the fish or other species. Fish may be culled because of the damage. In some cases, portions of the fish must be cut away with time-consuming hand labor. Water that isn't properly managed in the haul tank can lose oxygen resulting in the death of the aquacrop. Processors reject those that are dead on arrival at the plant.

After processing, proper hauling is essential. Frozen products must be hauled in trailers or trucks that keep the product frozen. Likewise, products that have been refrigerated must be kept cold. No lapses in maintaining the proper hauling temperature can be tolerated. Failing to keep the right temperature can result in poor quality or spoiled products reaching the consumer.

Figure 10–15. This truck is equipped to maintain product quality when hauling processed fish to retail outlets.

PROMOTING
AQUACULTURE PRODUCTS

Marketing includes promoting consumption. Producers of aquaculture products want consumers to eat or otherwise use more of their products. Various promotional efforts are used. These are supported by farm or industry associations and processors.

Aquaculture promotion efforts often include advertising, special events, instructional literature, food service training, and incentives.

ADVERTISING

Advertising involves using radio, television, newspapers, magazines, or other means to provide appealing information about an aquacrop. Advertisements are usually carefully prepared to get attention and make positive statements about products. Advertising is very expensive. Only larger producers and processors can individually afford to advertise on a large scale. Lower cost advertisements in local newspapers are often used to tell consumers about the opening of a fee lake or products available at the local supermarket.

Regional and national advertising campaigns are often sponsored by associations of farmers or processors. The ads may be financed with part of the profits from the products that are sold or through a system of fee assessment. In aquaculture, promotional fees may be attached to feed. When a farmer buys feed, an additional amount is automatically charged that goes to an association for advertising.

SPECIAL EVENTS

Many kinds of special events may be held. These range from cooking contests to festivals. Festivals may include tours to farms, educational displays, eating contests, costume contests, talent contests, and entertainment. Supermarkets may have products available for tasting. Associations may donate products for use at a dinner in order to expose people to the fine qualities of the product (hoping they will later buy the product). Aquaculture associations may host dinners for government policy makers, news reporters, and other persons in key positions that feature aquaculture products.

INSTRUCTIONAL LITERATURE

Farmer or processor associations may offer brochures, pamphlets, and other printed materials. These provide cooking suggestions, nutritional information, storing information, and other details related to enjoying an aquaculture product. Sometimes universities provide information on food preparation or storage.

FOOD SERVICE TRAINING

Individuals who work in restaurants, cafeterias, or other institutional kitchens may need training in how to prepare certain food products. Aquaculture associations or processing companies may provide this training. In some cases, government marketing agencies get involved in printing information or providing educational programs.

The training helps individuals develop skills in preparing the products in tasty forms. New recipes can be distributed. As food service people are trained, they are more likely to use the products and prepare delicious new foods for their customers.

INCENTIVES

Special incentives involve a wide range of activities. Products are sold at reduced prices to encourage new customers. Reduced price coupons are placed in newspapers or mailed to people. "Buy one, get one free" sales are used. Some stores give away some other product with the purchase of fish, such as a bottle of cocktail sauce with a fish or seafood purchase. In-store demonstrations show customers how to prepare a product. The overall goal is to attract customers and help them to have a good experience with the product.

SUMMARY

Marketing aquaculture products is much like marketing other agricultural products. Understanding the nature of aquaculture products can help in marketing. Understanding what products the consumer wants and how the consumer responds to the products is essential. Markets must be available before an aquacrop is produced. In fact, decisions about going into aquafarming must involve locating an appropriate market. Most producers go a step further and sign contracts with processors or other outlets before they make large investments.

Unlike most agricultural products, aquaculture products must compete with similar species harvested from rivers and oceans. Farmers who produce aquacrops must invest in land, equipment, facilities, seedstock, feed, and other inputs. Those who capture wild fish and seafood do not have all of these costs; however, they cannot verify the quality of their product to the same extent as aquafarmers.

A number of marketing channels are available in aquaculture. Some can handle large volumes of aquacrop. Automated processing plants can handle several tons a day. Others can only handle small amounts of aquacrop and in specialized marketing situations. Some farmers bridge the entire gap from farm to consumer by operating on-farm stores and restaurants. These add new demands on the farmer because of the additional business that is operated. In addition to aquacrops that are used for food, opportunities exist for ornamental, laboratory and bait fish, and related species.

All who are involved with a product have a role in its marketing. Sloppy work at any one place can result in a poor-quality product. Success depends on producing a product that the consumer demands.

CHAPTER SELF-CHECK

Match the following terms with the correct definitions:

    a. baitfish

    b. aquacrop

    c. seafood

    d. hydroponics

    e. aquaculture niche market

    f. custom order aquaculture marketing

    g. live hauler

    h. recreational aquaculture marketing

    i. product form

    j. off flavor

_____ aquatic animals used for human food

_____ growing terrestrial plants with their roots in water solutions

_____ the way a consumer wants an aquacrop

_____ when the product doesn't have the right taste

_____ an aquatic plant or animal that is farmed

_____ a small, specialized market for certain aquacrops

_____ taking orders from customers for certain products

_____ someone who buys and hauls fish

_____ a substitute for sport fishing

_____ small fish used by sport fishers to catch other fish

QUESTIONS AND PROBLEMS FOR DISCUSSION

1. What is the relationship of seafood to aquaculture?

2. How is the kind of water important in aquaculture?

3. What kinds of water structures may be used in aquaculture?

4. How is water temperature important?

5. What is hydroponics and how is it distinguished from aquaculture?

6. What are the important aquaculture species?

7. What are the ways (channels) of marketing aquacrops? Briefly describe each and give its relative importance. Which marketing channel will handle the largest quantity of aquacrop?

8. What are the major areas to consider in selecting a market? Why is each important?

9. What are the common product forms in aquaculture?

10. What is dressing percentage? Why is it important?

11. What are the common forms of preparation for fish? Briefly describe each.

12. What is preservation? Why is it important? What are the common methods of preserving aquacrops?

13. What is packaging? What kinds of packages are used in aquaculture?

14. Why is labeling important? What information is presented in a label?

15. Why are consumer preferences important? What are the major areas of consumer preference? How do these influence consumption?

16. What is the role of the producer in product quality? What steps can a producer take to assure a quality product?

17. What is promotion? Why is it important?

18. What are several promotions that are used to market aquaculture?

ACTIVITIES

1. Select one of your favorite seafoods. Determine if it is aquafarmed. If so, write a short report on what is involved in producing it. If not, write a short report on where and how the seafood is captured wild.

2. Go to a nearby supermarket. Visit the fresh, frozen, and canned foods areas. Make a list of the different seafood/aquacrops by how they have been preserved.

3. Interview the operator of a recreational fishing facility. Determine the species that are stocked, source of the stock, fees for fishing, and other details of the operation.

Chapter 11

MARKETING TO THE CONSUMER

Consumers are the people, farms, agribusinesses, and other entities that use goods and services. They have certain needs and preferences. They make decisions about what and how much they will consume. Success in agrimarketing involves understanding the consumer and the role of consumption. You want to have a product that will be chosen over all other products!

Agrimarketing is the link between production and consumption. Products must be marketed in a variety of ways to satisfy all consumers. Understanding the many kinds of consumers and how their choices affect

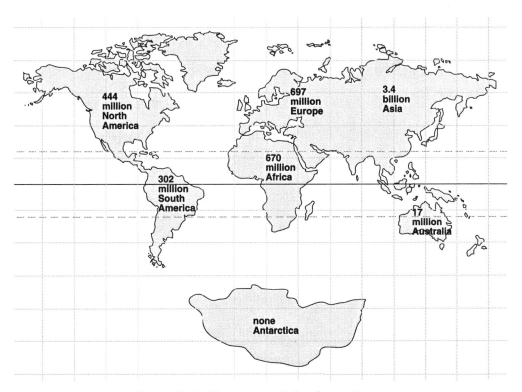

Figure 11–1. Human population by continent.

the marketing process is essential. All of us are consumers, and everyone needs clothing. Do you buy cloth and sew the items yourself or do you buy clothing ready to wear? Agrimarketing involves trying to meet the needs and demands of all consumers.

OBJECTIVES

This chapter outlines the role of consumers and consumption in agrimarketing. After reading it, you will be able to:

- Explain important population trends
- Describe problems and approaches in meeting the long-term needs of consumers
- Describe consumer behavior as related to agrimarketing
- List and explain major trends in consumer preferences
- Describe strategies used to market to consumers
- Explain consumer market segmentation
- Explain the role of world agricultural trade

TERMS

consumer behavior
consumption
decision making
difficult decisions
family
family life cycles
hunger
marketing mix
marketing strategy
market potential
market segmentation
mass marketing
multinational
per capita consumption
personal characteristics
population
product differentiation
product positioning
programmed decisions
segment positioning
sociocultural influences
sustainable agriculture
target market

POPULATION TRENDS
AND PREFERENCES

Agrimarketing technology is shaped by worldwide trends. Various forces shape agrimarketing throughout the world. What people want is influenced by their overall level of living and the characteristics of their cultures. This is partly determined by the productive capacity of agriculture in the various continents of the earth. Climate—particularly temperature, precipitation, and soil fertility—influence plant and animal production.

The technology used in agrimarketing varies by culture, just as agricultural production may vary. International trade involves making provisions for these differences.

CURRENT POPULATION

Population is the total number of people in a location. The population of the earth is 5.6 billion people. The population is primarily found on six of the earth's seven continents. North America (United States, Canada, and Mexico) has 444 million people. The continent with the largest population is Asia, with nearly 3.4 billion people. Antarctica has no resident population.

The population of the United States is nearing 260 million people. California has more people than any other state, with 30 million or 11.5 percent of the U.S. total. New York, Texas, and Florida follow California. Wyoming has the smallest population, with 450 thousand people—nearly 100,000 less than Alaska, which has the next to lowest population. Areas of Canada have very sparse population, particularly in the far north, which has a very cold climate.

POPULATION TRENDS

The world's population increases at the rate of 2.8 people every second! Each hour there are 10,080 more people on the earth. All of these people are consumers. They need food, clothing, and housing. Agrimarketing helps them meet these needs.

The world's population will double every 30 years at the current rate of population growth. This means that there will be nearly 10.3 billion people on the earth by the year 2030! Agricultural production and marketing must keep pace if the needs of these people are to be met.

Figure 11–2. Well-stocked grocery stores provide an
abundance of wholesome food in the
United States.

The rate of population increase is much greater in some countries than
in others. In some places, the supply of food is far below the amount
needed. People lack the bare essentials for proper nutrition. They are often
sick and die at a young age.

North America has been fortunate to have good agricultural production.
Except for a few isolated locations and disadvantaged people in large cities,
most people have adequate food, clothing, and housing. Fertile soil, a good
climate, and agricultural technology have made it possible for agriculture
production to keep pace with and exceed consumption in North America.

Agrimarketing technology plays a big role in getting the products to
consumers. Communication, transportation, processing, and other components of the marketing process are essential to meet consumer needs.

PREFERENCES

People eat a variety of foods, wear many styles of clothing, and live
in different kinds of housing. What they eat, wear, and use for housing
varies throughout the world. Preferences exist among countries as well as
within countries. Foods that are popular in one place may be disliked in
others. Preferences are shaped by climate, culture, income, and other factors.
For example, religious restrictions don't allow people of certain faiths to

eat foods such as pork or beef. Areas where such religious groups predominate have low consumption of these foods.

Food preferences in the United States are best illustrated with the per capita consumption of selected products. *Per capita consumption* is the average amount of a product that is consumed in a year by an individual in a nation. Comparing these amounts with previous years provides important information about trends in consumption. For example, in the last 20 years the per capita consumption of red meat has declined while consumption of poultry has increased. Table 11-1 summarizes per capita food consumption in the United States.

Table 11-1
**Per Capita Annual Consumption of Selected Food Products
in the United States**

Commodity	Annual Consumption	
	1970	1990
Red meat (beef, veal, lamb, mutton, and pork) (lbs.)	132.4	112.4
Poultry (chicken and turkey) (lbs.)	34.1	56.8
Fish and shellfish (wild catch and cultured) (lbs.)	11.8	20.0
Eggs (number of eggs)	309	234
Dairy products and milk (lbs.)	563.9	564.5
Fresh vegetables (lbs.) (does not include canned, frozen, or dried)	70.7	99.3
Fresh fruit and melons (lbs.)	100.6	118.4
Potatoes (includes sweet potatoes) (lbs.)	67.7	53.9
Mushrooms (lbs.)	0.3	2.1
Wheat (lbs.)	110.8	122.7
Rice (lbs.)	6.7	15.7

Sources: U.S. Department of Agriculture and U.S. Department of Commerce. Some rounding of information has been used. Information does not include: canned, frozen, and dried vegetables and fruit; peanuts; tree nuts; coffee; cocoa; fats and oils; certain cereal grains; and other non-reported foods, such as game animals.

In commercial agriculture, all producers and people involved in marketing should carefully study consumption trends. Commodities where increases have occurred may represent opportunities for continued increased production. Decreases in per capital consumption may be a signal to decrease production of a particular crop. Long-term analysis of these trends and a study of other factors are essential before an individual makes major production and marketing decisions.

One example is red meat. Even though the data indicate that per capita red meat consumption has declined, considerable demand still exists. Multiplying the population in the United States by the per capita consumption gives a good indication of the total involved: 29.2 billion pounds of boneless, ready-to-cook meat! Live animal weight would be near 100 billion pounds—a large number of hogs, cattle, and sheep!

Another example is mushrooms. The per capita consumption of mushrooms has increased considerably. The current demand for mushrooms is seven times higher than the 1970 consumption level. The total pounds of mushrooms consumed is now near 550 million pounds in the United States annually! This expanding market may represent a good opportunity to increase investment in the production and marketing of mushrooms.

Consumption data must always be carefully studied. Several factors can affect consumption. Production or marketing problems can suddenly cause huge changes in demand. Consumer patterns can change quickly if bad products reach the market. News reports that describe possible problems with foods such as chemicals on apples or bST used to produce milk also influence consumption.

MEETING CONSUMER DEMANDS

Providing for the needs of the world's people involves finding new approaches in agrimarketing technology. Population increases and declining supplies of some products have created major concern among world leaders. These leaders often address three areas of concern: hunger, the loss of agricultural productivity, and following sustainable agricultural practices.

HUNGER

Hunger is the human need for food. In many cases, hunger refers to a shortage of food or to famine. Some people are undernourished or malnourished. This means that they do not get adequate calories and proper nutrients and vitamins. There is hunger in some areas because agriculture is not productive or marketing systems are not capable of moving available food to locations where it is needed. A lack of adequate clothing and shelter are also associated with hunger.

Forty million people die of hunger each year in the world. Many millions of other people suffer diseases of hunger that lead to impaired life. Physical disability, mental retardation, stunted growth, and susceptibility to infectious disease are major consequences of hunger. Children who survive to adulthood are often retarded and capable of only menial labor.

Two major diseases associated with hunger are kwashiorkor and marasmus. People who have one of these diseases often also have the other.

Kwashiorkor results from a lack of protein in the diet. It is particularly a concern in small children. Kwashiorkor shows itself in children under age three as wasted arms and legs, swollen bellies, and sleepy eyes that move only occasionally. Small infants who are still nursing their mothers usually don't have kwashiorkor. The disease develops as they begin to eat solid food and are no longer nursing. The birth of another child may result in early weaning.

Children with marasmus have thin, wrinkled skin and visible ribs. Though the children may be active, they lack calories and protein. Children with marasmus often gnaw on their hands, clothes, and other objects in an effort to satisfy their hunger.

Most people in North America don't experience hunger firsthand. There is a generally adequate supply of food, clothing, and shelter. No more than 10 percent of the people in North America live in or close to hunger. This is not the case in other places of the world, where the hunger rate may be much higher.

Hunger is particularly a problem in areas of Asia, Africa, and Latin

Figure 11–3. Modern supermarkets in the United States may stock over 20,000 different food items.

America. Forty percent or more of the people may live in hunger. Many die as young children. Those who survive often lack the capacity to be productive citizens. They have been deprived of the ability to be highly productive people because they have not had adequate food.

Hunger is also associated with a high birth rate. Nations that lack sufficient food often have the highest birth rates. Family planning is often discussed as a partial solution for world hunger problems.

AGRICULTURAL PRODUCTIVITY

The major worldwide problems in providing adequate food, clothing, and housing are related to politics, loss of soil productivity, water shortages, and conversion of land to non-agricultural uses.

Policies

Government policies can restrict or encourage agricultural industry. Many of the world's hunger problems are associated with government control or lack of incentive to have a productive agriculture. Government regulations can restrict agricultural marketing even when adequate food supplies are available. Of course, people must be able to buy food that is produced. In some countries, this is very difficult because people have neither jobs to earn money nor land on which to produce crops.

Loss of Productivity

Soil erosion, loss of nutrients, and desertification are major areas in the loss of agricultural productivity. Erosion results when the soil is improperly managed so that it is washed away by rain, blown away by wind, or lost in other ways. Nutrients can be used up and leach out of the soil so that it is no longer productive. In some parts of the world, productive farm land is turning into desert, known as desertification. This occurs when the land is poorly managed resulting in the loss of productivity and return to a desert-like condition.

Water

Water shortages include both surface and below the surface supplies of freshwater. Only about one percent of the water on earth is available freshwater. Of the remaining 99 percent, 97 percent is saltwater and two percent is frozen as glaciers and polar ice. Freshwater may be used faster than it is restored through natural processes. It may be lost to pollution and salt. Agricultural productivity requires attention to water use and management as much as it does to the soil. Aquaculture, rice farming, irrigation of cotton, and other uses of water are contributing to a future shortage.

Non-Agricultural Land Use

Many acres of productive farmland are converted to other uses each year. The land is lost from production agriculture. It is used for housing, industry, business, recreation, and other purposes. In the United States, 5,280 acres of farmland are converted to non-farm use every day. These are important uses, but they result in major impacts on agricultural production.

SUSTAINABLE AGRICULTURE

Sustainable agriculture refers to managing agricultural production so that the long-term food, clothing, and shelter needs of people can be met. Production practices are used that reduce the loss of land and its productivity. Land that is not now in production is made productive, including the reclaiming of severely eroded land. New and alternative crops are produced that make more efficient use of resources. More aquatic crops may be produced. Loss to pests (insects, rodents, etc.) is reduced through proper control measures, harvesting, and storage. (Estimates are that up to 30 percent of agricultural production is destroyed by pests, spoilage, and disease.)

CONSUMER BEHAVIOR
IN AGRIMARKETING

The final consumers of all agricultural products are people. How people respond to available products is important in many ways. Careful study of consumers helps in making agrimarketing decisions.

Consumption is the use of goods and services that have value. Consumers exchange something of value for products and use them up or convert them into another form. For example, fertilizer is consumed when it is bought and applied to a crop. The increase in crop production more than pays for the fertilizer. Another example of consumption is a farm tractor. The tractor may be bought new and used for several years on the farm. The tractor no longer has the same value once it is used though it contributes to the production of other products that have value. People also buy food and clothing, although these products are consumed somewhat differently from the fertilizer and tractor.

Consumer behavior is how people make decisions about buying and using products. The decisions consumers make are often more detailed than they appear on the surface. Both personal and sociocultural influences influence decisions.

CONSUMER DECISIONS

Some decisions are easy for consumers to make; others are difficult to make. All decisions can be placed on a continuum between difficult and easy. Marketing processes help people make decisions. Understanding the consumer can help people in agrimarketing technology position a product in the market so that it is attractive to the consumer. This increases consumption of the product.

Decision making involves selecting among different alternatives. Several choices may be available. Decisions include whether or not to buy and, if

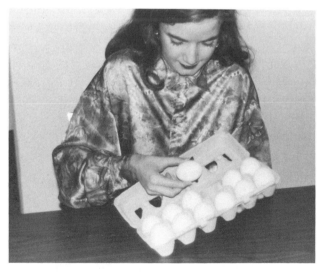

Figure 11-4. Buying graded eggs in convenient protective
packages is a routine decision for most
consumers.

to buy, which products to purchase. Financing the purchase is also often a part of decision making.

Easy decisions are said to be routine or *programmed decisions.* These decisions don't involve high risk or a lot of money, and are made frequently. For example, buying a loaf of bread at the supermarket is a routine decision for most consumers. Reduced prices, advertising, and other means are used to help consumers change their routine and buy another brand or kind of bread.

Difficult decisions are more complex and often require people to go through a fairly detailed process of problem solving. In many cases, these decisions involve large sums of money, risk, and long-term implications. For example, buying a new farm tractor requires a person to consider a number of factors before making a decision. Being aware of the difficulty of a decision is beneficial in marketing to the consumer. (Chapter 13 presents additional information on consumer decision making from the standpoint of selling.)

Figure 11–5. Buying an expensive new suit is a difficult
decision that is made easier when it is
properly fitted.

PERSONAL INFLUENCES

Personal characteristics are the traits of individuals that influence their behavior as consumers. The major personal characteristics are education, attitudes, lifestyle, motivation, perceptions, and personality. These tend to apply to decisions in the home as well as in the agricultural industry; however, decisions in the larger agricultural industries may be somewhat removed from personal influences. Regardless, people may be loyal to a particular brand or style. For example, many consumers repeatedly buy the same products, such as bread or milk. In agriculture, people tend to buy the make of equipment, seed, feed, chemicals, or tractors that they bought the last time.

SOCIOCULTURAL INFLUENCES

The personal characteristics of consumers are a product of their social and cultural environment, known as *sociocultural influences.* The major sociocultural influences are family, reference group, culture, and social class. A reference group is any group that has some influence on a person, such as clubs, churches, and friends. Culture includes the values, attitudes, and artifacts (material things) that help people adjust to their environments.

Social class refers to general groups of people who share similar attitudes and values as well as income and lifestyles. General measures of social class status are occupation, source of income, housing and where it is located, education, and family history. Three major social classes are found in the United States: upper, middle, and lower or marginal. The upper class is 15 percent of the population, while the middle class is 65 percent, and the lower and marginal class is 20 percent. These classes can be further divided into two groups each. People can move from one social class to another; however, only people born into it attain the highest level of the upper class.

THE CHANGING FAMILY

The *family* is the most basic group to which an individual belongs. Traditional views of family are changing. Family members are assuming different roles. More females are working, creating new and increased demands for products, such as convenience foods and ready-to-wear clothing.

Families go through cycles. The *family life cycle* is the series of stages people pass through in their lives. Children grow up in families and typically break away to form their own family units. In a typical lifetime, a person will go through several family stages:

1. Young single
2. Young married without children

3. Young married or divorced (under age 35)

   a. Without children

   b. With children

4. Middle-aged married or divorced and with or without children (age 35–64)

5. Older married, divorced, or widowed (over age 64)

More people in the United States are living longer. The number of people over age 64 is increasing. The kinds of goods and services older people want varies from that of younger people. Producers of food, clothing, and shelter must consider these population changes when considering the market demand.

TRENDS IN
CONSUMER PREFERENCES

Consumers change. Their preferences are associated with changes in personal and sociocultural variables. In general, consumers want quality products that are easy to use and priced within their ability to buy them. Major consumer trends are associated with health, ease of use or preparation, and standard of living.

HEALTH

Citizens of the United States are increasingly concerned about their health. They are better informed on many health-related issues such as nutrition and exercise. They want products that will contribute to their health.

Eating patterns are changing to foods and methods of food preparation that reportedly contribute to good health. People want foods with less fat, more fiber, and free of hazardous substances, such as pesticide residues. Declines in the consumption of red meat and increases in poultry and fish consumption are associated with the desire to consume less fat. Skim milk and other low-fat dairy products are increasingly popular. Fresh fruits and vegetables are demanded year-round.

Health-conscious people are willing to pay more for foods that were grown a certain way. For example, run-about eggs receive a higher price than other eggs. (These eggs are from hens that are allowed to range outside

Figure 11–6. The needs of consumers concerned about too much fat
are met by providing low-fat ground beef (on the left)
along with regular ground beef.

rather than being confined in buildings and cages. Run-about hens eat
insects, grass, and other items instead of an exclusive commercially-manufactured feed.)

Exercise, such as jogging and walking, has created the demand for new
styles of clothing and fibers. The use of cotton and other natural fibers
depends on producing clothing that meets consumer expectations. Older
citizens also have clothing preferences. They want comfortable clothing
that is easy to put on and take off.

EASE OF USE

The demand for products that are easy to use or prepare has created
new needs in agrimarketing technology. Ready-to-cook and ready-to-serve
food products are rapidly expanding even though they cost more than those
that may require preparation. Microwavable food products are popular. A
good example is popcorn. The consumption of popcorn has increased
drastically with the development of popcorn in bags that can be put in a
microwave oven. Consumers have many choices of foods in convenient
packages that can also be used for cooking and serving the food.

The number of meals eaten away from home has increased sharply in
recent years. Eating out is associated with increased incomes, more women

in the work force, and less leisure time. Restaurants often have a wide range of foods that are cooked to the consumer's specifications and served in an attractive manner at the table. Fast food restaurants with pizza and sandwiches have become popular though the food may not always be particularly healthy from a nutrition standpoint. Restaurants are moving away from fried foods to those that are baked or broiled to cater to health-conscious consumers. Increasingly, fried foods are cooked in vegetable oil. This has resulted in decreased demand for cooking oil made with animal fat.

Figure 11–7. This small bag of seasoned popcorn will be a large serving of delicious, hot popcorn in just three minutes in a microwave oven—and there are no containers to wash!

STANDARD OF LIVING

The standard of living enjoyed by many people has changed. Two-income families have more money and are willing to spend it for different kinds of food, clothing, and housing. People with higher incomes demand different food products, such as boneless fish fillets, exotic or baby vegetables, and organically-grown foods. They are willing to pay higher prices for these foods and for the atmosphere of the restaurant they are served in. The finer restaurants (often referred to as "white tablecloth restaurants") have trained chefs, use menus with food for the health-conscious, and stay informed on changes in demand.

REACHING THE CONSUMER: MARKETING STRATEGIES

Marketing to consumers involves selecting and using appropriate plans of action. These involve strategies for reaching consumers and achieving a share of the market.

MARKETING STRATEGY

A *marketing strategy* is the plan of action for achieving marketing objectives. A specific target market is defined and strategies are selected to achieve the objectives.

Developing strategies requires attention to details in the market analysis. Consumers characteristics, product features, and other factors in the market shape how a market is to be reached. Information about consumers creates a market segment profile. The people in a segment are often very similar to each other on the basis of certain characteristics.

TARGET MARKET

A *target market* is the group of consumers that is to be reached. The market should be well defined. Both present and potential customers should be identified. Information should be collected about the consumers, including personal and sociocultural variables. The information should be used to develop strategies to reach the target market.

Target markets are important in selling farm supplies and services. The kind of crop or livestock produced is a major factor in defining the target market. Individuals who fit into the target market get attention in marketing; those that don't fit don't get attention. A manufacturer of wheat drills (planting machines) would not gain from marketing efforts with trout farmers.

MARKETING MIX

The *marketing mix* is the combination of variables used to reach a target market. Marketing mix is composed of the four Ps: product, place, promotion, and price.

Product refers to the ability of a product to satisfy the needs of consumers. The product has certain traits and the consumers have certain demands.

Place refers to making a product convenient for people to purchase. The product is available at the right place at the right time and in the right quantity.

Promotion is communication between the source of a product and the targeted potential consumers. Advertising, personal selling, and other means are used to make consumers aware of the benefits of the product and encourage them to buy it.

Figure 11–8. A smart agrimarketing mix has allowed grain to be marketed to homeowners in convenient containers as feed for wild birds.

Price is the amount of money that buyers pay for the product. Prices must be competitive and within reach of potential consumers. Policies on pricing may include the taking of trade-ins (such as used tractors), discounts for volume purchases, and the extension of credit to buyers.

More information on marketing mix is presented in Chapter 12, Developing Marketing Plans.

MARKET POTENTIAL

Market potential is the size of a market over a period of time. It is often measured in sales volume. Market potential is the sum of all consumers who are likely to use a supply, product, or service. For example, the market potential for farm tractors is all of the consumers who buy tractors. The different makes and models of tractors compete in the overall market for the largest share that produces the greatest profit.

MARKET SEGMENTATION

Markets are studied to determine how to best provide the desired food, clothing, and shelter. A market is often viewed as a group of individuals or organizations who desire a product and are willing and able to buy it. Within the group, there are many variations. A good example is with families. As presented earlier in the chapter, families vary considerably. Smart marketing focuses on particular individuals within the market.

MASS MARKETING

Food, clothing, and shelter may be marketed to the overall population. *Mass marketing* is offering one product to all people regardless of their various characteristics. Mass marketing assumes that all people share a similar need for the product and that their differences aren't sufficiently important to justify using varied marketing approaches.

Many agricultural products have been mass marketed. For example, milk has been marketed as whole milk. All of the population was expected to buy whole milk. Milk producers studied approaches for expanding the amount of milk sold. They began to remove part or nearly all of the fat from the milk. At this point, consumers had several choices of milk and dairy products. This allowed more health-conscious people to buy milk with reduced fat content.

Making similar products with small differences is known as *product differentiation*. In many cases, product differentiation is a marketing strategy identified with products of certain manufacturers. Consumers are encouraged to believe that certain characteristics make products superior to other products. For example, marketing strategies for both Florida and California citrus products focus on telling consumers which state the product is from. The stress is on getting consumers to believe that the product of one state is superior to that from another.

SEGMENTATION

Market segmentation is developing specific marketing efforts that target consumers with unique needs. The larger mass market is divided into smaller markets based on certain criteria. Specific products are developed for the smaller segmented market. Different promotional strategies are used for the segments, also known as target markets.

Consumers are often segmented on the basis of personal or sociocultural backgrounds. A segmentation variable is a characteristic of the people in the mass market that makes it possible to divide it. Family life cycle may be a major basis for segmentation. For example, clothing may be designed and marketed to young singles, young married people, or older people.

Marketing agricultural supplies and services often involves segmentation approaches. For example, farm machinery manufacturers segment their market on the basis of the crops or livestock that farmers are producing. This makes it possible for the manufacturer to focus limited advertising resources on the groups that are most likely to buy a particular product. A large machinery manufacturer may produce equipment suited to many different uses as well as that for particular uses. Farm tractors can be used in a wide range of farm situations; however, rice combines are limited to the market segment that produces rice. From a sales perspective, there is little need to promote rice combines to dairy farmers not involved with rice production!

Figure 11–9. Small bundles of firewood are attractive to a segment of consumers who want a fire only occasionally.

BASES OF SEGMENTATION

Consumers may be placed in groups on the basis of many different criteria. In agriculture, segments are often on the basis of geographic location, kinds of crops or livestock produced, and size of farm or agribusiness. Many criteria are used to segment the overall population; including age, sex, income, ethnic group, lifestyle, family life cycle, climate, and geographic location.

The segments or groups must be large enough to be profitably served. Dividing consumers into groups that are too narrow may not be a wise move. A good example is magazines for agricultural audiences. Successful magazines meet the needs of subscribers and advertisers. Subscribers are often asked to indicate their interests and the crops and livestock they produce. All of the subscribers are placed in groups or segments on the basis of this information. The magazine is then assembled with articles related to the segments. Computer systems for magazine production and mailing provide a magazine tailored to individual farmers' needs. People get magazines that have some articles for all subscribers and other articles targeted to certain interests. In some cases, farm magazines have segmented too narrowly. They may have too many segments with small numbers of subscribers.

The market segments must also be reachable. Dividing consumers into groups where the individual members can't be identified is of no value. Segmentation variables must be used that help products reach target markets.

PRODUCT POSITIONING AND THE CONSUMER

Consumers develop attitudes about certain products. How people view a product or service is important in marketing. Market position is how people (consumers) compare one product or brand to other products or brands. Marketing strategies may attempt to position a product or service a certain way in the eyes of a consumer.

PRODUCT POSITIONING

Product positioning is creating a certain image of a product in the minds of consumers. The notion is to get consumers to believe that the product has the desired features that will best meet their needs. This is true in marketing supplies and services to the farm as well as products of the farm to consumers. Even the color of the paint on farm tractors conveys certain images of the tractor as well as loyalty to a particular manufacturer.

Operators of fruit and vegetable stands can use various strategies to position their products as compared to the products of other outlets available locally. They may wish to stress the freshness or other desirable characteristics of their products. A product logo can be used to help establish a position. Including the outlet's logo on labels often helps to identify the outlet. Advertising and other means can be used to promote the position of a fruit or vegetable stand with local consumers.

Position maps or diagrams are sometimes used by agrimarketers to determine relationships between products and brands of products that are on the market. These maps show positions occupied by competitors and suggest where new brands or products might be needed.

SEGMENT POSITIONING

Marketing may involve positioning a product in a particular market segment, known as *segment positioning*. This is used when a product is suited to the needs of particular consumers. These consumers form a segment for the product. An example is disposable diapers (a product of forestry). The market segment would be the population of young adults with infants. The strategy would involve creating a position within the segment for a particular brand of diaper.

Producers of farm supplies and services position themselves in segment markets. Manufacturers of milking machines market to the segment of dairy farmers with a volume of milk production suited to the particular equipment. Manufacturers of pesticides position themselves in the appropriate market by targeting the segment that would use the pesticide being produced.

WORLD AGRICULTURAL TRADE AND THE CONSUMER

People all over the world are consuming similar products that are often available on a year-round basis. This is because transportation and communication have made world trade easier and a regular part of providing for the needs of consumers. Buyers and sellers from all areas of the world are involved.

TRADE

Trade often focuses on basic food items and raw materials. Diverse climates and agricultural capabilities create needs for commodities and also provide excess commodities that can be traded. The importance of world agricultural trade is evident in every supermarket. (A typical supermarket has over 20,000 food items to select from.) Food products are on sale from all parts of the earth. Products that are out of season in one nation or region may be in-season in another. For example, fresh persimmons are available year-round in some U.S. supermarkets because they are imported by air from Israel in the late winter.

The bulk of world trade involves important grains: wheat, rice, corn, and soybeans. Other important world trade items in the United States are fish and seafood, fruit and vegetables, cotton, lumber and wood products, oil and other fuels, and minerals. The products are both exported (sold to

Figure 11–10. Fresh persimmons in an Atlanta, Georgia, supermarket
in late winter were imported from Israel.

other nations) and imported (bought from other nations). In addition, farm
supplies are often imported. Examples of imported supplies include farm
tractors, barbed wire, fertilizer, and chemicals for formulating pesticides.

CONSUMER CONCERNS

Consumers appreciate the product quality and supply provided by
international trade. However, they want food products that are wholesome
and healthful to eat. They want to know that the foods are free of hazardous
pesticide residues and foreign materials that might create hazards. Consumers also want the products to meet certain standards of uniformity.

The movement of some products is restricted. Only products free of
disease and other pests are permissible in trade. Several pests have been
imported to the United States with food and other crops. Fruit flies and
fire ants are two examples of insect pests that came into the United States
with imported food products.

Inspection for wholesomeness may be lacking in some nations. Food
products that aren't appropriate for consumption might be produced. International trade has the responsibility of assuring that products conform
to minimum standards.

Human rights issues are sometimes associated with trade. Consumers
may not want goods manufactured in places where people don't receive
proper compensation for their work or are made to work in unsafe condi-

Figure 11–11. Multinational companies use modern methods of transporting materials that reduce handling and speed the process of marketing. This photograph shows large containers of bananas at the Port of Gulfport, Mississippi, being lifted for placement on a trailer for delivery to banana terminals in major cities in the United States. The containers will be returned and loaded onto a ship for refilling in South America.

tions. In many cases, labels on products shape consumer decisions to buy a particular product if it was made in a certain location.

MULTINATIONAL COMPANIES

World trade often involves multinational approaches. *Multinational* is when trade and manufacturing to produce one product are carried out in several nations. A multinational company is a business that produces its products in several different nations with each contributing in a unique way to the product. For example, a multinational clothing manufacturer may buy raw cotton in one nation, have it woven in a second, made into garments in a third, and then finally sold in a fourth location. Altogether, meeting the needs of consumers may involve work in several different nations. Again, product labels may provide the information on manufacturing locations.

SUMMARY

Agrimarketing is more efficient when information on the characteristics and preferences of consumers is considered. Important information includes general population trends and needs, as well as the preferences of the people.

Consumers must make choices. Some of the choices are programmed decisions; others are more difficult. Personal and sociocultural influences are a part of the decision-making process. Family life cycle, changes in product preferences, and increased standard of living are important in meeting market needs.

Various marketing strategies are used to reach consumers. Target markets may be explored. An appropriate marketing mix is developed to reach the consumer. Mass marketing and market segmentation may be used. Product positioning is used to attract consumers.

World agricultural trade helps meet consumer demand. The trade often involves important grains and related crops. Increasingly, seafood, ornamental flowers, and fresh fruit and vegetables are a part of international marketing.

CHAPTER SELF-CHECK

Match the following terms with the correct definitions:

    a. consumption

    b. population

    c. hunger

    d. consumer behavior

    e. family

    f. marketing strategy

    g. target market

    h. marketing mix

    i. market potential

    j. market segmentation

_____   size of a market over a period of time

_____   total number of people in a location

_____ specific marketing efforts that target consumers with unique needs

_____ need of humans for food

_____ use of goods and services that have value

_____ how people make decisions in buying and using products

_____ basic group to which an individual belongs

_____ plan of action for achieving marketing objectives

_____ the group of consumers who are to be reached

_____ the combination of variables used to reach a target market

QUESTIONS AND PROBLEMS FOR DISCUSSION

1. What are the major population trends?

2. How are changes in preferences for food important in marketing? Select two foods and compare per capita consumption changes in the United States.

3. Why is hunger important in agrimarketing? What are the effects of hunger on people?

4. What are the major worldwide problems in providing adequate food?

5. What is sustainable agriculture?

6. What are consumer decisions? What kinds of decisions do consumers make?

7. What important personal characteristics influence consumer behavior?

8. What sociocultural influences are involved in consumer behavior?

9. What stages are involved in the family life cycle? How do these relate to consumer demand?

10. What are the three major consumer trends? How do these impact consumer demand?

11. What plans of action may be used to reach consumers?

12. What is the distinction between mass marketing and market segmentation? Why and when are they used?

13. How is product positioning important in agrimarketing?

14. Why is world agricultural trade important to consumers? What are consumer's major concerns about imported products?

ACTIVITIES

1. Draw a map of the earth's continents, using Figure 11–2 as a guide. Visit the local supermarket and list at least two food items that you find from the continents on the map. Read the labels on the products to help identify where they are from. (You may also use other reference materials, including an atlas or geography book.)

2. Survey your class members or friends on the difficulty of consumer decision making. Have them rate decisions to buy items on a five-point scale (with 1 = easy, 2 = somewhat easy, 3 = average, 4 = somewhat difficult, and 5 = difficult). The items to rate include: loaf of bread, carton of milk, pair of shoes, fast-food hamburger, new pickup truck, and farm land. Feel free to add other items to the list. Analyze your information to determine the level of difficulty of making decisions. Ratings of all people you survey can be averaged for each item. The higher the average number, the more difficult the decision is to make.

3. Invite the person in charge of marketing for an agribusiness to serve as a resource person in class and explain the procedures used in marketing by his or her company.

Chapter 12

DEVELOPING MARKETING PLANS

How do you get where you want to go? How do you build something the way you want it? How do you get the money to buy something you want? The best way is to develop a plan and use it!

Success in agrimarketing involves planning. Without plans, people lack direction much as an individual who leaves on a trip without a destination. Going in any direction will get you some place. But you really won't know when you have completed the trip because you didn't know where you wanted to go.

Developing marketing plans is a way to figure out how to get more money from your work. And everyone wants more money!

Figure 12–1. Students are shown presenting a marketing plan before judges in national competition. (Both the National FFA Organization and the National Agricultural Marketing Association [NAMA] have student marketing plan competitons.) (Courtesy, National FFA Organization)

OBJECTIVES

The focus of this chapter is on developing plans for marketing in agriculture. After reading the chapter you will be able to:

- Describe the fundamentals on which marketing plans are based

- Explain the importance of developing marketing plans

- Describe the kinds of marketing plans

- List the major parts of a marketing plan and explain how each is developed

- Explain how a marketing plan is developed

- Identify the characteristics of a good marketing plan

- Explain marketing plan alternatives for farm commodities

TERMS

action plan
analysis of the market
annual marketing plan
budget
business plan
business proposition
evaluation
income
marketing expense
marketing objective
marketing plan
marketing strategy
net profit
new product plan
place
planning assumption
price
pricing strategy
primary research
process evaluation
product
product evaluation
promotion
research
secondary research
total returns

MARKETING PLANS

A *marketing plan* is a written statement that guides the marketing process. Marketing plans focus on moving products from the producer to the consumer. Sometimes they are prepared to market a new product—people have got to know about the product if we expect them to try it! At other times they focus on getting people to use more of a product that has been available for a long time.

Most marketing plans involve careful attention to a number of details. Information is collected in various ways to use in developing the plan. The information may be about consumers and competitive products. Experts in marketing are often consulted in preparing the plan. Written marketing plans may range from 5 to 50 or more pages in length.

Marketing plans are based on several fundamentals: business plan, marketing strategy, target market, and marketing mix.

BUSINESS PLAN

The first fundamental in developing a marketing plan is to have a business plan. A *business plan*, often known as a strategic plan, focuses on how the farm or agribusiness will be operated so that it is successful. The plan typically consists of several goals and ways and means of reaching them. It includes a time schedule to help in meeting deadlines along the way.

The objectives of a farm or agribusiness are part of its business plan. The overall plan of operation usually involves having a written or unwritten business plan. A written plan is best. Writing a plan forces people to be more specific and give careful attention to details.

A business plan specifies what is to be produced. Knowing what to produce requires studying consumer needs and preferences. A business plan describes how something is to be produced. Expansion and possible new directions in production may be included. In the agricultural industry, the overall objective is to produce a product or service that can be marketed. Consumers must want what you have available. Success in marketing leads to financial success or profit for the farm or agribusiness. Profit results when consumers are willing and able to buy a product or service at a price that more than covers the cost of production.

A business plan should include marketing strategies. Even though you may have the best product, it won't provide returns (profit) unless consumers know about it.

MARKETING STRATEGY

Marketing strategy explains how a farm or agribusiness will use its resources to meet its objectives. In most cases, farm produce loses its identity at the first handler or with the processor. Once the identity is lost, farmers have little opportunity to influence product value to buyers at other levels of the marketing system. Farmers must focus on maximizing value at the point of first sale. Some farmers choose to perform additional steps and sell directly to the consumer. For example, a farmer who markets "fresh from the farm" vegetables at a roadside stand can maintain identity with the consumer. Those who sell to processing plants lose their identity.

Agribusinesses that provide supplies and services to the farm or serve in the marketing channels may have advantages over farmers in preparing marketing strategies. Their products typically retain identity, such as with brand names. There is also a disadvantage: The companies' reputations are at stake because labels provide names and other identification. Companies can suffer if there is publicity about a product with a severe problem.

A marketing plan details strategies that will be used to market a product. A key element in developing a strategy and plan is to identify a target market.

TARGET MARKET

Some farms and most agribusinesses have a specific group or groups they wish to target for their products. These individuals are the target market. A target market is a well-defined group of present and potential customers for a product. In many cases, defining target markets is a part of the overall business plan. Defining a market determines what is produced.

Here are a few examples of target markets:

- **Feed manufacturing**—A feed mill that specializes in producing feed for horses would target its marketing efforts toward owners of horses. Advertising would be directed at horse enthusiasts. Feed would be produced in bags that can be easily handled. The product would be especially formulated to meet the nutritional needs of horses.

- **Fish fee lake**—An aquafarmer might establish a fee lake as part of a food fish farm. This would provide additional income for the aquafarmer and meet the needs of customers who like sport fishing. The target market is sport fishers who are busy and don't have time and money for long trips to fishing areas.

- **"Run about eggs"**—Some customers want eggs produced by chickens that are not confined in houses or cages. The hens are free to "run about" in large outside pens where they eat grass, insects, and other items rather than a controlled grain feed, as they would get in confinement. Farmers producing "run about eggs" would target their marketing to consumers who are willing to pay more for eggs in order to get this specific product.

MARKETING MIX

Many things influence marketing. Some can't be controlled; others can. Those variables that can be controlled form the marketing mix. The successful farm or agribusiness focuses on those things that can be controlled, such as the kind of product produced and how it is packaged.

Four variables can be controlled in marketing most products and services: product, place, promotion, and price. These are known as the four Ps. Marketing specialists frequently cite the importance of the four Ps. Farmers typically focus on the point where ownership first changes, such as at the grain elevator or stockyards. Unfortunately, they may have little say over the price they are offered. Many farmers don't have large volumes or don't link directly with consumers. Regardless, the four Ps are a part of marketing agricultural products.

Product

Product refers to what is produced. It is the good or service that can fill the needs of a consumer. Consumers are willing to pay more for a product that better meets their needs. The nature or form of a product can be changed to attract more consumers. Much of agricultural industry attempts to make products more satisfying to consumers. All of the processing activities deal with getting products into forms that consumers want.

Poultry can be used to describe the importance of product. Processing chickens allows consumers to eat chicken without having to deal with a live bird. People eat much more chicken now than they did years ago. They do so because the product is prepared and easy to cook. Most consumers do not want to buy a live chicken and go through the process of preparing it for cooking. A huge poultry industry has developed to meet the needs of consumers for easy preparation.

Place

For the convenience of consumers, a product must be readily available to them. *Place* is product availability to consumers. Marketing specialists frequently say that the right product must be at the right place, at the right time, and in the right amount. Products that are not available to customers can't be sold. This means that the producer doesn't make any money.

Many agricultural products are seasonal. Various approaches are used to overcome seasonality. The fresh tomato is a good example. Some producers grow tomatoes in greenhouses for marketing in the winter. Others may grow tomatoes in warm climates for shipping into the United States. Fresh tomatoes bring a higher price in the winter. This can offset the higher cost of greenhouse production or greater transportation. The tomato must be available in the supermarket when the customer goes shopping.

Figure 12–2. Outdoor advertising is used to promote low-cholesterol eggs to consumers.

Promotion

Promotion is trying to influence people to buy a product. It involves the producer communicating with potential customers. Advertising is very important in getting the word to masses of people. Radio, television, and newspapers are used to communicate with masses of people. Trade and farm magazines may be used for advertising to people in agricultural industry. Personal selling may be used with large items or when large amounts are involved, such as farm tractors and fertilizer.

Promotion makes people aware of a product or service. It focuses on providing information that will convince a person to try the product or service. Many times the information is targeted to a particular group. Farm machinery manufacturers target advertisements to farmers and related audiences. It does little good for them to advertise to the general public because most members of the general public never buy tractors.

Most farms don't have a large enough share of the market to justify promoting their products. As mentioned earlier, most farm products lose identity when they leave the farm. The broilers grown on one farm are like those grown on another after they have been graded and processed. Associations of farmers may promote consumption of a certain product. For example, beef producers may form associations to promote beef consumption.

Price

Price is the amount that the buyer will have to pay for a product or service. Many factors go into determining price. Certainly, the cost of producing a product must be considered. It can't usually be sold for less than the cost of production! Transportation costs also affect price. The

Figure 12–3. Labels on individual bananas are used to promote consumption.

price must provide a profit to the producer as well as all who handle the product in marketing.

The price also must be in line with that of competing products. Discounts and other incentives may be used to attract customers. Attractive prices are as important as the other Ps: product, place, and promotion. For example, farmers are going to buy from a supplier with the best price (assuming that product quality is equal). If one supplier sells ammonium nitrate for $220 a ton and another for $195 a ton, the farmer will buy at the lowest price.

REASONS TO DEVELOP MARKETING PLANS

Marketing plans are the result of planning marketing activities. The plans help farms and agribusinesses use limited resources in the most productive ways. Several reasons for developing marketing plans are:

- The farm or agribusiness is more likely to make a profit if careful attention has been given to planning.

- Limited resources are given the highest priorities. A plan specifies what is to be done. Resources aren't used on doing things that don't contribute to the objectives of the plan.

- All attention can focus in one direction. People know what their objectives are and can readily go about their work.

- Managers can better coordinate their work toward achieving objectives. Those without direction may move in several directions which never lead to the objectives.

- Changes in the environment can be handled more easily. Response can be made to new, competing products. Other factors can be dealt with.

- Careful planning assures that products are appealing to consumers. Planning forces people involved with marketing to study consumer preferences. Research provides good information for making decisions.

KINDS OF MARKETING PLANS

In general, there are two kinds of marketing plans: the new product plan and the annual marketing plan. New product development usually includes an investigation of the market and development of a plan. Farmers should always have a market before they produce a product. Agribusinesses need to determine if there will be customers before they produce something.

NEW PRODUCT PLANS

A *new product plan* should be developed before a product is produced. Determining whether or not to produce a product is a part of planning. If several new products are being considered, planning should be used to determine which is likely to be most profitable. If information developed in the plan shows that the product will not be profitable, the product should not be produced. Of course, many products aren't profitable the first year. Several years may be required to pay the costs of development and production. New product plans should cover a period of several years—often five or more.

Once a product is available, another approach to marketing plan development is needed. This is the annual marketing plan.

ANNUAL PLANS

The *annual marketing plan* is developed each year for continuing product

Figure 12–4. Boards of directors may be involved in approving marketing plans, such as this board for an association.

lines. Situations change. Consumers change. Products that were once popular may no longer be in demand.

Annual marketing plans are prepared for products or services that are already being marketed. These plans address changes in competition, consumer preferences, and improvements made in products.

Annual plans are sometimes parts of long-term plans that are revised each year. For example, a plan may be developed for a span of five years. Each year it is revised adding one year and removing the year that has passed.

PARTS OF A MARKETING PLAN

Marketing plans typically contain five parts. The focus is on starting with the current situation, determining the direction (goals), establishing ways and means of reaching goals, and assessing the level of success in achieving the goals. The parts of a marketing plan are often stated as both topics and questions, as follows:

Topic	Question
1. Analysis of the market	What is the situation?
2. Business proposition	Where are we going?
3. Action plan	How do we achieve our objectives?
4. Projected budget	What is the financial situation?
5. Evaluation	How well did we do?

PROCEDURES IN DEVELOPING A MARKETING PLAN

Each of the five parts of a marketing plan should be carefully prepared. In most cases, these are best applied in marketing to the final consumer. Supply manufacturers and service distributors use them for marketing to the farmer or rancher. Processors and distributors of food and fiber use them to market to the consumer. The procedures described here apply to farmers who market directly to consumers. Since many farm products are sent through processing and distribution channels, all of the details presented here may not apply. (A section later in the chapter gives more details on marketing farm products.)

ANALYSIS OF THE MARKET

Analysis of the market is collecting information about the market and studying it for meaning. Careful attention to details is required. The environment in which a product or service is to be marketed is determined. Considerable information is needed for this. The information must be accurate. If not, decisions may not work out as planned. A decision can be no better than the information used in making it!

Figure 12–5. Market analysis may be used to determine demand for live fish products such as tilapia or German carp.

Research

Research is careful and diligent study to gain knowledge about a market. Information is collected about the potential of the product in the marketplace. Two kinds of research may be used: primary and secondary.

Primary research involves gathering information directly from potential consumers. Scientific procedures should be used to survey people. Questionnaires may be developed and sent through the mail. Personal interviews using interview schedules may be conducted. First-hand observations may be made of potential customers, such as visiting farms to see what the situation is like. For example, observing weeds in crops may be just the information that is needed to market a new herbicide. It is very important to collect good information. Individuals trained in research may be needed to assist in various phases of primary research. Collecting primary information for marketing plans typically involves six steps.

STEP 1. Determine the information that is needed. Don't collect information that won't contribute to the plan. The information needed varies with the product to be marketed and the potential customer. Some general areas of information that may be included are:

- Identification of potential customers for the product or service
- Number of potential customers and their characteristics
- Problems the potential customers face related to the intended product
- Competing products the potential customers now use
- Experiences the potential customers have had with similar products
- Trends in areas related to the intended product

STEP 2. Develop a means for getting the needed information. This may include developing written questionnaires, interview schedules, and guidelines for making personal observations.

Mailed questionnaires are often used. However, getting the names and mailing addresses of people to be surveyed can pose a problem. Also, printing and mailing questionnaires requires money. The following suggestions will help to make questionnaires effective. Limit questionnaires to one or two pages. Include instructions so that the person receiving the questionnaire knows what to do. Word questions carefully and make them easy to answer. Provide an envelope with return address and postage paid. Find a way to encourage people to fill out questionnaires— reminder cards and telephone calls may be used. Remember that even with considerable effort, no more than 20 or 30 percent of the general population may return useable questionnaires. (A sample survey form is shown in Appendix B.)

Personal interviews can provide good information. Unfortunately, this approach is time consuming and may be met with resistance by some people. There are ways to make personal interviews successful. Contact individuals ahead of time to make an appointment to do the interview. Use a carefully worded written interview schedule. This assures that all people are asked the same questions. Limit personal interviews to a few minutes. An alternative to going to farms, agribusinesses, and homes for interviews is to conduct the interview by telephone.

First-hand observations can provide useful information. Windshield surveys are sometimes conducted. These involve driving through a community and observing conditions to get general background information. This approach isn't very scientific but can provide good input in decision making if the observations are carefully made.

STEP 3. Word the questions carefully. Make sure the questions get the information you want. Rating scales can be used to get the opinions of people about products or services. Questions followed by blanks for answers can be used to get more detailed information. Checklists can be used to assess opinions or interests. All questions should be field-tested and reviewed by experts prior to being used. This helps assure that the questions consistently get the correct information. Of course, information is no better than the accuracy of the answers. Question wording can influence accuracy. Respondents may not give exact information. Questions about income and related areas are threatening to people, and they don't like to answer them. When they do, they often give inaccurate information.

STEP 4. Gather the information. This involves implementing steps 1–3. Step 4 may require more time than thought. It may take six weeks to collect information by mail. Personal interviews require varying amounts of time, but several weeks may be needed to interview the necessary number of people even in a small community.

STEP 5. Tabulate and analyze the information. First, organize and categorize the information according to the questions asked. Various simple procedures can be used to summarize the information. Averages and frequencies (number indicating a certain response) are often used. More advanced statistical procedures can also be used, such as standard deviations, Chi Square, and analysis of variance. The services of a statistician may be needed for more advanced analysis. Once data have been compiled and analyzed, it is time to try to see what it means.

STEP 6. Draw meaning and interpret the findings. This involves making judgments that lead to conclusions and recommendations. Try to avoid personal biases and let the information speak for itself. Conclusions must always be based on the findings. Conclusions are statements about what the findings mean. Using conclusions, courses of action are developed. These are known as recommendations. The recommendations provide scientific direction for the marketing initiative.

Secondary research involves using information that has all ready been collected. This includes previous primary marketing studies, census data, chamber of commerce reports, courthouse records, research bulletins, employment and agricultural statistics services reports, and various publications. Secondary research is usually more economical than primary research. However, information from secondary sources may not be up to date. It also may focus on a different audience of potential customers than your main focus. Secondary information should always be assessed for accuracy. Most government documents provide good information. A general rule is to never collect as primary research information that is already available.

Areas for Analysis

Assessing the marketing situation requires looking at certain information about the potential customers. This information should be related to the product or service to be marketed. Four areas need to be analyzed in studying the market situation.

AREA 1. Potential customer profile and behavior. This summarizes the characteristics of potential buyers of the product or service being marketed. The information needed varies with what you are trying to market as well as the target market itself. It is collected through surveys of potential customers, reviews of census data, personal observations, interviews with authorities or key individuals who live or work in the area, and in other ways.

Here are two examples:

- **Lawn supplies for the home owner**—The retailer, distributor, or manufacturer of lawn supplies wants to know what customers need. Information on the age of the homes, income level of the owners, knowledge of the owners about home lawns, and climate are very useful. Age of the homes may indicate if lawns are being established for new homes or maintained and improved, as is the case with older homes. Information on income level indicates the amount of money available for lawn care. Home owners experienced in lawn care need less information, while those who don't know how to care for lawns need simple instructions and the assistance of sales representatives. Climate has a considerable impact on marketing strategy. Those in dry climates need sprinklers and those in cold climates need grasses that will grow in cool weather.

- **Livestock supplies for the farm or ranch**—Agribusinesses selling to farmers need to know the number and size of the farms, the kind of livestock produced, production practices that are followed, and other details. The skill of the producer and how the livestock are managed are other important considerations. Seasonal problems or outbreaks of disease could also influence marketing.

Figure 12–6. Barbed wire is stocked by this supplies store to meet consumer demand.

AREA 2. Strengths and weaknesses of the competition. Producers need to study the performance of similar products on the market. Knowing the characteristics of the products that compete with yours can help position your product. Here are some questions you should answer about the competition:

1. What are the prices of competing products?

2. What promotional strategies are competitors using?

3. How much volume do competitors sell?

4. Does the competition plan to expand?

5. Are competitors making a profit?

6. How do consumers view competitors' products?

7. What patents are involved with the product?

8. How would competitors react to a new product on the market?

9. Does the competition have adequate financing?

10. How strong is the management of the companies that produce the competing products?

Some of these questions will not be easy to answer. Sources of information include literature produced by the competitor, such as sales brochures; newspaper advertisements and articles; annual reports of the competitor; trade show displays; association and government reports; observations in stores where competitors' products are sold; talking with customers who use competitors' products; employees of the competitor; and friends and relatives.

AREA 3. Strengths and weaknesses of your product or service. Will your proposed product be successful? If the answer is "no," you should stop at this step or make changes to assure the success of your product. Personal biases must be overcome. You must look at your product objectively. The following questions may be helpful in assessing your strengths and weaknesses:

1. Will adequate finances be available to market the product?
2. Who are the major competitors?
3. What is the reputation of the competition?
4. What is your reputation with potential buyers?
5. How is your product unique and superior to that of the competition?
6. Will you be able to produce the volume needed?

AREA 4. Trends and forecasts. Careful attention to trends can provide valuable information. You should study data from the last few years to determine if the market is growing or shrinking. Changes in livestock or

Figure 12–7. Ornamental and vegetable plants are displayed in front
of a drug store in a rapidly-expanding residential area
of California. Many citizens in the area will be buying
plants to landscape their new homes.

crop production can have a huge impact on marketing. You want to produce something that is expanding in use, not shrinking. Study changes in amounts produced over the last 10 years or so. Investigate government policies as related to the product. Determine if new diseases or other threats to the livestock or crop have been discovered. Assess the general profit level of the farms and ranches. If farms are unprofitable and less of a product is being produced each year, it is not a good idea to invest in marketing something that would support that product. The demand simply won't be there!

DEVELOPING THE BUSINESS PROPOSITION

The *business proposition* is a statement of what is to be accomplished. It requires careful thought and study. Information obtained in the analysis of the market is very useful. The advice of close, trusted associates should be sought. Sometimes consultants are hired to help with this important part of the marketing plan. A draft of the proposition should be reviewed and rewritten until the final copy is the best that can be produced.

The business proposition typically has four sections: key planning assumptions, description of target market, listing of objectives, and a statement of the strategy to be used in marketing the product or service.

Planning Assumptions

A marketing plan must be based on good judgments about what is going to happen in the future. After the market has been analyzed, some sort of future direction is stated. These are known as *planning assumptions*. They are based on conclusions from the information obtained about the market. Typically, planning assumptions are the best possible predictions about future markets for a particular product or service.

Areas to consider when preparing planning assumptions for agricultural industry are farm numbers and production trends, availability of competitive products and services, how technology will likely change production methods, experience in other areas closely related to the product or service to be marketed, international developments related to the product or service, and the impact of government regulations. Three examples follow.

Assumption One. As the importation of rice increases, rice farmers in the United States will push to increase per acre yields while lowering the cost of production. Farmers will plant improved varieties of rice seed that are resistant to rice blast disease.

Assumption Two. As citizens become more health conscious, they will select foods that are known to contribute to good health. They will reject those that are high in substances that may harm health. Farmers and ranchers will receive higher prices for those products that contribute to health. The proportion of farm-raised fish in the human diet will increase.

Assumption Three. Middle-income consumers are becoming increasingly concerned about the sources of their food and production practices used. They will increasingly buy foods of known origin that are free of pesticide contamination and not typically available in chain supermarkets. Locally grown, on-farm vegetable sales will increase.

Target Market

The target market must be defined. This involves identifying and selecting customers who are most likely to buy what is produced. The "group" may be large and found all across the nation or small and based in a local community. Deciding on the target market includes assessing what is possible for the farm or agribusiness. Small farms or agribusinesses should focus on a local community or geographical area. Large farm cooperatives or corporations might focus on a national or international market. For example, one almond farmer would be unable to market beyond the local area. By joining with other almond farmers in a cooperative, the volume is large enough for a national marketing initiative. Three examples follow.

Target Market One. A supplier of rice used as seed determines that the target market for the new blast resistant rice variety will be all rice farmers.

Target Market Two. A local on-farm fish store chooses a target market of local citizens who are health conscious and like to eat fish. Nationally, a large processor or corporation may target groups of educated people who are most aware of health issues and have sufficient income to buy the fish product.

Target Market Three. A local vegetable farmer who operates an on-farm store and produces pesticide-free vegetables targets better educated and moderate income consumers who eat most of their meals at home. The target market may be further defined by where the people live and/or work.

Marketing Objectives

The *marketing objectives* are the goals stated in the business proposition. The objectives are what you aim to achieve with your marketing campaign. Objectives tell you where you want to "go." They are also the bases for determining if your marketing efforts have been successful. Results are compared to what you intended to do. Objectives influence how resources will be used in marketing. For example, if you are a small business and wish to reach local potential customers, advertising in the local newspaper, on radio, or with billboards may provide the most returns. It is obvious that advertising in a large national medium would not be a wise use of resources.

Marketing objectives must be written for easy comparison with outcomes. Objectives should be written for each supply or service that is offered, such as kind of pesticide sold by an agribusiness. Objectives should state the amount that is to be sold and the time by which this is to be done. The time is known as a deadline or time line, and is often stated by quarter, year, or five year period. Three examples follow.

Objective One. A supplier of rice used as seed sets a goal to sell resistant rice seed to five hundred farmers next year, with total sales for the company of $2.5 million.

Objective Two. A farmer who produces fish and has an on-farm live and dressed fish store determines that sales of fish will reach $3,000 per week by the end of December, 1996, with sales equally divided between live and dressed fish.

Objective Three. A local farmer who produces pesticide-free vegetables and operates an on-farm store projects sales of vegetables will reach $5,000 a week during the growing season in 1996. This objective could be improved by specifying the kinds of vegetables and the dollar amount for each. The amount of each vegetable the farmer plants depends on the estimate of sales of each. If there is more demand for tomatoes than onions, more tomatoes should be planted.

Marketing Strategy

The details of the plan for achieving the objectives make up the marketing strategy. It is the ways and means used in carrying out the marketing plan. (Chapter 11 presents additional information on marketing strategy.)

The strategy selected must make it possible to achieve the objectives. Strategy and objectives must be in balance. Strategy statements should lead to the fulfillment of objectives, but should not be overly ambitious. Of course, it is okay to exceed a goal but the strategy should not waste resources on things not needed to achieve the objectives.

Strategies vary for each farm or agribusiness and supply or service being marketed. Good judgment is needed. Being informed on trends in demand for the product or service and of the supply available from competitors is essential. Key points to consider in developing a strategy are overall agricultural economy, production trends, likely actions of competitors, government programs and policies, climate patterns and changes, and consumer income and preferences. Three examples follow.

Strategy One. A supplier of rice used as seed will take several steps to reach 500 farmers and convince them to plant blast-resistant seed. Target advertising will be placed in local newspapers and rice grower publications. The supplier will host field days in rice producing areas, small group meetings (with complimentary dinner), and exhibits at farm shows. On-farm calls by marketing representatives and direct mailings may also be used. A price discount will be offered those who buy their seed by March 1. In addition, incentives will be offered local distributors of the rice seed.

Strategy Two. A farmer who produces fish and has an on-farm live and dressed fish store will promote the product with advertisements in the local newspaper, on the local radio station, and with attractive signs on the road. A one-day open house will be held with demonstrations of how to cook fish and free taste-size samples of cooked fish for all who attend. A door prize drawing of $50 in free dressed fish will be given to someone who attends the open house.

Strategy Three. A local farmer who produces pesticide-free vegetables and operates an on-farm store will advertise in the local newspaper and on the local radio station as the season begins. Special price incentives will be offered during the first week of the season. Cooking demonstrations will be scheduled throughout the season. All customers will be extended an invitation to tour the farm where the crops are grown and inspect pesticide-free farming practices for themselves.

ACTION PLAN

The *action plan* is the product mix that will be used in marketing. It is based on the strategy that has been developed. Action plans include four areas of product mix, as presented earlier in the chapter: product, price, place, and promotion. Ways the four Ps are used in developing a marketing plan are presented here.

Product

The action plan must outline how to attract buyer (consumer) attention to your product. The product or service must be readily available and appealing to them. Customers must feel that your product is superior to the others on the market. The advantages of your product or service over that of your competition must be stressed. What you have must be something the consumer wants. It must also be attractively designed and easy to get and use. It must be of good quality and live up to expectations.

Figure 12–8. A variety of different milk products are offered to appeal to the wide range of consumer preferences.

Ways must be found to compete with other similar products or services for consumer attention. If it is a product that is displayed, space must be available for it. Competitive products may have to be moved to another location to make room. Shelf space must sometimes be bought and installed in the retail store.

Many agricultural products undergo processing before reaching the consumer. This gets the product into a desired form. If perishable, the product must be preserved to prevent loss of quality.

Price

Price is important. It must be accepted by customers and competitive with similar products on the market. It must also be high enough to make a profit for all who are involved over the long run. In some cases, prices are reduced to attract customers and promote sales. This is a short-run tactic to promote your product or service.

Prices are set with several factors in mind. General trends must be considered, especially those in agriculture related to your product or service. How competitors set prices is always helpful. Price is most definitely influenced by the cost of producing what you have. A general rule is to set the price at a level for an appropriate profit—not too low or too high. Discounts can always be given to promote sales. After the promotion, the price returns to the original level. Customers will see that the price hasn't increased, and will understand that the sale is over!

Place

In the marketing plan, place refers to getting the product to the customer. It may involve shipping it long distances or merely making it accessible at a local store.

Agricultural products and services are typically sold directly to the consumer or indirectly through wholesalers, retailers and other agents. Products must reach the consumer in good condition if marketed through indirect channels. All individuals involved in grading, processing, storing, hauling, and other areas share in assuring a quality product. Various wholesalers and retailers must be lined up to handle the product. Products must arrive on time at the right place and in good condition. Products that arrive late may be of little use. Those that get there early may spoil before they are used. Timing is a critical part of "place."

Promotion

The marketing plan must spell out how information will be communicated to potential customers. Various forms of advertising may be used. Personal selling may be appropriate for larger, more expensive items or for large quantities of less expensive items. Sometimes known as face-to-face selling, personal selling is time consuming but effective with some products and services. It is often used with farm machinery. Salespersons may call on farms that use large volumes of fertilizer, seed, or chemicals.

Figure 12–9. Supermarkets often use advertisements in newspapers to attract customers.

Most promotional activities require money. Advertising is expensive. Some people try to use publicity, which amounts to free advertising. A good example is a feature story in a local newspaper about a new farm product or the fine fruit available at a local orchard. Small town papers will often run stories and photographs of local interest.

Salespeople may be given incentives to sell a product or service. Commissions and bonuses may be increased to get additional sales activity.

PROJECTED BUDGET

A *budget* is a statement of anticipated expenses and income. In marketing plans, the budget refers to expenses and income for the marketing initiative.

Expenses

Money must be available to finance marketing activities. These are the *marketing expenses.* Budgets usually have several lines of expense. The product must be produced. Advertisements must be bought. Distribution channels must be developed. All costs must be accounted for and included. Marketing plan development includes a budget that estimates the costs involved in marketing the product or service. The cost items to include in a budget are:

- **Cost of obtaining and/or producing the products or services to be sold**—This is how much what you sell will cost you. It refers to the amount required to produce the product or service yourself or to buy it from another producer.

- **Advertising**—This refers to radio, television and newspaper advertisements; billboards; direct mail; posters for store displays; etc.

- **Sales promotion**— This includes incentives to sales personnel, participation in field days and trade shows, setting up demonstration plots on farms or other demonstrations of how a product is used, and other promotional activities.

- **Management and general areas**—This includes salaries for clerical and managerial personnel, travel, telephone, office and other rent, postage, printing, and supplies.

- **Human resource development**—Costs involved in training sales personnel are included here.

- **Sales personnel costs**—These are the costs associated with operating a sales force. It includes salaries and benefits, travel, telephone, and other items.

Income

Income is the return from marketing. The product or service will be exchanged for money, which provides income. The budget in a marketing plan will estimate the volume that will be sold and how much money will result. The budget is based on sales projections. It is very important to use realistic sales projections. Typically, sales projections are based on monthly, quarterly, or, at most, yearly sales. Accurate projections are essential. Otherwise, an unrealistic budget might be developed. A carefully planned budget will show anticipated results if the expenditures are made to implement the marketing plan.

The total income from the amount sold is known as *total returns*. After total returns are determined, all costs associated with marketing are deducted. This leaves what all businesses want: *net profit*! In some cases, the budget in the marketing plan may show a loss. This should occur only in the short run. If losses continue, the marketing plan should be carefully studied and possibly abandoned if it is unprofitable.

EVALUATION

Marketing plans should be assessed to see how well they are doing. This is known as *evaluation*.

Evaluation may occur in two ways: process and product.

Process

Process evaluation involves observing the plan as it is being implemented. Sometimes situations change and the plan will need to be modified.

A marketing plan should never be so inflexible that minor adjustments can't be made. People who are involved in implementing the plan can provide information. Clients and customers can provide input. Certainly, changes by competitors will require some minor adjustments. Sometimes new government rules will be issued that impact a marketing plan.

Product

Product evaluation involves determining how well the plan did. This is done after the plan has been implemented and carried to completion (or partial completion in the case of a multi-year plan). The process compares what was proposed with what actually happened. Good records are essential. Everyone involved will likely need to keep records. The records will need to be compiled and summarized into one final report.

The most important part of evaluation is determining how well the plan performed financially. Were the sales goals achieved? Was a profit made?

HOW A MARKETING PLAN IS DEVELOPED

Marketing plans should be written for most agricultural products and services. Small producers who don't write marketing plans typically have unwritten plans in their minds. They have thought through the process and arrived at a decision. Medium-size and large farmers may find marketing plans more difficult to prepare. This is partly because of unique characteristics of production agriculture. Regardless, everyone can benefit from a written marketing plan. When written, marketing plans force the writer to give more attention to the details of the entire enterprise.

Marketing plans may be written by individuals, teams of individuals (with one person serving as the lead writer), or by consultants hired to write a plan.

STEPS IN DEVELOPING A MARKETING PLAN

A step-by-step process should be followed in developing a marketing plan. This will assure that all areas are addressed. Also, following key steps makes the process easier.

Here are some suggested steps to follow in developing marketing plans:

1. Gather information related to marketing the proposed product or service. This may include information about general trends in society as well as international trade and government regulations. Newspapers, magazines, and other reports may be useful. Seminars, workshops, and field days may provide good information as well as the opportunity to network with other people who have knowledge and skill. Competitors' publications also may be useful.

2. Review the parts of a marketing plan. Know what you need to write. Sample marketing plans developed for use in other situations may be helpful.

3. Prepare for the writing process. This involves collecting secondary and primary information. Once collected, the information needs to be compiled and studied for meaning.

Figure 12–10. Computers are useful in writing marketing plans.

4. Begin writing.

   a. Prepare a tentative statement analyzing the market. This is based on the information gained through the primary and secondary research.

   b. Prepare a tentative business proposition. Write the planning assumptions, identify the target market, specify the objectives, and describe a marketing strategy.

   c. Develop a tentative action plan. Include the four Ps: product, price, place, and promotion.

   d. Develop a tentative budget. This involves careful assessment of anticipated costs and returns from the marketing venture.

   e. Prepare a tentative statement of evaluation procedures. Be sure that this will result in an accurate picture of how well the plan performed.

5. Carefully review the draft of the marketing plan. Get trusted associates to read it and provide suggestions. Assess the plan. Determine if it is realistic and practical. Note improvements that need to be made.

6. Revise the draft of the plan. Use the suggestions received from trusted associates. Make needed copies of the final document.

7. Prepare for implementation of the plan. Organize personnel and procedures for efficient and effective work flow.

8. Implement the plan. Use process evaluation to make needed adjustments along the way.

9. Evaluate the plan. Determine if the objectives were achieved and if a profit was made. This is product evaluation, which occurs after a plan has been carried out. Revise the plan as needed.

Steps 1-9 can be repeated for another year or product.

CHARACTERISTICS OF A GOOD MARKETING PLAN

A good marketing plan provides the best possible opportunity for success in marketing. A marketing effort can be no better than the plan that is used. (A sample marketing plan is presented in Appendix A.)

There are several criteria that can be used to assess a marketing plan.

- **Organization**—All five of the major parts of a plan should be used and sequenced properly, as described earlier in the chapter. Missing parts may mean that the item was not considered in developing the plan. Incomplete information may result in poor decisions. The five major parts form the body of the plan. Title and cover pages may be added as well as supporting tables and information in appendices.

- **Accuracy**—All supporting information must be as accurate as possible. Interpretations of the information must be correct. There is no room for errors in a written plan. Proper communication skills should be followed. Words should be spelled correctly. Attention should be given to proper grammar and punctuation. Any mathematics should be accurate, such as in the budget. Budget errors can present income and expenses above or below what is realistic.

- **Attractive**—Marketing plans should be neatly typed or prepared using word processing programs and quality printers. Manuscript arrangement on the page should be pleasing to the reader. Appropriate margins (one inch for the top, right, and bottom and one and one-half inches for the left margin) should be used. Marketing plans should have an attractive cover and be bound in some way, such as spiral bound or stapled. Plans are usually on white bond paper.

- **Length**—Marketing plans may vary considerably in length, with 5 to 50 or more pages being common. Plans should be written concisely so that the length is kept to a minimum; however, they should always be long enough to present the essential information.

- **Specifications**—Sometimes marketing plans are required to conform to certain specifications. Large corporations may require all departments to use a standard format. Agribusinesses and farms may be required to follow the directions of banks or other lending agencies. High school and college students sometimes prepare for marketing plan competition. In this case, the specifications should be carefully followed. If not, the plan may receive a lower score or be disqualified.

CONSIDERATIONS IN MARKETING FARM COMMODITIES

Farmers and ranchers must often consider additional areas in developing marketing plans. This is because most of them do not market to the final consumer. This doesn't mean that they don't prepare marketing plans. It means that they must consider additional areas in developing their plans.

Farmers and ranchers who produce crops and livestock that are sold to dealers or processors use different approaches in marketing. The emphasis is more on market analysis and influencing the price received at the first point of sale, such as at a packing shed or processing plant. The marketing plan must address these situations. They prepare the same plan but approach the market analysis and business proposition differently.

The major decisions farmers and ranchers must make in marketing plan development are deciding what to produce; deciding when, where, and how to market; and using pricing strategies.

DECIDING WHAT TO PRODUCE

The decision about what to produce is based on what has a reasonable chance of making a profit. Many things happen during a growing season. Crops or livestock can be lost. Production nationwide can exceed expectations and prices can be lower than anticipated.

Forecasting price is very difficult. The farmer must get the best possible information to use in decision making. With some products, forward contracting (signing a contract before production to establish a profitable price for the harvested product), and futures marketing can help overcome un-

Figure 12–11. Deciding what to produce involves considerable risk, such as the near total loss that was experienced by this tree farmer from an ice storm.

certainty. Deciding what to produce is not easy, but can be more systematic when marketing plan procedures are followed.

DECIDING WHEN, WHERE, AND HOW TO MARKET

Producers typically have several alternatives for crops or livestock that are grown. The producer must decide which of the marketing functions he or she is willing to perform.

Some producers market directly to consumers and perform all of the marketing functions. This is sometimes known as "cutting out the middleman." Performing these functions adds to the need for labor and equipment and may increase the risk. Additional management skills are needed for marketing directly to consumers.

Other producers market to packing sheds or processing plants. Producers must decide if it is better to take the price offered by those who will market to the consumer (middlemen) or if it is better to perform all of the functions.

It is impractical for most farmers to consider direct marketing of certain crops, such as marketing wheat as flour or milk as cheese. Just think what it would cost to have a flour mill or cheese plant! Farmers can't afford this approach unless they form cooperatives or make other arrangements. Sometimes farmers go into the processing business. They establish facilities that buy raw products from other farmers and process them into the desired products.

USING PRICING STRATEGIES

A pricing strategy is a plan for getting an acceptable price. Farmers usually can't set prices but they can select from a range of alternatives. This may involve using futures and options, marketing directly from farm to consumer, selling to processors or dealers, marketing through other products (such as feeding corn to hogs—the corn is marketed through the hogs), and other ways. Well-informed people will likely be better at marketing.

Some examples of how different marketing choices affect prices follow.

- **Market locally and avoid transportation**—The price paid may be lower but the cost of transportation is avoided.

- **Market a distance from the farm and pay transportation**—The additional price received over local marketing must be equal to or greater than the cost of transportation.

- **Market on the farm**—On-farm marketing is possible for some produce and for farms that are in good locations. For example, an on-farm store could be used to meet the needs of a niche market for particular products, such as farm-fresh, pesticide-free fruit and "baby" vegetables near a large city.

- **Use pricing contracts with buyers that delay decisions about price until after delivery**—The question here is, "Will the price go up after the crop has been planted and harvested?" Producers should only deal with buyers who have good reputations.

- **Use futures markets**—This requires considerable knowledge of buying and selling commodities, using brokers and traders, and dealing with commodity exchanges.

- **Store the produce on the farm for later delivery**—Corn can be stored on the farm until the price goes up. Of course, a good storage bin costs money to own. Further, a farmer may need the money now and can't delay selling the crop.

- **Form cooperative marketing associations with other producers in the area**—Farm cooperatives can help with marketing in several ways. Some provide all of the functions to connect the producer with the consumer. Others assemble, grade, and store produce and locate buyers for the growers.

SUMMARY

Marketing plans are written statements that guide the marketing process. A good understanding of marketing is needed to develop a plan. Understanding marketing strategies, target markets, and marketing mix (the four Ps) serves as the foundation for developing the marketing plan. Two kinds of marketing plans are used: new product and annual. The overall contents of each tend to be the same. The marketing strategies may vary.

Marketing plans contain five major parts: market analysis, business proposition, action plan, projected budget, and evaluation. These parts become the five major steps in developing the plan.

Marketing plans can be developed by individuals, teams or committees, consultants, or others. The procedures used should result in the best possible plan. A good plan is well organized and includes accurate information. A plan should also be attractive and only long enough to cover the subject.

Marketing plans have often been developed by agribusinesses or farms and ranches for use in marketing to the final consumer. Commercial farms and ranches that market in other ways have often failed to prepare marketing plans. They should develop marketing plans. Additional strategies may be needed related to pricing. Farm producers usually have a number of alternatives in selling to the processor or first handler in the marketing system. Decisions about these pricing strategies require accurate information and good judgment. Marketing cooperatives may be useful to some farmers and ranchers.

CHAPTER SELF-CHECK

Match the following terms with the correct definitions:

    a. pricing strategy

    b. promotion

    c. price

    d. marketing strategy

    e. annual marketing plan

    f. primary research

    g. business proposition

    h. marketing plan

    i. planning assumption

    j. marketing objective

_____   written statements that guide the marketing process

_____   how resources are used to meet objectives

_____   trying to influence people to buy a product

_____   plans developed each year for continuing product lines

_____   amount the buyer pays for a product or service

_____ gathering information directly from potential customers

_____ statement of what is to be accomplished

_____ statement of the ends or goals to be reached

_____ conclusions from information about the market

_____ plan for getting an acceptable price

QUESTIONS AND PROBLEMS FOR DISCUSSION

1. How are the following related to the marketing plan: business plan, marketing strategy, target market, and marketing mix?

2. Why are marketing plans important?

3. What are the kinds of marketing plans? Distinguish between them.

4. What are the five major parts of a marketing plan? What question does each answer?

5. How is an analysis of the market made? What research is needed? What areas of analysis should be included?

6. How is a business proposition developed? Name and describe the four major sections of a business proposition.

7. How is the action plan developed? What are the four major parts?

8. What is a budget? Why is a budget important? What areas are included in a budget?

9. What is evaluation? Why is it important? What two kinds of evaluation are used?

10. What steps should be followed in developing a marketing plan? Briefly describe each step.

11. What are the characteristics of a good marketing plan?

12. What are the major decisions that farmers and ranchers make as related to marketing? What is the importance of each?

ACTIVITIES

1. Prepare a marketing plan as a class or committee activity. Follow the procedures described in this chapter. If available, obtain copies of regulations for student marketing plan competitions, such as those of the National FFA Organization or the National Agricultural Marketing Association. Assistance is also available from the agricultural education or agricultural economics department at the land-grant college in your state. Present the plan developed to students in your class or in competition with students from other schools. (Note: Refer to Appendix A for an example of a marketing plan.)

2. Invite a marketing manager for an agribusiness to serve as a resource person in class and explain the marketing plan process used by his or her business.

Chapter 13

SELLING IN THE AGRICULTURAL INDUSTRY

Selling is a part of everyone's life. Most things are purchased from some type of salesperson. Salespeople have a great impact on the overall success of their companies. Salespeople provide the connection between producers and customers. Without competent, knowledgeable, and customer-oriented salespeople agricultural businesses cannot be successful.

Agricultural businesses in America are very competitive. In our free enterprise system, many businesses sell similar products and services. For example, you can purchase a rose bush from a specialty retail nursery, a wholesale nursery, a chain nursery, or a discount store. Because customers

Figure 13–1. This feed salesperson is helping a customer determine the type of poultry feed to purchase. The salesperson needs to have knowledge of the feed products, knowledge of the selling process, and an understanding of the customer.

can purchase the same product or service from more than one business, it is important that businesses provide courteous and friendly service to customers. If customers do not receive courteous and knowledgeable help from salespeople at one business, they will purchase from another business. To be an effective salesperson, you need to provide the assistance customers expect.

Competent agricultural salespeople have both product knowledge and knowledge of the selling process. Although on the surface selling may appear simple, it is a complex process that involves an understanding of human psychology, communication, human relations, and economics.

TERMS

bartering
buyer benefits
buying excuse
buying motive
buying signals
cold call
cool calling
decided customer
emotional buying
hidden objection
just-looking customer
leads
manufacturing process
need
patronage buying
product buying
product composition
product features
product performance
prospecting
rational buying
real objection
sales resistance
salesperson
selling
targeting customers
trial close
undecided customer
want

OBJECTIVES

Knowledge of the selling process will help you prepare for a career in sales and assist you in becoming a more efficient consumer. This chapter provides information about the selling process and the role that selling plays in the success of an agricultural company. Upon completion of this chapter, you will be able to:

- Describe the functions of selling in agriculture

- Explain the history of selling

- List the four groups of customers dealt with in agriculture

- Describe what motivates people to buy

- Select questions and methods for determining customer needs and wants

- Explain the five steps in making a sale

- Describe the types of customers that salespeople deal with daily

- Explain the process of prospecting for customers

- Describe the kinds of product information a sales person needs

- Explain at least three approaches for opening a sales presentation

- Describe common ways of handling customer objections

- Describe common closing techniques used in selling

- Explain how to give a sales presentation using an agricultural product or service

OVERVIEW OF SELLING

When a customer goes into a store to purchase pet food or bedding plants, the person who waits on the customer is called a *salesperson*. Salespeople assist customers in selecting products that fulfill their needs. As payment for the products, the customer gives the salesperson money. This process of exchange is termed *selling*. Although the process of selling appears simplistic, if customers do not know what they want selling becomes more complex. For example, a customer wants to buy a lawnmower and has seen an advertisement about a new quiet electric mower. This customer may want to know if that mower will work on a one-acre lawn. The salesperson must provide information to assist the customer in making the best buying decision. Selling also may involve negotiating price, assisting with credit arrangements, or arranging for a trade in of an old lawnmower. Selling is a problem-solving process. During this process the salesperson: (1) finds out what the customer needs, (2) provides the customer with choices, (3) helps the customer select the best solution, and (4) solves the problem.

The customer is "king" of the selling process. Customers are the reason companies are in business. Therefore, selling must center around customers—their needs, tastes, and buying habits. The ultimate goal is to satisfy the customer.

HISTORY OF SELLING

If every person was self-sufficient and did not interact with others to acquire food, clothing, and shelter there would be no need for selling. However, in our society selling is a necessary part of the process through which we obtain the things we need to live. Trading or *bartering* were the earliest forms of selling. These involve exchanging one item for another. Trading and bartering still go on today. Many local newspapers publish

Figure 13–2. Bartering in ancient civilizations of the Middle East was the accepted way to do business. (Courtesy, The Bettmann Archive)

daily or weekly columns. Some neighborhoods have well-established systems of trading or bartering. Examples include trading a portion of a crop for labor in harvesting the crop, and trading the use of vacation homes in different parts of the United States or world.

To move from a system of trading to one of selling, there needs to be an acceptable medium of exchange. In the United States, our medium of exchange is the dollar. Because the dollar is accepted worldwide, Americans enjoy a secure medium of exchange for goods and services.

In early America, most food purchases did not require a middleman or salesperson because the farmer sold directly to the consumer. The role of the salesperson evolved as agriculture and other industries became more specialized. Specialization encouraged producers to become more efficient by directing all of their time and energy toward efficient production. This allowed processors to focus full-time on processing. These changes made salespeople necessary between suppliers, producers, and processors. Some of the major functions of salespeople in the agricultural industry include establishing product prices, bringing buyers and sellers together, and providing information and education on new innovations.

In early American agriculture, salespeople traveled from town to town demonstrating and informing farmers about new inventions, such as the cotton gin and the reaper. Today, salespeople often demonstrate new technology to customers at retail stores, wholesale markets, or national and international trade shows. It is interesting that Uncle Sam, the symbolic personification of the United States of America, is based on a salesman,

Figure 13–3. The symbolic personification of our country, Uncle Sam, is based on Samuel Wilson, a salesman from Troy, New York.

Samuel Wilson, of Troy, New York. He sold provisions to the army during the War of 1812.

Selling has evolved from trading and bartering to an exchange of goods for money. Agriculture has always been at the center of evolution and change in the selling of goods and services. As agriculture has changed from a production oriented industry to a service oriented industry, more sales and marketing personnel have been added to the selling process. They insure the efficient movement of goods and services from one level of activity to the next.

SELLING FUNCTIONS IN THE AGRICULTURAL INDUSTRY

Producers are the focus of the agricultural industry at all levels. Salespeople relate to producers in three ways: they sell supplies and services to producers; they market food and fiber products to wholesalers, retailers, or consumers; and they sell the services that producers provide for others or need themselves.

SELLING TO PRODUCERS

Farmers and ranchers are the largest group of producers in the agriculture industry. However, such production segments as food and fiber processors, timber producers, aquaculture producers, and nursery and floral crop producers are also significant parts of the agricultural industry. All production segments of the agriculture industry require salespeople to sell them supplies, services, and materials that enable them to produce food and fiber products. For example, salespeople sell nursery producers such things as equipment and nursery supplies, seed and plant materials, fertilizer, plant media, and greenhouses.

Salespeople who sell to producers work in a variety of environments. Some work in retail farm supply stores and wholesale nursery supply outlets, while others travel to production locations and meet with producers. Many salespeople are employed by catalog companies or as telephone marketers. Agricultural salespeople sell products ranging from fertilizer and lumber to tractors and floral supplies. Regardless of the product, it is important that the salesperson know the product and the needs of the producer. To understand the needs of the producer, the salesperson must learn about how producers in that segment of the agricultural industry interact and communicate. It is important to know what challenges face the industry and what specific problems producers need help to solve.

SELLING FOR PRODUCERS

Most agricultural products are sold several times before reaching the final user, the consumer. For example, some farmers sell directly to consumers through farmers' markets or roadside produce stands. Other farmers sell to brokers or wholesalers who, in turn, sell to retailers. Wholesalers buy from individual producers and assemble large quantities of products. They often add value to the products and resell them to retail stores. The retail store then sells the product to the consumer.

There are millions of jobs in agricultural sales that are invisible to the public. Salespeople sell agricultural products for producers to processors, wholesalers, and retailers. Without salespeople working at each level of the selling process the consistent flow of product from the producer to the consumer would not be possible. For example, a dairy producer sells milk to a processor who manufactures several different products (adds value to the milk) such as cheese, whipping cream, and sour cream. The processor employs a team of salespeople who sell the milk products to food wholesalers. In turn, wholesalers employ teams of salespeople to sell the products to retail stores. Retail stores employ sales forces to sell to consumers. In summary, agricultural salespeople work with four major groups of customers: producers, wholesalers, retailers, and consumers.

PROVIDING SERVICES

The success of a salesperson is based on his or her ability to solve problems for customers. In the process of problem solving or selling, a number of different services are provided. The most common and essential service is providing technically accurate and up-to-date information. However, a range of services are provided by salespeople. Salespeople may provide credit and financial services. Soil and leaf tissue analysis to determine soil nutrient deficiencies for making fertilizer recommendations may be offered. Ration formulation is another service. Some salespeople produce newsletters featuring issues and challenges of various commodities or offer seminars and short courses for producers. Competitive companies have recognized that they must provide services to the customer. These services assist customers in making the right choice of product for their situation today. Producers that know how to properly use the product or service are motivated to be customers over a long period of time.

Figure 13–4. Sales representative in the San Joaquin Valley of California examining cotton plants for insects and disease. Successful sales representatives provide services to producers to assist them in solving problems. (Courtesy, Merek Company, AgVet Division)

CUSTOMER BUYING PROCESS

Every customer consciously or unconsciously follows a series of four steps prior to buying a product: (1) figuring out needs, (2) looking for facts to fulfill needs, (3) finding a solution, and (4) reaffirming the choice.

Success in sales is directly related to how well a salesperson understands the mental process that the buyer goes through. The salesperson then must respond to the customer in a positive and persuasive manner. Therefore, the buying motive becomes the bases for the selling process that will be discussed later in this chapter. The steps that customers go through in making a buying decision are listed in the order that customers generally complete them. However, every customer will go through these steps differently, and each customer may require different facts in order to make a choice.

STEP ONE: FIGURING OUT NEEDS

No customer will buy unless he or she feels a need. Sometimes people do not know they have needs until they are helped to realize them. They may not know there is a product or service that can make them more productive or profitable, increase their personal satisfaction, or alleviate problems. The salesperson plays an important role in helping customers become aware of their needs and assisting them in selecting products or services to satisfy their needs. The scenario in Figure 13-5 demonstrates how a salesperson greets a customer and determines her need to purchase bedding plants.

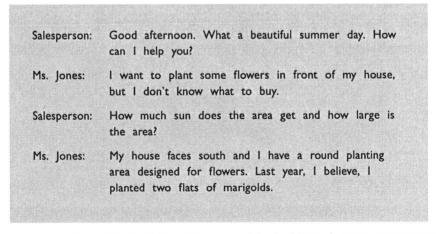

Salesperson:	Good afternoon. What a beautiful summer day. How can I help you?
Ms. Jones:	I want to plant some flowers in front of my house, but I don't know what to buy.
Salesperson:	How much sun does the area get and how large is the area?
Ms. Jones:	My house faces south and I have a round planting area designed for flowers. Last year, I believe, I planted two flats of marigolds.

Figure 13-5. Determining a need for bedding plants.

Figure 13–6. This customer discusses her need for bedding plants
with a salesperson.

In this situation, the customer had a need for bedding plants to beautify
her front yard. The salesperson has begun to help the customer identify
her need, but now she is looking for ways to fill that need

STEP TWO: LOOKING FOR FACTS

Once a customer identifies a need, he or she will look for information.
If the facts are not available immediately, the customer may move on to
another store. Customers obtain information about agricultural needs from
friends and neighbors, radio and television, magazines, cooperative extension experts, private consultants, salespeople, agricultural instructors, librar-
ies, and product brochures.

In some cases, a lot of facts are needed before a buying decision can
be made. For example, if you are investing several thousand dollars in a
new tractor it may take a month to assemble all of the facts. However only
a small investment is at stake if you are buying a flat of bedding plants.
You may be able to obtain the necessary facts from the salesperson to make
the buying decision in a few minutes. If the salesperson is not attentive
to the customer's need for facts, the customer may lose interest and desire
to buy. Using questions, salespeople are able to provide the information
necessary to satisfy the customer's needs and determine the interest and
the desire of the customer to purchase the product. Also, the salesperson
can stimulate interest and desire to purchase by demonstrating how the

product will meet the needs of the customer. Figure 13–7 shows how a salesperson uses questions to find out what the customer needs.

Salesperson:	Were you pleased with the marigolds you purchased last year?
Ms. Jones:	No, I did not like the color. They were too gold, I wanted bright yellow.
Salesperson:	We have yellow marigolds and many other kinds of bedding plants. May I show you our selection?
Ms. Jones:	Well, I would be interested in seeing your yellow marigolds and other yellow flowering plants.
Salesperson:	Here are three yellow marigold varieties that you might be interested in purchasing.
Ms. Jones:	I don't see any flowers, how do they differ in color?
Salesperson:	Can I show you our demonstration garden where we have these varieties flowering? It will help you decide which variety to purchase.
Ms. Jones:	I like the shortest yellow variety, but how do I know that the plants I buy will be that color and size?
Salesperson:	We guarantee that the plant varieties sold will perform the same as in the demonstration garden. Do you think the short yellow marigold variety will work for you?

Figure 13–7. Questions are used by salespeople to assist customers in determining their needs.

Note that the salesperson involved the customer in this step. Information was provided and the customer selected the variety that she preferred from the demonstration garden.

STEP THREE: FINDING A SOLUTION

Customers must be convinced that the product meets his or her need and then decide to purchase it. In this step, the salesperson determines the customer's convictions by obtaining positive responses to questions about the product's features and benefits. This step will take more time when more than one person is involved in making the decision. Educated, informed, and more progressive customers often ask additional questions. Salespeople should also expect to spend more time with customers making long-term purchases that require large investments or with cautious people when the purchase involves considerable risk. If answers to questions are positive, the salesperson should ask the customer to buy. It is important for the salesperson to recognize the step that the customer is at so the sale can be closed as quickly as possible. For further insights into this step, Figure 13–8 continues the bedding plant sales example.

Ms. Jones:	I like the way it looks, but does it require much care and is it disease resistant?
Salesperson:	Marigolds require very little care. However, they do require regular watering and fertilization to insure continuous blooms throughout the summer. They tend to be disease resistant. Marigolds are a good choice and this variety is new this year.
Ms. Jones:	How expensive are two flats?
Salesperson:	These marigolds are on sale today, $8.95 per flat. You are getting an excellent value. Normally, these sell for $12 per flat. How many flats can I get for you today?
Ms. Jones:	I would like two flats of the short yellow marigolds and some mulch and fertilizer.
Salesperson:	You have made an excellent choice. Be sure to let us know how well these marigolds perform for you. If you have any problems with them, please give me a call or stop by the nursery. Let me show you the fertilizer and mulch options that we have available.

Figure 13–8. The salesperson assists the customer in finding a solution to her bedding plant needs.

STEP IV: MAKING THE RIGHT CHOICE

In the final stage customers want to know that they made the best choice or the smartest buy. The salesperson needs to reassure the customer that he or she has made the right decision and that the company will stand behind the product. It is not only important for this sale, but will help obtain sales with that customer in the future. An example of how salespeople should reinforce the customer's choice is presented in Figure 13-8.

Figure 13–9. The salesperson reassures the customer that she has made a good selection. Both the customer and the salesperson express their positive feelings through their smiles.

Buying Decision Steps	Selling skills
Determining Needs	Greet the customer. Ask questions. Listen to what the customer needs or wants.
Looking for Facts	Provide up-to-date information. Demonstrate features and benefits.
Finding a Solution	State how features and benefits will meet the customer's needs. Be aware of signs that the customer is ready to buy. Ask the customer to buy.

Figure 13–10. Selling skills used by salespeople to assist customers in making a buying decision.

Making the Right Choice	Restate to the customer why this product was the right choice. Assure the customer that the company stands behind the product. Inform the customer of other services that enhance the product.

Figure 13–10 (Continued)

Successful salespeople are able to identify their customers' mental buying steps. Then they use specific selling skills to assist in meeting customers' needs. Each step in the buying process requires the use of special sales skills.

THE SELLING PROCESS

Just as there is a natural process to buying, there is also a process to selling. By learning the steps of the selling process, a salesperson will know more about their product and customer, feel and appear at ease and confident when working one-on-one with the customer, and have more satisfied customers who want to buy again and again.

Good salespeople use a step-by-step process for many reasons. It provides new salespeople with a guide to making a sales call. By knowing what should come next in the presentation, the salesperson is better able to concentrate on the needs and wants of the customer, rather than on the presentation. It is also time efficient. A well-prepared salesperson will spend less time looking for the answers to questions which are keeping the customer from buying. However, the salesperson must be careful to listen to the customer at all times. Many times customers know what they want to buy and will give signals that will allow the salesperson to ask for the sale in the early stages of the selling process.

There are five steps in the selling process: (1) preparation, (2) opening, (3) presentation, (4) closing, and (5) follow-up.

Each step is important to the success of a sales call. Therefore, it is important that salespeople have a complete understanding of each step and have the practical knowledge of how to implement each step in actual selling situations. The remainder of this chapter will focus on a discussion of the steps in the selling process.

STEP ONE: PREPARATION

Preparation is the work that a salesperson must do to get ready for selling. In other words, preparation is the work done before the salesperson actually meets the customer. According to Ditzenberger and Kidney (1992), selling is 90 percent preparation and 10 percent presentation. Time spent preparing for the selling opportunity will mean increased sales in the long-term. The three primary questions that must be answered in the preparation step are:

1. Who is the customer and how can I identify them?
2. What are the customer's buying motives?
3. What are the product's features and benefits?

Figure 13–11. Sales representative uses a laptop computer to assist him in preparing for a sales call. (Courtesy, Merek & Company, Inc., AgVet Division)

Types of Customers

The selling process begins and ends with the customer. Without customers businesses could not operate. Therefore, salespeople should learn everything they can about their customers. The goal of every sale is to satisfy the customer. The salesperson must provide products and services that meet the customers' needs in a friendly and courteous manner. Satisfied customers will return to make additional purchases in the future. Today, customers have high expectations of salespeople due to the highly competitive environment that exists at all levels of business. A good salesperson welcomes customers with a friendly smile and greeting, demonstrates interest and concern for each customer's needs, is eager to find just the right product or service for each customer, and focuses on the customer and avoids idle conversation with other employees or unrelated telephone calls.

Customers have many choices of stores, merchandise, and services today. Salespeople need to be aware that customers are influenced by many things beyond the ability and skill of the salesperson. Some of the major influences on today's customers in retail or discount stores include: store image in the community, advertising and promotion, attractiveness of store interior and displays, and merchandise availability and services offered. Customers want to take pride in where they shop. They want it to be a comfortable experience which is rewarded with a good selection of quality products and services.

It has been emphasized that customers are a very important part of the process of selling. Retail and wholesale agricultural stores sell directly to producers and consumers. Their customers come into the stores to buy. Examples of agriculture retail stores include farm and ranch supply stores, nursery and floral shops, and lumber and hardware stores. The customers of these stores can be categorized as decided customers, undecided customers or just-looking customers.

Decided Customers. *Decided customers* know what product or service they want to purchase. Generally, this type of customer can be identified easily because they will ask to see a particular product or request to speak with a certain salesperson. Also, the customer usually has considerable knowledge about the product or service and will ask specific and detailed questions. It is important that the salesperson not try to take complete control of this selling situation because the customer has already made a buying decision. With a decided customer, it is best for the salesperson to listen carefully and provide precise technical answers to any questions. If the customer's information is false or misleading, the salesperson should suggest alternative products that will satisfy the customer's need. Often the salesperson can learn much from this type of customer. New information about the product can be used in future sales situations. With this type of customer, knowledge is the most important ingredient in closing the sale. The customer is looking for product knowledge to confirm the facts that he or she has in order to make the final decision. It is important not to rush the customer, he or she will let the salesperson know when they are ready to purchase.

Undecided Customers. *Undecided customers* have little understanding about what they want to purchase. Generally, they are uncertain about what technical questions to ask and are dependent on the salesperson to select the product or service that will best fit their needs. It may be tempting for the salesperson to encourage the undecided customer to purchase an unnecessarily expensive product. However, the salesperson should remember that if the customer later discovers that a less expensive model would have been adequate, it may mean the permanent loss of a customer.

The undecided customer can be easily confused because of his or her lack of technical knowledge. Salespeople must be sure to understand the specific need of the customer and avoid confusion by selecting only one or two products for them to consider. Often salespeople want to show the undecided customer an entire line of products or services. This approach often overwhelms the customer to the point that they cannot make any buying decision.

Asking undecided customers questions about products is risky due to their limited knowledge. Generally, it is best for the salesperson to make short summary statements about the benefits and features of the products selected. This approach will set the stage for the customer to compare their needs with the benefits of the product. Also, offering to demonstrate or provide trial use of the product may assist the undecided customer to reach a positive buying decision.

Just-Looking Customers. Some customers are described as *just-looking* or casual customers. These customers are shopping for nothing specific, but are in the store to become familiar with the products or services offered. They may be decided or undecided customers or just need something to do for a short time. Today, many customers prefer to look at the selection of products or services available before the salesperson becomes involved. This trend is not difficult to understand given the large number of discount wholesale stores that feature low prices and little service or contact with a salesperson who is knowledgeable of the products offered. As a result, customers tend to feel that they must always make their product or service selection without the assistance of a trained salesperson.

Regardless of the type of customer, salespeople should greet all customers by saying, "Hello" or "Good Morning," and offer to show them anything special that interests them. If customers insist that they are "just-looking," encourage them to look around and to feel free to ask questions. When a customer shows interest in a product by picking it up or by asking questions, the salesperson should not hesitate to volunteer to demonstrate any of the products. Remember, the customer who is just looking today may be buying tomorrow.

Prospecting for Customers

Some businesses do not operate through a store. They must depend on salespeople to make one-on-one contact with the customers at their places of business, homes or over the telephone. Agricultural businesses that depend on prospecting for customers include companies that sell feed, seed, chemicals and fertilizer; insurance and real estate brokers; and farm equipment and building dealers. Salespeople need to learn how to identify, target, and contact customers to keep their companies successful. The process of finding new customers is termed *prospecting*. There are as many ways to prospect as there are different salespeople. However, the most common ways are cold calling, cool calling, leads, and targeting and/or market segmentation.

Cold Calling. A *cold call* is when a salesperson stops by to visit with a prospect without an appointment or any prior knowledge of the prospect. A livestock feed salesperson unexpectedly calling on a dairy producer is an example of a cold call. Cold calling is a valuable method to identify possible new customers. It introduces products or services and opens doors for new salespeople. Cold calling is very time consuming, but every salesperson should regularly make cold calls to identify new customers.

Cool Calling. Calling on prospects with or without an appointment, who fit a certain criteria is referred to as *cool calling*. For example, a feed salesperson calls on hog producers that market 200 or more hogs each year in a specific county. Cool calling is useful because it concentrates on prospects who have common needs. The prospects can identify with one another, and they fit a profile of the kind of customer that the company presently sells to or would like to sell to.

Leads. *Leads* are prospective customers who have been suggested by current customers, fellow salespeople, or prospects themselves. Often, salespeople ask customers to identify producers who they think could benefit from a product or service. It is also common for a company to target specific producers and mail promotional materials to them. Prospects are asked to return a postcard to receive further information, a free gift, or a product demonstration. Leads allow salespeople to find potential customers quickly,

Figure 13–12. Sales representative making a sales call on a prospective
distributor in his office. (Courtesy, Merck & Company, Inc.,
AgVet Division)

build trust, establish credibility, and recognize customers who have purchased.

Targeting and/or Market Segmentation. Targeting and market segmentation
are a lot alike. Each concentrates on customer characteristics, identifies
customer needs, judges customer buying potential, and develops a strategic
game plan for selling. However, targeting and market segmentation are not
the same thing. *Targeting* is the process of selecting a specific prospect and
developing an individual selling plan for that person. Market segmentation
is the process of targeting groups of people with similar buying habits so
that overall marketing and selling strategies can be developed. The salesperson can further individualize a sales call by recognizing what product
or service the customer is currently buying. Both targeting and market
segmentation help salespeople find potential customers who could be profitable for the company. High-potential prospects have some or all of the
following characteristics: buy enough for a salesperson to make a long-term
profit, are not credit risks, have done business with the salesperson in the
past, do not switch companies or products, need a company's products or
services, have a location the salesperson can easily reach, would gain from
a change, are good managers, and/or offer significant potential for additional
profit.

The targeting and market segmentation prospecting method allows the best investment of time in calling on prospective customers. However, the target must have the authority to buy, the ability to pay, and the need. In addition, the prospective customer must be able to recognize his or her own needs. In other words, the prospective consumer must be ready to make a change. Often, the task of the sales professional is to make the customer aware of a need that is obviously there, but which may not be clear to the customer. Staying active in the field with prospective customers helps the salesperson to stay in touch to know when a prospect is ready for a change.

Figure 13–13 shows an example of a prospect importance evaluation form that a salesperson could use to rate a list of potential customers. Prospects can be rated on several criteria using a scale of 0 to 10 (0 meaning least potential and 10 meaning greatest). The highest total score indicates the customers with the highest buying potential. Unless the salesperson has some tangible way of evaluating the list of potential customers, it is difficult to determine who should receive a sales call. Also, it is easy for the salesperson to become discouraged if he or she targets every possible customer and produces no sales. Although several criteria are suggested in the example, the criteria must be modified to fit each situation.

Prospect Importance Evaluation (PIE) Form

	Prospect #1	Prospect #2	Prospect #3
Product: _____			
Name	_____	_____	_____
Criteria			
1. Does prospect need my product?	_____	_____	_____
2. Can prospect pay?	_____	_____	_____
3. Size of order needed by prospect?	_____	_____	_____
4. Is prospect conveniently located?	_____	_____	_____
5. Is prospect likely to buy again?	_____	_____	_____
Total Scores	_____	_____	_____

Figure 13–13. Prospect importance evaluation form. (Rate each prospect using a 0 to 10 scale, with 0 meaning least potential and 10 meaning highest potential.)

Customer Buying Decisions

Before customers can buy any agricultural product or service they must find the answers to five questions.

1. What product or service should I buy?
2. Where should I make the purchase?
3. How much should I pay?
4. When during the year should I buy?
5. How much should I buy?

In order to make a sale, it is important that the salesperson understands the meaning of the buying questions and is prepared to assist the customer in finding answers to the questions. Many times, customers are not aware of the questions, but will not buy unless the salesperson can guide them in a positive way to the answers.

Product or Service. This refers to the item or utility that the customer purchases to satisfy a need. Quality, size, color, brand, model, and other characteristics are all part of the decision. Also, reputation and image are considered by the customer. Salespeople should be aware of the need to sell quality products that have a positive public image.

Place. The customer must choose the place (business or store) to purchase the product. The salesperson prepares for this decision by developing a good reputation for fair and honest sales coupled with a good service record. Also, the pride that the store or company takes in the physical appearance and cleanliness of the display area, store, or office can make a difference in the customer's decision to buy from one store or company instead of another.

Price. The price is the amount of money a product or service costs. It is a key factor in determining whether or not the customer will buy. Salespeople spend considerable time developing rationale to justify the price of a product or service based on its quality.

Time. Time of purchase is an important question to consider in buying agriculture products. Due to the seasonal nature of agricultural production, producers must determine when it is to their advantage to purchase production supplies, services, and materials. By purchasing in advance or out-of-season there is often a price advantage for the customer. Salespeople can use time of purchase and time of payment as incentives to the customer to purchase prior to the time needed. For example, an agricultural producer may decide to purchase a new combine just prior to harvest if the payment becomes due two or three months later.

Quantity. The amount of a product that the customer buys often determines the price. Some firms allow discounts if the customer can consolidate purchases of products. The salesperson should offer price discounts on quantity purchases as a benefit of purchasing the product from their store or company. Also, price discounts are given to customers who purchase an entire package of products rather than one item. For example, a customer may purchase a small garden tractor for $800. If the customer purchases a tractor with a mower attachment, it may only cost $900. Whereas, the mower attachment, if purchased separately, would cost $250.

All agriculture customers have different wants and needs and are influenced by a variety of factors. Therefore, a customer's buying decisions regarding product, place, price, time, and quantity have different levels of importance in every buying situation. For example, a farmer wants to finish planting a small field of wheat before a rain storm and needs some seed wheat to finish. The farmer may not place much importance on the variety of wheat (product) or price. However, time, place, and quantity may be of utmost importance because the seed wheat is needed immediately to complete planting.

Understanding Buying Motives

Behind every customer purchase is a motive or reason for buying. The reasons that influence customer's purchases are called *buying motives*. These buying motives are based on the customers' needs or wants and the ability of the product or service to satisfy them. A *need* is something that is considered basic to maintaining one's life, such as food, clothing, and shelter. A *want* is something desired, but not essential to maintain one's life. As an agricultural producer, a tractor is needed to engage in crop production. However, many farmers want a new tractor when they may only need a used tractor to be an efficient and profitable producer. It is important for salespeople to understand the motive or reason customers buy in order to assist them appropriately. For example, a customer may need to purchase a lawnmower for a small yard and the salesperson emphasizes low price and small size. However, the salesperson may find that the customer wants a larger self-propelled model like his neighbor purchased. Customers purchase the same product for different reasons or motives. A good salesperson must learn to recognize the customer's buying motives.

Some of the most common buying motives for agricultural products include: increased profitability, security, prestige and recognition, and comfort and convenience.

Profitability. All customers want to increase profits, save time and become more efficient. Salespeople can use this basic motive to show that by purchasing the product the customer can see an economic gain or improved efficiency.

Security. Customers desire products that will increase health and safety or physical well-being. Today, protection of the environment, and protection of agricultural workers and consumers from harmful pesticides is a high priority for producers. As a result, salespeople can use health and safety features of a product as an incentive to buy if the increase in cost is reasonable.

Prestige and Recognition. All customers like to feel good about the products they purchase. Also, customers obtain prestige from the recognition they receive from others about the products they buy. Purchasing a brand name tractor with the latest equipment, instead of a used tractor, carries more prestige and recognition of success. Although customers often do not reveal prestige and recognition as buying motives, it plays an important role in the sale of most products.

Comfort and Convenience. Comfort and convenience is a powerful buying motive. Agricultural work has historically been difficult with few comforts. However, through technology, agricultural work has become highly mechanized and requires much less manual labor than it did twenty years ago. Consider the large round baler innovation. By using this machine, the hay producer can cut, bale, and move the hay without ever physically touching it. The convenience that the large round baler provides is a major motive for buying this machine. There are many other examples in agriculture where comfort and convenience provided by purchasing the product becomes one of the reasons to buy.

Categories of Buying Motives

Buying motives are the reasons why customers buy. A product's features and benefits are what the customer buys. Salespeople use no specific order in appealing to buying motives of customers. However, as a salesperson it is useful to classify buying motives as a means to understand them in assisting customers. The four categories include: rational motive, emotional motive, product motive and patronage motive.

Rational Motive. *Rational buying* is based on the facts involved in the situation. Often customers make lists of the advantages and disadvantages of a product or service. Also, salespeople appeal to this motive by focusing the sales presentation on rational facts promoting a purchase. This approach leads to rational decision making based on facts rather than emotions.

Emotional Motive. *Emotional buying* is the desire to buy a particular product or service without any conditions attached. Although most people believe that rational reasoning determines what a customer purchases, in reality, emotional motives may have more influence. Some of the common emotional motives are fear, protection, appearance, recreation, comfort, recognition, variety, adventure, prestige, and popularity. Salespeople must determine the buying motives that have the greatest appeal to customers and use them in their presentations of the products.

Product Motive. *Product buying* refers to a customer buying a specific product with no regard to where it is purchased. A customer with this motive feels the product to be satisfying because of its price, quality, reputation, or other attributes. The salesperson appeals to this motive by having extensive knowledge of the product. An example of a product motive is often seen in buying tractors. Once the customer is convinced that only a certain name brand tractor will satisfy their needs, the customer focuses only on that product.

Patronage Motive. *Patronage buying* is the desire to make a purchase only from a particular firm. This motive is influenced by a firm's ability to offer a quality product at a fair price and with excellent service. A salesperson uses this motive in combination with the motive for a particular product to promote a sale. A salesperson develops patronage buying motives by expressing several favorable qualities of the firm. A knowledgeable salesperson knows the firm gains a good reputation by always providing excellent products and services. For example, a farmer purchases seed corn from only one firm in the community, although various stores in the area sell the same brand and variety of seed corn. Characteristics of a firm that wants to establish a positive patronage motive include: helpful salespeople, positive store image, variety of merchandise or services, and accessible store locations.

Buying motives of customers are strong selling points for sales personnel. If the salesperson identifies the customer's motive(s) for purchasing, the salesperson satisfies the customer's wants or needs and makes a sale.

The Importance of Product Knowledge

Customers expect salespeople to be knowledgeable about products and to assist them in finding answers to questions. Most customers have some knowledge about the product or service that they are purchasing. However, customers base most of their product knowledge on their own experience, experience of friends, and product literature or brochures. Salespeople should strive to be more knowledgeable of the products they sell than their customers. This knowledge base will reinforce the customer's confidence in the product or service. Knowledgeable salespeople often find their jobs more rewarding, develop higher degrees of self-confidence, and increase sales and opportunities for promotion.

Figure 13–14. Sales representatives must be knowledgeable of the products that they sell. This picture illustrates the available materials that inform sales representatives about fleas and the products that control them.

Some of the basic questions that all agriculture retail salespeople should be able to answer about the products before they sell to customers include:

- What products or services are carried by the store?
- What is the location of all products in the store?

- How much reserve stock is available for popular items?
- Where is the reserve stock?
- How long does it take to special order products?
- What are the specials for the week?

Sources of Product Knowledge

Knowing what products are sold by the store or business and their location is only the beginning. Customers expect salespeople to be experts about the products and services that they sell. This requires salespeople to spend time learning about their products. This education may be obtained through special training sessions provided by the company, self-study, or personal experience. The best way to learn about a product is through experience. Also, customers can provide valuable information to the salesperson. This information can be gathered after the sale through follow-up telephone calls or questionnaires. Salespeople can educate themselves about their products by reading publications about them and how they are manufactured. Also, trade magazines provide comparisons of products. This allows salespeople to become knowledgeable about competing products.

Kinds of Product Knowledge

It is important to approach learning about a product from a customer's point of view. Customers expect salespeople to know about product appearance, composition, manufacturing process, purposes, performance, maintenance, and price.

Appearance. Product appearance is important to customers. Style, color, size, and shape are features that can influence the buying decision of the customer. Agricultural products are generally functional in design and color. Appearance is important to the customer because it communicates and reflects on the image of the individual and the business.

Composition. *Product composition* is the material of which the product is made. Customers are interested in composition because it relates to the quality of the product. Salespeople should use product composition as an advantage for the customer. For example, if the customer is choosing between plastic or steel fence posts, the salesperson should be able to explain the advantages and disadvantages of each based on the composition of the product.

Manufacturing Process. The *manufacturing process* is the way the product is made. It includes quality control, testing, and inspection that the product undergoes before it is sold to the customer. Salespeople use their knowledge of the manufacturing process to help customers understand the quality of the product and the kind of performance that they can expect. If possible, salespeople should tour the manufacturing plant where the product is produced. As a result, they can share personal insights with customers about how quality is built into the product.

Purposes. A product may have several purposes or uses for the customer. Every purpose becomes a benefit that the salesperson can point out to the customer during the sales presentation. For example, a customer may want to purchase a riding lawnmower. The salesperson demonstrates that the lawnmower being considered can also be used as a small garden tractor with several additional attachments. This benefit or feature may assist the customer in making a buying decision.

Performance. *Product performance* refers to the length of product life and what the product will do. Often performance of the product will explain the difference in price and quality. If a farmer is buying a new feed grinder and intends to grind several tons of grain daily for a swine confinement operation, performance of the grinder over time may be the determining factor in making the buying decision.

Maintenance. Customers like products that require little or no maintenance. When maintenance is needed, customers expect the company to have a plan for providing it conveniently at a reasonable price. Many products have guarantees that assist the customer in developing confidence in the product. Salespeople use guarantees and service programs as benefits to the customer in purchasing the product.

Price. Many stores carry two or three different product lines to give customers a choice of price. Generally, the quality of the product changes as price changes. Salespeople are expected to know the price of the products and why one product line is more expensive than another. Customers are interested in buying products that have value for the price. If salespeople can explain the value of the product, customers will have fewer price objections.

Product knowledge is essential to the salesperson in assisting the customer in finding a product or service that will meet their needs. However, the salesperson should be careful not to make the customer feel stupid or to give the impression that the salesperson is always right. This attitude will cause the customer to seek other places to do business. Salespeople should be careful not to give too much information to the customer. This will cause customers to become confused and delay buying. Rather, the salesperson should listen carefully to the customer's questions and provide clear, accurate, and concise answers.

Summary

Preparation is the first step in the selling process. Salespersons must anticipate a selling situation by learning who the customer will be, the buying motives that the customer will bring, and by knowing the product from the customer's perspective. Preparation gives the salesperson confidence in assisting customers with their needs. This means that the salesperson will be more likely to make a sale. Remember, 90 percent of selling is preparation and only 10 percent is presentation. Successful salespeople are always prepared before they meet the customer.

STEP TWO: OPENING

The first step in the selling process is preparation to meet the customer. The second step is meeting the customer and opening the sales presentation. This initial contact with the customer is very important. During the first few minutes of the sales call the salesperson must earn the right to advance to the next step of the selling process. Therefore, the salesperson must create a good impression and get the prospect's attention. This creates a willingness on the part of the customer to become interested in the product or service.

During the opening, the salesperson also wants to probe for the customer's needs and wants. If you are working in a retail store, the customer may tell you their needs immediately. However, if you are making a cold call on a producer who you do not know, determining customer need may be difficult to achieve in the first sales call.

Types of Opening Approaches

There are many different ways to open a sales call. Sales experts have classified most openings into three approaches: the welcome approach, the product approach, and the service approach.

Welcome Approach. Most agricultural sales presentations are opened with a friendly greeting, "Good morning" or "Good afternoon." If possible, the customer's name should be used to show respect and a genuine interest in the person. Customers who feel welcome and comfortable will share their needs and wants more willingly with the salesperson.

A brief pause following the opening greeting is very important. This pause gives the customer time to adjust to the store environment. If the salesperson does not delay after the initial greeting and immediately asks, "What do you need?" the customer may feel pressured or rushed to buy and lose interest in buying or looking at products. However, if the salesperson delays too long customers may feel that the salesperson is not interested in making a sale. Generally, salespeople should determine quickly what the customer needs and assist the customer with the purchase. The welcome approach encourages the undecided or just-looking customer to tell the salesperson what they need. Also, this approach works well if the salesperson is busy with another customer. The salesperson could say, "I'll be with you in just a moment."

Product Approach. The product approach focuses the opening on a specific product. Sales experts consider it the most effective way of opening in a retail store. If the customer is looking at a pruning shear, the salesperson could say, "That is the best pruning shear sold" or "That pruning shear is our best seller." This type of opening does not give the customer a chance to reply. Instead, it provides an opportunity for the salesperson to begin selling the product. Using the product approach requires that the salesperson have good knowledge of the product and a lot of experience with customers in order to relate product features to customer needs. This approach is especially good for customers who are just looking or undecided.

Service Approach. The service approach is based on offering assistance to the customer. It is a very popular way of approaching selling and can be over used. Common opening questions are: "How may I help you?" and "Has someone helped you?" Often customers will respond, "No, I am just looking," unless they want immediate help. A follow-up response by the salesperson could be, "Is there anything special you are looking for?" This question indicates a sincere interest in assisting the customer and will often yield a positive response. Generally, it is best to avoid questions that require a yes or no response. The service approach works best with decided customers, because the customer's immediate wants and needs can be addressed quickly.

Every sales presentation has a beginning and an end. The opening is the beginning. Salespeople can use one of the opening approaches mentioned or a combination of approaches. The most important aspects of any sales opening is for the customer to feel welcomed and respected. Also, it is important for the salesperson to be sincere and project a warm smile. Using the customer's name, when possible, makes it is easier to take control of the selling situation. The goal of the opening is to establish a feeling of honesty, trust, and open communications.

STEP THREE: PRESENTATION

This sales presentation step includes three major components: (1) determining customer needs and wants, (2) presenting product features and benefits, and (3) handling customer objections.

Determining Customer Needs and Wants

Following the opening, the salesperson must determine the customer's needs and wants. Successful salespeople obtain a clear understanding of the customers' needs at the very beginning of the sales presentation. To determine needs and wants, the salesperson observes the behavior of the customer, presents a selling statement or questions, and listens carefully to the customer throughout the sales call or presentation. Sales experts call this process qualifying the customer.

Observing the Customer. Observation of the customer is important for the salesperson. The customer's body language, eye contact, and conversation all communicate information about needs and wants. Salespeople in a retail store should observe the movements of customers in the store. A customer who moves quickly through the store or dealership obviously looking for something generally is a decided customer. Whereas, a customer slowly walking through the store looking at many products is generally a just-looking customer. Also, customers who pick up products two or three times may be signaling that they are undecided and need assistance from a salesperson.

Customer's facial expressions and eye contact may communicate satisfaction, disapproval, or doubt about products and services. A smiling customer whose eyes sparkle with interest or excitement usually is showing satisfaction and approval for a product. Customers who look away, move away from a product, or frown are showing disapproval. A salesperson should make eye contact with the customer during the sales presentation to communicate sincere interest.

The way a customer is dressed often influences salespeople to make false judgments about the type of customer that they are serving. People have different values and, therefore, it is difficult to predict from outward appearances what the customer will purchase. It is best to treat all customers with respect regardless of personal appearance.

Presenting a Selling Statement. The initial observation of the customer and opening of the sales presentation usually occur quickly. The salesperson has to decide whether to make a selling statement or ask a question. Both approaches are ways to get the customer to talk with the salesperson about their needs or wants. For example, a customer enters a garden store and is looking at a lawnmower. The salesperson could make this selling statement.

Salesperson: This is our best selling lawnmower and it is on sale today.

Customer: It looks like a good buy. But I need a self-propelled mower.

In the example, the selling statement caused the customer to reveal their interest in buying a lawnmower. The next step for the salesperson is to show the customer the self-propelled model.

Using the same selling situation, consider how the salesperson could use a selling question.

Salesperson: How can I help you?

Customer: I am interested in looking at your lawnmowers.

The selling question revealed that the customer was interested in a lawnmower, but additional follow-up will be needed to reveal the true needs of the customer. Questions that ask who, what, where, when, how, and why require customers to reveal needs and wants quickly. Questions like, "May I help you?" require only a yes or no response. These should be avoided because they tend to provide no information about customer wants or needs. Salespeople should be aware that too many questions may put too much pressure on the customer and create a negative selling situation. It is best for the salesperson to ask one or two key questions in a sincere and patient manner using direct eye contact with the customer.

Listening. Listening is key to any sales presentation. Remember that the customer cannot reveal their needs or wants if the salesperson is talking.

Also, customers want to be heard and often will leave the store or end the sales call if they sense that the salesperson is not listening. Five tips to developing good listening skills include:

1. Listen attentively. When a customer talks, listen attentively by looking at the customer and thinking about what they are saying.

2. Show active interest in what the customer is saying by smiling, nodding your head in a positive way, and occasionally saying yes.

3. Don't interrupt. Patience is required in listening to customers. Often customers talk about unrelated problems or situations before they feel comfortable in telling a salesperson about their needs. Interrupting the customer is rude and will cause the customer to lose interest.

4. Allow time to think. Customers like to have time to think and consider the facts before making a buying decision. When a customer completes a response do not immediately begin talking or asking another question. Instead, wait a few seconds to see if the customer has additional questions or responses. It is appropriate to let the customer have time to think over the decision. The salesperson can attend to other matters for a few minutes after the product or service has been selected and all information has been given.

5. Respond. The salesperson indicates that he or she is listening to the customer by summarizing what the customer's needs are using phrases such as, "I understand you are looking for . . . ," or "Did you say . . . . ?"

Selecting a Product or Service. Following the identification of customer needs, the salesperson assists the customer in the selection of a product or service. Based on information given by the customer, the salesperson should select one or two products or services that solve the customer's problem. The customer may disagree and respond, "No, that isn't what I had in mind." This gives the salesperson an opportunity to show the customer other products or services. If too many products are presented at one time, the customer will become confused and may leave the store or conclude the sales call by saying, "I need some time to think this over."

Customer Buying Signals. Throughout the sales presentation the salesperson should watch for customer buying signals. *Buying signals* are signs of product or service approval. Buying signals are given in several ways. The customer may use body language, such as nodding approval, picking-up the product, and/or smiling. Verbal buying signals, such as the customer saying, "This is the one," "I can't wait to try it," or "Can I use my old ____ as a down payment?" are the most obvious. If the customer does not give a buying signal, the salesperson should attempt to show other products or services. It is also a good idea for the salesperson to restate the customer's needs or wants to be certain that they are clearly understood. Should the store or company not carry the product or service that the customer needs, it is best to refer the customer to a business that carries the product or service. As a result, the customer will feel that the salesperson was fair and generally will return to the business in the future.

Attempting to Close. Once the customer has given buying signals, the salesperson must either attempt to close the sale or continue the selling process with a feature-benefit presentation. Usually, the satisfied customer has no additional questions and is ready to buy. The salesperson can use a statement or question to attempt a trial close. Examples include: "How much can we deliver to your farm today?" "Will this be cash or charge?" "What else can I help you with?" "Can I answer any more questions before I write this up?" and "I'm sure you will receive many years of service from this selection." These questions do not put pressure on the customer, they simply allow the customer to purchase at this point or ask more questions. Closing statements should be given using a smooth conversational approach. This takes practice and experience.

Presenting a Feature-Benefit Presentation

A feature-benefit presentation by a salesperson provides additional information needed by the customer to make a buying decision. The feature-benefit presentation is based on buyers needs or wants rather then the product. Therefore, the salesperson focuses on translating product features into buyer benefits. *Product features* are the physical characteristics of a product (or service). *Buyer benefits* are the product (or service) features that satisfy the wants or needs of the customer. For example, a customer needs a yellow flowering bedding plant that grows well in a sunny part of her garden. The salesperson states, "Marigolds are hardy annuals that thrive in sunny locations and come in many shades of yellow. Planted in mass they are beautiful." The salesperson has translated the features of marigold bedding plants into benefits (yellow flowers and grows in the sun) for the customer. Customers buy benefits (anything that increases customer satisfaction) not product or service features. Another example of a customer benefit is a beef producer who reduces veterinary expenses (the benefit) after using a shipping fever vaccine on weaning calves. Figure 13–15 displays examples of common buyer benefits that motivate customers to buy.

Example Buyer Benefits

Profit	Appearance
Health	Prestige
Safety	Pleasure
Pride of ownership	Enjoyment
Convenience	Comfort

Figure 13–15. Example buyer benefits.

The feature-benefit presentation is a two step process. The salesperson first prepares the feature-benefit presentation and then practices to adapt it in a variety of selling situations based on customer needs.

Planning the Feature-Benefit Presentation. In planning the feature-benefit presentation, the salesperson must recognize product or service features, identify buyer benefits, and translate features into benefits.

Examples of product or service features in the section above define them as physical characteristics. In other words, a product feature is something that can be seen, felt, heard, smelled, or tasted. Features give a product value to the customer. Salespeople must know the features of the products they sell and be able to identify buyer benefits. Benefits motivate the customer to purchase the product or service.

Giving a Feature-Benefit Presentation. In order for salespeople to give feature-benefit presentations effectively, they must study the features and benefits of all major products they are selling. This allows the salesperson to concentrate on the customer and the processes involved in the feature-benefit presentation. Each customer has different needs; therefore, each presentation will be different. When making a feature-benefit presentation, the salesperson should generally follow this procedure:

1. Greet the customer and determine needs by asking a few probing questions or presenting a selling statement. If the customer does

not show buying signs, proceed with the feature-benefit presentation.

2. Ask questions to qualify the customer (determine what the customer likes).

3. Listen to the customer and analyze their needs.

4. Select a product and involve the customer in the demonstration of the product or service.

5. Appeal to the customer's buying motives with buyer benefits.

6. Demonstrate the product or service and reinforce how the benefit will solve the customer's problem. Be sure to properly handle the product and use showmanship to keep the customer interested. Showmanship refers to the use of body language, voice, and special props to create enthusiasm in a product or service. Often selling aids such as pictures, video tapes, and graphs or tables that show results of tests completed by unbiased laboratories or universities can be used in the demonstration.

Handling Customer Objections

During the sales presentation, customers often raise objections to buying the product or service. At this point in the sales presentation some salespeople actually stop selling, because they think the customer has lost interest in buying. This is usually not true. The customer is showing interest by voicing questions about the product or service. It emphasizes an important customer want or need. The objection may come because the customer did not understand a portion of the sales presentation or does not feel that the product's value exceeds its cost.

Salespeople consider objections by customers to be sales resistance. *Sales resistance* is the customer's way of expressing a concern or objection about a product or service presented. Some of the major forms of resistance are real objections, excuses, and hidden objections.

Real Objections. A *real objection* is a concern or problem the customer has about the products features. A real objection to buying a product or service generally stems from concern about the price, color, style, quality, quantity to buy, or service availability. Examples of this type of customer objection include, "I like the lawnmower, but the price is too high." "Do you have a truck like this one in a different color?" "I like this baler, but it looks too complicated to operate and maintain." Customers generally state real objections late in the sales presentation after the features have been demonstrated and the price stated.

Excuses. *Excuses* are insincere reasons given by the customer to delay a purchase or avoid becoming involved in a sales situation. Most excuses are not related to the product or service. Some common excuses used by customers in retail stores include: "I am just shopping," "I can't afford it," "I want to shop around a little more," or "I'll think about it." Excuses are generally given by customers near the beginning of the sales presentation. Salespeople should take the excuses seriously and continue selling until they are sure the customer is no longer interested in the product. Sometime customer's needs or wants have not been understood and this presents a good opportunity to ask a few more questions to determine the exact needs of the customer.

Hidden Objections. *Hidden objections* are reasons that a customer has for not buying, but the reason is not verbally expressed to salespeople. If salespeople feel that the customer has hidden objections to buying a product or service, the best approach is to attempt to close the sale. Often, this approach will encourage the customer to express the need or want to the salesperson.

Customer objections are an important part of the selling process and salespeople must be prepared to respond to objections whenever they occur in the selling process. In responding to customer objections, salespeople prepare in three areas: (1) product knowledge, (2) identifying areas of customer objections, and (3) procedures for answering objections.

Product Knowledge. Customers expect salespeople to know everything about the products or services that they are selling. Failure to answer questions about the product will often give the customer a reason to object. Also, customers will lose confidence in the salesperson's ability to sell.

The best way of anticipating customer objections is to plan a sales presentation that includes information that customers need to make smart buying decisions. Salespeople often develop lists of product features and the frequent objections that customers have voiced. Using this list of objections, a positive sales statement is developed for each objection. Salespeople practice using the positive sales statements in sales presentations to answer customer objections. By anticipating objections, salespeople build the confidence of customers in them. Also, the better prepared the salesperson is, the fewer objections they will receive.

Identifying Areas of Customer Objections. Customers must make five decisions before they buy a product or service: what to buy (product), where to buy (place), what price to pay (price), when to buy (time), and how much to buy (quantity). Customer objections usually stem from one or more of these five general areas.

1. **Product.** Objections that stem from the product are really objections about the product's features, style, color, size, quality, etc. The salesperson handles the objection to the product by understanding the needs and wants of the customer and turning the product features into buyer benefits.

2. **Place.** The customer that objects to purchasing the product or service from a place of business is reflecting a negative experience that they or someone else has experienced. The customer must feel that the business is there to serve them. This feeling and image is developed by the design and layout of the store, advertising, the helpfulness of the salespeople, and the willingness of the business to satisfy customer needs.

3. **Price.** Price of the product or service is usually the major objection customers have when buying. However, many customers treat price as more of a frustration, because it is often connected to the value of the product. Salespeople must be able to show customers what the value is for the price. The salesperson's ability to point out special features that give the product value are ways of answering objections to price. If the product or service is on sale, the salesperson can use price to show how much the customer will save and how much value they will receive.

4. **Time.** When to buy is an objection that is seldom expressed. In selling agricultural products and services, time of purchase is frequently a critical point that can be used by salespeople in a positive way to sell a product. For example, agricultural chemicals for crops, fertilizers, and other plant related products are sold to farmers during specific seasons of the year. Salespeople can reassure the customer that by buying early they will lock in a specific price that is lower than that during the peak of the growing season.

5. **Quantity.** How much to purchase is a difficult decision for some customers. Salespeople need to be able to reassure the customer that the quantity purchased is a good choice. Many agricultural companies give quantity discounts to customers who purchase a certain

quantity of feed, fertilizer, seed, etc. However, customers may object because of other concerns. For example, livestock feed purchased in quantity must be stored over a period of time and chance of spoilage is a common objection. Salespeople must be able to see the idea of a quantity purchase not only from the perspective of price, but from the customer's perspective of how long the feed must be stored before it is fed.

Understanding the buying decisions that customers must make before they purchase a product or service gives the salesperson insights into preparing for customer resistance. In addition, the salesperson who is aware of the common customer objections to a product will incorporate answers to those objections into the sales presentation.

Procedures for Answering Objections. Salespeople must be alert to customer objections throughout the sales presentation. This requires the salesperson to listen carefully and focus on the customer at all times. When a customer's objection is offered, the salesperson should pause before answering the objection. By pausing, the salesperson is indicating to the customer that the objection is being taken seriously. Also, it provides time for the salesperson to mentally outline a solution. If the answer is given too quickly, it may appear that the salesperson is trying to prove the customer wrong or that the salesperson is not taking the objection under serious consideration. It is important for the salesperson to demonstrate patience with the customer in answering an objection.

The next step in answering the customer's objection is to show empathy for the customer. The customer is emotionally involved when voicing an objection. It is important for the salesperson to let the customer know that their feelings are understood. Some of the common phrases used by salespeople to communicate this understanding include: "I know just how you feel," "I'm glad you asked that question," "You've made a good point," "I understand your concern," and "Yes, that is important." When a salesperson shows respect for a customer's opinions the customer will tend to be more open and honest.

Before a customer's objection can be answered, the salesperson must understand the objection. The best way to handle this is to simply restate or rephrase the objection. If it is restated correctly, the customer will know that the salesperson understands the objection. Also, restating the objection gives the salesperson time to find a solution. Generally, it is best to restate the objection in the form of a question. By stating it as a question, the customer knows that you understand their point of view. For example, the customer may object to buying a new brand of market hog feed because his neighbor's hogs got sick. The salesperson might respond: "I can appreciate your concern because of your neighbor's experience. Will your hogs get sick from this feed?" If the customer has several objections at once, do not try to restate all of them. Instead, use empathy statements to express concern.

Answering the customer's objection is important. If the answer is delayed, the customer may concentrate on the objection rather than the purchase. Also, the customer may believe that the salesperson is not interested in selling the product. The customer who feels that the salesperson is not being truthful will leave the store or end the sales call. The answer should be given with empathy, in a sincere, concise manner using words that the customer will be able to understand. The salesperson should observe the customer's facial expressions to see if they indicate understanding and satisfaction. Usually, a smile or movement toward the product will indicate approval, while a frown or movement away from the product indicates disapproval. Follow-up questions that are often asked include, "Have I answered your question?" or "Is this clearer?"

It is important for salespeople to answer customer objections promptly and honestly. As a result, customers will understand that the salesperson is sensitive to their point of view. At this point, the customer generally will become more open to expressing needs or wants. The procedure for answering objections is an important process in communicating with the customer. The primary steps are: listen to the customer's objection, pause before answering, show empathy, restate the objection, and answer the objection. By helping customers overcome buying objections, you will be able to assist them in making the best buying decision.

STEP FOUR: CLOSING THE SALE

The primary objective of the sales presentation is to close the sale and to have a satisfied customer. Therefore, the successful salesperson looks for opportunities to close the sale throughout the sales presentation. Customers often provide buying signals to the salesperson indicating product approval. Some of the common signals include approving facial expressions, a tone of voice that indicates approval, eyes that show approval, questions that reflect a feeling of ownership and/or use, and handling of the product or trial use of the service indicating a high degree of interest. When these buying signals occur, the salesperson should attempt a trial close. A *trial close* is asking customers buying questions in a casual and conversational manner: "How much can we deliver?" "Would you like some fertilizer to go with the flat of bedding plants?" "Will this be cash or credit card?" If the customer is not ready to buy, generally they will tell the salesperson the reason. Then the salesperson can adjust the sales presentation to meet the customer's needs.

Help Customers Make the Decision

Closing a sale should be a natural part of the sales process. It is not pressuring the customer to buy. If the salesperson has determined the customer's needs and asked a series of questions to determine product approval, it is only natural that the customer will purchase the product or service. Some of the actions that a salesperson can take to assist the customer in making the final decision to purchase follow.

Don't Show New Merchandise. If it appears that the product or service meets the customer's need, do not show additional products or services. Showing additional products may confuse and overwhelm the customer and delay the buying decision.

Help the Customer Narrow the Selection. Based on what the salesperson knows about the needs and wants of the customer, the salesperson should assist the customer in narrowing the selection to one or two products or services. Having three or four products or services to chose from complicates the buying decision for the customer. Expressions used by salespeople to assist customers in narrowing choices include: "Can I put those away, so you can look at these closely?" and "Which of these interest you the most?"

Create an Image of Ownership. Salespeople can assist customers in making the final decision to buy by helping them to visualize ownership of the product or service. Example statements of ownership include: "Your garden will be beautiful with the new hybrid tea roses," "Your new truck will provide you with years of service," and "The milk production of your herd will increase with the new protein supplement."

Ask the Customer to Buy. If salespeople wait for customers to tell the salesperson when they are ready to buy, the sale may never happen. Asking customers to buy is not pressuring the customer. It is providing the opportunity for the customer to buy or to voice objections. Salespeople who are confident about their products or services will naturally want to ask customers to buy.

Have Confidence. Most salespeople who have trouble asking customers to buy lack confidence in themselves or the products and/or services that they are selling. If salespeople do not believe that their products or services are worth the price charged, they may be selling the wrong product or working for the wrong company. Salespeople must be enthusiastic, positive, convinced the product or service will benefit the customer in specific ways, and willing to help the customer solve problems.

Understand Buying Resistance. As a salesperson, you are solving problems for people and not just selling products or services. When customers resist buying or cannot make up their minds, it is reasonable to ask them why. For example: "You seem to like the lawnmower. Why don't you feel it will work for you?" or "This hog feed will save you money compared to the brand you are using. Why can't we deliver some to you?" If the salesperson knows the reason why the customer is resisting buying, often a solution can be found. If the salesperson is expecting to actually close the sale, it is important to understand the customer's needs and wants from the very beginning.

Approaches to Closing

Salespeople who know how to close a sale will have a greater chance for success. Also, salespeople need to remember that they should close a sale the way they would like to be treated if they were the customer. Salespeople should not pressure the customer. However, standing and saying nothing is also irritating to the customer. Salespeople should be available to answer questions and demonstrate products or services as the customer's needs and interest dictate.

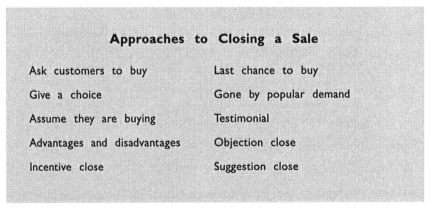

Approaches to Closing a Sale	
Ask customers to buy	Last chance to buy
Give a choice	Gone by popular demand
Assume they are buying	Testimonial
Advantages and disadvantages	Objection close
Incentive close	Suggestion close

Figure 13–16. Summary of approaches to closing a sale

Some widely used approaches for closing are displayed in Figure 13–16. It is possible that more than one approach will be used during a sales presentation or that two will be combined. It is important for the salesperson to have a good understanding of these approaches in order to close a sale efficiently.

Ask the Customer to Buy. Customers who give clear signals that they are ready to buy should quickly be asked to buy. Often, salespeople continue to sell when the customer is ready to buy. Buying questions used in this type of close are simple and conversational, "Can I start the contract?" "Shall I write this order-up?" "Do you want one or two pair?"

Give a Choice. The choice close is the most common close used by salespeople. The reason it is used frequently is because the emphasis is on which item the customer prefers, rather than on the decision to buy or not to buy. When the salesperson asks the customer which color or model is preferred, the salesperson is asking the customer to make a series of small choices or decisions. These decisions will result in a natural decision to buy the product or service. This means that the salesperson should remove products that do not meet the customer's needs and assist the customer in narrowing the choices to one or two. The salesperson's preference should not be given unless requested by the customer. The salesperson should respond honestly with the customer's needs in mind.

Assume They Are Buying. Using this approach, the salesperson is placing the buyer in a position of ownership. If the customer is ready to buy, the sale will be completed quickly. If the customer is not ready to buy, the salesperson will have some idea of the customer's objections. Some of the common statements used by salespeople in this type of close include, "We can have your new combine ready by this afternoon," and "How much fertilizer can we deliver tomorrow?"

Advantages and Disadvantages. Customers like to make rational buying decisions. In making a buying decision, many customers weigh the advantages and disadvantages of buying one product or service over another. A salesperson who has excellent product knowledge can encourage the rational buying approach by assisting customers with the identification of advantages and disadvantages of products or services. Often these are written down for the customer. A salesperson will focus on the advantages of the products rather than the disadvantages. Generally, the customer will bring the disadvantages to the forefront.

Incentive Close. In using this close, the salesperson offers something extra to the customer. For example, lawnmowers purchased today receive a gasoline storage container and six cans of lawnmower oil. Note, the price of the product in this example was not reduced. If the price had been reduced, the customer may believe that the price is up for negotiation or that the product is not worth the price. Incentives are created to convince customers to buy now. Generally, incentives are used for products that are expensive and sold in stores that specialize in the product. The incentives are controlled by the businesses management and salespeople must follow certain guidelines.

Last Chance to Buy. This close is used when a product or service is in high demand or short supply. Increased demand is often caused by a price reduction that stimulates buying. Salespeople must remember to be ethical in this situation. It is important for salespeople to continue to talk to customers about their needs rather then making the sale. Customers appreciate being informed of special offers, but may hold the salesperson responsible when they purchase a product and later discover that it does not meet their needs.

Gone by Popular Demand. Gone by popular demand is a close that infers that the customer demand is high and the product is in short supply. Because the supply is limited, it encourages customers to buy now before the supply is exhausted. Salespeople use statements like, "This is our most popular tractor model" or "This is the last of the special edition fertilizer spreaders." These statements tell customers why the product is in short supply and encourages them to purchase now.

Testimonial Close. Testimonials are natural ways to close a sale. Customers like to know that the product or service has satisfied other people's needs. Salespeople often have success stories of customers who have purchased products or services that they relate to new customers. Many times these are videotaped and shown in stores and businesses to prospective customers. Also, on-farm or business demonstrations are presented to convince customers that this is the right product or service. This approach to closing is often combined with closes discussed above.

Objection Close. During the course of a sales presentation, customers raise objections and salespeople generally answer them. If only one objection remains to buying, salespeople often take the opportunity to close the sale by offering to remove the objection. This should be done as part of the normal sales conversation. If the customer believes that the salesperson is trying to trap or pressure them, this close will surely fail. An example of this approach to closing follows.

Salesperson:	"Is the price of the seed corn your only objection?"
Customer:	"Yes."
Salesperson:	"We offer a 10 percent discount on orders of 50 bags or more. How many bags would you like?"

Suggestion Close. Customers often appear unsure of their decision to buy a product or service because they are not sure that they will get full use of it. Salespeople need to be sensitive to this type of problem and be ready to suggest related products or services that will assist the customer to obtain full use. For example, a customer wants to purchase a small garden tractor, but is concerned that he will not get full use of it. The salesperson suggests that he purchase an attachment with the lawnmower to till his garden. By being helpful to customers, salespeople not only increase sales, but help customers to make wise buying decisions because they can obtain full use of the products or services purchased.

STEP FIVE: FOLLOW-UP

Whether the salesperson closes the sale or does not, the successful salesperson continues to sell. When the customer has made the decision to buy, the salesperson asks the customer about purchasing related items. For example, if the customer purchased bedding plants fertilizer, potting soil may be needed. Customers that purchase market hog feed may need a new self-feeder or veterinary supplies.

During the closing of a sale, while the salesperson is completing the bill of sale, using the cash register, etc., conversation with the customer should continue. The salesperson should sincerely reassure the customer of the wise purchase and the benefits of the product or service. Also, the salesperson should remind the customer of the product or service guarantee and the policy that the business has to ensure satisfaction. If the customer feels uncomfortable with the product the salesperson should demonstrate the product or service to insure correct use.

If a customer does not buy, continue to sell. This customer may buy tomorrow and you want their business. It is best to tell the customer that you enjoyed showing them the product or service and to invite them to

Figure 13–17. Sales representative collects feed sample for analysis as a follow-up service to insure customer satisfaction. (Courtesy, Moorman Feed, Quincy, Illinois)

stop again at the store. If you called on the customer at their place of business, it may be possible to make a future appointment to call on the customer again.

After the customer leaves the store or the salesperson leaves the customer, it is good for the salesperson to reflect on how the sales presentation flowed and what could be done to improve it. By reviewing incomplete sales, salespeople will learn how to improve their selling skills and not make the same mistake in the future.

SUMMARY

A completed sale is not something that happens by chance, but by design. It includes five important steps: preparation, opening, presentation, closing, and follow-up. From the time a salesperson greets a customer, until the customer leaves the store or the salesperson leaves the customer's place of business, it is critical that the salesperson continue to sell the products or services.

CHAPTER SELF-CHECK

Match the following terms with the correct definitions:

     a. selling

     b. bartering

     c. prospecting

    d. cool calling

    e. need

    f. product

    g. resistance

    h. product features

    i. buying motive

    j. buyer benefit

_____ the transaction that takes place when one person exchanges goods or services with another for some medium of exchange such as money

_____ presenting information to overcome anticipated objections

_____ the product features that satisfy the wants or needs

_____ the process a salesperson uses to find new customers

_____ the earliest form of selling that involved exchanging one item for another

_____ calling on prospects with or without an appointment, who fit a certain criteria

_____ the item that the customer purchases to satisfy a need

_____ reasons that influence customers' purchases

_____ Basic to maintaining one's life such as food, clothing, and shelter

_____ the physical characteristics of a product

QUESTIONS AND PROBLEMS FOR DISCUSSION

1. Describe the problem-solving process that a salesperson follows.

2. What functions do agricultural salespeople perform?

3. Describe the four groups of customers that salespeople deal with in agriculture.

4. What are the four steps that customers follow in buying a product or service?

5. What are the five steps in selling?

6. What are the characteristics of a good salesperson?

7. Describe the three types of customers that all salespeople must be prepared to work with.

8. What are the methods of finding new customers?

9. What five questions must a customer find answers to before making a decision?

10. What is the difference between a want and a need?

11. What are three common openings used in selling agricultural products or services? Describe each briefly.

12. What are the three major components of the presentation step in the selling process? Describe each briefly.

13. List five or six closing approaches that are commonly used.

ACTIVITIES

1. Invite an agricultural salesperson to the class to talk about the sales process and the challenges of selling. Prepare a brief written report summarizing the salesperson's role.

2. Practice agricultural selling presentations by dividing the class into groups of three. Each member of the group plays a different role. One acts as the salesperson, one listens, and one is the customer. Every five to ten minutes the roles rotate until everyone has had a chance to play all three roles. Each group can discuss how to improve their sales presentations.

Chapter 14

DISTRIBUTING IN THE AGRICULTURAL INDUSTRY

Most agricultural supplies and products aren't produced where they are needed. They must be moved from the point of production to the final consumer. In most cases, there are many processing steps along the way. These are essential steps in agricultural marketing.

Your food, clothing, and shelter get to you through a complex distribution system. Many of the products we use are combinations of raw materials from a number of different places. Products must be manufactured and delivered to a convenient location for you to get them. Producing raw materials or a finished product isn't adequate alone. To be useful, it must get to the consumer.

The manufacturing and distribution process requires people who are

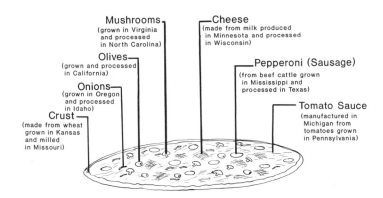

The Pizza: U.S. Agricultural Marketing in Action

(Ingredients may be varied to suit your preferences. Many times the ingredients are imported from foreign lands.)

Figure 14–1. Many distribution functions are involved in making a pizza.

377

skilled and work to assure good products. Knowledge of the functions in physical distribution will help you to be more efficient in the marketing process.

OBJECTIVES

To help you understand the physical distribution of agricultural products, several important areas are covered in this chapter. Upon completion of this chapter, you will be able to:

- Describe physical distribution and list major distribution functions
- List and describe distribution outlets
- Explain the elements of a physical distribution system
- Describe packaging and labeling
- Evaluate transportation methods
- Describe important areas of safety in physical distribution

TERMS

auction
bill of lading
biodegrade
catalog ordering
channel of distribution
container
dealership
distribution intensity
distribution outlet
inventory
inventory control
materials handling
order buyer
package
packaging material
pallet
physical distribution
physical distribution system
retailer
sales ticket
transporting
wholesaler

THE NATURE OF PHYSICAL DISTRIBUTION

Physical distribution is all of the functions in the actual movement of materials from the point of origin to the point of consumption. A number of functions may be needed to assure a good flow of materials. Raw products may change forms. Value is added to products through processing and through transportation to places where there is greater demand.

Having a product available for the consumer when and where it is wanted is as important as the ability to produce the product. For example, farm tractors sitting on a lot at the assembly plant are of little benefit to farmers and don't make a profit for the manufacturer. The same is true with grain and any other farm product. It is of no benefit if it can't be moved to a consumer.

INCLUDES SUPPLIES AND PRODUCTS

Physical distribution includes both the supplies that are used in production as well as the products of production agriculture, ornamental horticulture, and forestry.

Manufacturers of seed, feed, chemicals, equipment, and other inputs often have elaborate *physical distribution systems* to reach customers. A physical distribution system is a combination of functions that are coordinated to achieve a distribution goal. Agribusinesses may market to international, national, regional, or local markets. The nature of the physical distribution system depends on the marketing area and the kind of material being marketed.

Food, fiber, and wood materials that are produced often move through a many-faceted physical distribution system. Here are a few examples:

- **Food**—Foods produced in a local community may be marketed worldwide. Horse radish, which is produced in a small area in western Illinois, is distributed throughout North America in various products. Pineapples grown in Hawaii are shipped to many countries in fresh or processed forms. Shrimp grown in Asia are shipped to major population areas where demand exists.

- **Ornamental horticulture**—Ornamental plants tend to be produced in relatively small areas with unique climates. Shrubbery produced in Florida is shipped to many parts of the United States. Cut flowers grown in tropical areas, such as Hawaii and Central America, are shipped to places where they aren't grown.

- **Forestry**—Some places grow timber with highly desired qualities in abundance. It is cut, processed in varying amounts and shipped to many places. Valued walnut and cherry hardwoods of Virginia and North Carolina are made into furniture for wide use. Lumber for building construction is produced in the southeastern United States and shipped to other places.

Procedures used with supplies and products vary. There is no one physical distribution system that can be used for all products. The systems vary with the kind of product, geographical area of the market, and available infrastructure for physical distribution. For example, grain can be shipped by rail only if there is an accessible railroad.

Figure 14–2. Manufactured lumber may be shipped by rail under protective materials to assure that quality is maintained.

MAJOR FUNCTIONS

Physical distribution includes a number of functions. The functions vary according to the product being marketed. Some products are sold directly to the consumer with very little preparation, such as tomatoes sold at an on-farm roadside stand. Other tomatoes may undergo considerable preparation, such as those that are processed into catsup or salsa.

Physical distribution is made up of related marketing functions that deal with the movement of a supply or product from the source to the consumer or final user. The functions are sometimes described as marketing functions that deal with the flow of products and supplies.

The following functions are a part of physical distribution (but may not apply to all products): assembling, material handling, packaging, warehousing, order processing, inventory control, and transporting. In addition, customer services, procurement, demand forecasting, inventory control, salvage, and scrap disposal may be included with physical distribution. (These functions are covered in this chapter and elsewhere in the book.)

RELATIONSHIP TO MARKETING

Physical distribution includes several major functions in the marketing process. This cluster of marketing functions deals with physically moving products. Further, the functions included vary with the kind of product being marketed.

Each of the functions in physical distribution is a part of marketing. Without these functions, materials would not reach the consumer in the desired forms.

CHANNELS OF DISTRIBUTION

A *channel of distribution* is the route that a supply or product goes through between the producer and consumer. Some channels of distribution are simple; others are complex.

The most efficient and effective channel should be selected. Efficiency deals with getting the product to the consumer economically. The goal is to keep the costs of physical distribution as low as possible. This will allow the producer to sell at a lower cost and make a profit. Effectiveness deals with getting the product to the consumer in a timely manner. The product must be available when needed. If it is late, the consumer may buy from another source or not buy at all. A good example is cut Christmas trees. Trees that arrive after the holiday have no value. Consumers don't want them.

DISTRIBUTION OUTLETS

The *distribution outlet* is the point of contact between the producer and consumer. An outlet is at the end of the physical distribution system. Both supplies and products go through outlets.

The most common outlets in agricultural marketing are described here.

Dealerships

A *dealership* is a sales agency that has the authority to sell a supply or product. Dealerships often have a quantity of the item on hand and provide important services for the customer.

The most common dealerships in agriculture sell equipment and machinery. Most of these dealerships have exclusive rights to sell the particular brands of equipment in a local area. Equipment dealerships usually maintain a supply of parts and provide repair services.

Figure 14–3. Dealerships often handle one or a few lines of
equipment.

Seed, feed, chemicals, and other supplies are also sold through dealerships.

Farmers may sell through specific stores. This is especially true in niche marketing. A good example is run-about brown eggs. A producer of run-about eggs may supply the product to only a few stores in the area. These stores are dealers for the farmer.

Wholesalers

A wholesaler sells large quantities to retailers and volume buyers. Wholesalers may handle supplies or products. Many wholesalers deal with only a few products but do so in large quantities. A seed wholesaler rarely sells equipment. The seed wholesaler markets seed and closely related supplies to retail agricultural supplies stores, garden centers, and large farms.

Wholesalers are also involved with products originating on the farm: food, clothing, and wood products. They sell these products to smaller retail stores. The large store chains generally buy directly from the processor or manufacturer.

Retail Stores

A *retailer* sells to the general public. Many kinds of retail stores sell supplies and products. These vary from small convenience stores to large supermarkets and department stores. Lumber yards, garden centers, flower shops, farm supplies stores, forestry equipment outlets, and parts stores are examples.

Some farm producers operate retail stores and sell directly to the public. An on-farm roadside vegetable or fruit stand is a good example. Other farms may have "pick-your-own" sales that allow the consumer to harvest what they want. "Pick-your-own" approaches are often used with crops that require a lot of labor to harvest and need little processing for final consumption. Strawberries and peas are two examples.

Catalog Ordering

Some supplies and products are sold by having customers mail or telephone orders. This is known as *catalog ordering*. Catalogs provide details about the supplies or products. Customers look through the catalog and select the products they want. They may fill out an order form and mail it along with the payment or send it by facsimile with a credit card number or purchase order number. Orders may be made using on-line computer systems, particularly by dealers from their suppliers. The products are delivered to the customer by mail, courier, truck, or other means. The cost of shipping is usually added to the cost of the merchandise.

Seed, equipment, repair parts, food, lumber, and other items can be ordered from catalogs. Special packaging materials may be used to prevent spoilage and assure that products are delivered in good condition.

The reputation of a catalog order business is important. Customers expect to receive quality products in a timely manner.

Auctions

An *auction* is a public sale where people bid on the supplies or products being sold. People may compete with each other to buy at the lowest price.

An auctioneer is a person who conducts an auction. Auctioneers take bids, promote bidding, and describe products being auctioned. They try to get the highest possible selling price. Auctioneers have assistants who do such things as identify and label items, keep careful records of all sales, weigh animals, receive payments, and write checks to pay the owners of the products auctioned.

Most auctions involve starting at a low price and raising the price until no one will pay more. The auctioneer moves the action along and solicits additional bids to get the highest price for the seller.

Dutch-type auctions involve starting at a high price and reducing the price until a person bids. There is only one bid in a Dutch auction.

Silent auctions are also used. In this type of auction, people write down the price they are willing to pay. The person offering to pay the highest amount gets the product or supply.

Auctions are used to sell many different supplies and products. Used farm equipment, land, timber, harvested crops, livestock, and many other items are sold by auction.

Auctions are commonly used to market livestock. Producers may haul their livestock to a central location, known as an auction barn. Buyers representing feedlots, slaughter houses, and others regularly gather to bid against each other on the animals. Of course, individuals can buy for themselves. Some auctions are held on the farm. A good example is with valuable purebred cattle.

Buyers

Buyers may purchase from producers for resale to a processor, wholesaler, or others, or they may buy from a supplier representing a producer. Buyers represent the needs of the individuals they are buying for. They often don't own what they buy; the company or person they are buying for is the owner.

Some buyers get more involved by owning products themselves. They buy and sell to make a profit. This means that they buy at the lowest price

Figure 14-4. Feed is often delivered in bulk to poultry farms that use automated feeding equipment. (Courtesy, Michael Stevens, McCarty Farms)

and sell at the highest price they can get. They may buy and sell the products without ever taking possession of them.

Many buyers are known as *order buyers* because they have been hired to buy only certain grades of products, such as stocker cattle. Buyers are skilled in getting a good deal for their clients. Buyers may go to auctions, have stations at packing sheds, or go to farms to make purchases.

DISTRIBUTION INTENSITY

Some goods are available from many sources; others from only a few sources. The number of sources is known as *distribution intensity*. Most distribution is one of three types: intensive, selective, or exclusive.

Intensive distribution occurs when there are many dealers for a particular item. Consumers can go to almost any store and get the product. Most food items are sold at many places. People can buy fresh fruit at most grocery stores. When many customers are frequently exposed to a product, it is said to be intensively distributed.

Selective distribution occurs when a limited number of outlets handle a product. It is most often used to control the quality of the item as it reaches the consumer. If an outlet has poor facilities, some distributors may not allow it to handle their products. For example, frozen food quality must be retained. Stores without adequate freezers would not meet the standard that has been set.

Exclusive distribution occurs when only a few outlets carry a product. Small- and medium-sized towns and cities may have only one outlet for the item. In some cases, they may not have any outlets. Farm equipment is a good example. Dealerships are located only in farming areas because this is where demand exists for the equipment. The dealer is said to have a franchise or the exclusive right to market in a certain territory.

CHOOSING A DISTRIBUTION CHANNEL

In some cases, producers are able to choose a distribution channel for their products. In other cases, there is little choice of distribution channel. Four factors considered in choosing a distribution channel are given here.

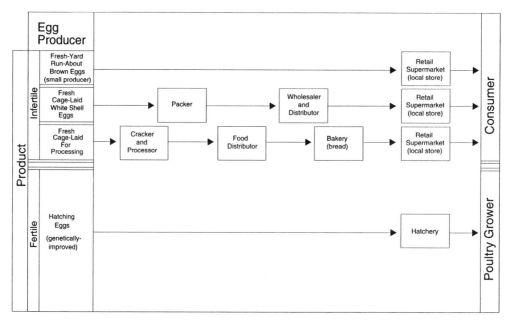

Figure 14–5. Various channels can be used in distributing eggs depending on the kind of egg, available channels, and preferences of the producer.

- **Customers**—How many customers and where they are located are important in a distribution channel. The amount customers will buy is another factor to study. Of course, the volume produced must be considered. Fresh vegetables may be marketed directly to consumers from the farm. However, large farms often find that marketing through a processing plant with nationwide distribution is best for them.

- **Kind of product**—The distribution channel selected varies with the nature of the product. Highly perishable products, such as berries, must be marketed quickly. If not, the product may spoil before it reaches the consumer. Products which don't spoil quickly, such as wool, can go through a much longer, more complex distribution channel.

- **Competition from other products**—When several people are involved in marketing a product, the various producers may compete for customers. Agriculture tends to have many producers who furnish the same product. The identity of many products can not be distinguished from one farm to another. Distribution channels that allow many producers to use the same channel reduce individual competition.

- **Experience**—Some producers have considerable experience in marketing and using the distribution channels; others aren't very knowledgeable of the processes. Those who understand distribution may wish to select a channel where they are more involved. Personal preference is also an important factor in deciding on the channel to use. For example, a grower who doesn't want to operate a roadside stand should sell through a processing plant, packing shed, or central farmers market. In some cases, growers sell to buyers or directly to supermarkets.

ELEMENTS OF A PHYSICAL DISTRIBUTION SYSTEM

Goods are moved from the producer to the consumer in a variety of ways. Some may be hauled long distances and stored in processed form for a time. The more steps involved in getting a product to the consumer, the more complex the physical distribution of the product.

Physical distribution is often described as a system. Many elements may be involved. When the elements work well together, goods are efficiently and effectively distributed. If one part of the system fails, goods aren't delivered as they should be. The elements involved in distributing particular goods vary depending on the kind of product and its qualities.

The major elements of physical distribution are described here.

ASSEMBLING

Assembling involves ordering and receiving supplies and products. It varies with the kind of supply or product.

In a farm supplies business, assembling involves ordering and receiving supplies from various sources. A quantity of all the items to be sold is usually on hand. Shelves and bins may need to be stocked. Knowing what, when, and how much to order is important in a farm supplies business.

With farm products, assembling involves soliciting crops from farmers and properly receiving them. This may involve having farmers sign contracts to provide a certain quantity of product at a given time. This assures that a supply will be on hand for distribution. When received, a procedure must be in place to determine how much was received, to keep accurate records, and to assure that the farmer is paid.

MATERIALS HANDLING

Materials handling is the unloading, lifting, moving, and loading of goods. All supplies and products must be moved about. Trucks, wagons, barges, and other vehicles must be loaded and unloaded. Once unloaded, the materials must be put in the right place for storage or manufacture. Forklifts, augers, compressed air, water, and other means are used to move supplies and products within factories and warehouses.

Feed, fertilizer, and other supplies can often be moved in bulk form.

Figure 14–6. Materials handling is a major activity at a large manufacturing plant, such as this paper mill. The raw materials and finished products must be moved from one location to another as a part of manufacturing. (Courtesy, Weyerhaeuser Company)

Specially designed truck beds and storage bins are used. Augers and other means may be used to move the materials. In some cases, these materials are put in bags, cans, or other containers. For example, bags of feed are moved with forklifts, conveyor belts, and in other ways. Most places use power equipment to move materials, keeping hand lifting to a minimum.

Harvested crops, livestock, and related products must be moved to get them from the farm to the consumer. Grain may be hauled by truck to an elevator where it is unloaded and conveyed to a bin. Livestock may be shipped by truck or rail, unloaded at ramps, and herded through the fenced alleys of cattle barns. Milk is held in bulk storage tanks and pumped through clean pipes to the tank on the milk truck.

PACKAGING

Packaging involves putting materials into containers—cans, boxes, barrels, or tanks. The containers must protect the material as well as prevent loss. Most supplies and products are put into containers of a certain size. This makes it easy to determine the amount that is on hand. Examples are apples, which are measured in boxes (weight = 44 pounds), and cotton, which is measured in 500-pound bales.

Containers may have labels attached that describe the supply or product and give the amount that is in the container. Products reaching the final consumer usually must have carefully designed labels that give accurate information about the product.

Figure 14–7. Plastic bags are often used as containers for small amounts of fertilizer, such as this container for use by home owners and those with small gardens.

STORING

Storing, also known as warehousing, involves keeping a supply or product until it is needed. The conditions of storage must be appropriate for the material. Milk must be stored under refrigeration and cotton cloth must be kept dry and where it can't be soiled.

Grain is often stored on the farm, usually in bulk in bins. Some farmers use this to delay sale until the price has gone up. Others store the grain until it is needed for livestock feed or other uses.

Producers who don't own storage facilities may use central storage facilities located near railroads, highways, or in other strategic places. The produce from several farms may be stored together in one place. Grain elevators store grain in farming areas, near processing plants, and at ports. Compresses have warehouses for storing bales of cotton. In most cases, farmers pay a fee for use of the storage facilities.

Supplies and products are stored in many different kinds of structures. Some are stored in large tanks, such as raw milk; others are stored in bags in warehouse buildings, such as sacked feed.

The quantity of a supply in storage must be appropriate to meet the demands of the customers and the goals of the owner. Many agricultural businesses have reduced the amount of products held in warehouses because of the money that may be required to buy and store the products. On the other hand, adequate products or supplies must be on hand to meet the immediate demands of customers. When a customer wants to buy a product or supply and it isn't in stock, the customer may buy from another source. A sale has been lost!

Inventory is the term applied to the supplies and products that are stored or on-hand. An inventory is the complete list of all materials that are on-hand. The total number of bushels of grain on a farm is the farm's grain inventory. The inventory in a farm store must reflect the anticipated demands of customers. Having too much in the inventory may result in waste and ties up money that may be needed for other uses. Not having enough inventory may result in customers going elsewhere when their orders can't be filled.

Many warehouses use a perpetual inventory. This involves keeping a record of all materials that are received and shipped. The quantity on-hand at any time should be equal to receipts minus shipments. In some cases, losses may occur and these should be accounted for. Theft, damage by insects and rodents, and other losses that don't result in a sale must be accounted for and eliminated, if possible.

ORDER PROCESSING

Order processing refers to the procedures followed when an order is received. The cost for the materials must be calculated accurately and the payment collected. Careful records must be kept of all payments. Payments may be made in cash (currency or check). Some customers may charge the purchase to a credit card. An established customer with a good credit rating may be mailed a bill for what was ordered.

Sales tickets are prepared to document a sale. Multiple copies are needed–one for the buyer and one or more for the seller. A sales ticket should include the buyer's name and address, date, method of payment, and description, quantity, and price of the goods. Sales tickets are used in order picking, loading trucks, making deliveries, billing, and tax records. In some cases, register tapes are used in place of sales tickets.

Order processing also involves picking what the customer wants from the inventory and preparing it for shipment. Warehouses that stock many products may require considerable organization to make order picking efficient. Once the materials have been selected, they must be prepared for

______ 19 ____ **Allen's Farm Supply** No.: 008-0961

3809 Donner Road
Truckee, CA 95616
Phone (916) 555-1234
FAX (916) 555-4321

Bill to: Ship to:

Sold by	Cash	C.O.D.	Charge	On Account	Mdse Ret'd	Paid Out	

Qty	Description	Price	Amount
	Tax		
	Total		

Received by ______________

Figure 14–8. Sample sales ticket for a retail agricultural supplies business.

Figure 14–9. Small orders are here being packed for shipment by the
shipping department of an agricultural supply business.

delivery to the customer. In some cases, this involves boxing the items for
shipment, such as the supplies for a florist. Small amounts may be sent by
a parcel delivery service. In other cases, the material may be loaded in bulk
on a truck for delivery, as with feed or fertilizer.

INVENTORY CONTROL

Inventory control is maintaining an adequate stock of materials. Records
of receipts and shipments must be kept. These vary with the nature of the
supply or product. A garment plant must have sufficient cloth on hand to
make the desired clothes. If the plant runs out of cloth, the people who
operate the sewing machines won't have work to do.

Inventory control also involves producing what is needed. Making too
much hog feed when the demand is for horse feed results in a warehouse
full of feed that can't be sold. Feed that can be sold may not be available.
Many feed mills keep an inventory of feed ingredients and manufacture
the feed only after an order has been received. Not only does this reduce
inventory but it allows the feed mill to meet the specific needs of a
customer.

Computer systems are used by most agribusinesses to keep inventory
records. All receipts are entered in the computer. All shipments are entered.
A statement of the volume in the inventory can be quickly obtained from
the computer.

Maintaining inventory requires careful study of the market situation. Decisions must be made about what and how much to stock. Of course, the materials must arrive at the proper time for the inventory. Seed received after the planting season is of little value!

TRANSPORTING

Transporting is hauling materials from one place to another, usually from the seller to the buyer. The term, "make delivery," is sometimes used.

Transportation is often a major cost in marketing agricultural supplies and products. Many food products are perishable and require more sophisticated means of transportation. Some must be kept refrigerated.

Costs vary with the kind of transportation used. Air shipment is more expensive than truck, rail, or barge transport, but is much faster. Speed of delivery is often an important consideration in marketing. Quick delivery is important with some parts and materials, such as a part being shipped overnight to repair a broken harvester.

PACKAGING AND LABELING

The method of packaging is determined by the nature of the material. Solid materials can be packaged one way, while liquids must be packaged another. Live plants and animals require special consideration. Live fish are packaged in oxygenated water in tanks or plastic bags. Hazardous materials, such as motor fuel, also require special consideration in handling.

CONTAINERS AND PACKAGING

A *container* is anything that contains something. Commonly, containers are large units that hold packages or bulk quantities of materials. Containerization is used to ship large "packages," such as entire trailer loads of materials. The containers are lifted by a giant crane from rail cars onto truck beds or onto ships and barges. The containers may be filled with smaller crates, boxes, or other units of materials.

Packages are containers for materials. Larger packages may be known as cases or cartons. A case may contain a number of smaller packages. Several cases may be stacked on a *pallet* (small movable platform) and bound together as one unit. Here is one example: food may be in cans, twelve cans may be put in a case, twenty cases may be stacked and bound

Table 14-1
Standard Containers Used With Selected Agricultural Products
(weights and measures)

Commodity	Container/Unit	Weight
		(pounds)
Apples	Northwest box	44
Apricots	Lug (wooden box)	24
Bananas	Folding fiber box	40
Cabbage	Open-mesh bag	50
Coffee	Bag	132.3
Corn, shelled	Bushel[1]	56
Cotton (lint)	Bale	500
Grain sorghum	Bushel[1]	56
Maple syrup	Gallon	11.02
Milk (raw)	Gallon[1]	8.6
Oranges:		
California and Arizona	Box	90
Florida and Texas	Box	75
Peaches	Lug	20
Pineapples	Crate	70
Potatoes	Bushel[1]	60
Rice	Bushel[1]	45
Soybeans	Bushel[1]	58
Strawberries	12-quart crate	10
Tobacco	Hogshead	775
Turpentine	Gallon	7.23
Tomatoes (slicer)	Crate	60
Wheat	Bushel[1]	61

Source: U.S. Department of Agriculture.

[1]Though measured in bushels, most of these products are marketed in bulk quantities and are not typically put in bushel containers.

together on a pallet, and a number of pallets put into one container. This method of shipping is designed to move goods at the least cost in a timely manner.

PURPOSES OF PACKAGING

Packaging materials fulfill several purposes in physical distribution.

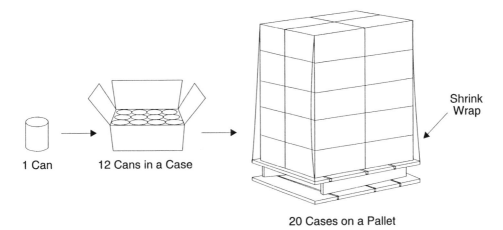

20 Cases on a Pallet

Figure 14–10. Cans, cartons, and pallets are often combined in shipping to facilitate handling.

Protection

Packaging helps prevent damage. This includes protecting the product from being damaged as well as keeping the product from damaging other materials.

Packaging may hold products in position so that they don't bump together and cause damage. Some products need to be cushioned against vibration. Various kinds of packaging materials may be used. Shredded paper and wood have largely been replaced with plastic-type sheet material with air bubbles and particles of plastic (often called "peanuts") or similar materials.

Portioning

Most materials are desired in certain quantities, known as portions. Large quantities are divided

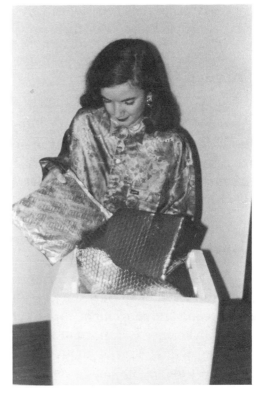

Figure 14–11. Packaging materials for perishable food items may include a styrofoam chest, insulated packaging material, and a small container of ice.

into portion-size packages. These packages hold a quantity of the materials together, such as asparagus spears in a can. The size of a package is often the one that is most convenient for the customer to use and came about through tradition.

Portions may be based on weight or other measures. Bags of feed usually are sold on the basis of weight, such as a 50-pound bag of hog feed. Foods may be sold in standard-size containers, such as bushels, lugs, and baskets. Many containers have standard sizes as established by the U.S. Department of Agriculture. All people involved in trading the product know that a bushel or other container holds a certain quantity.

Selling

Packages divide materials into quantities for customers. A bale of cotton is the appropriate size for a textile mill. A box of blueberries is what a consumer typically wants at the supermarket. Attractive and convenient packages make products appealing to consumers. Clean, colorful packages increase appeal and sales of many supplies and products.

Product Identification

Packages should provide a place for the material to be properly labeled. The label will contain specific information about the product, including the name of the product, how much product is in the container and, in the case of food, nutritional information. Labels may also provide important information about product storage (such as "keep refrigerated") and how to store the packages (such as "this side up").

Convenience

Packages are sized for convenience in using the product. Truck loads of fresh-picked snap beans are convenient for processing plants. Baskets of snap beans are convenient for supermarket use.

Convenience is important to the consumer. Many products are packaged for ease of use. Frozen foods may be in containers that can be used to cook the product. In some cases, packages can be used as serving containers.

PACKAGING MATERIALS

Packaging material is the material used to make packages. Various materials are used depending on the qualities of the product being packaged, how it is to be stored, and the way it is to be transported. Liquids require certain kinds of materials, while dry products can be packaged in other kinds of materials. The containers used must meet certain standards established by the Interstate Commerce Commission and the carriers of the products.

Common kinds of packaging materials are presented here.

Paper

Many kinds of paper packaging are used in agricultural marketing. Some products are put in the containers on the farm, others after they leave the farm. Fresh vegetables and fruit may be packaged on the farm or at a nearby packing shed. Frozen products may be put in paper containers after freezing or as a part of the freezing process. Cans may be put in paper boxes for shipping. Flour, sugar, and similar products may be put in paper bags.

A stiff paper known as cardboard is often used in making boxes and cartons. Heavier boxes are made of corrugated cardboard material. Lighter boxes are made of thinner material, such as shoe board or bending board.

Flexible paper is used to make bags and similar materials. Some packaging is designed to be used for the final preparation of the product, such as popcorn that can be prepared in the microwave. Fertilizer, feed, and other supplies often are packaged in paper bags.

Figure 14–12. These strawberries have been packaged in carefully designed cardboard containers.

Metal

Various metal containers are used, with aluminum and cans coated with tin or enamel being most common. Coated cans are often used for canning meats, fruit, vegetables, juices, and similar products. Some cans are designed for ease of opening, such as a can of snack food sausages.

Cans vary in shape and size. Pesticides may be in five-gallon cans or large drums. Smaller cans are used for other products, such as food. Metal containers may be used for other materials, such as oil, fuel, and grease.

Specialized canning equipment is needed to put materials in cans and properly seal them. Automated assembly line procedures where many cans can be quickly packed and sealed are the most popular.

Plastic

Increasingly, containers are made of plastic materials. Boxes, cans, baskets, bags, bottles, and other containers may be plastic. Pesticides, feed, equipment parts, oil, foods, and other materials are often packaged in plastic containers. Plastic materials also may be used to seal and bind containers together.

Perishable supplies and products may be put in styrofoam containers that provide good insulation and keep the product frozen or cold. Additional insulation material may be used. Frozen water-filled bags may be put in the containers to prevent thawing of the product.

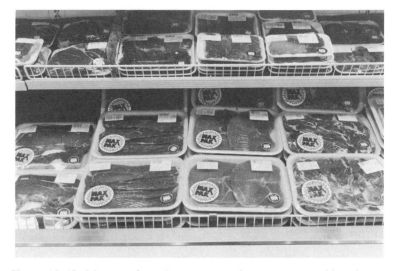

Figure 14–13. Meat products in a supermarket are protected by plastic packaging materials.

Plastic materials are light weight and easy to use. They can create a water-tight package that keeps the product in and foreign materials out. For example, seed packaged in plastic is protected from water while being shipped or stored. Water would damage the seed and make it worthless.

Disposal of plastic containers is sometimes a problem. Empty containers shouldn't be thrown into creeks or left in fields and pastures. Containers that have had poisonous materials in them must be washed and handled according to instructions on the labels. In some cases, the manufacturer of the poisonous material will take the container back after it is empty.

Some plastic materials are slow to *biodegrade* (rot or disintegrate). Once in the environment, they may stay a long time. Manufacturers of plastic now add corn starch and other materials to speed bio-degrading.

Plastic containers can be recycled. Of course, those that once contained dangerous materials must be separated from those containing other materials, such as milk or soft drinks. Recycling involves sorting the containers according to the code located on them and returning them to a recycling center.

Glass

Glass has been used successfully to package agricultural supplies and products for a long time. Jars, bottles, jugs, vials, ampules, and other glass containers are used. Glass prevents spoilage of foods and other materials. It is economical and can be re-used and recycled. Major disadvantages include breaking and environmental dam-

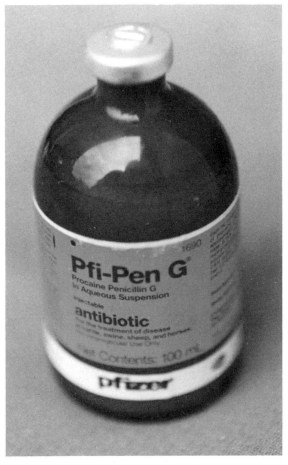

Figure 14–14. Animal biologicals are often packaged in glass containers with carefully designed tops that allow the filling of syringes.

age when improperly discarded. Specialized equipment is often needed to use glass for packaging. Foods are preserved by canning and sealing them in glass. Animal medicines are kept viable in glass containers.

Fibers

Cotton, jute, hemp, and other fibers are used to make bags and sacks. Containers from jute and hemp fibers are known as burlap, a coarse woven material. Jute is frequently used to make sacks for coffee beans, potatoes, and other products.

Bags and sacks are both containers that can be closed at the top. Sacks are larger than bags and usually made of stronger material. Bags have the disadvantage of allowing products to be contaminated, as when water gets on a burlap bag filled with rice. Most fiber bags are biodegradable and decay in a few months when exposed to moisture or buried in the earth.

Wood

Wood is used in making boxes, barrels, baskets, crates, and other kinds of packages. The use of wood has declined in recent years, though it is still used in many ways. Thin wooden strips are used for crates and baskets. Heavy boards may be used in building crates for large pieces of equipment. Pallets are strong, easily moved wooden platforms that support hundreds of pounds of supplies and products. Many warehouses store and transport boxes and bags of materials on pallets using forklifts and other power equipment.

LABELS

Labels are used to identify products and provide important information for the consumer. All containers should be properly labeled. Truthful labeling is essential. The U.S. Department of Agriculture, Federal Trade Commission, Food and Drug Administration, and the Consumer Product Safety Commission have regulations on labeling. In addition, many states have specific requirements.

Labels on fertilizer, seed, chemicals, and other products should provide essential information about the product. All labels should give the quantity of product in the container and the name and address of the manufacturer. In addition, labels provide information unique to the product. Fertilizer labels provide details on the analysis of the fertilizer, including the amounts of nutrients it contains. Seed labels describe the specific variety of seed, foreign material (trash), noxious weed seed, germination percentage, date prepared and other details, including planting procedures. Chemical labels describe the product, tell how to use it, and list safety procedures and other precautions.

Labels on food products are carefully designed to provide an accurate description

Figure 14–15. Sample label from a meat product packaged for retail sale includes a product identification bar code as well as name of product, price, weight, date, and other details.

of the contents. The name of the food, ingredients used to make the food, weight, and other details are nearly always listed. Information about nutrition must be included on most foods, especially those that have been processed. Storage and preparation instructions are often included.

Labels may be printed directly onto the container or attached in a secure manner to the container. Boxes often have label information printed on them. Jars and cans often have paper labels glued to them. Bags may have labels which have been sewn into the top as it was sealed after filling.

TRANSPORTING SUPPLIES AND PRODUCTS

Transporting is the moving of agricultural supplies and products from one geographic location to another. Marketing agricultural supplies and products depends on a good system of economical transportation.

METHODS OF TRANSPORTATION

Three major ways are used to transport materials: land, water, and air. Combinations of the three ways are often used to get materials where they are needed.

Figure 14–16. A truck-tractor with semi-trailer used to haul pulp
         wood.

Land

Land transportation primarily involves trucks and railroads. Some agricultural produce may be transported by tractors pulling wagons, with
animals used to a lesser extent to pack materials or pull wagons or sleds.
Animals are used in places where motor vehicles can't go and in lesser-de-
veloped nations that don't have other transportation. Pipelines, found all
across North America, are important in moving oil and related materials.

Trucks and truck-tractors with semi-trailers and trailers are most frequently used. These are commonly referred to as motor carriers. Roads and
highways must be passable for trucks, as they bog down on wet ground
and can't travel over rough terrain. Trucks and trailers are often designed
for the specific product or supply to be hauled. Raw milk is hauled from
farms in refrigerated tanks. Livestock are hauled in vehicles with sides and
often covers. Logs and poles are hauled on strong trailers with supports.
Grain, feed, and other materials may be hauled in bulk in specially-designed
truck bodies that are easy to load and unload.

Rail transportation is possible only where railroads are located. It is
an economical way to ship large quantities of materials, such as grain,
lumber, and feed. In some cases, a piggy-back approach is used so that rail
flat cars transport trailers or semi-trailers. This combines the advantages of
economical rail transportation and ease of final delivery by truck. The
trailers are removed from the flat cars, hooked to a truck-tractor, and driven
to the delivery point.

Figure 14–17. Rail cars being loaded at a canned food processing plant.

Water

Water transportation relies primarily on boats, ships, and barges. Other forms are occasionally used; sometimes large shipments of logs are bound together and floated to their destination. Water transportation can only be

Figure 14–18. Barges are often used to transport raw materials and manufactured products. These barges are being moved into a lock on the Tennessee-Tombigbee Waterway by a tug boat. (Courtesy, Weyerhaeuser Company)

used when goods are located near rivers, large lakes, oceans, and where other water resources are available. Port facilities are needed to load and unload supplies and products.

Water transportation is an economical way to move large quantities of products, including raw materials. Grain, logs, lumber, paper, and minerals are frequently shipped on rivers and lakes. International trade may involve large ships that transport machinery and equipment, foods, fertilizers, and other materials.

Air

Air transport is used when products need to be moved quickly. Shipping by air is often known as air freight. Airplanes are the most common carriers, although helicopters are sometimes used. In many cases, air transportation is used for high-value, perishable materials. Live plants and small animals may be shipped by air. Fresh fruit, seafood, flowers, animal medicines, seed, and other products may be shipped by air.

Figure 14–19. These packages are being loaded into an airplane for quick delivery.

Large airplanes can transport many tons of cargo. Specialized package delivery services use airplanes to ship materials overnight to many places that are thousands of miles away.

Helicopters are occasionally used to move poles in rough terrain, feed cattle in remote areas, or apply pesticides to crops.

TRANSPORTATION PROCEDURES

All transportation is subject to various regulations. Some of the regulations are from the federal government, while others are state and local. Agricultural marketers must conform to the regulations. In addition, all materials must be properly shipped and received.

Transportation facilities and equipment may be owned by a farm, agribusiness, or transportation company. Since the needed facilities and equipment are expensive, many farmers and agribusinesses use the services of transportation companies. These companies may be common carriers that haul for many different people or contract carriers that haul only specialized materials for one or a few customers. When a farm or agribusiness owns its own equipment it is a private carrier. It can haul only its own materials in either raw or processed form.

Regulations

Many regulations apply to transportation.

- **Licensing**—Operators and vehicles must be licensed. Operator licensing is used to insure that the operator is qualified to operate the vehicle. Many operators attend special schools on vehicle operation, such as truck driving school. Governments license vehicles in order to collect taxes and insure that the vehicles are safe. The kind of license needed varies with where the vehicle is operated. Trucks that travel into many states may need a license for each state.

- **Quarantine and product quality**—Agricultural products are subject to inspections and quality control. Raw products may be prohibited from entering a state or local area. Some fruit can't be hauled from one region to another without appropriate inspection and authorization. Unauthorized raw products can introduce new crop pests. Insects, rodents, diseases, weeds, and other problems have been spread by hauling. A good example is the pesky fire ant that is found across the southern part of the United States. The ant was reportedly brought to the United States with a boat load of bananas.

- **Operation regulations**—Vehicles must be operated according to safety regulations. Speed and weight limits on highways must be observed. Under-age drivers aren't permitted in certain places, such as on a log and pole yard.

- **Service and delivery obligations**–Common carriers are legally obligated to haul and deliver materials properly. All deliveries must be made within a reasonable time. Carriers must serve the needs of all shippers regardless of size. Materials must be delivered in good condition.

Record Keeping

Careful records must be kept of all transported materials. The most important record is the *bill of lading*. This document serves as a receipt to the shipper and a contract for the carrier to deliver the materials. Bills of lading typically include the name of the shipper, the consignee (who will receive the materials), name of carrier, description of material being shipped, charges for shipment, and other information. Upon receipt, the consignee should carefully document the amount and condition of the materials received.

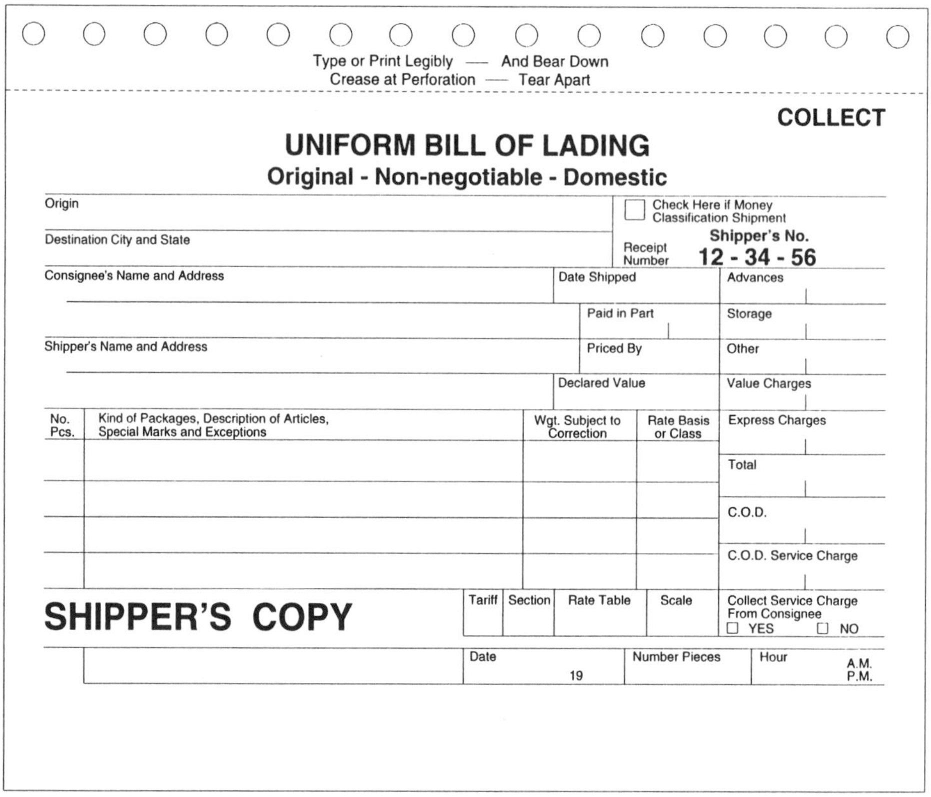
Type or Print Legibly — And Bear Down
Crease at Perforation — Tear Apart

COLLECT

UNIFORM BILL OF LADING
Original - Non-negotiable - Domestic

Origin
Check Here if Money Classification Shipment
Destination City and State
Receipt Number
Shipper's No. 12 - 34 - 56
Consignee's Name and Address
Date Shipped
Advances
Paid in Part
Storage
Shipper's Name and Address
Priced By
Other
Declared Value
Value Charges
No. Pcs. | Kind of Packages, Description of Articles, Special Marks and Exceptions | Wgt. Subject to Correction | Rate Basis or Class
Express Charges
Total
C.O.D.
C.O.D. Service Charge
SHIPPER'S COPY
Tariff | Section | Rate Table | Scale
Collect Service Charge From Consignee ☐ YES ☐ NO
Date 19 | Number Pieces | Hour A.M. P.M.

Figure 14–20. Sample bill of lading.

MAINTAINING QUALITY

The quality of supplies and products must be maintained during shipment. Many products must be shipped using special kinds of equipment. Further, they must be packaged to prevent damage.

Protection from Weather

Weather can damage products. Live plants and animals must be transported in conditions that minimize stress and loss. Cut flowers must be kept fresh and appealing to the florist and customer. Protection from weather extremes is often needed.

- **Protect from water**—Some materials must be kept dry. Seed, fertilizer, and other materials are destroyed or greatly damaged if they get wet from rain or snow. Cotton, wool, and other products must also be kept dry to prevent loss of quality.

- **Control temperature**—Below freezing temperatures can damage many products. Fruits, vegetables, bedding plants, and milk must be protected from freezing. High temperatures also can damage many products. Heat will kill animals and cause foods to spoil. Some products must be transported in refrigerated trucks, ships, airplanes, and rail cars.

Provide for Life Needs

Live plants and animals must be hauled under conditions that protect life. Plants need to be protected from wind and extreme temperatures. Animals need much the same protection. Specialized animal crops may need specific care. Fish are shipped in tanks of water with oxygen. Stops for rest and feeding may be necessary for animals on long trips.

Buyers may reject shipments that don't arrive in good condition. Processing plants will not use dead chickens, hogs, cattle, fish, or other animals. All animals should be transported in equipment that protects them from injury. Cattle, chickens, and other animals that have bruises, cuts, broken bones, and other injuries may be rejected or severely discounted in price.

FOLLOWING SAFE PRACTICES

Physical distribution often involves using and working around dangerous equipment. Following appropriate safety practices can help reduce the possibilities of injury.

THE WORK ENVIRONMENT

The physical distribution work environment can be a source of injury if safe practices aren't followed.

- **Observe safety rules**—Always follow safety rules in operating equipment and handling materials. Larger agricultural marketing firms may put up posters listing safety rules for the benefit of employees and customers. Smaller firms, though the rules may not be posted, may pose the same dangers.

- **Wear safety protection**—Certain work environments present hazards that require special safety protection. Hearing protection should be worn in places with a lot of noise. Eye protection should be used where objects, liquids, or small particles might harm vision. Respirators may be needed in dusty places or around chemicals. Wear protective clothing as needed, including gloves, hats, and shoes or water-proof boots.

- **Know the dangers associated with the work**—Some supplies and products are more hazardous than others. Large animals can attack people by kicking, biting, hooking, or in other ways. Chemicals and other materials may contain poisons that could be dangerous to health. Know about what you are working with and the dangers involved.

- **Keep a clean and orderly work environment**—Many safety hazards result when people don't keep the work environment neat and orderly. All safety devices should be in good working condition, such as the fire extinguisher. Materials should be stored properly so that people don't trip over them.

- **Ventilate the work area**—Proper ventilation assures that the air is safe. Grain elevators, feed mills, cotton gins, and other places may have a build-up of dust in the air. In some cases, the dust is explosive. In all cases, the dust is hazardous to breathe. Ventilation fans should operate properly and be used as appropriate.

- **Have a first aid kit**—A well-stocked first aid kit should be available on the work site.

- **Know emergency procedures**—All people should know the procedures to follow in case of an emergency. Know the location of shut-off valves and switches, releases, and other safety devices and how to use them. Post emergency telephone numbers by the telephone.

EQUIPMENT OPERATION

Physical distribution often involves using power equipment and machinery. Safety hazards can be reduced by following certain rules.

- **Have training in operation**—People need to know how to properly operate equipment. Be sure you are trained before operating forklifts, tractors, trucks, conveyor belts, augers, and other devices.

- **Use equipment properly**—Equipment is designed and built for certain uses. It should always be used as intended. Do not operate equipment unsafely, such as too fast, on steep inclines, and over slippery surfaces. Don't overload the equipment as this could cause it to break or turn over.

- **Guards**—Equipment usually has safety guards in the most dangerous locations. Belts, chains, pulleys, drive shafts, and other moving parts are often covered with guards. Be sure the guards are in place.

- **Keep equipment in good repair**—Equipment should be in good

Figure 14–21. Forklift being used to move a pallet with bags of feed. (Courtesy, Moorman Feed, Quincy, Illinois)

operating condition. Broken or inoperable equipment should be repaired. Also, do not modify equipment so that it is unsafe.

- **Properly tend equipment**—Power equipment may use motors or engines to operate moving parts. Equipment that is on should always be observed. Leaving a conveyor belt or auger running unattended is inviting danger. Visitors, including customers, should be restricted in terms of where they can go so that they are not exposed to the dangers of equipment.

SUMMARY

Physical distribution is a cluster of marketing functions that involve physically moving supplies and products from the point of origin to the point of final use. This includes supplies that are used in agricultural production as well as the products of farms, ornamental horticulture, and forestry.

Most agricultural supplies and products reach the consumer through specific channels of distribution. Each has distribution outlets, which are at the end of the distribution system. Outlets include dealerships, wholesalers, retailers, catalogs, auctions, and buyers. The intensity of the distribution channels varies. Some are intensive because the materials are available at a number of places. Others are selective because a limited number of outlets have the material. Some are exclusive when only a few carefully chosen outlets are involved.

CHAPTER SELF-CHECK

Match the following terms with the correct definitions:

a. bill of lading

b. inventory

c. container

d. physical distribution

e. pallet

f. materials handling

g. dealership

h. channel of distribution

i. inventory control

j. transporting

_____ supplies or products that are stored or on hand

_____ receipt for shipper and contract for carrier

_____ hauling materials from one place to another

_____ anything that contains something

_____ functions in moving materials from point of origin to point of consumption

_____ route that a supply or product goes through

_____ sales agencies that have the authority to sell a supply or product

_____ maintaining an adequate stock of materials

_____ small movable platform

_____ unloading, lifting, moving, and loading of goods

QUESTIONS AND PROBLEMS FOR DISCUSSION

1. What is physical distribution? Why is it important?

2. How does physical distribution apply to supplies and products?

3. How is physical distribution related to agricultural marketing?

4. What is a channel of distribution? What are distribution outlets?

5. Describe the major distribution outlets in agriculture.

6. What is distribution intensity? How does it work?

7. Why is physical distribution described as a system?

8. List and briefly describe the elements in a physical distribution system.

9. What is a container? Why are they important?

10. What major purposes are served by packaging?

11. What kinds of packaging materials are used?

12. What kinds of transportation are used in agriculture?

13. What safety practices should be followed in physical distribution? Visit an agricultural marketing business and observe the possible safety hazards and how they have been handled.

ACTIVITIES

1. Prepare a display of different packaging materials used with agricultural supplies and products. Label the different materials, describing the kind of container and its use.

2. Construct a poster or bulletin board with labels from various food containers. Write a short paper that summarizes the general information on the labels.

3. Tour a packing shed, processing plant, livestock auction, or other agricultural marketing facility. Prepare a report of your observations.

Chapter 15

ADVERTISING AND DISPLAYING

Advertising is a part of everyone's life. In fact, we all receive advertisements daily in the mail. Every store that we shop in has displays promoting products. Advertising has become so commonplace through radio, television, newspapers, magazines, billboards, clothing, and store displays that most people have accepted it as part of their environment.

The movement of agricultural goods and services from producers through processors, manufacturers, wholesalers, and retailers to customers is a major economic activity in the free enterprise system. Most agricultural businesses use advertising to communicate information about products and services that they are offering for sale to potential customers. It is the intent and purpose of this form of promotion to bring together buyers and sellers so that a product or service can be sold.

According to the American Marketing Association, *advertising* is defined as "any form of nonpersonal presentation and promotion of ideas, goods or services by an identified sponsor." Three basic forms of media

Figure 15–1. Print media is an important tool in attracting customers to purchase animal feeds. (Courtesy, MoorMan's Feed, Quincy, Illinois)

413

are used in presenting the advertising message: (1) *print media*, such as newspapers, magazines, trade journals or brochures; (2) *broadcast media*, commonly referred to as radio and television; (3) *visual media*, defined as billboards, signs, or displays.

In general, these forms are termed mass media. *Mass media* can be defined as forms of media utilized to reach large numbers of people.

OBJECTIVES

This chapter will assist you in understanding advertising and display of agricultural products and services. Upon completion of this chapter, you will be able to:

- Explain advertising and its relationship to marketing.

- Describe the role of advertising and display in selling agricultural products.

- Describe the major elements of a good print advertisement.

- List the types of newspapers and categories of advertisements.

- Describe the rough layout of a newspaper advertisement.

- Describe the use of radio and television advertising.

- Explain the purpose and use of direct mail in advertising.

- List the types of displays used in agribusinesses and describe considerations in designing a display.

- Explain how to develop a plan for an agricultural display.

TERMS

advertising
balance
black space
body copy
broadcast media
business magazines
circulation
classified advertising
clip art
column inch
consumer magazines
contrast
cooperative ad
copywriter
direct mail
display
display advertising
display classified
  advertisement
emphasis
exhibit
focal point
harmony
headline
illustration
line art
logotype
mass media
point-of-purchase
print media
promotion
proportion
publicity
rough layout
selling points
slicks
target audience
typeface
visual media
white space

RELATIONSHIP BETWEEN AGRICULTURAL ADVERTISING AND MARKETING

Agricultural products generally follow a path from the farmer or producer to the processor or manufacturer. After processing, products go to wholesalers, then to retailers, and finally to consumers. Marketing includes all of the activities from the time the agricultural product is produced until it reaches the final consumer. The flow of agricultural products and services can be simple or complex depending on whether the path followed is direct or some alternate flow is used. For example, wheat is produced by farmers and sold to grain elevators or wholesalers, who in turn sell the wheat to processors for milling into several different products, such as flour. Flour, along with the other products, is sold to wholesalers who package and sell some directly to grocery stores or retailers. They, in turn, sell it to consumers. Also, some of the flour is sold to manufacturers, who add value by baking bread and making other food items. These value-added items are sold to retail stores that sell them to consumers. Sometimes the manufacturer also sells directly to the consumer. From this example, you can see that there are a lot of activities that must take place in order for the product to reach

Figure 15–2. Agricultural products follow a variety of paths from the producer to the consumer and from the retailer or wholesaler to the producer.

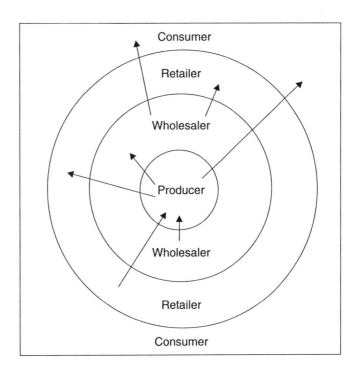

the consumer. Some of the activities include transporting, pricing, and financing of products; formulating product information; establishing title or ownership; and obtaining insurance.

The activity that connects all of the different paths from the producer through the processor and/or manufacturer to the wholesaler and retailer and finally to the consumer is communication. Advertising is one of the major ways that communication is established between the seller of agricultural products and the potential buyers. Producer groups advertise to processors. Processors or manufacturers advertise to wholesalers, and retailers advertise to consumers. However, farmers often organize into commodity or producer groups and conduct advertising and promotion campaigns directly to consumers and retailers. Examples of farmers organizing at the local, state, and national levels to advertise and promote agricultural products include the National Dairy Council, Blue Diamond Almond Growers, beef and pork producers associations, and peach producers.

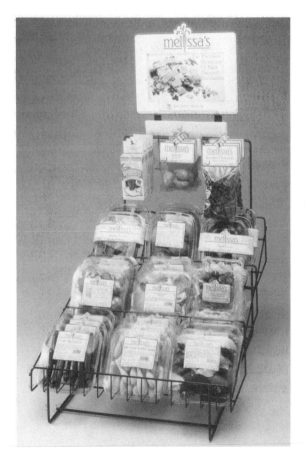

Figure 15–3. Display of value added produce. (Courtesy, Melissa's World Variety Produce, Inc., Los Angeles)

IMPORTANCE OF ADVERTISING

Good advertising has been proven to be important to the success of many businesses. Successful businesses do not wait for customers to come to them. Instead, they motivate and invite customers through quality advertisements that are used in a planned, targeted, and consistent manner. There are four reasons advertising is important to the success of businesses.

1. Advertising makes it possible to seek new customers from large masses of people.

2. It helps develop a positive public image, and build customer confidence and reputation in the community.

3. Potential customers are informed about the products and services that are sold, acquainted with the price, and encouraged to buy from a specific business.

4. Advertising is economical.

Although advertising is important, it does not compensate for low-quality products or inefficient sales service. Advertising is primarily a vehicle to attract potential customers into a business and to answer basic questions such as: what is the product or service, who is selling it, where is it located, and how much does it cost. When customers come into the business it is important for sales and service people to meet customers in a positive manner, determine their needs, and assist them in understanding, selecting, and buying the product or service that will meet their needs. Through this type of customer-oriented team effort, businesses are able to realize successes such as increased sales, repeat customers, and ultimately increased profits.

PROMOTIONAL ACTIVITIES USED IN AGRIBUSINESS

According to Samson and Price, "*promotion* is the coordination of all seller-initiated efforts to communicate with potential customers." In other words, the firm selling the product or service is attempting in some way to communicate with all potential buyers and influence them to make contact with the company or store to seek out the product or service. Products and services are promoted primarily through advertising, face-to-face selling, displays, and publicity.

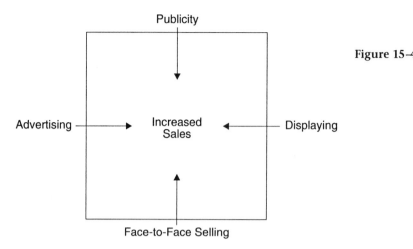

Figure 15-4. Promotion includes publicity, displaying, advertising, and face-to-face selling. All parts working together can increase sales.

ADVERTISING

Advertising is any message communicated to potential customers about a product or service that uses mass media (radio, television, magazines, direct mail, newspapers, etc.) and is paid for by a sponsor. The purpose of this form of product promotion is to inform the potential customer about a product or service and to motivate them to connect with the business that is selling that product or service.

Advertising is important to agribusinesses because they obtain much of their sales through advertisements in the mass media. Also, agribusiness is important to mass media because much of the cost of operating radio and television stations and newspapers is paid for by selling advertising space. Therefore, the next time that you watch your favorite television show or listen to your favorite radio station try to identify the sponsor. Generally, if there is no sponsor there is no program.

FACE-TO-FACE SELLING

In the chapter on selling, you learned that face-to-face selling is working directly with customers to assist them in solving problems by buying products or services. Because the role of advertising is to attract potential customers to the business and selling is helping customers satisfy needs, the two work in tandem to increase sales. Figure 15-4 illustrates the various aspects of product and service promotion.

DISPLAYS, EXHIBITS, AND DEMONSTRATIONS

Store (point-of-purchase) displays, including window arrangements and in-store special promotional exhibits and outdoor demonstrations are used by retail and wholesale agricultural businesses to promote products or services to potential customers. Displays offer the advantage of letting customers see the actual product. Demonstrations help them gain an understanding of how to use it. Just like advertisements, displays and demonstrations bring potential customers into a business and connect them with salespeople who can assist them with their buying decisions.

PUBLICITY

Publicity is mass media news coverage that includes the name of the business or product at no cost to the business. Creating positive publicity about a product, business, or industry does not happen randomly. Businesses develop plans and strategies to promote positive publicity that will build customer confidence. Often publicity and advertising are confused. It is important to remember that advertising is communication about a product or service with potential customers that is paid for by the business. Whereas, publicity is gained when news stories and other mass media mention the business or product at no cost to the business.

To create positive publicity, businesses sponsor activities of community

Figure 15–5. This point-of-purchase display is important in attracting customers to buy apples.

interest such as athletic events, music and cultural activities, and youth activities that attract a large number of potential customers. News coverage that results from these types of events will generate positive publicity for the product or business. This publicity builds customer confidence in the product or business.

Product promotion is a complex area of marketing that involves advertising, face-to-face selling, publicity, and display. Promotion can only become successful if it is teamed with effective face-to-face selling. When all four aspects of promotion are linked together in an integrated plan for product promotion the business can find true success.

DECIDING TO ADVERTISE

When an agricultural business, whether wholesale or retail, decides to advertise, six basic questions must be answered.

1. What products or services should be advertised?

2. Why is it necessary to advertise this product at this time?

3. To whom should the advertising be directed?

4. Which advertising media will be most effective?

5. When is the best time for the advertisement to appear?

6. How will the advertisement fit with the overall promotional calendar?

Advertising plans must address all of the above questions if sales and profits are to increase. Since advertising is expensive and subtracts from the profit, it is important that money spent on advertising show results. Therefore, each question must be carefully considered and an advertising plan developed that will meet the above objectives. Following is a brief discussion of each of the advertising decision-making questions.

DECIDING WHAT PRODUCTS OR SERVICES TO ADVERTISE

Many agricultural businesses sell a variety of products and it is difficult to determine which to advertise. Research has shown that most businesses are ahead to advertise the products that sell the best. In most businesses, nearly 70 percent of the gross sales comes from only 25 to 30 percent of the products or services offered by the business. Therefore, it makes good sense to advertise those products that are the best sellers. Although advertising what sells best appears simple, many businesses continue to focus their advertising on over-stocked items or end-of-season specials. People will not buy products that they don't want. Advertising such products will not increase profits or improve the image of the business in the community.

WHEN TO ADVERTISE

Once the product or service to be advertised is determined, the seller must ask, "Is this the best time?" Every product or service has a pattern of sales during the year. The ideal time to advertise is when the largest number of customers are making their buying decisions about that product. For example, most seed corn is generally sold after harvest, from November to February. During other months of the year, little seed corn is sold. Therefore, the ideal time to advertise seed corn is in late fall or early winter when the majority of customers are making buying decisions. Just as certain agricultural products are associated with specific months of the year, so are agricultural services. For example, fertilizer for most crops is sold in the spring. This is also the same time that fertilizer application services are in demand. Often both are featured jointly in an advertisement. Ideally, the seller must be knowledgeable of the requirements of the buyers so the advertising plan can be timed to meet the customers' needs. By so doing, the business can take full advantage of an advertisement and generate the most sales possible.

DIRECTING THE ADVERTISING

The seller of the product or service must identify the segment of the people in the market that are likely to buy. *Target audience* is the term used to describe to whom the advertising message is directed. In agriculture, there are many different target audiences, because agriculture is such a large and diverse industry. For example, the target audience for a specific brand of tractors is farmers. However, depending on the size and use of the tractor, the target audience may be a relatively small number of farmers.

To identify the target audience, the advertiser must consider the potential user of the product and who will make the buying decision. In the case of milking equipment for dairies, the target audience is the owners of dairies and their employees. The owner is interested in reducing labor costs and making the dairy more profitable, while the employees are interested in convenience and reducing manual labor.

SELECTING ADVERTISING MEDIA

Selecting the media that will be most effective in advertising various products and services is a difficult decision for every business. Large national agribusiness firms contract with advertising agencies to conduct detailed market research that assists in determining the best advertising media for the products and services sold. However, most small businesses do not have the resources to hire external consulting firms. They must rely on past experience and information from advertising salespeople to determine the best media mixes for their community, target audience, and products. As a result, no two businesses have the same advertising plan. Figure 15-6 presents a summary of the major kinds of advertising media and the advantages and disadvantages of each.

Major Advertising Media Choices

Media	Advantages	Disadvantages
Radio	Can motivate easily Accommodates changes Easy to saturate target audience	Message depends on announcer Possible waste in distribution

Television	Utilizes movement and sound
	  effectively
	Product featured can be
	  demonstrated realistically
	Highly motivational
		Cost is high
		Quality dependent on expertise
		  of producer

Newspaper	Wide circulation Consistent illustration Dependable Economical	Some waste in circulation

Direct Mail	Easy to target
	Color and illustrations are
	  limitless
		High cost
		Some customers may have
		  negative image of the business

Magazine	High quality color Can saturate large audience	Cost varies depending on circulation Planning must be done early Changes are difficult

Figure 15-6. Advantages and disadvantages of major advertising media are presented.

THE ADVERTISEMENT AND
THE OVERALL PROMOTIONAL CALENDAR

It is essential to know how advertisement fits with the overall promotions of the business. Much of the advertising any agricultural retail or wholesale business does is linked to the seasons of the year. However, most agricultural businesses have opportunities for special promotions. Celebrations featuring agricultural products produced in their area, such as peach days or turkey days are popular. Sometimes a business creates its own events featuring new product introductions, a grand opening and/or anniversary, remodeling celebration, or an end-of-season clearance. These kinds of promotions assist in attracting new customers and in keeping existing customers by helping them save money and/or fulfill needs. Special promotions sometimes involve not only special prices on selected products or services, but free gifts, refreshments, famous people, and special prizes. All of these ideas for promotion attract more potential customers into the business and encourages them to stay and become acquainted with the products and services. Special promotions often attract news media representatives and can give the business free news coverage that will assist in building a positive public image. The cost of special promotions can be very high. Therefore, the costs must be budgeted carefully to maintain a profitable business.

Making the decision to advertise requires that the agricultural business manager determine what, why, where, when, to whom, and how to advertise. These questions are not always easy to answer, but when addressed carefully can lead to a successful advertising promotion program.

HOW AGRIBUSINESS USES
PRINTED MEDIA
FOR ADVERTISEMENTS

The three major types of printed media are newspapers, magazines, and direct mail. Newspaper advertising is the largest single form of printed advertising in the United States. It is estimated that there are over 1,700 daily papers with a total *circulation* (number of people that purchase and read a newspaper or magazine) of about 63 million copies. Also, there are many weekly newspapers and community shoppers or advertising papers available to consumers.

ADVERTISING IN NEWSPAPERS

Newspapers play an important role in peoples' lives. They help to form public opinion, educate, entertain, provide a window to view the world, and bring buyers and sellers together through advertisements. Approximately 30 percent of all advertising dollars are spent on newspaper advertising. Billions of dollars are spent on newspaper advertising, and because newspapers sell 50 to 70 percent of their space to advertisers, consumers pay a relatively low price for a newspaper.

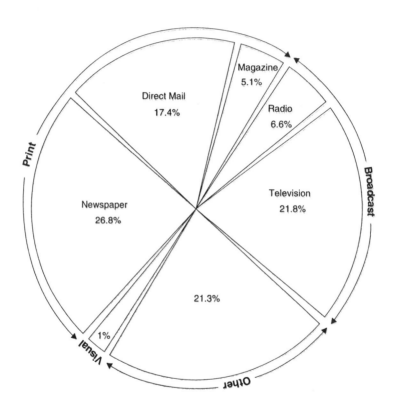

Figure 15-7. Summary of United States advertising expenditures in major advertising media. (Source: Statistical Abstract of the U.S., 1991).

The advantages of newspaper advertising include:

1. Low cost per reader due to large circulation.
2. Wide market coverage in most communities.

3. Quick customer response.

4. Flexibility in advertisement style, size, and format possible up to press time.

5. Detailed information and referral.

6. Consumers can refer to it easily.

7. Best media choice for most agricultural businesses.

Types of Newspapers and Uses

Newspapers can be classified into five types. National newspapers, such as *The Wall Street Journal* and *USA Today,* are national in scope and circulation. Daily newspapers originate in a specific city and have circulation in that city and region. Weekly newspapers are published once per week, usually in smaller communities and suburbs. Shoppers' newspapers are published once per week and consist mostly of advertisements and announcements with distribution limited to a neighborhood or small community. Special interest newspapers are focused at a specific group, such as college students, religious organizations, or fraternal groups. Agricultural business managers need to understand the different types of newspapers, their purposes, and audiences in order to make wise decisions about where to place advertisements to reach potential customers.

Daily, weekly, and shoppers' newspapers are good for farms selling produce, pet stores, feed dealers, farm Realtors, garden supply stores, nurseries, landscapers, and farm supply stores. Daily or weekly newspapers, which are regional in circulation, are good places for farm machinery dealers, fertilizer businesses, and agricultural building contractors to run their ads. National and large daily newspapers carry ads for manufacturers, such as seed corn companies, name brand farm machinery, and irrigation systems.

Kinds of Newspaper Advertising

Advertising in newspapers is divided into two primary groups: display and classified. *Display advertising* is the use of illustrations, headline, copy, and white space to promote a product or service to a potential customer in a newspaper advertisement. *Classified advertising* is the use of only the printed selling message to promote a product or service. Usually, the classified ads are grouped together in one section of the newspaper.

Figure 15–8. Display advertisements are designed uniquely for selling each product. Classified ads have one basic design and are located in one section of the newspaper.

There are three major types of display advertisements: local, national, and cooperative. Local ads are the type that agricultural businesses in the community place to sell specific products or services identified with their store in daily, weekly, and shoppers' newspapers. Generally, local ads are prepared by the newspaper, but may utilize nationally prepared advertisements, called, *slicks*. National ads feature a product or service, but do not connect it with a specific business. The ad usually focuses on features and benefits and promotes the national brand such as John Deere machinery, Scotts lawn fertilizer, or Holstein dairy cattle. *Cooperative ads* combine both national expertise in advertising and brand identification with the local business. Often the local agricultural business arranges for and purchases the advertising space in the newspaper and the national company designs the ad and may provide some funding.

Advertising Cost

Newspaper advertising is sold by the column inch. A *column inch* is the width of a column of print and 1 inch in length. A typical newspaper might be nine columns wide and 22 inches long. This would be almost 200 column inches on a single sheet. Rates vary widely, and there are different rates for display and classified ads. Ads placed in a Sunday edition of a daily newspaper may cost more per column inch than ads run other days. Companies that advertise frequently and consistently may be offered a special discounted rate.

MAGAZINE ADVERTISING

The second largest print medium is magazines. Currently, there are over 6,000 magazines in the United States with a total circulation per issue of about 265 million copies. Magazines are typically developed for a specialized audience that share a common interest. Traditionally, the highest quality magazines were national in scope due to the high cost of production and the need to have a large circulation to make the magazine financially feasible. Today, many high-quality agricultural magazines are being published for state and regional audiences.

The major types of magazines in the United States include consumer, business, and agriculture. *Consumer magazines* focus on a specific area of consumer interest and/or lifestyle. Examples include *MacUser, Better Homes and Gardens, Sunset,* and *Field and Stream.* Business magazines or trade journals are similar to consumer magazines, but are focused around industry groups. Some examples include *Appaloosa News, Modern Tire Dealer,* and *Walnut Growers.* These magazines promote a higher level of audience selectivity and therefore businesses who advertise have a more focused audience. Agriculture magazines are organized into general and industry or commodity groups. For example, general agriculture magazines include *Farm Journal, Successful Farming, California Farmer,* and *Farm Futures.* Industry or commodity magazines are the same as trade journals described above. They focus on specific agricultural commodities or specialized occupational groups of the agricultural industry. Examples include *Agri-Finance, Agricultural Education Magazine, Hoard's Dairyman,* and *Hampshire Herdsman.*

Types of Magazine Advertisements

The types of magazine advertisements are generally the same as newspaper ads: display and classified. However, magazines have a type of ads that are unique. These are termed display classified advertisements. *Display classified ads* use simple illustrations, varying type sizes and fonts, and limited white space. They are placed in the back of the magazine with the classified ads. In general, illustrations and photographs used in magazines are of much higher quality than those used in newspapers. Display ads in magazines have the advantage of using four color printing and high-quality

Figure 15–9. Display classified
advertisements are
placed in magazines
to attract customers.

paper. The audience and advertiser have come to expect the latest in style
and technology.

Advantages of Magazine Advertising

Some of the major advantages of using magazine advertising include:

1. Ability to produce high-quality color or black and white display ads.

2. Ability to selectively target a specific audience when needed.

3. Relatively long life span compared to other media.

4. Possible special effects and dramatic impact on potential customer.

DEVELOPING
A PRINTED ADVERTISEMENT

Agricultural business owners and advertisers agree that the ultimate
goal in developing a successful ad is to (1) reach out and attract the
attention of potential customers and (2) motivate them to visit the store
or business to buy the products or services offered for sale. There is no
guarantee that any advertisement will accomplish the above two goals
because of the many consumer and market variables that are constantly
changing. Companies spend large amounts of money to research why customers buy certain products and services and how different kinds of ad-

vertising impact the sales of various products and services. Although there is no magic formula for a perfect advertisement, advertising professionals agree that the major essential components of a good advertisement are:

1. Background knowledge of the product or service, selling points, and customers to be targeted.
2. A headline that attracts attention.
3. Clear and simplistic copy.
4. High quality illustrations that link ideas together.
5. Clearly stated price.
6. Identification of the business.

FACTORS INFLUENCING ADVERTISING COPY

Before any advertisement elements can be written, it is important for the *copywriter* (the person who creates the written information that goes into advertisements) to be knowledgeable of the product or service, have an understanding of the customer that is being targeted, and understand the primary selling points of the product or service.

Product or Service Knowledge

An ad that reflects incomplete product knowledge is doomed. Therefore, copywriters who are preparing ads need to have knowledge of the agricultural product or service. For example, to prepare ads for combines used to harvest wheat, corn, soybeans, and sorghum, the copywriter needs to know such things as size and capacity, engine specifications, cost, warranties, service availability, and other types of harvest head attachments. The copywriter who develops an ad for a quarter horse ranch will need to know pedigrees, birth dates, show placing, and training and handling practices. Every product or service has unique features which should be the focus of the advertisement.

Targeted Audience

The better an agribusiness knows its customers' needs for specific products or services, the easier it is for the copywriter to prepare the advertisement. Customers for agricultural products and services vary from farmers and ranchers to urban home owners and consumers. Also, customers' education level, needs, and ability to pay varies greatly. For example, a commercial corn producer purchases fertilizer and herbicide in large quantities. The corn producer may go to the farm supply business seeking only limited information about the fertilizer and herbicide, but wanting to know detailed information about price, quantity discounts, and credit applications. The same business also may sell lawn and garden fertilizer and herbicides. The targeted audience for these products may be primarily home owners who need a product that will both fertilize and kill the weeds in their lawn. They are more interested in product knowledge that will insure a beautiful, weed-free lawn, than a quantity discount.

Advertisements for the two examples above will be very different because the customers are different. Also, the display ads will appear in different places in the newspaper. The ad targeted for corn producers will appear in the farm section, whereas the ad targeted for homeowners will appear in the garden section. Without considerable knowledge of the targeted customers and their needs, it is almost impossible to prepare an ad that will be effective in increasing sales.

Selling Points

All successful advertisements have *selling points* (customer benefits) that are the focus of an advertisement. These selling points are what interests and motivates the customer to come into the business and seek more information to make a buying decision.

Selling points vary based on the purpose and nature of the product or service. Some of the common selling points stress economy, dependability, efficiency, ease of operation, low maintenance, service, comfort, and reliability. Selling points are most convincing when they are stated in terms of customer benefits. For example, lawn fertilizer ads stress how green and healthy the lawn will look, rather than how the fertilizer smells or looks. Market cattle feed supplements stress increased weight gain efficiency and increased producer profits and not feed appearance and composition.

Selling points are usually of three types: rational, emotional, and testimonial. Rational selling points focus on such logical ideas as low maintenance, efficiency, lower costs, increased profits, and environmental safety.

Emotional selling points focus on the way customers feel. Pride of ownership, recognition in the community, environmental friendliness, and improved appearance or health are common emotional selling points. Usually, these are not stated directly in ads, but inferred to customers through statements such as, "Get into the winner's circle!" "Milk, it does a body good," and "Eat more turkey, dance more tangos."

Testimonials are used in agricultural ads to endorse or recommend the use of specific products or services. For example a famous ice skater, Dorothy Hamill, is quoted in a plant fertilizer ad, "Like mother used to say, there's nothing like Miracle-Gro." Successful farmers are often quoted in ads for hybrid seed, fertilizer, animal feeds, and farm equipment to assist other farmers in picturing themselves using the product or service.

Agribusinesses that can give the copywriter the major selling points of a product or service for special groups of customers will enhance the chances for ultimate success of the ad—increased sales.

Figure 15–10. Major elements found in good advertisements: headline, copy, illustration, and business identification.

DEVELOPING ADVERTISEMENT HEADLINES

Advertising experts agree that one of the most important features in an ad is the headline. The *headline* is that part of any ad that attracts potential customers and stimulates the customer to continue to look or read further. Copywriters who develop headlines for national ads often spend several days reviewing background materials about the products or services and their selling points. The writers also study research about the buying habits of the targeted customers. Local agribusinesses and newspapers also need to be aware of the importance of headlines and take adequate time to prepare them. Headlines should (1) speak personally and directly to the potential customer, (2) stress the product's best selling points, (3) strive to be innovative and different, and (4) motivate the reader to seek more information.

Speak Personally and Directly to the Potential Customer

For headlines to be effective, they must get the attention of the potential customer. One way of getting attention is to speak to the customer directly. By using the word "you," the headline automatically becomes more personal and grabs the reader's attention. For example, if a farm supply store is having a sale on fence posts, the headline might read, "You can save 50 percent on fence posts!" Perhaps a corn seed dealer is introducing a new variety of corn. The headline might read, "You can take the first step to increased corn yields!" or "Do you want an extra $1 per bushel for your corn crop?"

Personalizing a headline can make a big difference in persuading the reader to take a few seconds and continue reading the ad. However, to hold the readers interest you will need to tell them more.

Stress the Best Selling Points

People read advertisements because they are looking for a solution to a particular need or want. Therefore, if the headline promises benefits that will satisfy needs or wants it will hold the readers attention. It has been often said, "Businesses sell the benefits derived from owning products or services." Headlines can take advantage of this statement by stressing benefits. The major challenge for copywriters and agricultural businesses is to identify the most important benefits. They need to determine what is most appealing to potential customers. For example, an ad for a garden tractor may read, "Landscaping was never so easy." This headline might appeal to landscape contractors. However, by changing one word it will attract a broader audience: "Gardening was never so easy." If other benefits are also important, the wording might read, "Gardening was never so easy and economical."

Try to be Innovative and Different

Customers are attracted to new and innovative products and services. Experienced copywriters know that new and different products and services are exciting to the public and frequently use the words, "new," "now," and "at last" to get customer attention. Examples of how agricultural businesses use these powerful words in headlines include: "To increase tomato yields try our new variety KL100!" and "At last a 40 horsepower tractor with 20 percent improved fuel efficiency!"

Motivate the Reader to Seek More Information

Consumers hear or see hundreds of advertisements each day if they listen to the radio or watch television. Also, most daily newspapers consist of 50 to 70 percent advertisements. Because people are exposed to a large number of ads daily, they spend only seconds viewing or listening to an individual ad. If the headline does not grab the consumer's attention and motivate them to seek more information in the ad, they move on to other activities.

Copywriters must think of themselves as potential buyers when they develop headlines. Unless they can envision how consumers will react to the ad headline, the ad's chances for effectiveness is limited.

In summary, remember that attention-getting headlines speak directly, stress the most important selling points, are as unique as possible, and stimulate the potential customer to seek more information.

DEVELOPING THE SELLING MESSAGE IN ADVERTISEMENTS

The selling message in advertisements is often referred to as the *body copy*. The body copy is useful in keeping the readers' attention and assisting them in understanding the benefits of owning the product or service. Copywriters should prepare a selling message that (1) sticks to the headline theme in a friendly way, (2) stresses key selling points, and (3) asks the reader to buy.

Stick to the Headline Theme in a Friendly Way

The selling message should build on the headline that captured the readers attention. For example, if the headline were, "The Best Self Mulching Lawn Mower Built for Home Owners !" The selling message that follows this headline could read, "This deluxe self-mulching lawnmower has a 5-hp engine, easy recoil starter, and easy-to-read oil dipstick. The seven-inch wheels adjust to five cutting heights. The handles are easy to fold for storage and tempered dual steel blades provide clean cutting and mulching, even in heavy grass."

It is important for the selling message to be written in natural, concise, and clear language, using simple words that the audience will understand. Often it is not what is said that makes potential buyers question or distrust the ad, but how it is stated. Read the copy out loud. Have others read it to determine if it flows and expresses the facts in a way that you would talk to a prospective customer. Figure 15-11, provides several examples of headlines and body copy.

Stress Key Selling Points

Just as headlines stress the most important benefits customers will receive from owning the product or service, so does the body copy of the advertisement. Customers must be able to quickly obtain information on how they will benefit, since they will not read an ad for more than a few seconds. Therefore, as few words as possible should be used to give the reader the features and benefits. The more specific the information given in the ad, the more responsive the customer will be. Some of the questions that may be addressed for product or service ads include: How much will it cost? How much money will be saved? How many years will it last? How will it add to the beauty of your home, farm, or business?

One major benefit or theme should be stressed in an advertisement. The body copy should reinforce that benefit. Other benefits can be mentioned, but care should be taken to not confuse the overall benefit of the product or service. If the ad is effective and customers visit the business, additional benefits can be discussed in the sales presentation. Figure 15-11 shows examples of body copy that support the headline concisely.

Ask the Reader to Buy

As potential customers read ads, they need to become so highly motivated that they will take the next step and come into the business to buy or contact the business by telephone. In order to get this level of motivation in the body copy of an advertisement, words and phrases need to be used to stimulate action on the part of the reader to buy. There are hundreds of motivating words and phrases. Example phrases include:

- Come in soon—limited quantities.

Dog Food
(Headline)

"The beauty of Softcoat is more than skin deep."

(Body Copy)

"Think of Softcoat as a way to get obedience from the inside of your dog. The correct balance of nutrients commands the correct response. Now, you have far more control over your dog's health and well-being."

Grass Trimmer
(Headline)

"Trim It Right With Clean Cut Trimmers & Brushcutters"

(Body Copy)

HLT-15

- Dependable 25cc 2-cycle engine
- Carburetor primer bulb for easy starting
- Twenty-three ounce fuel tank for longer run time
- Automatic line advancing

Lawn Irrigation System
(Headline)

"Install It Yourself
It's Easy, And
You'll Save Money"

(Body Copy)

"Your irrigation system will be trouble-free and economical, and you'll enjoy it even more because you did it yourself!"

Figure 15–11. Example body copy follows the theme of the headline. Copy needs to be concise, clear, and tell the customer how they will benefit and what the product or service will do.

- While supplies last.

- Stop in anytime—we're open 24 hours.

- Give us a call—we deliver.

- Come to the grand opening—free hot dogs and popcorn.

- Test drive a new tractor and get a free movie pass!

- Stop in and let our experts design a drip irrigation plan for your yard.

- Free installation with the first 25 purchases.

ILLUSTRATING ADVERTISEMENTS

Americans are visual people due to the availability and time spent watching television. Research has revealed that when most people look at an ad they first see the *illustration* (picture), then the headline, and finally the body copy, price, and business identification. When you consider that the illustration is the first thing that attracts a potential customer to an ad, the importance of selecting the right illustration becomes essential. Beyond attracting attention and creating interest, illustrations show the product or service, its uses, and possible benefits to the buyer.

Determining What to Illustrate

Generally, the agricultural product or service is the main feature of the advertisement. However, before an ad illustration can be developed, a decision must be reached on which aspect of the product or service will be the major theme of the advertisement. Some of the common themes used for agricultural product or service ads include:

- The product or service pictured in an idealized setting.

- Economics of the product or service.

- Safety of the product or service.

- Uses of the product or service.

- Benefits of ownership that are captured in images of idealized buyers.

- Quality (dependability, durability, manufacturing process, and materials used).

Although advertisements commonly have illustrations of the product or service, illustrations of people with the product are also important. The rationale for having people pictured using the product is to assist the reader in visualizing themselves as an owner of the product. Often space is limited and only a portion of a person is used in the ad. For example, only the head of a person is often used to advertise safety glasses, and only the upper part of the body is seen in tractor ads.

Obtaining Illustrations for Advertisements

Effective ads must have high-quality illustrations that are relevant to the product in the ad and the overall theme. Illustrations used for advertisements generally come from three primary sources: clip art, original drawings, and photographs.

Clip Art. *Clip art* is art produced by specialized businesses for advertisements that is ready to use and copyright-free. Clip art is the least expensive means of illustrating advertisements. Agricultural businesses and newspapers can buy books of clip art on a variety of subjects for use in developing ads. Also, manufacturers and national companies provide prepared *line art*. These drawings made with solid lines can be used by dealers and smaller agribusinesses by adding the local business identification prior to sending it to the newspaper. Many weekly and small community newspapers use primarily clip art to develop advertisements. This allows high-quality ads to be developed quickly with lower production costs.

Original Drawings. Original drawings provide the best opportunity to develop highly effective illustrations for advertisements. Several options for creating the art are available. The most obvious is to have an artist create illustrations or to work with a newspaper or advertising company to create the original drawings. Most large newspapers and advertising firms employ artists that will work with the agricultural business so that the feature of the product or service to be advertised and the style of the ad meets the needs of the audience and the business. Original drawings for advertisements are composed twice as large as the finished illustration. This allows detail in the drawing to be clearer when the drawing is reduced in size for the advertisement.

Computer generated illustrations have become popular for use in advertisements. Computer graphics software is widely available and many types of line drawing now can be created and reproduced using high-quality laser printers. In addition, manufacturers and other businesses may prepare

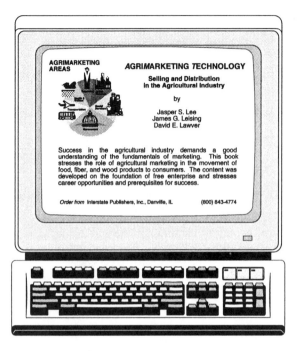

Figure 15–12. Computer graphic software has provided designers with a powerful tool for creating line drawings for ads.

computer diskettes for newspapers and businesses that contain entire advertisements, specific graphics of products, headlines, and body copy. This enables businesses to view all of the graphics and select the illustrations, headlines, and formats that they prefer. As computer graphics software is further adapted to the development of advertisements, other forms of illustration may become outdated.

Photographs. Photographs are used more for illustrations in magazines and other media then in newspaper advertisements. Magazines use high-quality paper and printing processes that take advantage of color photography. Newspapers use some color pictures, but due to high cost, normally pictures are printed in black and white. In most newspaper agriculture ads, photographs are used primarily to show some kind of action. As a result, photographs can be good attention getters in ads, because people like to see pictures of people they know or can identity with.

Each photograph should have a single purpose in an advertisement. The photo must relate clearly to the theme of the ad to avoid distraction. Photos suitable for advertisements are commonly taken by a professional photographer. The photographer may be hired by the advertiser, or may be obtained from an advertising firm or manufacturer. Usually, the photo is planned carefully and taken specifically for the advertisement. In smaller communities, newspaper photographers often take photos for ads during slow periods.

PRICE

Price of agricultural products and services is an important factor that customers consider in making a buying decision. The decision to include price in an advertisement is based on the purpose of the ad. If the ad's primary purpose is to attract customers to purchase specific products or services, price is highly important. If the primary purpose of the ad is to develop a positive image and build public confidence in the business or to advertise services such as installation and delivery, price is not important in the ad.

If price is used in the ad, it should be placed boldly so it is clear and accurate. If a number of different products are being featured, the price should be placed next to the copy describing the product. Often reduced or special priced products are of limited supply. To encourage customers to buy early, phrases such as, "Only two stock trailers at this special price" and "Supplies are limited" are added to the body copy. If the price changes frequently, the phrase, "Please call for price quotations," is sometimes used.

BUSINESS IDENTIFICATION

Businesses use identification logos that serve as a source of public recognition. This identification is termed a *logotype* or signature. Many national companies use their logos on all advertisements and materials produced. Figure 15–13 shows an example logo for the MoorMan's Feed Company.

Logos used in advertisements should be large enough so the customer can identify them easily. They should be used consistently over a long period of time to promote company recognition by the customer. Besides the logo, most businesses also list their

Figure 15–13. MoorMan's Feed Company logo appears near the top and bottom of the advertisement, "MoorMan's. The efficiency experts of animal agriculture."

address, telephone and facsimile numbers, and business hours. Commonly, the logo and location information is located together near the bottom of the advertisement.

The primary purpose of an advertisement is to attract and encourage potential customers to take some action toward buying a product or service. For an ad to be effective, six essential elements are included: accurate knowledge of the product and customer, a headline, selling message, illustration, price (if appropriate), and business logo or trademark.

DEVELOPING ROUGH LAYOUTS
OF PRINTED ADVERTISEMENTS

Agricultural businesses who advertise in newspapers and magazines work closely with the advertising staff to insure that the ad meets their needs. Once the decision about which products or services to be advertised has been reached, the advertising staff works with the business to prepare a rough layout of the advertisement A *rough layout* is a draft arrangement of the ad parts that will appear in the finished advertisement. The purpose of developing a rough layout is to give a perspective of the ad's size; the position of the headline, body copy, and illustrations; and its overall ability to attract customers.

Agricultural businesses that understand the basic principles of how to develop a rough layout are able to develop their own layouts of ads and communicate more efficiently with newspapers and magazines. Some of the basic ideas that need to be included in layouts are focal point; design flow; arrangement of the ad elements; use of white space, black space, and borders; proportion; and price and coupon placement.

FOCAL POINT

In placing the elements of an ad, one of the major considerations is creating a focal point. A *focal point* is the part of the advertisement that stands out and attracts the viewer to other parts of the ad. Often the focal point is either the illustration or the headline. If an ad lacks a focal point, it is easy for the reader's eyes to pass over the advertisement. Figure 15–15 shows two advertisements. One has a definite focal point. The other does not. Try to discern which has the focal point and what it is.

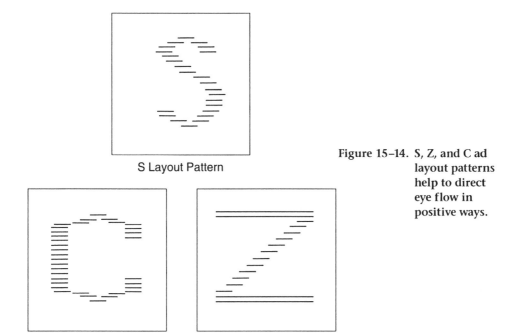

S Layout Pattern

Figure 15–14. S, Z, and C ad
layout patterns
help to direct
eye flow in
positive ways.

C Layout Pattern   Z Layout Pattern

DESIGN FLOW

How a reader's eyes flow over an advertisement is very important
Research has demonstrated that most readers look at an ad from top to
bottom. Some of the patterns that have been found to help direct eye flow
in positive ways are the S, Z, C, or their reverse shapes. Also, the most
critical part of the ad is placed generally in the center of the advertisement.
This spot is referred to as the optical center. It is slightly above and to the
left of the center of the ad.

ARRANGEMENT OF THE AD ELEMENTS

How the elements of an advertisement are arranged is critical for its
success in attracting customers.

Headline

The most important thing to remember is that the headline should be
placed immediately above the selling message. The two should not be
separated by an illustration. For an example, see Figure 15–15.

Figure 15–15. All advertisements need a focal point. In the ad on the right, it is difficult to determine the focal point. The ad on the left has a definite focal point. Note what you see first, the illustration and headline.

Type

When laying out the selling message, type lines should be three to four inches long because this length is easier to read. The *font* (shape or style of type) is not critical as long as it can be read with ease and the font fits the mood and style of the advertisement.

Illustrations

Illustrations are placed generally near the focal point of the advertisement. One large illustration usually is better than several smaller ones. Often, several different views of the product are shown. If this type of illustration or photograph is inviting and dynamic, it may be considered. Also, the direction of the subjects in illustrations is very important. If the people or objects in the illustration face inward rather than outward, they tend to keep the reader's attention on the advertisement.

Use of White Space, Black Space, and Borders

The amount of *white space* (unfilled parts of an advertisement) and *black space* (unfilled black parts of an advertisement) in an ad is important.

White space works as a tool to make the illustrations and typed messages in the advertisement readable and dynamic. Also, it assists the reader in reading the ad. If the white space is more than 50 percent, the ad appears cold and uninviting. If the white is less than 30 to 40 percent it appears crowded, unattractive, and difficult to read. Black space is created by a reverse process that printers sometimes use to add boldness and appeal to an advertisement. In other words, the normal white space becomes black and what is normally black becomes white.

Many ads in newspapers have borders around the outer edge. Borders help to keep the reader's eyes focused on that particular ad rather than looking at other ads surrounding it. Smaller ads often have distinctive borders because it is difficult for them to compete for the reader's attention if surrounded by larger ads. Since it is difficult to know where the ad will be placed in a newspaper, many businesses request a particular border for all of their ads. By using the same border for all advertisements, the border can become an identifying symbol of the business that the reader relies on for quick identification.

CHOOSING THE PROPORTION AND SIZE

Those in the advertising industry generally agree that the width-to-depth proportion of three to five works well for most ads. This general proportion is used because it is visually attractive to the reader. Ads that vary significantly from this proportion can look awkward and the ad layout is difficult.

Newspapers and magazines have different sizes of advertisements based on the size of paper used for the publication. A minimum display ad in a newspaper is usually one column wide by one inch deep. A newspaper minimum classified ad is one column wide by three lines, or one-quarter inch deep. Magazines allow a range of ad sizes and have a variety of page sizes. Both newspapers and magazines allow full-page ads.

PRICE AND COUPON PLACEMENT

Advertisements that feature a specific product or service generally use price as one of the major selling points to attract customers. To assist the customer in relating the price to the product, it is important that the product appear near the price. If price is the primary selling point, it is listed in large type and often a different color of ink to attract the reader.

Many agricultural retail stores place coupons in their ads to bring more prospective customers into the store or business. The coupons in the

Figure 15–16. A coupon offering a $10 discount is being used by the Green Valley Nursery as the primary selling point to attract new customers.

advertisement generally give customers discounts on the purchase of specific products or services. Also, coupons may offer a free product if a certain amount of other products are purchased. Coupons are placed near the bottom of an advertisement and usually toward a corner. This allows the reader to detach the coupon without tearing the ad, so it can be retained for future reference. Also, the coupon should have a border (dotted or solid line) to separate it from the ad. An expiration date should be clearly printed on the coupon.

SUMMARY OF ROUGH LAYOUT

The rough layout of an ad contains the essential elements of an ad such as the headline, selling message, logo, price, and illustrations. It is sized to represent the finished ad. To obtain a real understanding of how it compares to other ads in a newspaper and to determine if it meets the expectation of the business, it can be glued or taped to an actual copy of the newspaper. This will give the business a feel for how it will actually look in print. It is important to note that the entire selling message and coupons are generally not written or typed on the rough layout. This makes the layout look too messy and is too time consuming. The selling message or body copy is written or typed on a separate sheet of paper and attached to the layout along with illustration originals (drawings and negatives). Usually, numbers on the elements of the rough layout correspond to the attached elements to assure that no confusion will exist when the final ad is printed by the newspaper or magazine.

CONSIDERATIONS IN PRINTING THE ADVERTISEMENT

Following approval of the rough layout, the advertisement is ready to be printed by the newspaper or magazine. The publication's technical staff will take the rough layout and produce the ad based on specifications given on the layout. To work effectively with the technical staff of a newspaper, it is helpful if people in the agricultural business understand the use of different typefaces, ways of insuring readability, illustration preparation, and possible ways of positioning ads in newspapers or magazines.

TYPEFACE SELECTION

Typeface is a term used to describe the design or shape of the letters used in printing the different elements of an advertisement. Selection of the typeface is important in attracting prospective customers to read the advertisement. Books of different typefaces are available from the printing departments of newspapers and magazines. After looking at the typefaces, it will be easier to communicate with the newspaper staff about what best represents the business and the product or service to be advertised. Today, most final ads are composed on a computer terminal and drafts of the actual typefaces can be printed for review by the business in advance of the finished product. There are some important guidelines for choosing a typeface that will improve the ad's readability.

- **Use bold face type sparingly**—Bold face type is the dark, heavy type used for emphasis. If bold face type is used for the entire selling message, it is difficult to read and the emphasis is lost.

- **Avoid using capitalization to add emphasis**—Generally, it is best to capitalize only the words that are capitalized when the English language is used correctly.

- **Use italic type to add emphasis**—Using italic type for all of the body copy is not wise because many people find it difficult to read.

- **The size of the type is important**—If the type is too small, usually less than eight point, it is difficult to read. Ads that use small type sizes will discourage the reader because it takes too much time to focus on the small type. Generally, headline type is the largest and bold. Smaller, but easily read, type is used for the selling message. The written message on the coupon is the smallest because it is near the bottom of the ad. The rationale is that the reader who has read the top portion of the ad is interested enough to spend slightly more time reading.

- **Balance the spacing between letters and lines**—The ideal line length is three to four inches. As the line length increases more space is needed between lines. It is important that there is consistent spacing between letters and lines throughout the copy. High-quality type-setting makes an ad look more attractive, enhances the businesses image, and increases the chances for its success. It is better to have less copy and more balance in spacing than to crowd the copy.

ILLUSTRATIONS

Newspapers generally use line drawings for advertisements or computer generated images that are similar to line drawings. Halftone illustrations, those with shadings, are seldom used for newspapers. The reproduction process used by newspapers results in an illustration that is dark and not as focused as a line drawing. Magazines use halftone illustrations more successfully because of higher quality paper and a different more expensive reproduction process.

Most illustrations are produced larger than the illustration in the finished ad. This ensures a sharper, more detailed illustration in the final ad. If the illustration is an original drawing, it should be in high contrast, black ink on white paper. Computer graphic illustrations need to be laser printed to have enough contrast for quality reproduction. When using photographs, a glossy finish works best.

POSITIONING NEWSPAPER ADVERTISEMENTS

The size and location of a newspaper ad is important to an agricultural business. Generally, the newspaper will decide where to place the ad. However, the advertiser can request a specific section of the paper. For example, garden product or service ads will appear in the home and garden section and agriculture production products or services ads will appear in the agriculture section of the newspaper. Since newspapers sell advertising space, it is in their best interest to place ads in the locations that obtain the highest readership for the business. Businesses that want to insure a specific location for their ad pay higher costs, but preferred space is limited.

The size of the ad is the major factor that determines location on the page. Newspapers generally place the largest ad in the lower right-hand corner of the page. News stories and smaller ads are located above and to the left of the larger ad. Figure 15–17 shows an example of a typical newspaper page layout.

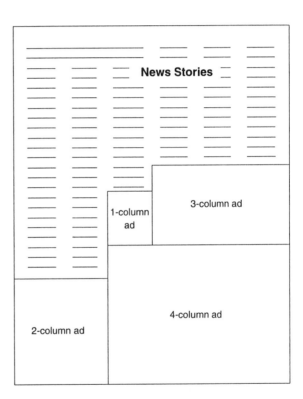

Figure 15–17. Newspapers position ads commonly as shown. Businesses need to be aware that the size of the ad will impact where it is placed in the newspaper.

POSITIONING MAGAZINE ADVERTISEMENTS

Magazine advertisements are generally located throughout an issue. Like newspapers, magazines are divided into sections with different topics of interest. Advertisements are displayed in the various sections based on the type of product or service to be advertised. If the advertiser requests a specific section, the request is normally honored. However, the position of the ad in a magazine is usually a decision of the magazine. Sample positioning of ads for a magazine are shown in Figure 15–18.

Size of a magazine ad is selected by the advertiser and the cost is determined by size, frequency of advertising, and color/illustration requirements. A higher price is charged for the cover positions (inside the front cover or back cover on either side) in a magazine. All other areas have a similar cost.

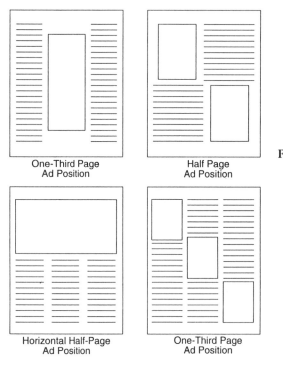

One-Third Page
Ad Position

Half Page
Ad Position

Horizontal Half-Page
Ad Position

One-Third Page
Ad Position

Figure 15–18. Magazine ads are positioned differently than in newspapers. Four common positions are shown.

PLANNING DISPLAYS FOR AGRICULTURE SALES

Agricultural businesses use displays in a variety of ways to attract customers to purchase products or services. A *display* is defined as an exhibit of merchandise (products or services). Some of the major types of displays used by agricultural businesses include: window displays, point-of-purchase displays, wall and ceiling displays, and shelf displays.

WINDOW DISPLAYS

Window displays are important in attracting customers into an agricultural retail or wholesale business. Also, the window display assists the business in developing a positive image in the community and gives potential customers their first impression of the business. As a result, the window display's general appearance is very important so that the customer obtains a positive impression.

The window display features sale products or seasonal items of interest to many customers. Simplistic designs with attractive colors are used to grab a person's attention as they walk by or enter the business.

POINT-OF-PURCHASE DISPLAYS

Displays set-up near the check-out areas, on counters or aisles, and in other open areas of the store are referred to as point-of-purchase displays. This type of display advertises specific products or services that the business is promoting for a period of time. The distinguishing feature of point-of-purchase displays is that only one product is being displayed. Therefore, the entire display is centered on the product. Often the product is arranged neatly with signs posted that clearly identify the product and price. Price discounts on products are often advertised in point-of-purchase displays.

Figure 15–19. A point-of-purchase display is being used by Calgene to introduce the new MacGregor's Flavr-Savr Tomato (the new tomato is the first FDA approved genetically altered food product).

Also, this type of display allows customers to touch and handle the product and sets-off the product from others in the store.

WALL AND CEILING DISPLAYS

All available space in a business must be used efficiently and effectively due to the high cost of renting or owning a building. Walls present an ideal location for display of products. Usually three walls are available for display, plus any additional temporary walls that are added to enhance display areas. Wall displays are used for hanging products (rakes, hoes, and other kinds of garden tools), for displaying signs, and seasonal decorations. Also, shelves and enclosed display cases are attached to walls. If enclosed cases are used for display, they must be kept clean, have good lighting, and look fresh. In addition, large pieces of equipment are displayed along walls. This allows the equipment to be seen and provides a backdrop for advertisements, but does not stop traffic flow through the store.

Ceiling displays are used effectively in stores with high ceilings. Also, ceilings are used for hanging signs, for seasonal decorations, and to call attention to products that are being discounted or are on clearance.

SHELF DISPLAYS

Shelf displays are used throughout stores to stock merchandise. In

Figure 15–20. Vegetable seeds are displayed using a space-efficient wall unit.

many stores, shelves are set-up in rows facing each other with aisles down the center. This allows a large quantity of different products to be displayed at eye level for easy customer access. Although shelves contain the actual products that customers will take to the check-out area, there is some space available for display arrangements. The wall behind and above the merchandise frequently is used for signs advertising the products. Also, products may be arranged uniquely on the shelf to attract customers. Other methods of attracting customers to shelf displayed products include such things as a free-standing floor sign in front of the shelf which advertises the product, or a small red blinking light that indicates special discounts or pricing.

PRINCIPLES OF DESIGN USED IN DISPLAYS

Successful displays incorporate the basic principles of design. When each of us look at a display these principles assist us in determining if we are attracted to it and the merchandise for sale. The primary principles that are involved in causing people to be attracted to a display include: balance, contrast, emphasis, harmony, proportion, and unity.

BALANCE

Balance is a term that refers to equal attention or weight of the elements within a display or advertisement. When people look at a display, it is most pleasing when equal attention is given to all parts. For example, if a seed corn display uses a bag of seed corn on one side, something that appears equal in size is needed on the other side to ensure balance. This might be achieved by using a stack of hats with the seed corn brand on them.

CONTRAST

The principle of *contrast* refers to the differences among items in the display that show the positive benefits of the advertised product or service. For example, the display may feature a brand of weed killer. The display has samples of weeds before and after spraying. The contrast being displayed is between the dead weeds and the live weeds.

Contrast can also mean working with different shapes, sizes, and colors. Display backgrounds are generally made-up of a color that contrasts with the other elements in the display. Parts of displays that are the same color as the background do not contrast with the background and are difficult for customers to see.

EMPHASIS

Emphasis in a display means that one main product or idea is being stressed. Every successful display has one emphasis or focal point, just like a newspaper advertisement. There are many ways to create an emphasis in a display. Some techniques include making the product featured the largest part of the display, placing arrows or other graphics around the area of emphasis, placing the product on a raised platform or area and surrounding it with smaller items, and using color to add emphasis to the product or item.

HARMONY

A principle of design that give balance and uniformity to the display is referred to as *harmony*. Harmony is the total effect that you see and feel when looking at a display that is pleasing to the eye. All parts of the display blend and fit together to form a whole. Harmony is achieved through the combination of shapes, lines, colors, textures, and sizes. No formula for harmony in a display exists. Through experimentation and observing displays, it can be attained.

PROPORTION

Proportion means that items in the display are of the proper size and scale when compared to each other. When possible, actual merchandise should be used. If the business display area is not large enough for the real products, the products can to be scaled down to fit the display area. Rectangles are generally better shapes for displays then squares. Again, by looking at the display, proportion can be judged in relation to the other principles of design.

UNITY

All the parts of a display must fit together to form a whole. This is termed unity. It is best for a display to give one impression and not to be overwhelmed by several main ideas. For displays to have impact on the customer, they must be simplistic, follow the principles of design, and get the attention of the customer immediately.

COMPONENTS OF A SUCCESSFUL DISPLAY DESIGN

The principles of design can only be made to come alive if the components of design are understood. The major components include the use of color, direction, line, shape, size, texture, and weight. Each will be discussed in terms of applying them in developing agricultural displays.

COLOR

Color is an important component in developing a successful display. Color can have a positive or negative impact on the emotional feelings of people who are in the process of making buying decisions. People who work in the planning and development of agricultural displays need to have a basic understanding of color and how color can be used effectively to influence buying decision.

The basic colors, red, yellow, and blue, are termed primary colors. Secondary colors are green, violet (purple), and orange. These colors are obtained by mixing the primary colors on either side of it on the color wheel (see Figure 15-21). Depending on how much of each color is mixed, many different shades of primary and secondary colors can be created. The two colors that are opposite each other on the color wheel are referred to as complementary.

It takes years of experience to learn what colors work best in different kinds of displays. Most important is to select colors that harmonize and are complementary. Limit the colors for any display to two or three and use bright colors only as accents. Warm colors (colors with brown, orange or yellow tints) are used for emphasis. Cool colors (colors with blue or green tints) are used for background.

Some of the characteristics associated with the use of popular colors are described briefly.

- **Black**—Black is a neutral color that is frequently used for backgrounds and lettering. When other colors are outlined in black they tend to stand out more. Black can be mixed with other colors to make them darker and change the mood. For example, black mixed with orange

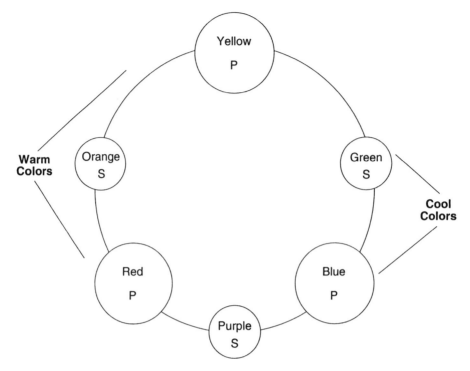

Primary (P) and Secondary (S) Colors

Figure 15–21. Knowledge and understanding of the primary and secondary color wheel is important in designing a quality display.

will give a display an autumn mood. Also, black objects appear smaller than white objects.

- **Beige**—Brown and white mixed together form the color beige. It is used in backgrounds for agricultural displays because it is neutral and complements many of the color shades found in agricultural props, such as soil, sand, brick, western wear, livestock equipment, and lumber. Also, beige complements brown, green, and orange.

- **Blue**—Blue is associated with the sky and water. It is used in combination with green to give a spring feeling to a display and in combination with white to give a winter mood.

- **Brown**—The color brown is commonly used to represent soil and tree bark in displays. Because it is a darker color, too much brown will give the display a dull look. Brown is generally used on the bottom of a display and beige and other brighter colors are used on the upper parts.

- **Green**—Green is a powerful color because it can represent money, crops, growing things, spring, and summer. Agricultural displays use shades of green extensively to suggest plants and healthy plant growth. Also, green is used as a background color for autumn colors.

- **Orange**— Orange is a warm color that attracts lots of attention. When it is mixed with yellow or red it becomes even brighter. Orange is one of the basic colors used for fall displays.

- **Red**—Red is the attention-getting color. It is used for traffic lights to mean stop or to indicate danger. Red is used in almost all displays to call attention to important elements. It complements most colors when used in small amounts.

- **White**—White is a neutral color and works well as a background for displays. However, it can make the display appear bleak or sterile unless other colors are mixed with it. There are many different shades of white—from grays and yellows to pinks. White is commonly used as a background for black and mixed with darker colors to lighten them. For example, the color gray is made by mixing white with black.

- **Yellow**—Yellow is an emotionally uplifting color that suggests energy and sunshine. It is used as an accent color in displays for green and brown.

DIRECTION AND LINE

The attention of viewers can be directed in displays by the way that the display items are arranged or pointed. Common lines used in displays are vertical, horizontal, diagonal, and curved. Vertical lines give the impression of height and dignity. Vertical lines are created in displays by stacking products or raising products vertically on platforms. Vertical lines are good because the viewer tends to make eye contact from top to bottom.

Horizontal lines tend to infer order and formality. Horizontal and vertical lines are frequently combined in displays. This results in a display element that has both height and formality.

Diagonal lines are another way of directing attention in displays. A left diagonal line encourages the viewer to scan the display from left to right. Right diagonal lines are possible, but caution must be exercised because they appear distracting unless combined with a vertical line.

Curved lines in a display tend to indicate that the display is informal

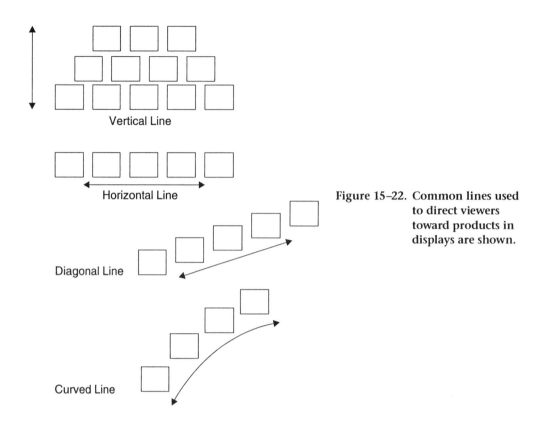

Figure 15–22. Common lines used
to direct viewers
toward products in
displays are shown.

and fun. Also, it may be indicative of the type of businesses and appeal to the public. Figure 15–22 summarizes the different types of lines.

SHAPE AND SIZE

There is no one shape that is best for a display. Circles, hexagons, octagons, ovals, rectangles, squares, and triangles are some of the shapes that can be used. Displays can use one shape or combinations of shapes for different elements in the display. The important thing is to keep the display in balance.

Size of elements in the display need to be large enough for the viewer to see easily. The size of each part of the display must also be considered in relation to other parts of the display. Generally, a ratio of 2:1 is considered pleasing in appearance. For example, a machine that is six feet tall and a sign that is three feet tall should look in correct proportion, as long as the width has a similar ratio as the height.

TEXTURE

Texture in displays conveys the feel or look of the surface of an object. The choice of texture is based on the product to be sold and the image that the product or service is trying to promote. For example, if the display is promoting horse showing equipment, the display may have a background made of barn siding and grass or wood chips on the floor.

The texture of the barn siding and wood chips provides a foundation to display the leather halters, brushes, and other equipment that is the feature of the display.

VALUE AND WEIGHT

Lightness and darkness of color is expressed as value. We commonly use the phrase, shade of color, to indicate color value. Effectiveness of color can be enhanced in displays by paying careful attention to value. Also, businesses should be sensitive to how customers react to products promoted in display areas using different color values.

Weight does not refer to pounds, but to the color, shape, and texture of an item. Small items that are a light color and have a smooth-texture create a light effect in displays. Items that are dark color and rougher in texture, appear heavier and larger.

DEVELOPING A PLAN FOR AN AGRICULTURAL DISPLAY

A good knowledge of design principles and an understanding of the elements of design are important for planning agricultural displays. However, without a plan describing the display it will be difficult to construct and communicate ideas to others.

Steps in developing a plan for an agricultural display include (1) determining the product or service to be featured, (2) establishing a theme, (3) incorporating seasons and current events, (4) selecting a display arrangement, (5) identifying and selecting materials, and (6) drawing the plan.

DETERMINING THE PRODUCT OR SERVICE

The first step in designing any display is to determine which product(s) or service(s) will be featured and to find answers to questions that will assist in designing the display. Some of the questions commonly asked by designers are: "What is it?" "Where is it used?" "How is it used?" and "What are its main selling features?" Answers to these questions give the designer ideas about the kind of setting, props that will be needed, and the space required.

THEME

The purpose of a display is to assist in the selling of products or services to customers. Displays play the role of creating a setting and environment that help customers to feel and see themselves as the owner of the product or service. As a result, customers are psychologically motivated to buy. A central idea or theme for a display will relate the product or service to the needs of the customer. For example, a lawn fertilizer display may have a theme of growing a beautiful green lawn in the spring. The display assists the customer in visualizing the green lawn and the pride that the home owner feels.

SEASONS AND CURRENT EVENTS

Agricultural displays can take advantage of the seasons of the year for themes and settings that relate to the customer. Agricultural displays in spring feature products related to planting and growing crops, the birth of animals, and repair and construction. Summer means irrigation of crops, insect and disease control, vacations and recreation, and the selling of produce. Fall is harvest time; harvesting equipment and preparation for colder weather and holidays are on peoples minds. Winter is a slower time when customers are making plans, thinking about the production season ahead, and completing indoor projects and repairs. Because the different seasons of the year are so important to agriculture, they naturally provide display settings that assist the customer in relating to the featured product or service.

Current events are difficult to anticipate, but provide excellent opportunities for businesses to stimulate customer buying. These displays are generally simplistic and single-product oriented. For example, if farmers are having an outbreak of calf scours, medication for that disease may have good selling potential and a point-of-purchase display can be constructed in a few hours. Other examples of current events that can be related to agricultural products or services include weather problems, fairs and shows, and sporting events in the community.

SELECTING A DISPLAY ARRANGEMENT

Using the design elements of direction, line, and shape, it is possible to develop a variety of arrangements for displays. Six major arrangements are commonly used: wedge, pyramid, radiation, repetition, stair step, and zigzag. A brief definition of each and its common use follows.

Wedge Arrangement

The wedge is a V-shaped arrangement that is used to show related products or services or a team approach. The viewer's eyes focus on the center object, which is closest, and then looks at the related items on both sides.

Pyramid Arrangement

A pyramid arrangement takes advantage of vertical and horizontal lines and forms a three dimensional triangle. Displays in the shape of a pyramid are tall and draw the viewer's eyes to the top and then down the sides. A pyramid draws attention because the product is usually stacked in this arrangement and urges the viewer to buy now.

Radiation Arrangement

Radiation arrangements develop the focal point of the display in the center with rays or strands coming off the center that show related or complementary products or services.

Repetition Arrangement

Repetition arrangements are simplistic displays that show repetition of the product using straight or curved lines or a mass. They are easy to set up. They have impact because the customer sees the product many times and remembers it better. Repetition arrangements also include repeating products at specific intervals, using the same container or other accessory throughout a display.

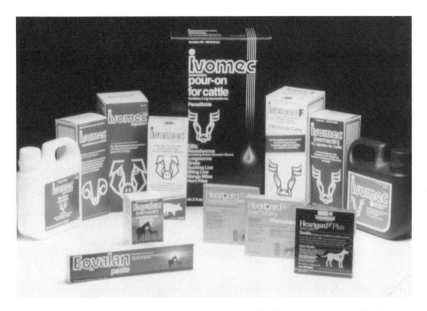

Figure 15–23. Animal medical products are displayed using a radiation
            and repetition arrangement. (Courtesy, Merch Ag Vet
            Division)

Stair Step Arrangement

Arrangements use stair steps to indicate progress, different quality products, production of a product, and different prices of products. Displays using stair steps have height and are easy for viewers to see and to understand. Construction of the stairs is easily completed by using concrete blocks, bricks and boards, or different sized barrels or cubes.

Zigzag Arrangement

Zigzag arrangements are created by setting the product in uneven lines that look informal and fun. This arrangement is good for relaxed, outdoor display settings.

The arrangement is important because it gives an overall shape to the display. The arrangement is based on the product, its major selling point, and the theme and setting that will best relate to the customers needs.

IDENTIFYING AND SELECTING DISPLAY MATERIALS

A wide variety of materials can be used to construct displays. All of the materials selected must complement the theme and product featured.

Background

Once the display structure is designed, the background materials are chosen. Background for displays is like paint for a room in your home, it must complement and provide a setting for the furnishings in the room. Agricultural exhibits use a variety of backgrounds for the floor from off-white paint to wood chips, burlap, canvas, and carpet. Background for the walls include such things as pictures or murals of skies, woods, fields, buildings, and barns. Some background walls are painted with neutral colors to complement the product. Real or artificial plants are frequently added to displays to give them color, as accent to break up sharp corners, or to fill in bare space.

Product Display Props

Props are needed to display the product arrangement. Props refer to the supports used to display the products or services. Common props include stands, tables, steps, panels, mannequins, easels, and cubes. Props must coordinate with the products and display theme or be hidden from sight. Also, props need to be strong enough to support the product and last for as long as the display is used. Care must be exercised to be certain that the display is safe and will not harm customers or be a potential fire hazard. Portability of display props is a consideration because they will have to be stored from time to time and space is often limited.

Accessories

Accessories add interest and attract attention to the display. However, the accessories should not overpower the display or take the focus from the products being displayed. Examples of the kinds of accessories used in agricultural displays include plants, produce, books, baskets, saddles, and antique equipment. The accessories chosen for a display should complement and fit the theme and season. For example, a decorated tree could be added during the Christmas season. Potting soil and gardening tools can enhance bedding plant displays, and spring flowers are a colorful accent to garden fertilizer displays.

Signs and Lettering

Signs that are accurate, attractive, and easy to read help customers learn quickly about the products or services being offered. Information cards that are used in displays to give the product name, price, key selling point, and other brief information are referred to as show cards.

Show cards can be made in a variety of sizes. No one size is correct, but signs should complement the display and be large enough to attract attention and be easily read. Key ideas in designing show cards are simplicity, neatness, and brief facts. Signs can be printed by hand or designed using a computer graphics program. More businesses are using the computer designed cards because of the advantages of neatness, spelling accuracy, and consistency throughout the store.

Figure 15–24. A sign clearly identifies the price of the landscape timbers being displayed at a farm supply store. Attractive and accurate signs are important in convincing customers to buy.

DRAWING THE DISPLAY PLAN

Prior to actual set-up of displays a drawing or sketch needs to be made. The drawing shows what the display will look like and the materials needed to assemble it. Without the drawing, it is difficult for people setting up displays to understand how to put it together. Therefore, drawings become a communication link between the designer, management, and those constructing the display. The drawing is used by management to determine if it represents the product being advertised and to calculate the cost of the display.

Drawings can be simplistic, showing the outline of the design, dimensions of all key elements, primary title or show card, and arrangement of the product. A list of supplies, materials, and any special accessories needed to assemble the display is important. Frequently, several drawings are made by the designer before the final drawing is approved by management. If the display is large, it is helpful to draw it from different angles.

SUMMARY

Advertising is the major way that producers and sellers of agricultural products and services reach out to customers. Therefore, advertising and displaying are thought of as forms of communication. The three basic forms of media used in advertising are print media, broadcast media, and visual media.

Advertising is important to the success of agricultural businesses because it identifies new customers, builds customer confidence and a positive image of the business in the community, increases sales, and informs potential customers of the products and services available. The ways that products and services are promoted in agriculture include advertising, face-to-face selling, displays, and publicity.

Newspapers and magazines are the two largest forms of printed advertising in the United States. The primary kinds of advertising are display advertising and classified advertising. The three major types of display advertisements are local, national, and cooperative. Essential components of a good advertisement include evidence of product knowledge, a strong headline, clear body copy, quality illustrations, clearly stated price, and business identification.

Development of rough layouts involves arranging the ad parts that will appear in the finished advertisement. Some of the basic ideas that are addressed in preparing the layout include focal point, design flow, arrangement of key elements, use of white and black space and borders, choosing the right proportions, and price and coupon placement. Following approval of the rough layout, the ad is prepared by the technical staff of the newspaper or magazine. It is important for agricultural businesses to have an understanding of typefaces, ways of insuring readability, illustration options, and ways of positioning ads. Knowledge of these areas will enhance communications between the business and the staff printing the publication.

CHAPTER SELF-CHECK

Match the following terms with the correct definitions:

a. advertising

b. promotion

c. display

d. circulation

e. selling points

f. headline

g. body copy

h. line art

i. logotype

j. rough layout

k. harmony

l. proportion

m. typeface

_____ the selling message of an advertisement. It usually appears after the headline.

_____ drawings or illustrations made of solid black lines and no shadings

_____ distinctive business identification symbol that is intended to be recognized by the public. A business trademark.

_____ a layout of an ad; it is a guide to a newspaper or

magazine for placing the elements that will appear in the finished ad

_____ the design or shape of the letters (type) used in printing the headline or copy of an ad

_____ a principle of design that places the display items in their proper positions

_____ a principle of design that gives balance and uniformity to the display

_____ the leading words or phrases in generally bold letters that attracts the potential customer to read the ad and is part of every advertisement

_____ customer benefits that are the focus of an advertisement

_____ the number of people who purchase and read a newspaper, magazine or other printed media

_____ any form of nonpersonal presentation and promotion of ideas, goods or services by an identified sponsor

_____ the coordination of all sell-initiated efforts to communicate with potential customers

_____ an exhibit featuring products or services

QUESTIONS AND PROBLEMS FOR DISCUSSION

1. Define the term *advertising* and explain its relationship to marketing.

2. Why is advertising important to agricultural sellers and buyers?

3. What are the differences between farmer, processor, wholesaler and manufacturer advertising?

4. Describe the major elements of a good print advertisement in a newspaper or magazine.

5. Discuss the different kinds of advertising that are available to agribusinesses in your community.

6. Explain how the cost of advertising is determined.

7. Describe the different kinds of displays that agricultural firms use.

8. What is harmony in a display?

9. Other than color, what are four other important elements in designing an agribusiness display?

10. Contrast and compare the different kinds of display product arrangements.

ACTIVITIES

1. Using a variety of agricultural magazines and the farm section of newspapers, cut out different advertisements and develop poster presentations describing the different elements of the ads and the strengths and weaknesses of each. Prepare a written or oral report.

2. Select an agricultural product or service, research its selling points and target audience, and prepare an advertisement for a local newspaper. Present oral reports explaining the rationale for the ad development and the rough layout of the advertisement.

3. Form teams of students to develop different types of displays in the school about FFA or develop a partnership with local businesses in which students have an opportunity to develop a variety of displays at local agricultural businesses. Make a bulletin board of the pictures of the different displays and present an oral or written report explaining the rationale for the design.

Chapter 16

HANDLING HUMAN RELATIONS

Marketing involves dealing with people. Some people are easy to get along with; others are difficult. People who are successful in agrimarketing develop skills in human relations.

Success in agrimarketing depends on the ability to handle many areas of human interaction appropriately. Good products aren't enough to ensure success in agrimarketing. Customers want to deal with knowledgeable salespeople. They want to feel good about the products they buy and the people associated with those products. Reaching agreement on price and other marketing details involves negotiation. When negotiating, there are many

Figure 16–1. Human relationships are important in many settings in agrimarketing. This shows a sample of feed being taken on the farm by a feed marketing representative. (Courtesy, Moorman Feed, Quincy, Illinois)

opportunities for differences of opinion to become conflicts. Minor conflicts can become major obstacles in agrimarketing. Handling human relations properly enhances the marketing process for everyone involved.

Have you ever gone into a store and felt that you weren't treated well? Did you go back? Business is lost when customers are made to feel uncomfortable.

OBJECTIVES

This chapter introduces basic concepts involved in human relations. After completing it, you will be able to:

- Explain the importance of human relations in agrimarketing

- Describe the role of communication in human relations

- Explain why people respond the way they do

- Identify the areas of personal development

- Understand how to deal with conflict and anger

- List rules for good human relations

TERMS

assertiveness
belonging
clothing
communication
conflict
conflict management
courtesy
empathy
feedback
grooming
health
honesty
human relations
human relations skills
interpersonal relations
medium
message
motivation
need
noise
on task
patience
personality
physical appearance
physical need
prompt
receiver
self-concept
self esteem
sender

HUMAN RELATIONS IN AGRIMARKETING

Human relations describes how people relate to other people. All contact with other people involves human relations. Sometimes it is referred to as group behavior. Relations can be good or bad. We want to have good relationships. Developing good human relations is based on showing respect for other individuals.

People are important. Treating other people properly is important for career and personal success in agrimarketing. The ability to establish good human relations is an essential skill. The overall goal is to create good feelings among people.

Human relations skills refers to the ability to understand people and favorably interact with them. People who have good human relations skills have empathy. This means that they can identify with the feelings of other people. The word vicarious is sometimes used, which is the ability to have the same, or nearly the same, feelings as another person.

INTERPERSONAL RELATIONS

Interpersonal relations refers to the relations among people. It includes the feelings and emotions that people have toward each other. It also includes how people view themselves as part of a group. How people respond when around other people reflects how they feel about themselves and other people either as a group or as individuals.

Interpersonal relations is important in the agrimarketing work setting. There are two major types of interpersonal relationships in agribusiness: relationships with fellow workers and relationships with customers or others who come into contact with a business.

Relating to Co-Workers

People enjoy their work more if they feel comfortable around the other workers. An agrimarketing business is more efficient if the people feel good about their work.

Relating to co-workers involves two factors: how they feel about you and how you feel about them. In many cases, how they feel about you is based on how you respond to them. Co-workers will show consideration for you if you show consideration for them.

How people respond to each other at the work site may be obvious to customers and the public. If a customer goes into a packing shed and hears people who work there arguing with each other, the customer will not feel comfortable dealing with them. The customer may leave without making a purchase or make a purchase this time but not come back.

Good relations with co-workers can usually be achieved by giving a little extra effort at work and showing courtesy to co-workers. Being friendly, saying "thank you," returning equipment and tools properly, staying on the work tasks, arriving on time and staying until the work is done, and not complaining are important in having good relationships with co-workers.

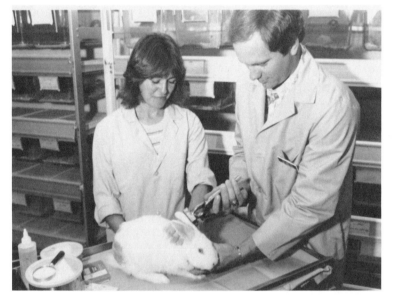

Figure 16–2. Providing veterinary services includes relating to technicians in a clinic as well as to the owners of animals. (Courtesy, Texas Veterinary Medical Center)

Relating to the Public

It is important to have good relationships with your customers. In one way or another, many people are customers.

Customers like to feel good about the people with whom they do business. They like to feel that their business is wanted and appreciated.

Greeting customers warmly and showing sincerity in helping them solve problems are very important. Customers like to be called by name. They like for others to look them in the eye and carefully listen to their concerns. Customers like for people to follow through on what they say they are going to do.

Relating to the public often involves a human quality known as *empathy*. Empathy is trying to imagine yourself in another person's situation. Agrimarketing people who understand the situations that farmers face can more effectively relate to them. If you understand what it is like for a crop to be flooded by too much rain, you can empathize with crop farmers.

Agriculturalists also like the people they are dealing with to be aware of common agricultural situations, such as the effect of an early frost or a high infestation of insects. Having practical experience in production agriculture is very useful in preparing to work in agrimarketing jobs.

Relating with the public also includes what people see in the work setting. Loud radios and talking indicate that people aren't really concentrating on their work. Joking and laughing are further indications of off-task behavior. Chewing gum and using tobacco products are turn-offs to some people. These influence how the public will relate to the people who work in an environment.

COMMUNICATION SKILLS

Communication is the exchange of information. It is more than speaking or writing effectively. Communication involves the other person in a process of sharing. People who are good communicators always consider the background of the person with whom they are communicating. They select words that the other person can understand. An eloquent speech is of little good if others can't understand it!

Communication Process

Communication is a process. As a process, communication is circular. Messages are sent to other people and you observe how they respond. Communication is much like a completed electrical circuit. If the circuit is completed, the electric light or appliance works. In communication, completing the process involves the exchange of information. In some cases, the responses people give are non-verbal— what people do is part of communication. This is also known as body language. It includes facial expressions, how people hold their hands, what they do with their feet, or where they focus their eyes.

The communication process involves four components:

- **Sender**–The individual who initiates the message; also known as the source.

- **Message**–A set of symbols that are interpreted for meaning; words have certain meanings; numbers have meaning; other symbols also have meaning, such as the "skull and crossbones" on a poisonous chemical.

- **Medium**–The channel that connects the sender with the receiver, such as written words, spoken words, and shapes (an example of shape is the octagonal stop sign at a road intersection).

- **Receiver**–The person or group that interprets the message; the receiver must be familiar with the codes or symbols in the message or the effort to exchange information will fail.

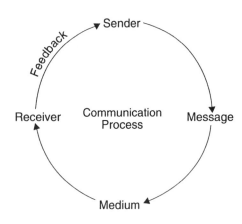

Figure 16–3. Communication is the process of exchanging information and includes feedback to assess how well the process worked.

The effectiveness of communication is assessed by feedback. *Feedback* is how another person responds to your attempt at exchanging information. Feedback allows you to determine if they understood what you intended. Feedback is the return channel from the receiver back to the sender.

Blockages sometimes occur in communication. Regardless of the kind of blockage, they are known as *noise*. Noise is anything that interferes with the exchange of information. It can be a loud sound, distracting pictures, unpleasant odors, or anything else that causes the attention of people to be distracted away from the attempted exchange of information.

Noise keeps people from effectively communicating. If you write a message to a person who can't read, you will not be able to communicate. Inability to read the symbols (words) is a blockage (noise).

Good communication involves considering the receiver and selecting messages and mediums that they understand. Communication cannot occur

Figure 16–4. Managers and employees must often communicate important information in planning marketing strategies. (Courtesy, Terra International, Inc.)

without both the sender and receiver drawing the same meaning from the message.

Good Communication

Communication is easier if people remember the communication process and follow a few basic rules in using it. Emphasis must always be on selecting communication approaches based on the traits of the receiver, the kind of information to be exchanged, and the channels that are available.

Consider the Other Person. Select a means of sending information that the other person can understand. Knowing the background of the other person is very important. If you know that a co-worker or customer is having a bad day, be extra considerate. Once you know a person well, you will adjust your way of dealing with them so that communication is better.

Use Feedback. This involves determining if the other person understands what you intended. Direct questioning may sometimes be used. How another person responds with facial expressions, shrugs of the shoulders, or in other ways is good feedback. When people send you information, you should respond with your interpretation of the message. Voluntarily give feedback!

Plan the Communication Effort. Select the right form for the message so that you exchange information. Use real things as substitutes for words. Show people how to do something rather than just telling them. Demonstrations are very effective for explaining such things as how to grade crops or set up displays.

Be Accurate. Communicate information that is truthful. Get the facts straight! Many decisions in agrimarketing require accurate information, otherwise decisions will not be as good as they could be.

Figure 16–5. People who work in food processing relate to each other in many ways and one problem can disrupt the flow of work.

Stick to the Point. This is also known as brevity. Don't cloud the attempt at communication with more details than are needed.

Be Clear. Planning the communication effort will help you to communicate clearly. Carefully select the communication channels. Use no more detail than is required.

WHY PEOPLE DO WHAT THEY DO

People respond the way they do for a reason. The way people relate to others varies with how they feel and what they need. People who excel in establishing good human relations understand other people as well as themselves.

MOTIVATION

Why do people do what they do? What we do results from our motivations. *Motivation* is all of the factors that cause us to behave a certain way. These factors are known as motives. They can cause us to change or continue what we are doing. Motives are the objects or goals of our actions. They are influenced by our attitudes and values. Most people like to feel they are doing the right thing.

Motivation deals with how people use their energy. In human relations, we can use energy negatively by saying ugly things, or we can use our energy positively by saying nice things to other people. People are often motivated by their needs.

NEEDS OF PEOPLE

People have certain needs. When a *need* is met, people feel satisfied. Needs are often referred to as a gap between what actually exists and what is desired. Some needs are obvious—we know about them. Other needs are unfelt. We may not be aware of them, but other people may say that we have them.

Physical Needs

Physical needs include the needs people have for the three major products of agriculture: food, clothing, and shelter. These are the basic needs for living. How people respond to others is influenced by how well these and other physical needs are being met.

Physical needs also include safety, sleep, and freedom from pain. When these aren't met, people are motivated to meet them. Their behavior is driven by their attempts to meet these needs to a level that is satisfactory for them. The level at which the needs are met varies with different people and with the culture in which the person lives.

People who feel that their physical needs aren't being met will be motivated to meet them. How they relate to other people is influenced by their needs. For example, people who have worked a long day will be tired and sleepy. Sometimes they are grouchy and want to be left alone. They want to rest and sleep to meet this need. People who don't have breakfast may be hungry and have low energy by lunch time. They won't be as productive in their jobs or as cheerful as those who had an appropriate breakfast. Eating the right food on a regular basis is important.

Need to Belong

People want to feel comfortable around other people. This is known as *belonging*. We want and enjoy the company of other people. Belonging gives people the feeling of being secure and important.

Feeling loved and liked is a part of the need to belong. Some of this need can be met through our work and co-workers. At other times, we meet this need through families, friends, clubs, and organizations.

Friends are important in helping people have a good feeling about themselves. Responding positively to other people can create a bond. If we are rude and respond negatively, no bond will be established with other people.

Need to Feel Good about Ourselves

How we feel about ourselves is reflected in how we treat other people. Successful people feel good about themselves. They have high self esteem.

Self esteem is how an individual assesses his or her own personal worth. People with high self esteem feel good about themselves, and this shows in their dealings with other people. People with high self esteem are less likely to become involved with illegal drugs. High self esteem helps people adjust to their social groups and avoid behavior that may have negative consequences. Teenage pregnancy is often associated with low self esteem. People who feel good about themselves are able to set desirable standards of behavior and follow them.

Self-concept is a part of how we feel about ourselves. *Self-concept* is an individual's feelings of himself or herself. People who have positive self-concepts are more likely to have good human relations.

Of course, people must keep their feelings of self in proper perspective. People need to avoid acting as if they are "better than other people."

RESPONDING TO NEEDS

People with good human relations skills respond appropriately based on the needs of other people and of themselves.

This means understanding that other people have needs and that these needs influence how they respond to you. It also involves "reaching out." Reaching out means having empathy or trying to understand the situation of the other person. If we know a person has been sick we can respond to them with support and understanding. If we know they have a problem with a crop pest or livestock disease, we can show that we sincerely care.

People need to accurately assess their own needs and how these influence the way they respond to other people. We sometimes have to "mask" or cover-up our real feelings. Being critical of others or complaining about our own situations will not result in good human relations. Even though we may not feel well, we need to "put a smile on our face and happiness in our voice!"

DEVELOPING HUMAN RELATIONS SKILLS

Good human relations skills can be learned. People can make conscious efforts to develop these skills by knowing the appropriate way to respond. Once the skills are developed, we need to use them.

Figure 16-6. Examining growing crops for disease and other conditions often requires people to work together. (Courtesy, American Association of Cereal Chemists, St. Paul, Minnesota)

PERSONALITY

Personality is how a person appears to the rest of the world. It is a person's pattern of behavior with other people. Personality is the visible part (sometimes called a picture) of a person's character. It is made up of all of the social, mental, emotional, and physical traits of a person.

Personality is learned. It is a product of our childhood, present environment, education, self-concept, and needs. It might be necessary to change your personality to establish better human relations. It isn't easy, but we all have room for improvements.

A few personality traits that are useful in agrimarketing are included here. With conscientious effort, you can improve in these areas.

Being Courteous

Courtesy is being considerate and respectful of other people. There are many simple things that make other people feel respected. Courtesy often requires little extra effort but does require remembering the feelings of other people. We commonly think of courtesy as holding doors and letting other people go first. Courtesy also includes many workplace behaviors, such as returning tools and equipment to the right places and keeping other people informed.

Being Patient

Patience is dealing with other people without complaining or showing anger. We don't show that another person is annoying us. Patience often involves taking extra time to help people. It includes keeping a positive attitude toward other people and their problems.

Being Pleasant

Who likes a person who complains all of the time? *Pleasant* means that a person has agreeable personal qualities. They are sociable and friendly. They have a smile on their face and cheerfully greet people. Pleasant people aren't critical of others and they don't put other people down. A good, positive attitude toward life, other people, and work is most beneficial. Pleasant people are cheerful and show that they are happy!

Being Honest

Honesty means that a person is forthright and doesn't cheat, lie, or steal. Honest people are truthful. An honest person seeks out accurate information. Honest people keep their promises. Honesty is essential in agrimarketing; many dollars of agricultural products are at stake!

Being Prompt and On Time

Prompt means that something is done without delay. People who are prompt are quick to act and do things as promised. Keeping appointments is essential. Being at work on time and staying until the work is done is an essential personal quality. Making agricultural deliveries and providing services when promised builds goodwill for your company.

Being On Task

Being *on task* means that a person is going about the expected work duties in an efficient and effective manner. People who spend a lot of time talking to others and not concentrating on their work are off-task. Work gets done when people are on-task. Agricultural producers like to market through people who are on-task. They feel that people who are off-task are costing them money because they aren't being productive.

APPEARANCE

All people have unique physical traits that make them who they are. Some people don't feel that they are as attractive as they would like to be. Improving appearance doesn't require elaborate clothing and cosmetic surgery. It can be achieved with simple, economical attention to details of our physical appearance.

Physical appearance is what we look like on the outside. It is made up of our natural features as well as how we dress and groom ourselves. Our physical appearance influences how we relate with other people. We need to present the appropriate physical appearance for work in agrimarketing.

Three important areas related to physical appearance are presented here.

Clothing

Clothing is the covering people put on their bodies, sometimes known as garments. How we relate in agrimarketing depends on how we dress. The right clothing helps overcome other shortcomings a person may have. It can also help a person to feel more confident about what they are doing.

Selecting Clothing. Select clothing that is appropriate for your work in agrimarketing. This depends on your job duties and the kind of image you want to project. The clothing should also provide protection and meet the requirements of the work site.

People working in processing and manufacturing should meet the safety and sanitation requirements of the employer. This may include wearing clothing that is provided for the work. In some cases, specific safety shoes with steel toes or water-proof boots may be needed.

People in sales and management may wear clothing that is stylish and presents a business appearance. In general, people are more successful if they avoid high-fashion clothing that will go out of date quickly. The style of dress should be appropriate for the audience; most farmers don't expect someone coming to the ranch to buy cattle to wear a fancy, expensive suit.

Clothing should be durable and comfortable. It should also meet the needs of the climate and the work environment. The clothing should fit properly, be of a good color that won't fade quickly, and priced within your budget.

Young people who want to be upwardly mobile in their careers are encouraged to dress slightly better than others in their work setting. Dress appropriately for the next level of job you aspire to hold.

Maintaining Clothing. Properly caring for and wearing clothing is essential. Neat, well-cared for clothing helps people relate well with others.

Clothing should be properly washed or dry cleaned and neatly ironed. Small tears should be repaired and missing buttons should be promptly replaced. A success-oriented person in agrimarketing has no use for torn and worn out clothing. Dirty clothing detracts from your appearance and becomes an obstacle in good human relations.

Grooming

Grooming is the neatness and cleanliness of the body. It includes taking baths, brushing teeth, using deodorant, and combing hair. How the clothes are worn is also a part of grooming.

Human relations may be greatly damaged by body odor. Situations vary in different countries and cultures, but in North America body odor is considered offensive. Regular baths and deodorant help prevent body odor.

Brushing teeth is important in maintaining good teeth as well as personal appearance. Clean teeth help keep your breath smelling pleasant.

Properly combing the hair is important. Hair varies in its nature, and this must be considered in the hair style you use. The hair should always be conservatively combed in agrimarketing occupations. Both males and females should keep hair neat and acceptably short!

Health

Healthy people are more productive in their work and relate better to other people. *Health* is the absence of disease. How we eat and live influences our health. People in poor health may miss a lot of work and be inefficient in their agrimarketing responsibilities.

The body needs proper food to provide for its nutritional needs. Eating the right food helps to keep people healthy and more productive in their work. Eating regular meals also helps people stay healthy. Missing breakfast or lunch isn't a good practice in the long run.

Sleep and rest are essential so that the body restores itself and stays healthy. Sleep and rest also help a person concentrate on their work and on human relationships. Staying out too late at night reduces a person's effectiveness the next day. An individual who didn't get enough sleep is more likely to be grouchy and fail to follow safe practices in using machinery.

Drugs, tobacco, and other substances that abuse the body should be avoided. Not only are these addictive and damaging to health, their use can cost people their jobs. Some employers test employees for drugs because they realize the value of a drug-free workforce.

Preventative health care practices should be followed. Regular check-ups by a physician can catch minor health problems before they become serious. Regular visits to a dentist can do the same for your teeth.

Exercise is important to the body. Walking, jogging, mowing the lawn, riding a stationary bike, and other activities provide exercise. In some cases, the work may provide sufficient physical activity. Most people should have

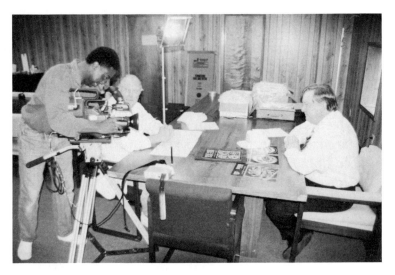

Figure 16–7. All details for a good appearance in this on-site
interview of the marketing manager of a food
processing company are being carefully arranged.

a medical check-up before they begin an exercise program. If they haven't
been active, they may need to start exercising gradually.

A person who has good health is much more likely to enjoy success
in an agrimarketing career. When you feel better, you relate better with
people!

DEALING WITH CONFLICT

People don't always get along. When they don't, conflict may come
out in the open. Arguments and disagreements may disrupt the work place
and interfere with agrimarketing. People may oppose each other and clash.
In most cases, the conflict is verbal and may not be obvious. However,
sometimes conflicts become violent.

CONFLICT MANAGEMENT

Conflict is when people become competitive and oppose each other. It
is disruptive and certainly doesn't contribute to good human relations.

Conflict may occur between employees in an agrimarketing firm or
between an employee and a customer. Disagreements over weights, grades,
prices, and other product characteristics may cause conflicts between people

in the marketing process. Conflicts with customers are definitely damaging in the agrimarketing process.

Conflict management involves preventing conflicts from occurring and, if they do occur, solving them. Work environments can be arranged to reduce the chance of conflicts occurring. Following good human relations practices is a big first step.

People can help reduce conflict by expressing ideas in non-threatening ways. Some differences of opinion will always be present. Providing opportunities for people to bring up problems before they become major concerns can help reduce conflict. When issues come up, they should be addressed promptly. Of course, good human relations includes the ability to tolerate differences of opinion without letting them become conflicts.

Here are a few pointers on managing conflict:

- Be a good listener.

- Be willing to compromise.

- Respect differences of opinion.

- Consider the appropriateness of your response before speaking.

- Never criticize a person; criticize their behavior if necessary.

- Be open and non-defensive.

- Choose the right time and place for what you do.

- Be assertive; not combative.

ASSERTION SKILLS

Assertiveness involves defending oneself through direct expression of positive and negative feelings. It allows people to protect their rights without aggressive behavior that causes conflict. People can express their needs in non-threatening ways. Assertiveness can prevent head-on fights.

Assertion skills are often learned in training programs that provide skill development. Conflicts can be avoided when people understand assertion skills. It isn't always what a person does, it is how they go about doing it. For example, if you were preparing to write a short article for the local paper about agrimarketing and you wanted a good place to write, you might say to the people around you, "I am going to write the article and would appreciate your keeping the noise down." This is not a threat or a command. It appeals to people to cooperate so that you can get your work done. Suppose you had said, "Shut up so I can write." How would the other people feel? They would likely be offended and ready to have an open conflict.

HANDLING ANGER

People sometimes get angry. The anger may be kept inside or come out as rage and fury. People often get angry because they think they have been wronged. People with good human relations skills can help calm the angry person. Anger is sometimes expressed as a physical attack on another person. Situations involving anger should be handled carefully. People who are angry don't have good judgment at the height of their emotion. They may say or do things that they later regret.

In handling anger, be a good listener. Let people explain why they are upset. Hear their side of the story, and you may agree that they have a reason to be upset. Let the angry person do most of the talking; never hurry them along. When confronted with anger, keep calm. You don't need to get angry, too! Encourage the angry person to propose a solution to the problem that caused the anger. If the anger is too great, postpone discussion of solutions until another time when heads are cooler.

Anger between customers and employees in the agrimarketing process can result in long-term damage to reputations and the loss of business. It's a good idea to practice the motto that, "The customer is always right."

Figure 16–8. Some agrimarketing occupations involve relating to many people in fast-paced situations, such as on this trading floor. (Courtesy, Chicago Board of Trade)

ATTRIBUTES OF PEOPLE WHO ARE GOOD IN HUMAN RELATIONS

Good human relations skills can be learned. Some practice of the basic rules may be needed, however. Here are ten rules for good human relations:

1. Be genuinely interested in people. Try to like everyone. All people have good traits even though they may have traits that you don't like. Showing genuine interest develops long-term friendship and customer loyalty.

2. Speak to people. Saying "hello" or "good morning" in a cheerful voice makes everyone feel better. Be friendly and helpful.

3. Smile at people. A smile helps open the door to good human relations.

4. Look people in the eye when you talk to them. Eye-to-eye contact is important in communicating respect and honesty in our culture.

5. Call people by their names. Most people like to hear their names and when you pronounce them properly it helps people feel better. Younger people should also be respectful and include Mr. or Ms. when speaking to adults.

6. Be generous with praise and cautious with criticism. People like to hear that what they have done is good. Even when people fail, try to find something good that was done.

7. Be considerate of the feelings of others. All people have feelings and values, and they appreciate other people respecting them.

8. Be alert to help people with their needs. Though it may be a small problem to you, a problem may be big to the person who has it. Take the time to talk and solve it.

9. Be cordial. Make it appear that everything you do is a genuine pleasure.

10. Be honest and fair with people. Dishonesty can damage relationships very quickly. Dishonesty in agrimarketing can involve breaking laws that could result in fines and jail terms. If you make a mistake, admit it and apologize. Always treat other people as you would like to be treated yourself.

SUMMARY

People are more productive when they relate well with each other. Having good human relations skills is important to success in agrimarketing. It includes both relationships with co-workers and with the public.

Communication is important to human relations. People are better at communication if they realize that it is a process and that the needs of the receiver must be considered. Feedback is used to assess the effectiveness of communication.

People do what they do for a reason. Motivations cause them to respond in certain ways. Important needs are physical needs, the need to belong, and the need to feel good about ourselves. How we respond to the needs of people is important. We can respond better if we understand our needs as well.

Human relations skills are learned. People can improve on the skills they have and develop new skills. Personality and appearance can be improved.

Conflicts sometimes occur. Preventing conflicts involves conflict management. Assertion skills are also helpful in establishing a good environment without creating conflict. Anger should be dealt with to minimize hostility.

Following a few simple rules can be helpful in improving human relations.

CHAPTER SELF-CHECK

Match the following terms with the correct definitions:

   a. human relations

   b. interpersonal relations

   c. communication

   d. feedback

   e. assertiveness

   f. self esteem

   g. personality

   h. courtesy

   i. physical appearance

   j. conflict

_____   defending oneself through direct expression of
            feelings

_____   occurs when people become competitive and
            oppose each other

_____   how people relate to other people

_____   the exchange of information

_____   the feelings and emotions people have toward
            each other

_____   used to evaluate the effectiveness of communication

_____   how individuals assess their own personal worth

_____   how a person appears to the rest of the world

_____   being considerate and respectful of other people

_____   what we look like on the outside

QUESTIONS AND PROBLEMS
FOR DISCUSSION

1. Interpersonal relations involves two major areas. List and explain these two areas. Indicate why they are important in agrimarketing.

2. What are the components of the communication process? Explain each and describe how they relate to each other.

3. What is used to assess the effectiveness of the communication process? Explain how it works.

4. What is motivation and why is it important in human relations?

5. What are the needs of people? How do they relate to human relations?

6. People who are good in human relations respond on the basis of at least two individuals. Who are they and why are they important?

7. What areas of personality can be developed? What should a person do to develop human relations skills in these areas?

8. Three areas contribute to appearance. List and tell why these areas are important.

9. Why does conflict occur? What can a person do when conflict occurs?

10. What is anger? How is it handled?

ACTIVITIES

1. Get a copy of the food guide pyramid. Study how foods are clustered for best nutrition. Compare your eating habits to the recommendations in the pyramid. Develop a plan for improving your eating habits.

2. Arrange to visit an agricultural marketing business, such as a processing plant or grain elevator. Observe how the people dress and assess if you feel their dress is appropriate for the work they are doing. How well does their dress relate to the customers of the business?

3. Invite a counselor to visit the class and discuss ways to improve personality and human relations. Prepare a bulletin board or poster that summarizes the major areas and how to make improvements.

4. Sponsor an occupational dress day at your school. Have students come to school dressed as they would in the first job in their career.

5. Invite a representative of a clothing store to serve as a resource person and describe how to dress for success. Ask for an explanation of the kinds of fabrics and how to care for them. Find out how to get clothes that fit well and are durable. Read and report on books that explain how to dress for success.

6. Prepare an oral or a written report on human relations. Your report can be from the standpoint of a manager or as a co-worker. A good reference is *Agribusiness Management and Entrepreneurship* by Michael E. Newman and Walter J. Wills, available from Interstate Publishers, Inc.

Appendixes

APPENDIX A

SAMPLE MARKETING PLAN

The following plan was adapted from the Instructional Packet: Marketing Plan Project released by the National FFA Organization in 1990. It is intended as a guide for student groups in developing marketing plans.

A Fictional Example
A MARKETING PLAN FOR
THE MISS-D ONION COOPERATIVE

This marketing plan for the Miss-D Onion Cooperative was developed by the Dalton FFA Chapter. It is aimed at expanding the cooperative's share of the fresh onion market in the Garthace, Missouri, area. The plan is presented in five parts: Analysis of the Market, Business Proposition, Action Plan, Budget, and Evaluation.

Analysis of the Market

Miss-D Onions have been produced in Dalton County since 1981, when one farmer planted one-half acre. The onion has unique qualities that make it particularly attractive to consumers. It is a mild, sweet, juicy onion with excellent storage qualities. It compliments salads, sandwiches, and other foods—cooked or raw—in a superb manner. Five farmers in Dalton County now grow 75 acres of Miss-D Onions. Gross sales in 1991 were $20,000 by the cooperative. As a profitable alternative for cash grain farmers, the Miss-D Onion Cooperative seeks to expand its share of the fresh onion market in the Garthace, Missouri, area and increase acreage planted to Miss-D Onions. This will result in a more profitable farm economy in Dalton County.

Miss-D Onions have been marketed under the Miss-D label since 1986. The name was originated by the first farmer to plant the onion, with "D" representing the words "Dalton" and "delicious." The onions are marketed on a limited basis in a seven county area through supermarkets. It is not used by any of the fast food restaurants even though Miss-D is known to enhance the flavor of many fast food products.

The cooperative currently has a small packing shed operated on a part-time basis. It is managed by one of the onion farmers with assistance from the local adult farmer teacher. The onions are bagged in 3-pound, 5-pound, and 25-pound mesh bags. Distribution is through two fruit and vegetable wholesale distributors. The cooperative has not developed a logo or other promotional materials. All bags are labeled as Miss-D Onions—a product of Dalton County, Missouri.

There are 18 fast food establishments in Garthace. Of these, 14 primarily sell sandwiches and salads. Four primarily sell pizza. The predominance of sandwiches sold are hamburgers followed by roast beef sandwiches, chicken fillet sandwiches, and hot dogs with onion and chili. The salads are primarily of the garden description and made of lettuce, radishes, cucumbers, tomatoes, and bean sprouts. A survey of the restaurants found only one that included an onion slice in its salad. All four of the pizza restaurants use some onion in certain pizza products. Certainly, all of the fast food restaurants could be using some Miss-D Onions!

At present there is very little promotion of premium onion products in Garthace. Each June–August all four of the supermarkets and 5 of the 11 convenience stores carry Vidalia Onions—a Georgia-produced onion somewhat similar to the Miss-D. Occasionally supermarkets carry Texas Sweet Onions. Usually, the supermarkets that do not handle the Miss-D have few premium onions. The stores now sell a combined total of approximately 550 3-pound bags and 525 5-pound bags of all kinds of onions each week.

This situation provides the Miss-D Onion Cooperative the opportunity to expand its share of the retail onion market in Garthace, a town of 21,000 citizens with another 26,000 in the surrounding trade area. In addition, highways through the town regularly bring tourist and business traffic that frequents the fast food restaurants and convenience stores. Could Miss-D become a product tourists would buy and take back to their homes?

Business Proposition

The opportunity to expand the consumption of Miss-D Onions appears to have two areas for growth: (1) supermarkets and convenience stores and (2) fast food restaurants. The objective for 1996 is to increase the sales of Miss-D by 300 percent in Garthace. This will involve having 100 percent of the supermarkets and convenience stores and 75 percent of the fast food restaurants selling or using Miss-D Onions. Since half of the supermarkets and convenience stores now have Miss-D Onions, the major target will be the remaining supermarkets and convenience stores followed by the fast food restaurants.

The major strategy will focus on developing a Miss-D logo, printing promotional posters for supermarkets and convenience stores to display where the onions are stocked, preparing ready-to-use ad copy for the stores to insert in advertisements, encouraging all stores to stock and attractively display Miss-D Onions, keeping all displayed onions attractive and fresh, and sponsoring a "Cook with Miss-D Contest" at the county fair. Small placards (tent cards) will be printed for those fast food restaurants using Miss-D Onions to display on their tables and counters.

Action Plan

The action plan for increasing the sales of Miss-D Onions will involve onion growers, the cooperative, supermarket, convenience store, and fast food restaurant managers. Due to the effort to sell more onions, the farmers will be asked to increase their acreage by 300 percent to meet the anticipated increased demand.

Product Positioning

The onion cooperative will employ a part-time marketing specialist to visit supermarkets, convenience stores, and fast food restaurants promoting Miss-D Onions. This individual will take promotional literature to the stores and assist in putting it up, discuss display procedures for onions, and describe how the cooperative is going to be involved in promoting the Miss-D—a premium onion. Attractive labeling and freshness will help sell the onions. The fast food restaurants will receive suggestions on how to use onions in food items and the use of promotional literature.

Price

Since the Miss-D is a superior onion, the shelf price will be established slightly above the other onion products. To encourage customers to buy Miss-D Onions, coupons offering 25 cent discounts on 3-pound and 5-pound bags will be run by the stores in their advertisements in the local newspapers. (With the coupon, particularly in stores with double coupon value incentives, the per pound price of Miss-D will be less than most other onion products.) The price to fast food restaurants for 25-pound bags will be competitive with other brands of onions.

Place

The Cooperative will make twice weekly deliveries to supermarkets, convenience stores, and fast food restaurants through the vegetable and fruit distributors currently handling the Miss-D. Bags with spoiled onions will be reclaimed and appropriate credit given the store. Stores will be encouraged to stock the 3- and 5-pound bags; fast food restaurants will be encouraged to buy the 25-pound bags.

Promotion

Promotion will include attractive newspaper advertisements, posters for stores, tent cards for restaurants, articles for the the food section of the local newspaper on cooking with Miss-D Onions, and sales promotion, including the use of discount coupons. High school home economics teachers and extension home economists will be given samples of Miss-D Onions.

A "Cook with Miss-D Contest" will be held. The managers of the stores and restaurants will be invited to be special guests at the contest at the county fair. The managers of the supermarket, convenience store, and fast food restaurant with the largest sales or use of Miss-D Onions will be invited to serve as judges for the contest. Newspaper coverage of the contest will be sought. The contest will be promoted through stores, newspaper announcements, the fair catalog, and the homemakers clubs of the Extension Service. A $100 savings bond will be awarded the first place winner.

Marketing Budget

The implementation of the marketing plan will require an investment by the cooperative; increased returns show that this investment will produce good results. A projected budget is presented on the following page. (Note: Due to the production cycle of onions, the budget is calculated for the year beginning in April and running through the next March.)

Evaluation

Each aspect of the marketing plan will be evaluated as it is implemented. This will include an assessment of each step as it is planned and initiated (with needed adjustments being made in the procedures) at the end of each quarter and at the end of the year. The marketing specialist will make regular contacts with the managers of stores and restaurants to determine their assessment of marketing progress. Further, the marketing specialist will maintain close contact with the two fruit and vegetable distributors that are involved in the physical distribution of the Miss-D Onion. These efforts in evaluation will allow the Miss-D Onion Cooperative to maximize returns to onion farmers and cooperative patrons/members.

MARKETING BUDGET

| Cost Items | Quarters | | | | Total (year) |
	First ($)	Second ($)	Third ($)	Fourth ($)	($)
Advertising					
Newspapers	200	400	200	100	900
Posters	400	0	0	0	400
Tent cards	200	0	200	0	400
Logo and label design	500	0	0	0	500
Total					2,200
Sales Promotion					
Discount coupons	100	200	200	200	700
"Cook with Miss-D Contest"	0	0	300	0	300
Marketing specialist (25% FTE @ $28,000/yr.)	1,750	1,750	1,750	1,750	7,000
Total					8,000
General and Administrative					
Clerical	300	200	250	250	1,000
Telephone	40	40	40	40	160
Postage	30	30	30	30	120
Office supplies	20	20	20	20	80
Travel (@ 20 cents/mile)	80	90	80	20	270
Total					1,630
Human Resource Development					
Workshop for farmers	150	0	0	0	150
Total					150
Sales Personnel	0	0	0	0	0
Total					0
Grand Total					$11,980
Sales and Returns Projections					
Sales of Miss-D by Cooperative*	8,580	15,210	18,720	18,720	61,230
Cost of onions sold**	(6,370)	(11,440)	(14,105)	(14,105)	(46,020)
Marketing costs	(3,680)	(2,730)	(3,070)	(2,410)	(11,890)
Net Income (before taxes)	(1,470)	1,040	1,545	2,205	3,320

*Sales are based on the following:

| Bag Size | Quarter | | | | Total |
	First	Second	Third	Fourth	
3-pound					
Pounds	11,700	23,400	27,300	27,300	89,700
Bags	3,900	7,800	9,100	9,100	29,900
5-pound					
Pounds	19,500	26,000	32,500	32,500	110,500
Bags	3,900	5,200	6,500	6,500	22,100
25-pound					
Pounds	32,500	65,000	81,250	81,250	260,000
Bags	1,300	2,600	3,250	3,250	10,400

Price received per pound by cooperative:
 3-lb. bag = $.15/lb or $.45/bag
 5-lb. bag = $.15/lb or $.75/bag
 25-lb. bag - $.12/lb or $3.00/bag

**The cost to the cooperative for the onions sold (includes product purchase from farmers, grading, packaging, transporting, etc.) will be $.10/lb. (The price paid to farmers equals approximately $.07/lb.)

APPENDIX B

SAMPLE SURVEY INSTRUMENT

The following sample survey was adapted from the Instructional Packet: Marketing Plan Project produced by the National FFA Organization in 1990. It is a simple example to guide student groups in learning about marketing plan development.

FARM EQUIPMENT REPLACEMENT PARTS

This survey is designed to determine how farmers might respond to a proposed on-farm parts delivery service. Your help in providing the following information will be appreciated.

1. What do you produce on your farm? (kind and acreage of crops and kind and number of head of livestock) _____
_____

2. When repair needs arise, how do you get your replacement parts? (check all that apply)

   _____ Make special trip to town
   _____ Get part on regular trip to town
   _____ Order by telephone for mail delivery
   _____ Other (specify) _____

3. Where do you get replacement parts now? (give name of business)
_____

4. How many dollars do you spend each year on replacement parts?
   $_____

5. How do you feel about on-farm parts delivery?

   _____ Good idea and I would use it   _____ Unsure
   _____ Good idea but I probably wouldn't use it   _____ Bad idea

6. Would you be willing to pay a small amount more for parts if they were delivered to your farm?

   _____ Yes   _____ No   _____ Unsure

7. How do you normally pay for parts?

   _____ Charge to account and pay monthly
   _____ Pay cash at time of purchase
   _____ Charge to account and pay at end of season
   _____ Charge to credit card
   _____ Other (specify) _____

APPENDIX C

SAMPLE COMPETITION ANALYSIS SHEET

This form was adapted from the Instructional Packet Marketing Plan Project produced by the National FFA Organization in 1990.

FARM EQUIPMENT REPLACEMENT PARTS

Use this form to help assess the strengths and weaknesses of competitors. List the name of each competing business and its strengths and weaknesses.

Names of Businesses Selling Parts	Strengths	Weaknesses
1. _____	1. 2. 3.	1. 2. 3.
2. _____	1. 2. 3.	1. 2. 3.
3. _____	1. 2. 3.	1. 2. 3.
4. _____	1. 2. 3.	1. 2. 3.
5. _____	1. 2. 3.	1. 2. 3.

APPENDIX D

SAMPLE MARKET POTENTIAL AND SHARE ANALYSIS

This form was adapted from the Instructional Packet: Marketing Plan Project produced by the National FFA Organization in 1990.

STRENGTHS, WEAKNESSES AND ANALYSIS

Use this form to help assess your ability to compete. Identify the strengths and weaknesses of your agribusiness, supply, or service. Estimate how well you will compete with your competitors.

Your Strengths	Relationship to Gaining Share of the Market
1.	1.
2.	2.
3.	3.
4.	4.
5.	5.

Your Weaknesses	Relationship to Gaining Share of the Market
1.	1.
2.	2.
3.	3.
4.	4.
5.	5.

Glossary

Acclimatization–climatic adaptation of a plant to a new environment.

Action plan–The product mix that will be used in a marketing plan.

Actuating–A management function that involves getting people to work together toward a common goal; leading or directing.

Advertising–Any form of nonpersonal presentation and promotion of ideas, goods, and/or services by an identified sponsor.

Agribusiness marketing–Marketing supplies and services to the farm producer.

Agricultural chemicals–Various chemical compounds applied to areas where crops or animals are produced to control pests or other problems.

Agricultural education–Courses in schools that teach agriculture through classroom and laboratory learning activities.

Agricultural industry–All of the production and marketing activities that meet the needs of consumers for food and fiber.

Agricultural input industries–Businesses that manufacture, process, and/or supply inputs.

Agricultural marketing–Marketing the food and fiber products produced on farms; also known as agrimarketing.

Agricultural pharmaceutical–Medicine or other substance used to treat sick animals and otherwise maintain their health.

Agricultural revolution–Changes that have occurred in how food and fiber are made available to people.

Agrimarketing career–A sequence or progression of jobs in the area of agrimarketing that leads to personal success.

Agrimarketing functions–The series of steps involved in moving food and fiber from farms to consumers.

Agrimarketing technology–Agricultural marketing that emphasizes the use of technology in the process of marketing food and fiber.

Analysis of the market–Collecting information about the market and studying it for meaning; part of developing a marketing plan.

Annual marketing plan–A marketing plan prepared each year for continuing product lines.

Apprenticeship–A period of job training under the direction of a highly skilled worker.

Aquacrop–An aquatic plant or animal that is farmed.

Aquacrop label–The written description on a package that identifies the aquacrop product.

Aquacrop processing–All of the steps taken to get an aquacrop into the form consumers want.

Aquaculture–The culture of aquatic plants and animals.

Aquaculture niche market–a small, specialized market for certain aquaculture products.

Aquatic animals–Animals that grow in water.

Aquatic plants—Plants that grow in water.

Assertiveness—Defending oneself through direct expression of both positive and negative feelings; training may be needed to effectively use assertiveness.

Auction—Public sale where people bid on supplies or products being sold.

Baccalaureate degree—The degree received after completion of a prescribed curriculum; typically requires four years of study beyond high school.

Bait and tackle stores—Stores that sell bait and tackle for sport fishers; also known as bait shops.

Baitfish—Small fish used by sport fishers to catch game (wild) fish.

Balled and burlapped—Plants (usually small trees and shrubs) grown in a field that have been carefully dug and burlap wrapped around the ball of soil to protect the roots.

Bank financing—A bank lending a buyer money to purchase equipment or other items.

Bare root—Plants marketed without soil on their roots.

Bartering—Exchanging one item of value for another.

Bedding plants—Small, seedling plants that will be transplanted into flower and vegetable gardens.

Belonging—How one individual feels around other people; how comfortable people are together.

Bill of lading—Used in transportation as receipt to the shipper and a contract for the carrier to deliver materials.

Biodegrade—Rotting or disintegration of materials.

Black space—Unfilled areas of an advertisement that are black.

Body copy—The selling message of an advertisement; usually appears after the headline.

Brackish water—Where freshwater streams flow into saltwater; a mixture of saltwater and freshwater.

Broadcast media—Radio and television.

Budget—A statement of anticipated expenses and income; used in marketing plans.

Business magazine—A magazine focused on different industry groups.

Business plan—A written plan on how a farm or agribusiness will be operated so that it is successful.

Business proposition—A statement of what is to be accomplished in a marketing plan.

Buyer benefits—The wants or needs of a customer that a product satisfies.

Buying excuse—Insincere reasons a customer gives to avoid buying.

Buying motive—Reasons that influence customers to buy certain things.

Buying signals—Signs of product or service approval during the sales process.

Capital—Property used in agricultural production and the agrimarketing infrastructure; money and what money will provide.

Capitalism—An economic system in which individuals are free to establish a business to earn a profit (see "free enterprise").

Career—General course of a person's life as related to work.

Career advancement—Moving to higher levels of work in a career.

Career ladder—The sequential upward advancement of people in careers.

Cash contract—Agreement between farmer and buyer specifying a certain quantity of a commodity will be delivered on or by a certain date at a specified price.

Cash market—Traditional agricultural markets where producers can expect to receive current cash prices; examples are local grain elevators and livestock auctions.

Cash marketing—Delivering products and getting paid for them at the time of delivery.

Cash price—The price paid for products at the time of delivery.

Catalog ordering—Buying materials through the mail or by telephone after identifying them in a published listing of products.

Channel of distribution—The route a product goes through between producer and consumer.

Checkoff—Assessing fees when a commodity is sold or bought to make funds available for research or product promotion.

Circulation—The number of people who purchase and read a newspaper, magazine, or other printed media.

Classified advertising—An advertisement that uses only the printed selling message to promote a product or service.

Clip art—Artwork that is produced by specialized businesses and sold to advertisers in ready-to-use form and is copyright free.

Clothing—The covering people put on their bodies.

Cold call—When a salesperson calls on a prospective buyer without an appointment or any prior knowledge of the prospect's needs.

Column inch—The width of a column of print in a newspaper that is 1 inch (2.5 cm) in length.

Commercial greenhouse—Horticulture businesses that produce plants for sale in artificially controlled environments.

Commercial production—Producing crops and livestock to be sold, rather than consumed on the farm.

Commodities—Agricultural products such as wheat, corn, and cattle that can be traded.

Commodity commissions—Organizations formed by producers for promotion and research of a particular commodity.

Communication—The exchange of information; a process of exchanging information.

Company financing—When a manufacturer lends a buyer money to purchase equipment or other items.

Comparative advantage—The advantage that one location has over another in the production of a commodity.

Competition—Condition that occurs when several producers have identical or similar products and each tries to get people to buy their products.

Conflict—When people become competitive and oppose each other.

Conflict management—Striving to prevent conflicts from occurring and, if they do occur, appropriately solving them.

Consumer—People, farms, agribusinesses, and others that use goods and services.

Consumer behavior—How people make decisions in buying and using products.

Consumer magazine—A magazine that focuses on a specific area of interest or lifestyle.

Consumption—Use of goods and services that have value.

Container—Anything that contains something; cartons, boxes, crates, cans, jars, and other devices that are used in packaging.

Container grown—Plants that are grown in containers, such as plastic buckets and metal cans.

Continuing education—Education that an individual gets throughout a career.

Controlling—A management function that assesses how well goals of a business were achieved.

Cool calling—When a salesperson calls on a prospective buyer who might fit a certain criterion.

Cooperative—Form of business created and operated by an association.

Cooperative ad—Advertisement that combines a national company's expertise in advertising and brand name identification with a local business.

Copywriter—The person who creates the written information for advertisements.

Corporation—Way of doing business that involves one or more people creating a legal entity that is treated as an individual.

Cost-price squeeze—When prices producers receive are near the cost of production.

Courtesy—Being considerate and respectful of other people.

Current market values—What a commodity is currently worth.

Custom farming—Individuals who own equipment and perform a variety of farm functions for a fee.

Custom order aquaculture marketing—When producers take orders from buyers for specific kinds of aquacrops.

Daily newspaper—A newspaper originat-

ing in a specific city with circulation primarily in that city or region and published five or more days per week.

Dealer financing—When a dealer lends a buyer money to purchase equipment.

Dealership—A sales agency that has the authority to sell a product.

Debt structure—Amount and other characteristics of the debt of a farm or agribusiness.

Decided customer—A customer who knows the product or service they want to buy.

Decision making—Selecting among alternative courses of action.

Demand—Amount of a product that will be bought at a given price at a particular time.

Difficult decisions—Decisions that require people to go through a process of problem solving.

Direct action advertising—Advertising that encourages customers to buy specific goods or services now.

Direct mail—Printed ad materials sent to potential customers' homes by mail.

Direct marketing—When the producer markets directly to the consumer.

Display—A visual presentation prepared by a business to promote products or services and build goodwill.

Display advertising—The use of illustrations, different type sizes and fonts, and white space in an ad to promote a product or service.

Display classified advertisement—Advertisement that uses simple illustrations, varying type sizes and fonts, and limited white space; only appear in the back of magazines.

Distribution—Moving products to locations where consumers have access to them.

Distribution intensity–The number of sources of a particular good or service.

Distribution outlet–Point of contact between the producer and the consumer.

Economics–Creation of goods and services to satisfy human wants and needs.

Economic system–The way the government provides for goods to be owned, created, and exchanged; examples are capitalism, socialism, and communism.

Economy of scale–Larger quantities of products offer advantages associated with lowering per unit fixed costs.

Emotional buying–Making the decision to buy without any conditions attached; data aren't important.

Empathy–Identification of one person with another person's situation.

Employment application form–A written form that is filled out when applying for a job; asks about education, experience, and goals.

Evaluation–In marketing, a process used to assess how well a marketing plan is doing.

Family–Basic group to which people belong.

Family life cycles–Series of stages people pass through in their lives.

Farmers' markets–Large sheds, buildings, or other facilities where several producers can bring their products and operate retail direct markets; producers often rent a stall or small space that is similar to their own store.

Farm magazine–Magazine targeted toward farmers and agricultural production.

Farm/ranch problem–Unstable and relatively low prices and incomes for farms and ranches.

Feedback–In communication, return channels from the receiver to sender to aid in evaluating the effectiveness of the exchange of information; how another person responds to an attempt to communicate.

Fee lake–A type of recreational aquaculture market where sport fishers pay a fee to catch fish using hooks and lines as with wild fish.

Financial backing–Amount of funds available to operate an agribusiness or farm.

Food and fiber marketing sector–Agribusinesses involved in marketing food and fiber.

For-profit business–Farms and businesses that are privately owned and intended to make a profit for the owner.

Forward contracting–Marketing procedure used when producer and buyer enter into an agreement well before a crop is harvested.

Freedom of choice–Individuals are free to choose what they want to produce and buy and sell at prices they agree upon; part of free enterprise.

Free enterprise–Economic system that allows individuals to organize and conduct business with a minimum of government control; individuals privately own what they produce.

Free-rider–Farmers who receive the benefit of an action without making a sacrifice for the overall welfare of a group.

Freshwater–Water with little or no salt content.

Futures contracts–An agreement to take or make delivery of a commodity in the future at a specified price; involves use of futures trading on a commodity exchange.

Goal—A level of accomplishment an individual wants to achieve.

Goal setting—The process an individual goes through in describing what they want to accomplish and how they will accomplish it.

Grading—Marketing function to assure uniformity of products and quality.

Grooming—Neatness and cleanliness of the human body.

Headline—The leading words or phrases, generally in bold letters, that attract potential customers to read an ad; part of every advertisement.

Health—The absence of disease.

Hedging—Using the futures market to lock in a price.

Hidden objection—Reasons a customer has for not buying a product or service that aren't expressed to the salesperson.

Honesty—Character trait of being forthright; not cheating, lying, or stealing.

Human relations—How people relate to each other.

Human relations skills—The ability to understand people and favorably interact with them.

Hunger—The human need for food.

Hydroponics—Growing terrestrial plants with roots in water solutions.

Illustration—A drawing or photograph in an advertisement that attracts attention, creates interest, and shows the product or service.

Income—The monetary return received from marketing.

Indirect action advertising—Advertising that is intended to develop a positive image, confidence, and goodwill, as

well as build permanent patronage for a business.

Industry fragmentation—Lack of coordination in the agricultural industry caused by many different producers.

Infrastructure—Framework of roads, processing plants, trucks, and other structures that allows agricultural industry to function.

Inputs—Supplies and services farmers use to produce crops, livestock, and other items.

Interest inventories—Types of tests that help people understand themselves.

Interpersonal skills—Feelings and emotions that people have toward each other in their relationships.

Inventory—The quantity of supplies or products that are stored or on hand.

Inventory control—Maintaining an adequate stock of materials.

Job—Work in a paid occupation involving a specific site and employer.

Job interview—Personal conference between a job applicant and prospective employer.

Just-looking customer—A customer shopping for nothing specific; in a store looking to become familiar with the products and services that are offered.

Landscape contractor—Occupation that involves the installation and maintenance of landscapes.

Landscape design—Using plants and other materials to create a union between nature and buildings and other structures.

Leads—Prospective customers who have been suggested by current customers or others.

Leasing—Allowing another person to use

property over a period of time for a fee.

Letter of application—Business letter sent to prospective employer indicating that you are applying for a job.

Level of education—Amount of education by years and degrees completed by an individual.

Level of work—Amount of responsibility in an occupation.

Line drawing—Drawings or illustrations made of solid black lines and no shading.

Live hauler—Individuals who buy live fish from a farmer and haul them to another location to sell as live fish.

Live products—Aquacrops marketed live to consumers.

Local ad—Advertisement that promotes a product or service available in a given community.

Logotype or signature—Distinctive business identification symbol that is intended to be recognized by the public; a business trademark; also known as a logo.

Mail order—Method of marketing used when customers have a catalog to identify merchandise that is ordered by mail or telephone.

Management—The use of resources to achieve the objectives of a farm, agribusiness, or other business.

Management functions—Five roles of managers: planning, organizing, staffing, actuating, and controlling.

Managerial occupation—An occupation involving management responsibilities.

Manufacturing process—The way a product has been made, tested, and inspected.

Market area—The geographical area in which a supply or service is marketed.

Market information—Knowledge about conditions that influence market decisions.

Marketing—Providing the goods and services that people want.

Marketing approach—The result of marketing decisions about when, where, how, and the form in which commodities are sold.

Marketing cooperative—A kind of cooperative that markets farm commodities.

Marketing expense—Funds needed to finance marketing activities.

Marketing mix—The combination of four variables used to reach a target market: product, place, price, and promotion; known as the four Ps.

Marketing objective—The ends or goals to be reached by a marketing plan; stated in the business proposition.

Marketing plan—A written statement that guides the marketing process.

Marketing strategy—The part of a marketing plan that explains how a farm or agribusiness will use its resources to meet its objectives.

Market intervention—When the government takes steps to enhance the overall welfare of a nation by regulating certain aspects of marketing.

Market niche—A particular market for a unique product.

Market places—Where agricultural commodities are traditionally sold.

Market potential—The size of a market over a period of time.

Market segmentation—developing specific marketing efforts that target consumers with unique needs.

Market share—a business' portion of the sales of a supply or service.

Mass media—Forms of media used to reach large numbers of people, such as radio and newspapers.

Mass marketing—Offering products to all people regardless of how the people vary in characteristics.

Materials handling—The unloading, lifting, moving, and loading of goods.

Medium—In the communication process, the channel that connects the sender of the message with the receiver.

Message—In the communication process, a set of symbols that are interpreted for their meaning.

Method of delivery—The transportation of raw agricultural products.

Method of exchange—The way a seller is paid for a commodity.

Motivation—Factors that cause people to respond the way they do.

Multinational—When trade and manufacturing of a product are carried out in several nations.

National ad—Advertisement that points out features of a product or service but does not refer to a specific business; used in a large geographical area, typically all of the United States.

National newspaper—A newspaper that has national scope and circulation.

Need—Something that is considered basic to maintaining one's life, such as food, clothing, and shelter.

Net profit—The income after all costs have been deducted from gross profit.

New product plan—A marketing plan prepared for a new product.

Noise—Anything that blocks or interferes with the communication process.

Non-agricultural marketing—Activities in the flow and production of non-agricultural goods and services.

Nonprofit business—Kind of business that isn't intended to make a profit.

Occupation—Specific work that involves certain duties and can be given a title.

Off-flavor—When an aquacrop used for food doesn't taste the way it should.

On task—Going about work duties in an efficient and effective manner; not loafing.

Opportunity costs—Costs associated with delaying the sale of a commodity until a later date when prices may be higher.

Order buyer—An occupation that involves buying products to meet certain specifications for clients; often used with livestock.

Organizing—A management function in establishing roles and activities in a business.

Ornamental aquacrop—Aquatic plants or animals kept for ornamental purposes, including pet fish.

Package—A container for materials.

Packaging material—The material used to make packages.

Pallet—Small movable platform on which containers can be placed for moving and storing.

Parity—Equality of farm income with income in other sectors of the economy.

Partnership—When two or more individuals join together to start a business.

Patience—Dealing with other people without complaining or losing one's temper.

Patronage buying—Buying a product from a specific business.

Per capita consumption—The average amount of a product that is consumed in a year by an individual in a nation.

Personal characteristics—The traits of individuals that influence their behavior as consumers.

Personal data sheet—A written summary of an individual's education, experience, and goals.

Personality—How individuals appear to the people around them.

Personal property—Goods that people use in life, such as clothing, cars, and household furnishings.

Physical appearance—What people look like on the outside; includes posture, clothing, cleanliness, and grooming.

Physical distribution—All of the functions in the actual movement of materials from the point of origin to the point of consumption.

Physical distribution system—The combination of physical distribution functions to achieve a distribution goal.

Physical needs—Basic needs that people have for food, clothing, and shelter; includes sleep, safety, body elimination, and other bodily functions.

Pick-your-own—A form of direct marketing in which consumers do the harvesting.

Place—Product availability to consumers.

Placement service—An office or agency at a school, college, or university that helps people find jobs.

Planning—A management function in deciding on a future course of action.

Planning assumption—The best possible judgments about what is going to happen in the future in a market.

Point-of-purchase advertising—Special promotional displays located at strategic spots within a facility, usually at checkout registers or counters.

Population—The number of people at a location.

Postsecondary education—Education beyond the high school level; typically education in grades 13 and 14.

Preparation—Changes made in an aquacrop to meet consumer preferences.

Preservation—How a food is kept wholesome until it reaches the consumer.

Price—The amount of money that a buyer will pay for a product or service.

Price maker—An individual or organization that sets the price for a commodity.

Price taker—An individual or organization that has little control over the price of a commodity.

Pricing efficiency—Situation that exists when nearly every producer can expect nearly the same price for commodities.

Pricing strategy—A plan for getting an acceptable price for a product or service.

Primary research—Gathering information directly from potential consumers; used when developing a marketing plan.

Principle of supply and demand—Economic principle that price varies with the supply of a product and the demand for it.

Print media—Newspapers and magazines.

Private ownership—When individuals own property.

Private treaty—A market agreement arrived at by a buyer and seller in private negotiations.

Process evaluation–Assessing a marketing plan as it is being implemented.

Producer sector–Farmers and ranchers who are producers.

Product–Broad description of what is produced.

Product buying–Buying a specific product without regard to where it is purchased.

Product composition–Materials used to make a product; important in selling process.

Product differentiation–Making similar products with small differences to appeal to a larger market.

Product evaluation–Assessing a marketing plan after it has been implemented; answers the question, "How well did we do?"

Product features–The physical characteristics of a product.

Product form–The condition of a product when it is marketed, such as with or without processing.

Production control–Limiting the amount of a supply or service that is produced.

Production flexibility–Ability to change products after a production cycle has been initiated.

Product performance–The length of product life and what the product can do.

Product positioning–Creating a certain image of a product in the minds of consumers.

Product uniformity–Products that meet certain standards though they aren't identical.

Product wholesomeness–Food that is fresh, is free of harmful substances, and promotes good health.

Professional occupation–An occupation that involves a high level of education.

Programmed decisions–Routine decisions that are made frequently and don't involve a high level of risk.

Promotion–The coordination of all seller-initiated efforts (advertising, displaying, news publicity, and personal selling) to communicate with potential customers.

Prompt–Doing something without delay.

Proprietor–An individual who owns a business.

Prospecting–The process a salesperson uses to find new customers.

Publicity–Mass media news coverage that includes the name of a business or product at no cost to the business.

Purchasing cooperative–Cooperative that collectively buys supplies for farms and re-sells them to farmers.

Rational buying–Making the decision to buy after facts have been collected and studied.

Real objection–Concerns or problems a customer has about the features of a product.

Real property–Land and the improvements that have been made to it, such as buildings and fences.

Receiver–In the communication process, the individual who interprets a message and tries to draw meaning from it.

Recreational aquaculture marketing–Using ponds or other facilities where people pay a fee to catch fish.

Research–Careful and diligent study to gain knowledge about a market; used in developing a marketing plan.

Retail nursery–A horticultural plant business that sells directly to the end user of the plant.

Retail store–Store that sells to the general public.

Risk–The possibility of financial loss.

Roadside markets–Retail markets operated by producers on highways, roads, and other easy-access locations.

Rough layout–A layout of an ad; serves as a guide to a newspaper or magazine for placing the elements that will appear in the finished ad.

Salesperson–Occupation that involves assisting people in selecting products to meet their needs.

Sales potential–Predicted sales volume of a supply or service.

Sales resistance–The way a customer expresses objections or concern about a product during the selling process.

Sales ticket–Written statement that documents a sale.

Saltwater–Water with a high salt content and suited to certain species of plants and animals.

Seafood–Wide range of aquatic animals used for human food; usually grow wild in saltwater.

Secondary research–Using information that has already been collected and reported elsewhere; the information is used in developing marketing plans.

Segmentation–Dividing traditional farm functions so that some are carried out in off-farm agribusinesses.

Segment positioning–Positioning a product in a particular market segment.

Self-concept–How individuals feel about themselves.

Self esteem–How individuals assess their personal worth.

Self-sufficient–When farmers produce for their needs only; opposite of commercial production.

Selling–The process of exchanging goods or services for other goods, services, or money.

Selling points–Customer benefits that are the focus of an advertisement.

Semi-skilled occupation–An occupation that requires some skill and job training, but less than the skilled level.

Sender–In communication, the person who initiates a message and interprets feedback to determine the effectiveness of the exchange of information.

Shoppers' guide–A newspaper published once per week consisting primarily of advertisements and announcements, with circulation limited to a neighborhood or small community.

Single theme ad–An advertisement that features the single product or service a business hopes will be its best seller.

Skilled occupation–An occupation that requires specialized training or experience.

Sociocultural characteristics–The traits of people as related to their cultural and social environment.

Sole proprietorship–When one individual owns a business.

Special event ad–An advertisement that features headlines, body copy, and/or illustrations relating to a special event a business is holding.

Special interest newspaper–A newspaper that is developed to serve a specific group of people.

Specialization–When farms or agribusinesses produce only one or a few products.

Staffing–A management function involving selecting, training, and rewarding personnel.

Success—Achieving worthy goals.

Supply—Amount of a product that is available for sale in the market.

Sustainable agriculture—Managing agricultural production so that the long-term food, clothing, and shelter needs of people can be met.

Target audience—The audience to whom an advertising message is directed.

Targeting customers—When a salesperson selects a prospective buyer and develops an individual selling plan.

Target market—The group of consumers that is to be reached in marketing.

Task orientation—Dedication to work duties.

Terminal markets—Locations where large quantities of products are assembled; often located centrally in terms of the market.

Terrestrial animals—Animals that grow on land.

Terrestrial plants—Plants that grow on land.

Total return—The total amount of income received from marketing.

Trade leakage—When people leave their local area to shop.

Traders—People who work in futures markets linking buyers and sellers.

Transporting—The moving of supplies and products from one geographical location to another.

Trial close—Asking customers questions in a casual and conversational manner to close a sale.

Undecided customer—A customer who doesn't know the product or service he or she wants to buy.

Uniform species—When the fish or fish product in a container is all of the same species.

Unskilled occupation—An occupation that does not require specific education or experience.

Value-added—Increasing the value of a product through processing, packaging, or other improvement after the product leaves the site of production.

Visual media—Billboards, signs, and displays.

Volume of production—The amount of a commodity that is produced.

Want—Something that is desired but not essential to maintain one's life.

Water structure—Facility that holds the water for aquaculture.

Weekly newspaper—A newspaper published one time a week.

White space—Unfilled areas of an advertisement.

Wholesale marketing—Used when products go from the producer to some other business or businesses before reaching the consumer.

Wholesale nursery—A horticultural business that markets plants to individuals and businesses that later sell them to consumers.

Wholesaler—Middle person between producer and retailer; sells in large quantities to volume buyers and retail stores.

Work ethic—How people view work; attitudes toward work.

Bibliography

Aguayo, Rafael. *Dr. Deming: The American Who Taught the Japanese About Quality*. New York: Simon & Schuster, 1990.

Andersen, R. Clifton, and William P. Dommermuth. *Distribution Systems: Firms, Functions, and Efficiencies*. New York: Meredith Corporation, 1972.

Barnett, Steve (editor). *The Nissan Report: A Bold New Blueprint for Successful Innovation in American Business*. New York: Avon Books, 1992.

Beierlein, James G., and Michael W. Woolverton. *Agribusiness Marketing: The Management Perspective*. Englewood Cliffs, New Jersey: Prentice-Hall Inc., 1991.

Branson, Robert E., and Douglass G. Norvell. *Introduction to Agricultural Marketing*. New York: McGraw-Hill, Inc., 1983.

Bovèe, Courtland L., and William F. Arens. *Contemporary Advertising*, 4th ed. Homewood, Illinois: Richard D. Irwin, Inc., 1992.

Christopher, Martin. *The Strategy of Distribution Management*. Westport, Connecticut: Quorum Books, 1985.

Cohen, William A. *The Practice of Marketing Management*. New York: Macmillan Publishing Company, 1988.

Ditzenberger, Roger, and John Kidney. *Selling: Helping Customers Buy*, 3rd ed. Cincinnati, Ohio: South-Western Publishing Company, 1992.

Downey, W. David, Michael A. Jackson, and Carl G. Stevens. *Agri Selling*. Skokie, Illinois: Agri Business Publications, 1983.

Duft, Kenneth D. *Principles of Management in Agribusiness*. Reston, Virginia: Reston Publishing Company, 1979.

Hawkins, Del I., Robert J. Best, and Kenneth A. Coney. *Consumer Behavior: Implications for Marketing Strategy*, 5th ed. Boston, Massachusetts: Richard D. Irwin, Inc., 1992.

Heuser, C. W., Jr., and R. F. Stinson. *Nursery Production*. University Park: Pennsylvania State University, 1989.

Instructional Materials Service. *Advanced Agribusiness Management and Marketing*. College Station: Texas A&M University, 1991.

Instructional Materials Service. *Floral Design and Interior Landscape Development*. College Station: Texas A&M University, 1989.

Instructional Materials Service. *Fruit, Nut, and Vegetable Production*. College Station: Texas A&M University, 1990.

Instructional Materials Service. *Horticultural Plant Production*. College Station: Texas A&M University, 1989.

Johnson, James C. *Readings in Contemporary Physical Distribution*, 3rd ed. Tulsa, Oklahoma: The Petroleum Publishing Company, 1977-1978.

Johnson, James C., and Donald F. Wood. *Contemporary Physical Distribution*. Tulsa, Oklahoma: The Petroleum Publishing Company, 1977.

Hanagriff, Roger D., and Larry Ermis. *Agricultural Sales Handbook*. College Station, Texas: Instructional Materials Service, Department of Agricultural Education, Texas A&M University, 1993.

Jolly, Curtis M., and Howard A. Clonts. *Economics of Aquaculture*. Binghamton, New York: The Hawarth Press, Inc., 1993.

Katzenstein, Herbert, and William S. Sachs. *Direct Marketing*, 2nd ed. New York: Macmillan Publishing Company, 1992.

Kohls, Richard L., and Joseph N. Uhl. *Marketing of Agricultural Products*, 5th ed. New York: Macmillan Publishing Company, 1980.

Kohls, Richard L., and Joseph N. Uhl. *Marketing of Agricultural Products*, 6th ed. New York: Macmillan Publishing Company, 1985.

Kotler, Philip. *Marketing Management: Analysis, Planning, Implementation, and Control*, 7th ed. Englewood Cliffs, New Jersey: Prentice Hall, Inc., 1991.

Lee, Jasper S. *Commercial Catfish Farming*, 3rd ed. Danville, Illinois: Interstate Publishers, Inc., 1991.

Lee, Jasper S., and Michael E. Newman. *Aquaculture–An Introduction*. Danville, Illinois: Interstate Publishers, Inc., 1992.

Lee, Jasper S., and Diana L. Turner. *Introduction to World AgriScience and Technology*. Danville, Illinois: Interstate Publishers, Inc., 1994.

Lesser, William H. *Marketing Livestock and Meat*. Binghamton, New York: The Hawarth Press, Inc., 1993.

Miller, Larry E. *Selling in Agribusiness*. New York: Gregg Division, McGraw-Hill, Inc., 1979.

Mortenson, W. P. *Modern Marketing of Farm Products*. Danville, Illinois: The Interstate Printers & Publishers, Inc., 1968.

National Assessment Institute. *Handbook for Safe Food Service Management.* Englewood Cliffs, New Jersey: Regents/Prentice Hall, 1994.

National FFA Association. *Bulletin Four, National FFA Contest.* Alexandria, Virginia: National FFA Supply Service, 1991.

National FFA Center. *FFA Selling and Fund-Raising Guide.* Alexandria, Virginia: National FFA Supply Service, 1991.

Nelson, K. S. *Flower and Plant Production in the Greenhouse.* Danville, Illinois: Interstate Publishers, Inc., 1991.

Nelson, Raymond A. *Total Physical Distribution Management.* New York: AMACOM, 1975.

Newman, Michael E., and Walter J. Wills. *Agribusiness Management and Entrepreneurship*, 3rd ed. Danville, Illinois: Interstate Publishers, Inc., 1994.

Purcell, Wayne D. *Agricultural Marketing: Systems, Coordination, Cash and Futures Prices.* Reston, Virginia: Reston Publishing Company, Inc., 1979.

Rice, Craig, S. *How to Plan and Execute the Marketing Campaign.* Chicago, Illinois: The Dartnell Corporation, 1966.

Sager, Robert J., David M. Helgren, and Saul Israel. *World Geography Today.* Chicago, Illinois: Holt, Rinehart and Winston, 1992.

Sampson, Harland E. *Advertising Planning & Techniques.* Cincinnati, Ohio: South-Western Publishing Company, 1985.

Schoell, William F., and Joseph P. Guiltinan. *Marketing: Contemporary Concepts and Practices*, 5th ed. Needham Heights, Massachusetts: Allyn and Bacon, 1992.

Schoell, William F., and Joseph P. Guiltinan. *Marketing: Contemporary Concepts and Practices*, 4th ed. Needham Heights, Massachusetts: Allyn and Bacon, 1990.

Snowden, Obed L., and Alvin W. Donahoo. *Profitable Farm Marketing.* Englewood Cliffs, New Jersey: Prentice-Hall, Inc., 1960.

Spechler, Jay W. *When America Does It Right.* Norcross, Georgia: Industrial Engineering and Management Press, 1988.

Staten, Vince. *Can You Trust a Tomato in January?* New York: Simon & Schuster, 1993.

U.S. Department of Agriculture. *Agricultural Statistics 1991.* Washington, D.C., 1991.

U.S. Department of Agriculture. *Marketing U.S. Agriculture-1988 Yearbook of Agriculture*. Washington, D.C., 1988.

U.S. Department of Agriculture. *New Crops New Uses New Markets*. Washington, D.C., 1992.

U.S. Bureau of the Census. *Statistical Abstract of the United States 1991*. Washington D.C., 1991.

Willis, Roger. *Physical Distribution Management: An Analytical Approach to Cutting Costs*. Park Ridge, New Jersey: Noyes Data Corporation, 1977.

Wright, John W. (editor). *The Universal Almanac 1993*. New York: Andrews and McMeel, 1993.

Zeithaml, Valarie, A. Parasuraman, and Leonard L. Berry. *Delivering Quality Service*. New York: The Free Press, 1990.

Index